My
iPhone

SEVENTH EDITION

Brad Miser

800 East 96th Street,
Indianapolis, Indiana 46240 USA

My iPhone®, Seventh Edition

Copyright © 2014 by Pearson Education, Inc.

ISBN-13: 978-0-7897-5044-0

ISBN-10: 0-7897-5044-9

Library of Congress Cataloging-in-Publication Data is on file.

Printed in the United States of America

First Printing: October 2013

Trademarks

All terms mentioned in this book that are known to be trademarks or service marks have been appropriately capitalized. Que Publishing cannot attest to the accuracy of this information. Use of a term in this book should not be regarded as affecting the validity of any trademark or service mark.

Warning and Disclaimer

Every effort has been made to make this book as complete and as accurate as possible, but no warranty or fitness is implied. The information provided is on an "as is" basis. The author and the publisher shall have neither liability nor responsibility to any person or entity with respect to any loss or damages arising from the information contained in this book.

Bulk Sales

Que Publishing offers excellent discounts on this book when ordered in quantity for bulk purchases or special sales. For more information, please contact

U.S. Corporate and Government Sales

1-800-382-3419

corpsales@pearsontechgroup.com

For sales outside of the U.S., please contact

International Sales

international@pearsoned.com

Editor-in-Chief
Greg Wiegand

Senior Acquisitions Editor
Laura Norman

Development Editor
Laura Norman

Managing Editor
Sandra Schroeder

Project Editor
Mandie Frank

Technical Editor
Paul Sihvonen-Binder

Copy Editor
Megan Wade-Taxter

Indexer
Cheryl Lenser

Proofreader
Dan Knott

Publishing Coordinator
Cindy Teeters

Designer
Mark Shirar

Compositor
TnT Design, Inc.

Contents at a Glance

Table of Contents

Using This Book

This book has been designed to help you transform an iPhone into *your* iPhone by helping you learn to use it easily and quickly. As you can tell, the book relies heavily on pictures to show you how an iPhone works. It is also task-focused so that you can quickly learn the specific steps to follow to do all the cool things you can do with your iPhone.

Using an iPhone involves lots of touching its screen with your fingers. When you need to tap part of the screen, such as a button or keyboard, you see a callout with the step number pointing to where you need to tap. When you need to swipe your finger along the screen, such as to browse lists, you see the following icons:

The directions in which you should slide your finger on the screen are indicated with arrows. When the arrow points both ways, you can move your finger in either direction. When the arrows point in all four directions, you can move your finger in any direction on the screen.

To zoom in or zoom out on screens, you unpinch or pinch, respectively, your fingers on the screen. These motions are indicated by the following icons:

When you need to tap once or twice, such as to zoom out or in, you see the following icons matching the number of times you need to tap:

When you should rotate your iPhone, you see this icon:

Occasionally, you shake the iPhone to activate a control. When you do, you see this icon:

About the Author

Brad Miser has written extensively about technology, with his favorite topics being the amazing "i" devices, especially the iPhone and iPod touch, that make it possible to take our lives with us while we are on the move. In addition to *My iPhone*, 7th Edition, Brad has written many other books, including *My iPod touch*, 4th Edition; *iTunes and iCloud for iPhone, iPad, & iPod touch Absolute Beginner's Guide*; and *Sams Teach Yourself iCloud in 10 Minutes*, 2nd Edition. He has also been an author, development editor, or technical editor for more than 50 other titles.

Brad is or has been a sales support specialist, the director of product and customer services, and the manager of education and support services for several software development companies. Previously, he was the lead proposal specialist for an aircraft engine manufacturer, a development editor for a computer book publisher, and a civilian aviation test officer/engineer for the U.S. Army. Brad holds a bachelor of science degree in mechanical engineering from California Polytechnic State University at San Luis Obispo and has received advanced education in maintainability engineering, business, and other topics.

In addition to his passion for silicon-based technology, Brad is active in building and flying radio-controlled aircraft.

Originally from California, Brad now lives in Brownsburg, Indiana, with his wife Amy; their three daughters, Jill, Emily, and Grace; and a rabbit.

Brad would love to hear about your experiences with this book (the good, the bad, and the ugly). You can write to him at bradmiser@icloud.com.

Dedication

To those who have given the last full measure of devotion so that the rest of us can be free.

Acknowledgments

To the following people on the *My iPhone* project team, my sincere appreciation for your hard work on this book:

Laura Norman, my acquisitions and development editor, who envisioned the original concept for *My iPhone* and works very difficult and long hours to ensure the success of each edition. Laura and I have worked on many books together, and I appreciate her professional and effective approach to these projects. Thanks for putting up with me yet one more time!

Paul Sihvonen-Binder, my technical editor, who carefully reviewed the content in this book and made numerous suggestions to correct my mistakes and add valuable information to it.

Mandie Frank, my project editor, who skillfully managed the hundreds of files and production process that it took to make this book.

Mark Shirar, for the interior design and cover of the book.

Que's production and sales team for printing the book and getting it into your hands.

We Want to Hear from You!

As the reader of this book, *you* are our most important critic and commentator. We value your opinion and want to know what we're doing right, what we could do better, what areas you'd like to see us publish in, and any other words of wisdom you're willing to pass our way.

We welcome your comments. You can email or write us directly to let us know what you did or didn't like about this book—as well as what we can do to make our books better.

Please note that we cannot help you with technical problems related to the topic of this book.

When you write, please be sure to include this book's title and author as well as your name, email address, and phone number. We will carefully review your comments and share them with the author and editors who worked on the book.

Email: feedback@quepublishing.com

Mail:
Que Publishing
ATTN: Reader Feedback
800 East 96th Street
Indianapolis, IN 46240 USA

Reader Services

Visit our website and register this book at quepublishing.com/register for convenient access to any updates, downloads, or errata that might be available for this book.

You'll soon wonder how you
ever got along without one!

In this chapter, you get introduced to the amazing iPhone! Topics include the following:

→ Getting to know your iPhone's external features
→ Getting to know your iPhone's software

Getting Started with Your iPhone

Your iPhone is one of the most amazing handheld devices ever because of how well it is designed. It has only a few external features you need to understand. For most of the things you do, you just use your fingers on your iPhone's screen (which just seems natural), and the iPhone's consistent interface enables you to accomplish most tasks with similar steps.

Getting to Know Your iPhone's External Features

Take a quick look at the iPhone's physical attributes. It doesn't have many physical buttons or controls because you mostly use software to control it.

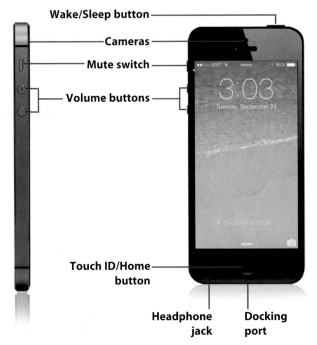

- **Cameras**—One of the iPhone's camera lenses is located on its backside near the top; the other is on the front at the top. The flash is located near the camera on the backside.

- **Wake/Sleep button**—Press this to lock the iPhone's controls and put it to sleep. Press it again to wake the iPhone from Sleep mode. You also use this button to shut down the iPhone and to power it up.

- **Mute switch**—This switch determines whether the iPhone makes sounds, such as ringing when a call comes in or making the alert noise for a notification, such as an event on a calendar. Slide it toward the front of the iPhone to hear sounds. Slide it toward the back of the iPhone to mute all sound.

- **Headphone jack**—Plug the iPhone's EarPods or self-powered, external speakers into this jack.

- **Volume**—Press the upper button to increase volume; press the lower button to decrease volume. This is contextual; for example, when you are listening to music, it controls the music's volume, but when you aren't, it controls the ringer volume. When you are using the Camera app, pressing either button takes a photo.

- **Docking port**—Use this port, located on the bottom side of the iPhone, to connect it to a computer or power adapter using the included USB cable. There are also accessories that connect to this port.

- **Touch ID/Home button (iPhone 5S)**—This serves two functions. The Touch ID sensor recognizes your fingerprint, so you can simply touch it to unlock your iPhone. You can also tap it to sign in to your Apple ID (no need to type a password). Additionally, it functions just like the Home button described in the following bullet.

- **Home button (iPhone 5C, 5, 4S, and 4)**—Press this button to move to the all-important Home screens. Press it twice quickly to show the Multitasking screen. When the iPhone is asleep, press it to wake up the iPhone. Press and hold the Home button to activate Siri to speak to your iPhone.

So Many iPhones, So Few Pages

The iPhone is now in its seventh generation. Each successive generation has added features and capabilities to the previous version. All iPhone hardware runs the iOS operating system. However, this book is based on the current version of this operating system, iOS 7. Only the iPhone 4 and newer can run this version of the software. If you have an older version of the iPhone, this book helps you see why it is time to upgrade, but most of the information contained herein won't apply to your iPhone until you do.

There are also differences even among the models of iPhones that can run iOS 7. For example, the iPhone 4 can't run Siri that enables you to use your voice to work with text, get information, and much more. The iPhone 5S is the only one with Touch ID that uses your fingerprint to unlock your iPhone and to sign in to your Apple ID.

This book is primarily based on the latest generation of iPhones, the iPhone 5S and 5C. If you don't use one of these, there might be some differences between the details you read in this book and your phone, but those differences shouldn't stop you from accomplishing the tasks described in this book.

Getting to Know Your iPhone's Software

You might not suspect it based on the iPhone's simple and elegant exterior, but this powerhouse runs very sophisticated software that enables you to do all sorts of great things. The beauty of the iPhone's software is that it is both very powerful and also easy to use—once you get used to its User Interface (UI for the more technical among you). The iPhone's UI is so well designed that after a few minutes, you may wish everything worked so well and is so easy to use.

Using Your Fingers to Control Your iPhone

Apple designed the iPhone to be touched. Most of the time, you control your iPhone by using your fingers on its screen to tap buttons, select items on lists, swipe on the screen, zoom, type text, and so on. If you want to get nerdy, this method of interacting with software is called the Multi-touch interface.

Going Home

Almost all iPhone activities start at the Home screen (or Home screens, to be more accurate, because the Home screen has multiple pages), which you get to by pressing the Touch ID/Home button. Along the bottom of the Home screen is the Home Screen toolbar, which is always visible when you move through the Home screen's pages. This gives you easy access to the icons it contains (more on the Home screen shortly); up to four icons can be placed on this toolbar. Above the toolbar are apps that do all sorts of cool things. As you install apps, the number of icons increases. You can also create bookmarks for websites and store them as icons on the Home screens. You can organize the icons on the pages of the Home screens in any way you like, and you can place buttons into folders to keep your Home screens tidy and so that accessing the icons you use most frequently is convenient. At the top of the screen are status icons that provide you with important information, such as whether you are connected to a Wi-Fi network and the current charge of your iPhone's battery.

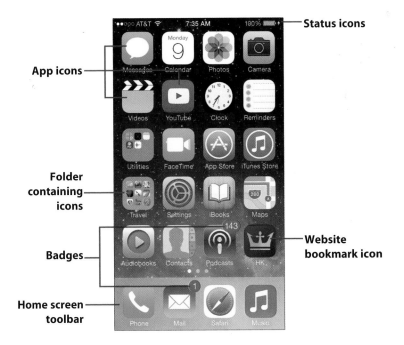

Touching the iPhone's Screen

The following figures highlight the major ways you control an iPhone. A tap is just what it sounds like—you briefly touch a finger to the iPhone's screen over the item you want to control and then lift your finger again. For example, to work with an app, you tap its icon. Sometimes, you double-tap, which is also exactly what it sounds like: you simply tap twice. To swipe, you touch the screen at any location and slide your finger in one direction, such as to the left to move to the next screen, which might show the next photo in an album you are viewing, for example. To drag, you tap and hold an object and move your finger across the screen without lifting it up; the faster you move your finger, the faster the resulting action happens. (You don't need to apply pressure, just make contact.) To pinch or unpinch, place two fingers on the screen and drag them together or move them apart; the faster and more you pinch or unpinch, the "more" the action happens (such as a zoom in). You can rotate the iPhone to change the screen's orientation.

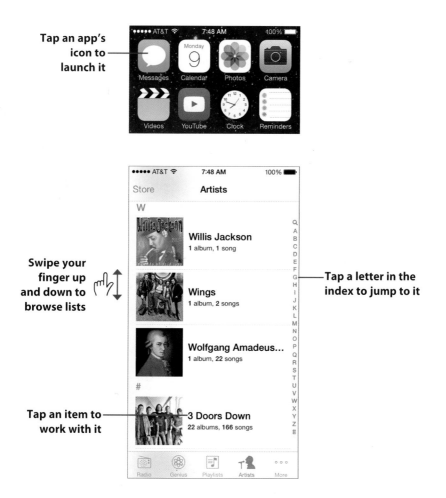

Tap an app's icon to launch it

Swipe your finger up and down to browse lists

Tap a letter in the index to jump to it

Tap an item to work with it

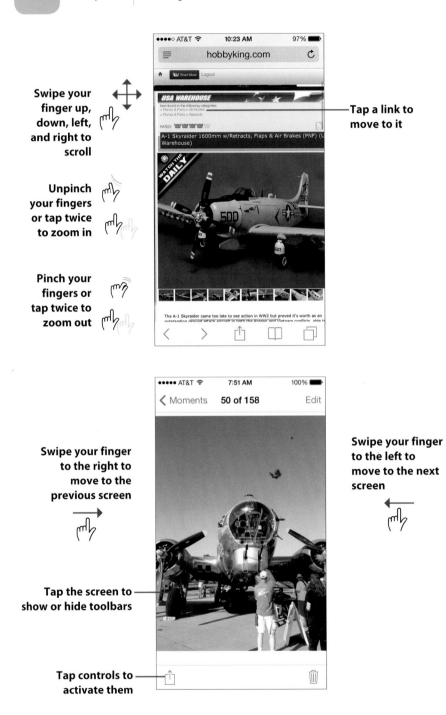

Swipe your finger up, down, left, and right to scroll

Unpinch your fingers or tap twice to zoom in

Pinch your fingers or tap twice to zoom out

Tap a link to move to it

Swipe your finger to the right to move to the previous screen

Swipe your finger to the left to move to the next screen

Tap the screen to show or hide toolbars

Tap controls to activate them

Rotate the iPhone to change the screen's orientation

Working with iPhone Apps

One of the best things about an iPhone is that it can run all sorts of applications, or in iPhone lingo, *apps*. It includes a number of preinstalled apps, such as Mail, Safari, and so on, but you can download and use thousands of other apps through the App Store. You learn about many of the iPhone's preinstalled apps as you read through this book. And as you learned earlier, to launch an app, you simply tap its icon. The app launches and fills the iPhone's screen.

When you tap an app's icon, it opens and fills the iPhone's screen

Tap a folder to access its icons

In Chapter 4, "Configuring an iPhone to Suit Your Preferences," you learn how you can organize icons in folders to keep your Home screens tidy and make getting to icons faster and easier. To access an icon that is in a folder, tap the folder. It opens and takes over the screen. Under its name is a box showing the apps or website bookmarks it contains. Like the Home screens, folders can have multiple pages. To move between a folder's pages, swipe to the left to move to the next screen or to the right to move to the previous one. Each time you "flip" a page, you see another set of icons.

Folder name

Open folder

Tap an icon to open it

Icons within the folder

Swipe to the right or left to move between a folder's pages

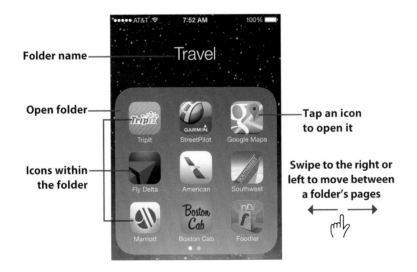

To launch an app or open a website bookmark within a folder, tap its icon.

When you are done using an app, press the Home button. You return to the Home screen you were most recently using.

However, because the iPhone multitasks, when you move out of an app by pressing the Home button, the app moves into the background but doesn't stop. So, if the app has a task to complete, such as uploading photos or playing audio, it continues to work behind-the-scenes. In some cases, notably games, the app becomes suspended at the point you leave it. In addition to the benefit of completing tasks when you move into another app, the iPhone's capability to multitask means that you can run multiple apps at the same time. For example, you can run an Internet radio app to listen to music while you switch over to the Mail app to work on your email.

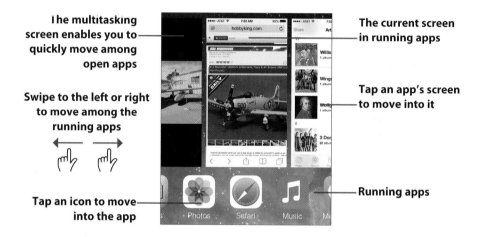

The multitasking screen enables you to quickly move among open apps

The current screen in running apps

Swipe to the left or right to move among the running apps

Tap an app's screen to move into it

Tap an icon to move into the app

Running apps

You can control apps by using the Multitasking screen. To see this, press the Touch ID/Home button twice. The Multitasking screen appears. At the bottom of this screen, you see the icons of all the apps that are currently running. Above the icons are the screens currently open in each app. You can swipe to the left or right on either the screens or the icons to move among the running apps.

To jump quickly into a different app, tap its icon or its screen. That app takes over the screen, and you can work with it, picking up right where you left off the last time you used it.

To close the screen without moving into a different app, press the Home button once. You move back into the app you were most recently using.

Swipe up on an app's screen to force it to close

In some cases (such as when it's using up your battery too quickly), you might want to force an app to quit. To do this, open the Multitasking screen and swipe up on the app you want to stop. The app is forced to quit, its icon and screen disappear, and you remain on the Multitasking screen. You should be careful about this, though, because if the app, such as Pages, has unsaved data, you will likely lose that data when you force the app to quit. The app is not deleted from the iPhone—it is just shut down until you open it again.

Using the Home Screens

Earlier, you read that the Home screen is the jumping-off point for many of the things you do with your iPhone because that is where you access the icons you tap to launch apps or to move to website bookmarks you've saved there.

The Home screen has multiple pages. To change the page you are viewing, swipe to the left to move to later pages or to the right to move to earlier pages. The dots above the toolbar represent the pages of the Home screen. The white dot represents the page being displayed. You can also change the page by tapping to the left of this dot to move to the previous page or to the right of it to move to the next page.

Swipe to the left or right to move between pages of your Home screen

Tap to the left or right of the current page (white dot) to move to the previous or the next page

When you move to a different page, you see a different set of icons and folders

The toolbar is visible on every page

Swipe down from
the center part
of the screen to
search your iPhone

You can use the Spotlight Search tool to search your iPhone. To open this tool, swipe down from the center part of the screen (if you swipe down from the top of the screen, the Notification Center opens instead).

To perform a search, tap in the Search bar and type the search term using the onscreen keyboard. As you type, items that meet your search are shown on the list below the Search bar. When you finish typing the search term, tap Search.

The results are organized into sections, each of which is labeled by the type of object it is, such as contacts, mail, music, and so on. To work with an item you find, such as to view contact information you found, tap it; you move into the associated app and see the information you found. The results remain in the Spotlight Search tool so that you can move back to the results screen to work with other items you found. To clear a search, tap the Clear button (x).

Type what you
want to search for

Current results

When you're done
entering your search
term, tap Search

Tap to clear a search

Contacts you found

Search results

To work with a
result, tap it

Email messages that
relate to your search

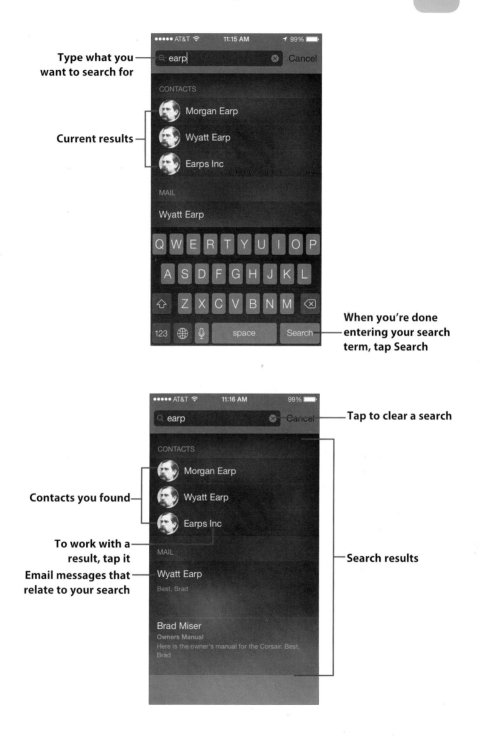

Working with the Control Center

The Control Center provides quick access to a number of very useful controls. To access it, swipe up from the bottom of the screen. If your iPhone is asleep, press the Sleep/Wake button to wake up the phone and then swipe up from the bottom of the screen. The Control Center opens and gives you quick access to a number of controls.

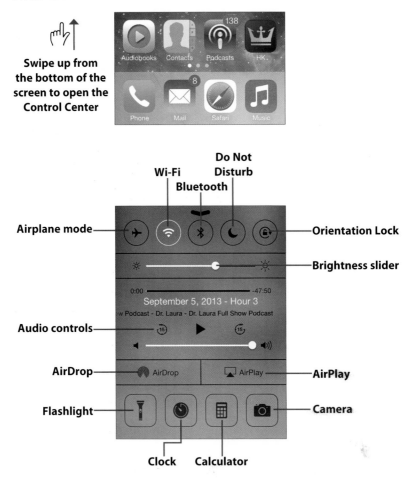

Swipe up from the bottom of the screen to open the Control Center

At the top of the Control Center are buttons you can use to turn on or turn off important functions. To activate a function, tap the button, which becomes white to show the function is active. To disable a function, tap the button so that it becomes dark to show you it is inactive. For example, to lock the orientation of the iPhone's screen in its current position, tap the Orientation Lock button so it becomes white. Your iPhone's screen no longer changes when you rotate the phone. To make it change when you rotate the phone again, turn off the Orientation Lock button. You learn about Airplane mode and Do No Disturb later in this chapter. Wi-Fi and Bluetooth are explained in Chapter 2, "Connecting Your iPhone to the Internet, Bluetooth Devices, and iPhones/iPods/iPads."

Below the function buttons is the Brightness slider. Drag the slider to the right to make the screen brighter or to the left to make it dimmer.

In the center of the Control Center are the audio controls you can use with whatever audio is playing, such as music from the Music app, podcasts from the Podcasts app, and so on. Music and podcasts are covered in Chapter 14, "Finding and Listening to Music," and Chapter 16, "Using Other Cool iPhone Apps," respectively.

The AirDrop button enables you to share content with other iOS device users in the same vicinity; this is covered in Chapter 2. The AirPlay button enables you to stream your iPhone's music, podcasts, photos, and video onto other devices, such as a TV to which an Apple TV is connected; using AirPlay is covered in Chapters 14, 15, "Working with Photos and Video You Take with Your iPhone," and 16.

At the bottom of the Control Center are four app icons; just as you do on the Home screens, tap an icon to open the app. The Flashlight app uses your iPhone's flash as a flashlight. The Clock app provides you with a number of time-related functions, which are world clocks, alarms, a timer, and a stopwatch. The Calculator does just what it sounds like it does; when you hold the iPhone vertically, you see a simple calculator while if you rotate the iPhone to horizontal, the calculator becomes more powerful. The Camera app enables you to capture photos and video (this is covered in Chapter 15).

Working with Notifications and the Notification Center

Your iPhone has a lot of activity going on, from new emails to reminders to calendar events. The iOS notification system keeps you informed of these happenings through a number of means. Visual notifications include alerts, banners, and badges. Alert sounds can also let you know something has happened, and vibrations make you feel the new activity. You can have all sorts of notification options for each app. You learn how to customize the notifications your iPhone uses in Chapter 4.

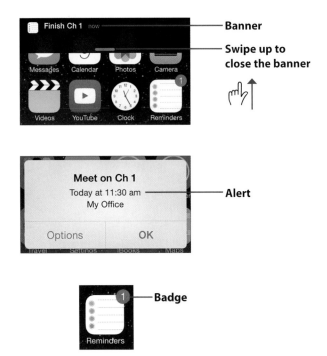

Banner

Swipe up to close the banner

Alert

Badge

Working with visual notifications is pretty straightforward. When a banner appears, you can do one of several things. You can view and then ignore it (it rotates off the screen after displaying for a few seconds). You can tap it to move into the app to take some action, such as to read an email. Or, you can swipe up from its bottom to close it. When an alert appears, you must either take action, such as listening to a voice message or tap the Dismiss/ Close/Ignore button to close the alert and keep doing what you were doing. Badges appear on an app's or a folder's icon to let you know something has changed, such as a reminder alert. Badges are purely informational as are sounds and vibrations; you can't take any action on these directly. They inform you about an event so that you can take action, such as to download and install an update to your iPhone's iOS software.

Notifications on the Lock Screen

Notifications can appear on the Lock screen. This is useful because you can see them even if your iPhone is locked. You can also press the Wake/Sleep button or the Home button to see your notifications without unlocking the iPhone. You can swipe up or down the screen to browse the notifications on the Lock screen or swipe to the right on them to move to the related app, too.

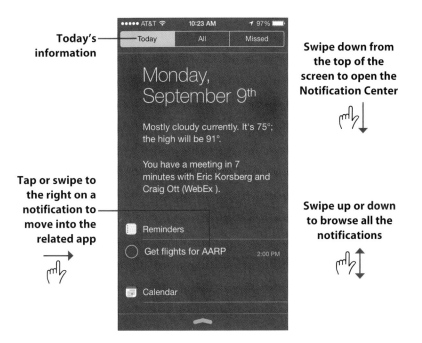

Today's information

Tap or swipe to the right on a notification to move into the related app

Swipe down from the top of the screen to open the Notification Center

Swipe up or down to browse all the notifications

The Notification Center organizes and displays a variety of information for you. To open the Notification Center, swipe down from the top of the iPhone's screen; if your iPhone is currently asleep, press the Sleep/Wake button and then swipe down from the top of the screen.

Tap the Today tab to see the day and date along with weather information. Under that, you see any notifications that impact your day; these are organized in sections based on their type, such as Reminders, Calendar events, and so on. On this tab, you see current notifications, too, such as when you receive a new email or text message. Swipe up or down the screen to browse the notifications. At the bottom of the screen is a summary of events on your calendar for the next day. You can move to a specific item, such as an email message, by tapping or swiping to the right on its notification.

All notifications ——

App from which the ——
notifications come

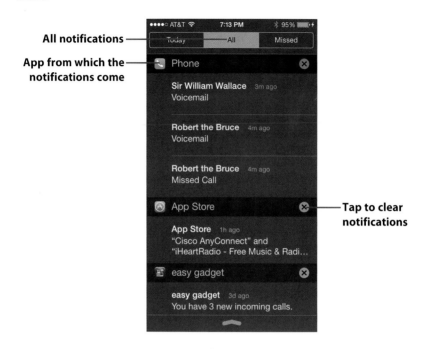

—— **Tap to clear**
notifications

Tap the All tab to see all your current notifications. These are organized by the app from which they come. Like the Today tab, you can swipe up and down to browse all the notifications, tap a notification to move to the related app, and so on. To remove all the notifications for an app, tap its Clear button (x) and then tap Clear.

Tap the Missed tab to see notifications about events you have missed, such as phone calls. To close the Notification Center, swipe up from the bottom of the screen or press the Home button.

Active Notifications

Some of the notifications can show more information than can fit on the screen (examples include the Weather and Stocks apps). Swipe to the left or right on these notifications to see more information. Some notifications have links that take you to the Web to get more detailed information.

Missed
notifications

Swipe up
to close the
Notification
Center

Using the Do Not Disturb Mode

All the notifications you read about in the previous section are useful, but at times, they can be annoying or distracting. When you put your iPhone in Do Not Disturb mode, its visual, audible, and vibration notifications are disabled so that they won't bother you. It won't ring if someone calls you, either.

Tap to keep your
iPhone from
bothering you

Do Not Disturb
is on

To put your iPhone in Do Not Disturb mode, open the Control Center and tap the Do Not Disturb button. It becomes white and the Do Not Disturb: On status flashes at the top of the Control Center. Your iPhone stops its notifications and does not ring if someone calls. To make your notifications active again, tap the Do Not Disturb button so it is black; your iPhone resumes trying to get your attention when it is needed.

In Chapter 4, you learn how to set a schedule for Do Not Disturb so that your iPhone goes into this mode automatically at certain times, such as from 10 p.m. to 6 a.m. You can also configure certain exceptions, including whose calls come in even when your iPhone is in this mode.

Working with Text

You can do lots of things with an iPhone that require you to type, and the iPhone's keyboard is quite amazing. Whenever you need it, whether it's for emailing, entering a website URL, performing a search, and so on, it pops up automatically.

Use the iPhone's virtual keyboard to type

Tap to dictate to your iPhone

To type, just tap the keys. As you tap each key, you hear audio feedback (you can disable this sound if you want to). The keyboard includes all the standard keys you expect. To change from letters to numbers and special characters, just tap the 123 key. Tap the #+= key to see more special characters. Tap the 123 key to move back to the numbers and special characters or the ABC key to return to letters. The keyboard also has contextual keys that appear when you need them. For example, when you enter a website address, the .com key appears so you can enter these four characters with a single tap.

The iPhone is taking dictation

Tap Done when you're done speaking

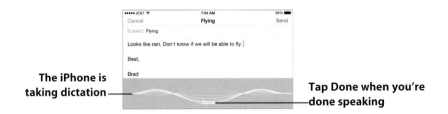

When you tap the Microphone key, you can dictate text into an app, such as Mail, Notes, and so on. After you tap the Microphone key, a gray bar with a line through it replaces the keyboard. Speak the text; as you speak, the line becomes wavy to show you that the iPhone hears what you are saying. Tap Done when you're finished, and the text you spoke is added to whatever you are working on. You can dictate text anywhere you can use the keyboard; this feature is amazingly accurate and can be a much faster and more convenient way to type.

What's Your Typing Orientation?

Like many other tasks, you can rotate the iPhone to change the screen's orientation while you type. When the iPhone is in the horizontal orientation, the keyboard is wider, making it easier to tap individual keys. When the iPhone is in vertical orientation, the keyboard is narrower, but you can see more of the typing area. So, try both to see which mode is most effective for you.

Your iPhone tries to be helpful as you type

Tap to reject the suggestion

If you type a word that the iPhone doesn't recognize, it makes a suggestion about what it thinks is the correct word in a pop-up box. To accept the suggestion, tap the Space key. To reject the suggestion, tap the pop-up box to close it and keep what you typed. You can also use this feature for shorthand typing. For example, to type "I've" you can simply type "Ive" and iPhone suggests "I've" which you can accept by tapping the Space key.

Typing Tricks

Many keys, especially symbols and punctuation, have additional characters. To see a character's options, tap it and hold down. If it has options, a menu pops up after a second or so. To enter one of the optional characters, drag over the menu until the one you want to enter is highlighted, and then lift your finger off the screen. The optional character you selected is entered. For example, if you tap and hold on the period, you can select .com, .edu, and so on, which is very helpful when you are typing a website address.

By default, the iPhone attempts to correct the capitalization of what you type. It also automatically selects the Shift key when you start a new sentence, start a new paragraph, or in other places where its best guess is that you need a capital letter. If you don't want to enter a capital character, simply tap the Shift key before you type. You can enable the Caps Lock key by tapping the Shift key twice. When the key is highlighted, everything you type is in uppercase letters.

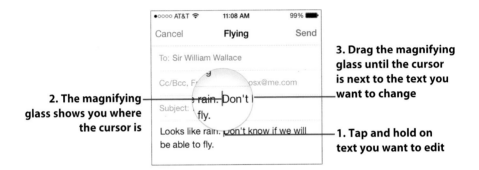

3. Drag the magnifying glass until the cursor is next to the text you want to change

2. The magnifying glass shows you where the cursor is

1. Tap and hold on text you want to edit

To edit text you've typed, tap and hold on the text you want to edit. A magnifying glass icon appears on the screen, and within it you see a magnified view of the location of the cursor. Drag the magnifying glass to where you want to make changes (to position the cursor where you want to start making changes), and then lift your finger from the screen. The cursor remains in that location, and you can use the keyboard to make changes to the text or to add text at that location.

Your Own Shortcuts

You can create your own text shortcuts so you can type something like "eadd" and it is automatically be replaced with your email address. See Chapter 4 for the details.

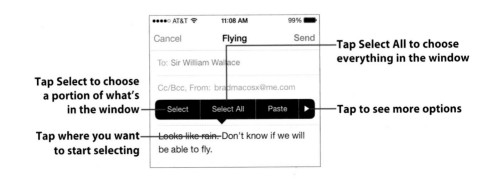

Tap Select All to choose everything in the window

Tap Select to choose a portion of what's in the window

Tap where you want to start selecting

Tap to see more options

You can also select text or images to copy and paste the selected content into a new location. Tap and hold down briefly where you want to start the selection until the magnifying glass icon appears; then lift your finger off the screen. The Select menu appears. Tap Select to select part of the content on the screen, or tap Select All to select everything in the current window.

More Commands

Some menus that appear when you are making selections and performing actions have a right facing arrow at the right end. Tap this to see a new menu that contains additional commands. These commands are contextual, meaning that you see different commands depending on what you are doing at that specific time. You can tap the left-facing arrow to move back to a previous menu.

The blue markers indicate where the selection starts and stops

Selected text

You see markers indicating where the selection starts and stops. (The iPhone attempts to select something logical, such as the word or sentence.) New commands appear on the menu; these provide actions for the text currently selected.

Magnified view of what you are selecting

Drag the markers so that they enclose what you want to select

Selected text (in blue)

Drag the two markers so that the content you want to select is between them; the selected portion is highlighted in blue. As you drag, you see a magnified view of where the selection marker is, which helps you place it more accurately. When the selection markers are located correctly, lift your finger from the screen. (If you tapped the Select All command, you don't need to do this because the content you want is already selected.)

Have I Got a Suggestion for You!

Tap the Suggestion option to see items that might be useful to you. These are also contextual. For example, when you have a word selected, one of the suggestions might be Define, which looks up the selected word in the Dictionary (tap Done to return to where you came from). As you use your iPhone, check out the Suggestions because you'll find some very useful options tucked away there.

Tap Cut or Copy

Selected text

Tap Cut to remove the content from the current window, or tap Copy to just copy it.

Format It!

If you tap the **B**/U button, you can tap Bold, Italics, or Underline to apply those formatting options to the selected text. You also can tap multiple format options to apply them at the same time. You might need to tap the right-facing arrow at the end of the menu to see this command, depending on how many commands are on the menu.

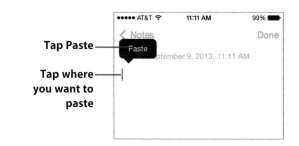

Tap Paste

Tap where you want to paste

Move to where you want to paste the content you selected; for example, use the Multitasking screen to change to a different app. Tap where you want the content to be pasted. For a more precise location, tap and hold and then use the magnifying glass icon to move to a specific location. Then tap Paste.

Pasted content —Don't know if we will be able to fly.

The content you copied or cut appears where you placed the cursor.

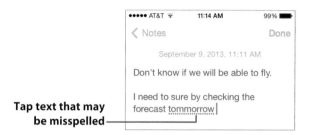

Tap text that may be misspelled — I need to sure by checking the forecast tommorrow

The iPhone also has a spell-checking feature that comes into play after you have entered text (as opposed to the autocorrect feature that changes text as you type it). When you've entered text the iPhone doesn't recognize, it is underlined in red.

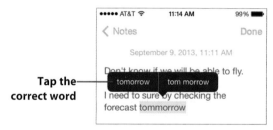

Tap the correct word

Tap the underlined word. It is shaded in red to show you what is being checked, and a menu appears with one or more replacements that might be the correct spelling. If one of the options is the one you want, tap it. The incorrect word is replaced with the one you tapped.

Contextual Menus and You

In some apps, tapping a word causes a menu with other kinds of actions to appear; you can tap an action to make it happen. For example, in the iBooks app, when you tap a word, the resulting menu enables you to look up the word in a dictionary. Other apps support different kinds of actions, so it's a good idea to try tapping words in apps that involve text to see which commands are available.

Meeting Siri

Siri is the iPhone's voice-recognition and control software. This feature enables you to accomplish many tasks by speaking. For example, you can create and send text messages, reply to emails, make phone calls, and much more. (Using Siri is explained in detail in Chapter 12, "Working with Siri.")

When you perform actions, Siri uses the related apps to accomplish what you've asked it to do. For example, when you create a meeting, Siri uses the Calendar app.

Siri is a great way to control your iPhone, especially when you are working in handsfree mode.

Your iPhone has to be connected to the Internet for Siri (and dictation) to work. That's because the words you speak are sent over the Internet, transcribed into text, and then sent back to your iPhone. If your iPhone isn't connected to the Internet, this can't happen and Siri reports that it can't connect to the network.

Using Siri is pretty simple because it follows a consistent pattern and prompts you for input and direction.

Siri is ready to do your bidding —— What can I help you with?

This line shows what Siri is hearing ——

Activate Siri by pressing and holding down the Home button or pressing and holding down the center part of the buttons on the right EarPod wire until you hear the Siri chime. This puts Siri in "listening" mode and the "What can I help you with?" text appears on the screen. This indicates Siri is ready for your command.

What Siri heard you say

Siri is thinking

Speak your command or ask a question. When you stop speaking, Siri goes into processing mode. After Siri interprets what you've said, it provides two kinds of feedback to confirm what it heard: it displays what it heard on the screen and provides audible feedback to you. Siri then tries to do what it thinks you've asked and shows you what it is doing. If it needs more input from you, you're prompted to provide it and Siri moves into "listening" mode automatically.

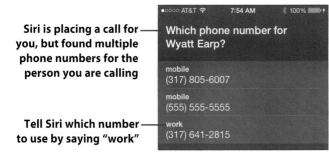

Siri is placing a call for you, but found multiple phone numbers for the person you are calling

Tell Siri which number to use by saying "work"

If Siri requests that you confirm what it is doing or to make a selection, do so. Siri completes the action and displays what it has done; it also audibly confirms the result.

What Siri is doing for you

Say "send" to send the email

Tap to speak to Siri again

Siri isn't quite like using the computer on the Starship Enterprise on *Star Trek*, but it's pretty darn close. Mostly, you can just speak to Siri as you would talk to someone else, and it is able to do what you want or asks you the information it needs to do what you want.

Understanding iPhone Status Icons

At the top of the screen is the Status bar with various icons that provide you with information, such as whether you are connected to a Wi-Fi or cellular data network, the time, sync in process, whether the iPhone's orientation is locked, the state of the iPhone's battery, and so on. Keep an eye on this area as you use your iPhone. The following table provides a guide to the icons.

Table 1   iPhone Status Icons

Icon	Description	Where to Learn More
●●●●●	Signal Strength—Indicates how strong the cellular signal is.	Chapter 2
AT&T	Provider name—The provider of the current cellular network.	Chapter 2
LTE	Cellular data network—Indicates which cellular network your iPhone is using to connect to the Internet.	Chapter 2
📶	Wi-Fi—Indicates your phone is connected to a Wi-Fi network.	Chapter 2
🌙	Do Not Disturb—Your iPhone's notifications and ringer are silenced.	Chapters 1, 4
✳	Bluetooth—Indicates Bluetooth is turned on or off and if your phone is connected to a device.	Chapter 2
97%	Battery percentage—Percentage of charge remaining in the battery.	Chapter 17
▭	Battery status—Relative level of charge of the battery.	Chapter 17
🔒	Orientation Lock—Your iPhone's screen won't change when you rotate your iPhone.	Chapter 1
▭⚡	Charging—The battery in the iPhone is being charged.	Chapter 17
➤	Location Services—An app is using the Location Services feature to track your iPhone's location.	Chapter 4
↻	Sync—Your iPhone is currently being synced with iTunes.	Chapter 5
✈	Airplane mode—The transmit and receive functions are disabled.	Chapter 1

Turning Your iPhone On or Off

If you want to turn off your iPhone, press and hold the Wake/Sleep button until the red slider appears at the top of the screen. Swipe the slider to the right to shut down the iPhone. The iPhone shuts down.

Swipe to the right to turn your iPhone off

To restart your iPhone, press and hold the Wake/Sleep button until the Apple logo appears on the screen, and then let go of the button. After it starts up, you see the Lock screen if your iPhone has a passcode or Home screen if it doesn't, and it's ready for you to use.

Sleeping/Locking and Waking/Unlocking Your iPhone

When an iPhone is asleep/locked, you need to wake it up and then unlock it to use it. How you do this depends on the type of iPhone you have.

If you have an iPhone 5S, press the Touch ID/Home button once and then touch the Touch ID button with your finger. When your fingerprint is recognized, your iPhone unlocks and you can start using it.

**Press once and
then touch
to wake and
unlock your
iPhone 5S**

Be Recognized

To use the Touch ID, you need to train your iPhone 5S to recognize your fingerprint. If you didn't do this when you first turned on your iPhone or you want to train your iPhone 5 to recognize other people's fingerprints so they can also unlock your phone, see Chapter 4.

If you have an iPhone 5C, 5, 4S, or 4, you first press the Wake/Sleep button or the Home button. The iPhone wakes up, the Lock screen appears, and at the bottom of the screen, the Unlock slider appears. Swipe on the slider to the right to unlock the iPhone so you can work with it.

If you require a passcode to unlock your iPhone—which you should for security—type your passcode at the prompt. (See Chapter 4 to learn how to configure a passcode.)

Swipe to the right to unlock your iPhone 5C, 5, 4S, or 4

Enter your passcode to unlock and start using your iPhone

If you enter the correct passcode or you don't require a passcode, when you unlock the phone, you move to the last screen you were using.

The Time Is Always Handy

If you use your iPhone as a watch the way I do, just press the Wake/Sleep button. The current time and date appear; if you don't unlock it, the iPhone goes back to sleep after a few seconds.

In most cases, you should just put the iPhone to sleep when you aren't using it instead of shutting it off. It doesn't use much power when it sleeps, and it wakes up immediately when you want to start using it again. Also, when you put your your iPhone to sleep, it can't be used until it is unlocked. If you set it to require a passcode to unlock, this also protects your information. (You seldom need to turn off an iPhone.) Even when the iPhone is asleep, you can receive notifications, such as when you receive emails or text messages. (See Chapter 4 to configure which notifications you see on the Lock screen.)

To put your iPhone to sleep and lock it, press the Wake/Sleep button.

Signing In to Your Apple ID on an iPhone 5S

As you learn throughout this book, an Apple ID is useful in many situations, such as to access iCloud services; purchase music, movies, and other content from the iTunes Store; download apps from the App Store; and so on. If you have an iPhone 5S, you can quickly sign in to your Apple ID by using its Touch ID/Home button. (As referenced in the prior note, you need to configure your iPhone to recognize your fingerprint to use the Touch ID; see Chapter 4 for details.)

When you need to sign in to your Apple ID, you see a prompt. Simply touch your finger to the Touch ID/Home button. When your fingerprint is recognized, you sign in to your Apple ID and can complete whatever your were doing, such as downloading music from the iTunes Store.

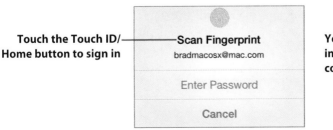

Touch the Touch ID/ Home button to sign in

You need to sign into your Apple ID to complete an action

Setting the Volume

To change the iPhone's volume, press the up or down Volume button on the side of the iPhone. When you change the volume, your change affects the current activity. For example, if you are on phone call, the call volume changes or if you are listening to music, the music's volume changes. If you aren't on a screen that shows the Volume slider, an icon pops up to show you the relative volume you are setting and the type, such as setting the ringer's volume. When the volume is right, release the volume button.

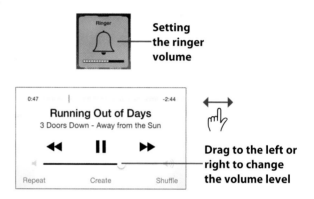

Setting the ringer volume

Drag to the left or right to change the volume level

When you are using an app that produces sound, such as the Music app, you can also drag the volume slider to increase or decrease the volume.

When you use the iPhone's EarPods, you can change the volume by pressing the upper part of the switch on the right EarPod's wire to increase volume or the lower part to decrease it.

Using Airplane Mode

Although there's a debate about whether devices such as iPhones pose any real danger to the operation of aircraft, there's no reason to run any risk by using your iPhone while you are on an airplane. (Besides, not following crew instructions on airplanes can lead you to less-than-desirable situations.) When you place your iPhone in Airplane mode, its transmitting and receiving are disabled, so it poses no threat to the operation of the aircraft. While it is in Airplane mode, you can't use the phone, the Web, Siri, or any other functions that require communication between your iPhone and other devices or networks.

Tap to put your iPhone in Airplane mode

To put your iPhone in Airplane mode, swipe up from the bottom of the screen to open the Control Center and tap the Airplane mode button. All connections to the Internet and the cell network stop, and your iPhone goes into quiet mode in which it doesn't broadcast or receive any signals. The Airplane mode button becomes white and you see the Airplane mode icon at the top of the screen.

In Airplane mode, you can use your iPhone for all your apps that don't require an Internet connection, such as iBooks, Music, Videos, Photos, and so on.

To turn off Airplane mode, open the Control Center and tap the Airplane mode button; it becomes black again and the Airplane mode icon disappears. The iPhone resumes transmitting and receiving signals, and all the functions that require a connection start working again.

Wi-Fi in Airplane Mode

Many airplanes are now supporting Wi-Fi onboard. To access a Wi-Fi network without violating the requirement not to use a cell network, put the iPhone in Airplane mode, which turns off Wi-Fi. On the Control Center, tap the Wi-Fi button to turn Wi-Fi back on. Wi-Fi starts up and you can select the network you want to join (see Chapter 2). You can use this configuration at other times, too, such as when you want to access the Internet but don't want to be bothered with phone calls. When your iPhone is in Airplane mode and Wi-Fi is on, all your calls go straight to voicemail but you can use your Internet-related apps. (I would never do this, you understand.)

Using the Settings App

Tap to open the Settings app

The Settings app is where you do almost all of your iPhone's configuration, and you use it frequently throughout this book. To use the Settings app, tap Settings on the Home screen. The app opens. Swipe up and down the screen to browse the various settings tools. Tap an item to configure its settings. For example, to configure your notifications, you tap Notification Center. (You use the Settings app in a number of chapters in this book, especially Chapter 4.)

Swipe up or down to browse all the settings options

Tap a setting to configure it

Printing from Your iPhone

You can also print from your iPhone to AirPrint-compatible printers.

First, set up and configure your AirPrint printer (see the instructions that came with the printer you use).

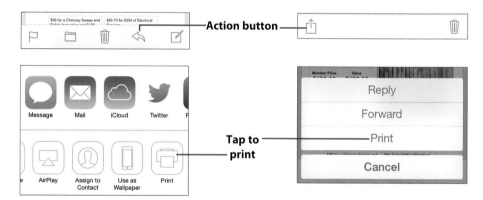

Action button

Tap to print

When you are in the app from which you want to print, tap the Action button and then tap Print on the resulting menu (if you don't see the Action button or the Print command, the app doesn't support printing). The Action button looks a bit different in some apps, but it works similarly in all apps.

The first time you print, you need to select the printer you want to use. On the Printer Options screen, tap Select Printer. Then tap the printer you want to use. You move back to the Printer Option screen and see the printer you selected.

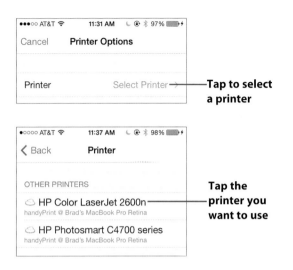

Tap to select a printer

Tap the printer you want to use

Don't Have an AirPrint Printer?

If you don't have an AirPrint printer, do a web search for a tool called "AirPrint for Windows" if you have a Windows PC or "handyPrint for Mac" if you have a Mac. Download and install the software on a computer that is capable of sharing its printers. Configure your computer to share the printer you want to use with your iPhone. Then launch the software on your computer and start it. The printers you configure in the AirPrint software are available for printing from your iPhone.

Current printer

Tap to set the number of copies

Tap to print

Tap the – or + next to the text "Copies" to set the number of copies. Tap Print to print. The document is printed.

The next time you print, if you want to use the same printer, you can skip the printer selection process because the iPhone remembers the last printer you used.

Connect to the
Internet via Wi-Fi or a
cellular network

Use AirDrop to
share content
with other iOS
devices

Take advantage
of an Internet
connection in
many different
apps

Tap here to join
Wi-Fi networks
to connect to
the Internet
and configure
Bluetooth to
connect to other
devices

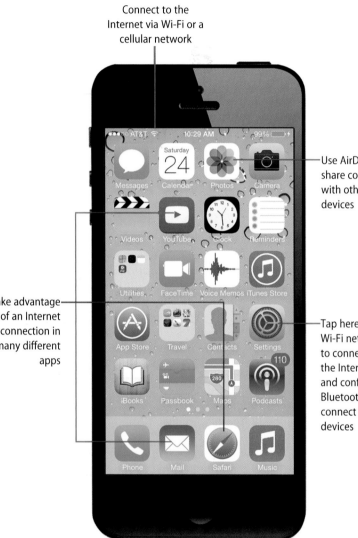

In this chapter, you explore how to connect your iPhone to the Internet; Bluetooth devices; and other iPhones, iPod touches, and iPads. Topics include the following:

→ Using Wi-Fi networks to connect to the Internet
→ Using cellular data networks to connect to the Internet
→ Using Bluetooth to connect to other devices
→ Connecting your iPhone to other iPhones, iPod touches, or iPads
→ Using AirDrop to share content with other iPhones, iPod touches, or iPads

Connecting Your iPhone to the Internet, Bluetooth Devices, and iPhones/iPods/iPads

Your iPhone has many functions that rely on an Internet connection, with the most obvious being email, web browsing, and so on. However, many default and third-party apps rely on an Internet connection to work as well. Fortunately, you can connect your iPhone to the Internet by connecting it to a Wi-Fi network that provides Internet access. You can also connect to the Internet through a cellular data network operated by your cell phone provider.

Using Bluetooth, you can wirelessly connect your iPhone to other devices, including keyboards, headsets, headphones, and so on.

There are a number of ways to connect your iPhone to other iPhones, iPod touches, and iPads. This is useful to use collaborative apps, play games, and share information. For example, using AirDrop, you can quickly and easily share photos and other content with other iOS devices.

Using Wi-Fi Networks to Connect to the Internet

Much of the iPhone's amazing functionality relies on an Internet connection. Fortunately, you can easily connect your iPhone to just about any Wi-Fi network to get to the Internet, and Wi-Fi networks are available just about everywhere these days.

Almost all Wi-Fi networks broadcast their information so that you can easily see them with your iPhone; these are called *open networks* because anyone who is in range can attempt to join one since they appear on Wi-Fi devices automatically. The Wi-Fi networks you can access in public places (such as airports and hotels) are all open, and you can see them on your iPhone. Likewise, any Wi-Fi networks in your home or office are very likely to be open as well. Connecting to an open network typically requires selecting the network you want to join, based on its name, and then entering its password (if required).

By default, when you access one of your iPhone's Internet functions, such as Safari, your iPhone automatically searches for Wi-Fi networks to join if you aren't already connected to one. A box appears showing all the networks available. You can select and join one of these networks, as you learn how to do in the following steps.

Connecting to Open Wi-Fi Networks

To connect to a Wi-Fi network, perform the following steps:

1. On the Home screen, tap Settings. Next to Wi-Fi is the status of your Wi-Fi connection, which is Off if Wi-Fi is currently disabled, Not Connected if Wi-Fi is enabled but your phone isn't currently connected to Wi-Fi, or the name of the Wi-Fi network to which your iPhone is connected.

2. Tap Wi-Fi.

Current Wi-Fi status

3. If Wi-Fi isn't enabled already, slide the Wi-Fi switch to on (green) to allow your iPhone to start searching for available networks. When Wi-Fi is turned on, a list of available networks is displayed in the CHOOSE A NETWORK section (it can take a moment or two for your iPhone to list all the networks in the area). Along with each network's name are icons indicating whether it requires a password (the padlock icon) to join and the current signal strength (the radio signal icon).

4. Tap the network you want to join. If multiple networks are available, you need to decide which one to join. If a network requires a password, of course, you must know what that password is to be able to join it. Another consideration should be signal strength; the more waves in the network's signal strength icon, the stronger the connection will be.

5. At the prompt, enter the password for the network. If you aren't prompted for a password, you selected a network that doesn't require one and can skip to step 7. This is common in public places (hotels, airports, and so on); see the next section for information on using these types of networks.

6. Tap Join. If you provided the correct password, your iPhone connects to the network and gets the information it needs to connect to the Internet. If not, you're prompted to enter the password again. After you successfully connect to the network, you return to the Wi-Fi screen.

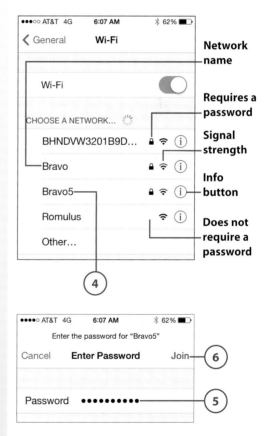

Typing Passwords

As you type a password, each character is hidden by dots in the Password field except for the last character you entered, which is displayed on the screen for a few moments. This is helpful even though you see each character as you type it, so you always see the most recent character you entered, which can prevent you from getting all the way to the end of a long password only to discover you've made a mistake along the way and have to start all over again.

7. Review the network information. The network to which you are connected appears just below the Wi-Fi switch and is marked with a check mark. You also see the signal strength for that network. (This indication is typically more accurate than the one you see before you are connected.) Assuming the Wi-Fi network is providing Internet access, you're able to use apps that require the Internet to work.

8. Try to move to a web page, such as www.weather.com to test your Wi-Fi connection. (See Chapter 13, "Surfing the Web," for details.) If the webpage opens, you are ready to use the Internet on your phone. If you are taken to a login webpage for a Wi-Fi provider rather than the page you were trying to access, see the following task. If you see a message saying the Internet is not available, there is a problem with the network you joined. Go back to step 4 to select a different network or contact the network's provider to see when the issue will be corrected.

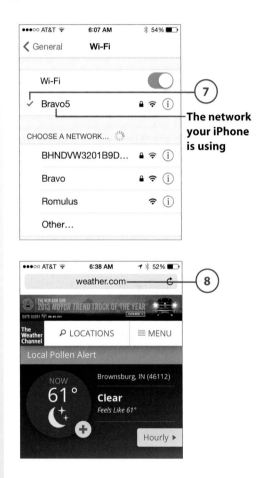

The network your iPhone is using

Be Known

After your iPhone connects to a Wi-Fi network successfully, it becomes a known network. This means that your iPhone remembers its information so you don't have to enter it again. Your iPhone automatically connects to known networks when it needs to access the Internet. So unless you tell your iPhone to forget a network (explained later in this chapter), you need to log in to it only the first time you connect to it.

Connecting to Public Wi-Fi Networks

Many Wi-Fi networks in public places, such as hotels or airports, require that you pay a fee or provide other information to access the Internet through that network; even if access is free, you usually have to accept the terms and conditions for the network to be able to use it.

When you connect to one of these public networks, you're prompted to provide whatever information is required. This can involve different details for different networks, but the general steps are the same. You're prompted to provide whatever information is required so you just follow the instructions that appear.

Following are the general steps to connect to many types of public Wi-Fi networks:

1. Use the steps in the previous task to move to and tap the public network you want to join. The iPhone connects to the network, and you see the Log In screen for that network.

2. If prompted to do so, provide the information required to join the network, such as a name and room number. If a fee is required, you'll have to provide payment information. In almost all cases, you at least have to indicate that you accept the terms and conditions for using the network, which you typically do by checking a check box.

3. Tap the button to join the network. This button can have different labels depending on the type of access, such as Authenticate, Done, Free Access, Login, and so on.

No Prompt?

Not all public networks prompt you to log in as these steps explain. Sometimes, you use the network's website to log in instead. After you join the network (step 1), your iPhone is connected to the network without any prompts. When you try to move to a webpage as explained in step 4, you're prompted to log in to or create an account with the network's provider on the webpage that appears.

4. Try to move to a webpage, such as www.apple.com, to test your Wi-Fi connection. (See Chapter 13 for details.) If the webpage opens, you are ready to use the Internet on your phone. If you are taken to a login webpage for the Wi-Fi network's provider, you need to provide the required information to be able to use the Internet.

A Closed Network

Some Wi-Fi networks are closed, which means they don't broadcast their names. You don't see closed networks listed in the CHOOSE A NETWORK on the Wi-Fi screen. To be able to access a closed network, you need to know its name, its password, and the type of security it uses. With this information in hand, tap Other in the CHOOSE A NETWORK section. Then type the network's name. Tap Security, choose the appropriate type, and tap Back. Enter the required password and tap Join.

Disabling Automatic Prompting

When your iPhone can't find a known network—meaning one that you've used before—it presents a prompt showing you the currently available networks. You can use this prompt to select and join one of these networks. This can be useful because you don't have to use the Settings app to find a network to which you are going to connect; instead, you can just tap a network at the prompt to join it.

However, this automatic prompting for networks can be as annoying as it is helpful. It is helpful In that your iPhone prompts you when it comes into range of a network it doesn't know, which can make it easier to know when a network is available to you. It can be annoying when you are moving around a lot because what you are doing can be constantly interrupted by the prompt, even if you don't want to connect to one of the available networks. For example, when you walk through an airport, the prompt can appear multiple times as you move between networks.

To disable automatic network prompting, perform the following steps:

1. Open the Settings app and move to the Wi-Fi screen.

2. Set the Ask to Join Networks switch to off (white). To connect to unknown networks, you need to use the Settings app as described in the previous tasks because your iPhone no longer prompts you to join unknown networks.

Forgetting Wi-Fi Networks

As you learned earlier, your iPhone remembers networks you have joined and connects to them automatically as needed; these are known networks. Although this is mostly a good thing, occasionally you won't want to use a particular network any more. For example, when in an airport, you might decide to connect to a network for which you have to pay for Internet access. Each time you move through that airport, your iPhone connects to that network again automatically, which might not be what you want it to do.

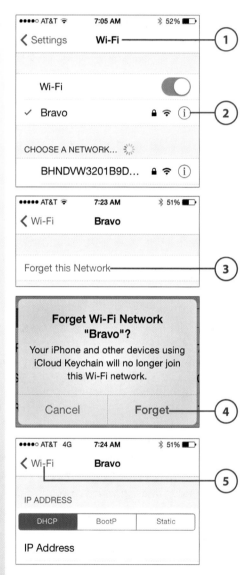

To have your iPhone forget a network so it doesn't automatically connect to it in the future, do the following:

1. Tap Wi-Fi in the Settings app to view the Wi-Fi screen.

2. Tap the Info button for the network that you want your iPhone to forget. (You can forget a network only if you are currently connected to it.)

3. Tap Forget this Network.

4. Tap Forget in the resulting prompt. Your iPhone stops using and forgets the network.

5. Tap Wi-Fi. You return to the Wi-Fi screen. If another known network is available, your iPhone connects to it automatically. If a network you've forgotten is still in range of your iPhone, it continues to appear in the CHOOSE A NETWORK section, but your iPhone will no longer automatically connect to it. You can rejoin the forgotten network at any time just as you did the first time you connected to it.

Cell Phone Provider Wi-Fi Networks

Many cell phone providers also provide other services, particularly public Wi-Fi networks. In some cases, you can access that provider's Internet service through a Wi-Fi network that it provides; ideally, you can do this at no additional charge. So, you can take advantage of the speed a Wi-Fi connection provides without paying more for it. You start connecting to these networks just like any other by selecting them on the available network list. What happens next depends on the specific network. In some cases, you need to enter your mobile phone number and then respond to a text message to that phone number. Check your provider's website to find out whether it offers this service and where you can access it.

Using Cellular Data Networks to Connect to the Internet

The cellular provider associated with your iPhone also provides a cellular Internet connection your iPhone uses automatically when a Wi-Fi connection isn't available. (Your iPhone tries to connect to an available Wi-Fi network before connecting to a cellular data connection because Wi-Fi is typically less expensive to use.) These networks are great because the area they cover is large and the connection to them is automatic; your iPhone chooses and connects to the best cellular network currently available on its own. Access to these networks is usually part of your monthly account fee. Usually, you choose from among various amounts of data per month at different monthly charges. The best case is where you have unlimited data, but not all providers offer this option.

Most providers have multiple cellular data networks, such as a low-speed network that is available widely and one or more higher-speed networks that have a more limited coverage area. Your iPhone chooses the best connection available automatically. (If a low-speed network is all that is currently available, you might find its performance unusable for web browsing or other data-intensive tasks; in which case, you should try to connect to a Wi-Fi network.)

The cellular data networks you can use are determined based on your provider, your data plan, the model of iPhone you are using, and your location within your provider's networks or the roaming networks available when you are outside of your provider's coverage area. The iPhone automatically uses the fastest connection available to it at any given time (assuming you haven't disabled that option, as explained later).

In the United States, the major iPhone providers are AT&T, Verizon, T-Mobile, and Sprint. There are also other smaller providers, such as Virgin Mobile.

All these companies offer high-speed Long Term Evolution (LTE) cellular networks (these are also referred to as *true 4G networks*) along with the slower 4G and 3G networks. In other locations, the names and speed of the networks available might be different.

As noted earlier, the speed of the cellular data network you can access depends on the model of iPhone you are using. The iPhone 5, 5C, and 5S can use the fastest possible connection. The iPhone 4S can connect to the next fastest networks.

The following information is focused on AT&T's LTE network because I happen to live in the United States, use an iPhone 5S, and use AT&T as my cell phone provider. If you use another provider or a different iPhone model, you are able to access your provider's networks similarly, though your details might be different. For example, the icon on the Home screen reflects the name of your provider's network, which might or might not be LTE.

This iPhone is connected to a high-speed LTE cellular network

AT&T's and the other providers' LTE high-speed wireless networks provide very fast Internet access from many locations. (Note: The LTE network is not available everywhere, but you can usually count on it near populated areas.) To connect to the LTE network, you don't need to do anything. If you aren't connected to a Wi-Fi network, you haven't turned off LTE, and your iPhone isn't in Airplane mode, the iPhone automatically connects to the LTE network if it is available in your current location. When you are connected to the LTE network, you see the LTE indicator at the top of the iPhone's screen. If you can't access the LTE network, such as when you aren't in range of it, the iPhone automatically connects to the next fastest network available, such as 4G. If that isn't available, it connects to the next fastest and so on until it finds a network to which it can connect if at least one network is available. If it can't connect to any network, you see No Service instead of a network's name.

Whenever you are connected to the LTE or other cellular data network, you can access the Internet for web browsing, email, and so on. The performance you experience depends on the speed of the specific network to which you connect and the strength of the signal through which you are connecting. In the best case, the performance of the cellular data network rivals or even exceeds that of a Wi-Fi network; in the worst case, it is so slow that you might find the performance unbearable or not available at all. The only way to know is to try it by using the Web, email, or other Internet-based activity.

One thing you do need to keep in mind when using a cellular network is that your account might include a set amount of data per month. When your data use exceeds this limit, you may be charged overage fees, which can be very expensive. Most providers send you warning texts or emails as your data use approaches your plan's limit, at which point you need to be careful about what you do while using the cellular data network to avoid an overage fee. Some tasks, such as watching YouTube videos or downloading large movie files, can chew up a lot of data. Others, such as using email, typically don't use very much.

An App for That

Various apps are available in the App Store that you can install on your iPhone that monitor how much data you are using. These apps are a good way to know where your data use is relative to your plan's monthly allowance so that you can avoid an overage situation. To get information on finding, downloading, and installing apps, see Chapter 6, "Downloading Apps, Music, Movies, TV Shows, and More onto Your iPhone." (To find an app for this purpose, search for "data monitoring app.")

When you move outside of your primary network's geographic coverage area, you are in roaming territory, which means a different provider might provide both cellular phone or data access or both. The iPhone automatically selects a roaming provider if there is only one available or allows you to choose one if there is more than one available.

When you are outside of your primary provider's coverage area, roaming charges can be associated with calls or data use. These charges are often very expensive. The roaming charges associated with phone calls are easier to manage given that it's more obvious when you make or receive a phone call in a roaming area. However, data roaming charges are much more insidious, especially if Push functionality (where emails are pushed to iPhone from the server as they are received) are active. And when you use some applications, such as Maps to navigate, you don't really know how much data is involved. Because data roaming charges are harder to notice, the iPhone is configured by default to prevent data roaming. When data roaming is disabled, the iPhone is unable to access the Internet when you are outside of your cellular network, unless you connect to a Wi-Fi network. (You can still use the cellular roaming network for telephone calls.)

You can configure some aspects of how your cellular network is used, as you see in this task. You can also allow individual apps to use, or prevent them from using, your cellular data network. This is important when your data plan has a monthly limit. You should be careful about enabling apps to use the cellular data network to help prevent overage charges (assuming you don't have an account with unlimited data). In most cases, the first time you launch an app, you're prompted to allow or prevent it from using cellular data. At any time, you can use the Settings app to enable or disable an app's access to your cellular data network.

To configure how your iPhone uses its cellular network for data, perform the following steps:

1. Open the Settings app.

2. Tap Cellular.

3. To disable all cellular data connections, set the Cellular Data switch to off (white). The iPhone is no longer able to connect to any cellular data networks. To use the Internet when this is off, you have to be connected to a Wi-Fi network that provides Internet access.

4. To disable the high-speed network, set its Enable switch (in this example, Enable LTE) to off (white). Your iPhone connects to the cellular data network using the next best available speed, such as a 3G network.

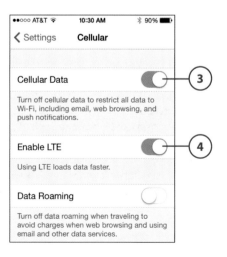

Higher-speed Networks Use More Power

Using a higher-speed network, such as an LTE network, also uses somewhat more battery power than using a slower network. If getting the absolute maximum time on a charge is important, you might want to disable the high-speed network.

5. If you want to allow data roaming, slide the Data Roaming switch to the on (green) position. When you move outside your primary network, data comes to iPhone via an available roaming network. You should disable it again by sliding the Data Roaming switch to off (white) as soon as you're done with a specific task to limit the amount of overage charges.

6. Swipe up the screen until you see the USE CELLULAR DATA FOR section. This section enables you to allow or prevent individual apps from accessing the cellular data network. It's a good idea to review this list and allow only those apps that you rely on to use the cellular data network to limit the amount of data you use. (Of course, if you are fortunate enough to have an unlimited data plan, you can leave all the apps enabled.)

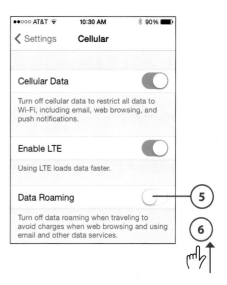

Monitoring Data Use

In the CELLULAR DATA USAGE section of the Cellular screen, you see how much data you've used for the current period and how much you've used while roaming. This can help you see where your use is compared to your monthly plan allowance so you know whether you are getting close to exceeding that allowance (thus incurring overage charges). This isn't proactive at all, so you have to remember to move to this screen to see the information. If you are concerned about data use, you're better off getting an app with more active monitoring.

7. Set an app's switch to on (green) if you want it to be able to use your cellular data network.

8. Set an app's switch to off (white) if you want it to be able to access the Internet only when you are connected to a Wi-Fi network.

9. Tap Settings when you're done configuring your cellular network use.

TETHERING (AKA PERSONAL HOTSPOT)

The iPhone supports tethering, which is providing an Internet connection through the iPhone to computers or other devices. This is useful when you are in a location where you can't connect a computer or other device to a network with Internet access (or don't want to spend the money to do so) but can access the Internet with the iPhone's high-speed cellular data connection.

There are a lot of caveats to this service, including whether your provider offers it, additional costs, and so on. Check with your provider to see if the personal hotspot feature is supported and if there are additional fees to use it. If it is provided and the fees are acceptable, this is a good way to provide Internet access to other devices when a Wi-Fi connection either isn't available or is too expensive.

First, add the tethering service to your cellular account. Second, move to the Cellular screen in the Settings app, and then tap Set Up Personal Hotspot. Follow the onscreen prompts to complete the configuration of the personal hotspot; the details depend on the specific provider you are using. After your iPhone is configured as a hotspot, it can share its Internet connection with other devices.

Using Bluetooth to Connect to Other Devices

The iPhone includes built-in Bluetooth support so you can use this wireless technology to connect to other Bluetooth-capable devices. The most likely devices to connect to iPhone in this way are Bluetooth headphones or headsets or car audio/entertainment/information systems, but you can also use Bluetooth to connect to other kinds of devices, most notably keyboards, headphones, computers, iPod touches, iPads, and other iPhones.

To connect Bluetooth devices together, you *pair* them. In Bluetooth, pairing enables two Bluetooth devices to communicate with each other. The one constant requirement is that the devices can communicate with each other via Bluetooth. For devices to find and identify each other so they can communicate, one or both must be *discoverable*, which means they broadcast a Bluetooth signal other devices can detect and connect to.

There is also a "sometimes" requirement, which is a pairing code, passkey, or PIN. All those terms refer to the same thing, which is a series of numbers, letters, or both that are entered on one or both devices being paired. Sometimes you enter this code on both devices, whereas for other devices you enter the first device's code on the second device. Some devices don't require a pairing code at all.

When you have to pair devices, you're prompted to do so, and you have to complete the actions required by the prompt to communicate via Bluetooth. This might be just tapping Connect, or you might have to enter a passcode on one or both devices.

Connecting to Bluetooth Devices

This task demonstrates pairing an iPhone with a Bluetooth keyboard; you can pair it with other devices similarly.

1. Move to the Settings screen. The current status of Bluetooth on your iPhone is shown.

2. Tap Bluetooth.

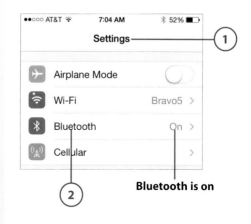

3. If Bluetooth isn't on (green), tap the Bluetooth switch to turn it on. If it isn't running already, Bluetooth starts up. The iPhone immediately begins searching for Bluetooth devices. You also see the status Now Discoverable, which means other Bluetooth devices can discover the iPhone. In the DEVICES section, you see devices with which your iPhone is currently paired. You also see the current status of their connections, those being Connected (the iPhone is currently communicating with the device) or Not Connected (the iPhone is not currently communicated with the device). A device must show Connected for your iPhone to work with it.

4. Put the other device in Discoverable mode. (See the instructions provided with the device.) The two devices find each other. On the iPhone, the other device is listed but is shown as Not Paired.

5. Tap the device to which you want to connect. If a passkey is required, you see a prompt to enter it on the device with which you are pairing.

6. Input the required passkey, such as typing the passkey on a keyboard if you are pairing with a Bluetooth keyboard.

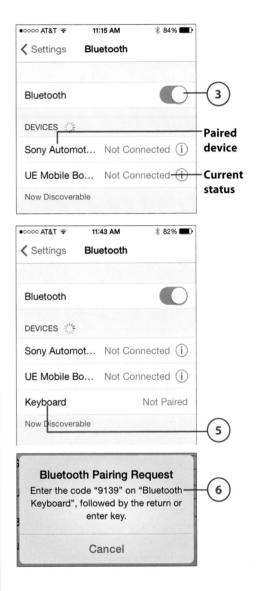

7. If required, tap Connect—some devices connect as soon as you enter the passkey and you won't need to do this. If a passcode isn't required, you tap Connect instead. You see the device to which the iPhone is connected in the Devices section of the Bluetooth screen.

●●●●○ AT&T 📶	11:43 AM	⚡ 82% 🔋
‹ Settings	**Bluetooth**	

Bluetooth	⬤

DEVICES ⚙

Bluetooth Keyboard	Connected	ⓘ
Sony Automot...	Not Connected	ⓘ
UE Mobile Bo...	Not Connected	ⓘ
Now Discoverable		

This keyboard is now connected and can be used

>>>Go Further

MANAGING BLUETOOTH

Following are a few pointers for using Bluetooth with other devices

- Like other connections you make, the iPhone remembers Bluetooth devices to which you've connected before and reconnects to them automatically, which is convenient—most of the time anyway. If you don't want your iPhone to keep connecting to a device, move to the Bluetooth screen and tap the device's Info (i) button. Tap the Forget this Device button and then tap Forget Device. The pairing is removed. Of course, you can always pair the devices again at any time.

- If a device is already paired but doesn't connect automatically, you need to connect it to use it. Move to the Bluetooth screen and tap the device. Once connected, your iPhone can communicate with the device again.

- You can use multiple Bluetooth devices with your iPhone at the same time.

Connecting Your iPhone to Other iPhones, iPod Touches, or iPads

The iPhone (and other devices that run the iOS software, including iPod touches and iPads) supports peer-to-peer connectivity, which is an overly complicated way of saying that these devices can communicate with one another directly via a Wi-Fi network or Bluetooth. This capability is used in a number of apps, especially multiplayer gaming, for information sharing, and for other collaborative purposes.

If the app you want to use communicates over a Wi-Fi network, such as a network you use to access the Internet, all the devices with which you want to communicate must be on that same network. If the application uses Bluetooth, you must enable Bluetooth on each device and pair them (as described in the previous section) so they can communicate with one another.

The specific steps you use to connect to other iOS devices using a collaborative app depend on the specific app you are using. The general steps are typically as follows:

1. Ensure the devices can communicate with each other. If the app uses Wi-Fi, each device must be on the same Wi-Fi network. If the app uses Bluetooth, the devices must be paired.

2. Each person opens the app on his device.

3. Use the app's controls to select the devices with which you'll be collaborating. Usually, this involves a confirmation process in which one person selects another person's device and that person confirms that the connection should be allowed.

4. Use the app's features to collaborate. For example, if the app is a game, each person can interact with the group members. Or, you can directly collaborate on a document with all parties providing input into the document.

Using AirDrop to Share Content with Other iPhones, iPod Touches, or iPads

You can use the iOS AirDrop feature to share content directly with other iOS device users. For example, if you capture a great photo on your iPhone, you can use AirDrop to instantly share that photo with iOS device users near you.

AirDrop can use Wi-Fi or Bluetooth to share, but the nice thing about AirDrop is that it manages the details for you. You simply open the Action menu—which is available in most apps—tap AirDrop, and tap the people with whom you want to share.

When you activate AirDrop, you can select Everyone, which means you will see anyone who has an iOS device running version iOS 7 or newer and is on the same Wi-Fi network with you (or has a paired Bluetooth device); those people can see you, too. Or, you can select Contacts Only, which means only people who are in your Contacts app are able to use AirDrop to communicate with you. In most cases, you should choose the Contacts Only option so you have more control over who communicates with you.

When enabled, you can use AirDrop by opening the Action menu while using an app. Then you tap the people with whom you want to share content.

Is AirDrop Safe?

Anything you share with AirDrop is encrypted, so the chances of someone else being able to intercept and use what you share are quite low. Likewise, you don't have to worry about someone using AirDrop to access your information or to add information to your device without your permission. However, like any networking technology, there's always some chance—quite small in this case—that someone will figure out how to use this technology for nefarious purposes. The best thing you can do is to be wary of any requests you receive to share information and ensure they are from people you know and trust before you accept them.

Enabling AirDrop

To use AirDrop, you must enable it on your iPhone.

1. Swipe up from the bottom of the screen to open the Control Center.

2. If AirDrop is not active, tap AirDrop. If it is active, which is indicated by the highlighted icon and its status (Everyone or Contacts Only), skip this step.

3. Tap Contacts Only to allow only people in your Contacts app to communicate with you via AirDrop, or tap Everyone to allow anyone running an iOS 7 device in your area to do so.

4. Swipe down from the top of the Control Center to close it. You're ready to use AirDrop to share.

Current AirDrop status (disabled)

Share and Share Alike?

You should disable AirDrop when you aren't using it, especially if you use the Everyone option. By disabling it, you avoid having people in your area be able to try to communicate with you without you wanting them to do so. Generally, you should enable AirDrop only when you are actively using it and disable it when you aren't. To disable AirDrop, open the Control Center, tap AirDrop, and then tap Off.

People in your Contacts app can use AirDrop to communicate with you

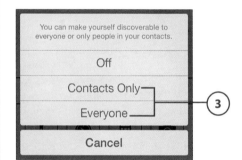

Using AirDrop to Share Your Content

To use AirDrop to share your content, do the following:

1. Open the app and move to the content you want to share. This example shows sharing a photo using the Photos app, but the steps to share in any app are quite similar.

2. Tap the Action button.

3. Tap AirDrop. The AirDrop button is replaced with icons for each person in your area who has AirDrop enabled that you have permission to access (such as being in her Contacts app if she is using the Contacts Only option).

4. If necessary, swipe to the left or right to browse all the people with whom you can share.

5. Tap the people with whom you want to share the content. A sharing request is sent to those people's devices. Under their icons, the Waiting status is displayed. When a recipient accepts your content, the status changes to Sent. If a recipient rejects your content, the status changes to Declined.

Photo selected to share

6. If the app supports it, browse and select more content to share.

7. Tap the people with whom you want to share the content.

8. When you're done sharing, tap Done.

Waiting for the recipient to accept or decline your sharing

Recipient has accepted your content

Using AirDrop to Work with Content Shared with You

When someone wants to share content with you, you receive an AirDrop sharing request. Respond by doing the following:

1. Make sure you know the person attempting to share with you.

2. Make sure the content being shared with you is something you want. In this case, a contact card is being shared.

3. To accept the content on your iPhone, tap Accept. To reject it, tap Decline.

4. If you accepted the content and the app enables you to review it in detail or edit it before saving it on your iPhone, swipe up and down the screen to see the detail of what you are accepting, or use the app's controls to edit it. For example, you can review the details of contact information being shared, you can edit photos shared with you, and so on.

5. Tap Save to save the content on your iPhone or Cancel to not save it. (Other apps provide different controls—for example, the Photo app provides the open to edit and delete photos shared with you options.)

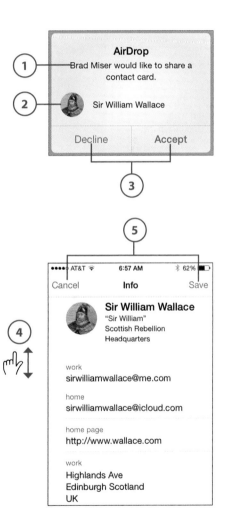

Use iCloud and other accounts to connect your iPhone to the Internet

Set up Facebook, Twitter, and other social networking accounts so you can share information, photos, and more

In this chapter, you learn how to connect your iPhone to various types of accounts, such as iCloud, Exchange, and Google. You also learn how to manage your accounts. The topics include the following:

→ Configuring iCloud
→ Setting up other types of accounts on your iPhone
→ Determining how and when your accounts are updated
→ Managing your accounts

Setting Up iCloud and Other Online Accounts

No iPhone is an island. Connecting your iPhone to the Internet enables you to share and sync a wide variety of content. Using iCloud, you can put your email, contacts, calendars, and more on the Internet so that multiple devices—most importantly your iPhone—can connect to and use that information. (There's a lot more you can do with iCloud, too, as you learn throughout this book.) There are lots of other accounts you might also want to use, such as Exchange and Google for email, calendars, and contacts as well as Twitter and Facebook for accessing social networks.

You need to configure each of these accounts on your iPhone to be able to use them; you'll see a section for a number of accounts you might want to use. Of course, you only need to refer to the section related to the accounts you actually use. You should also understand how you can determine how and when your information is updated along with tasks you might find valuable as you manage the various accounts on your iPhone.

Configuring iCloud Settings

iCloud is a service provided by Apple that provides with you with your own storage space on the Internet. In general, such Internet storage space is known as the cloud, so Apple's version of this space is called iCloud. You can store your information in your storage space on the cloud, and because it is on the Internet, all your devices are able to access that information at the same time. This means you can easily share your information on your iPhone, a computer, an iPad, and so on, so that the same information and content is available to you no matter which device you are using at any one time.

Although your iPhone can work with many types of online/Internet accounts, iCloud is integrated into the iPhone like no other type of account (not surprising because iCloud is also Apple technology). An iCloud account is really useful in a number of ways. For example, iCloud can be used for the following:

- **Email**—An iCloud account includes an @icloud.com email address. You can configure any device to use your iCloud email account, including an iPhone, an iPad, an iPod, a computer, and so on.

- **Contacts**—You can store contact information in iCloud so that you can access it from lots of different devices.

- **Calendars**—Putting your calendars in iCloud makes it much easier to manage your time.

- **Reminders**—Through iCloud, you can be reminded of things you need to do or anything else you want to make sure you don't forget. Like the other features, you can have the same reminders on any device you've connected to your iCloud account.

- **Safari**—iCloud can store your bookmarks, letting you easily access the same websites from all your devices.

- **Notes**—With the Notes app, you can create text notes for many purposes; iCloud enables you to access these notes on any iCloud-enabled device.

- **Passbook**—The Passbook app stores coupons, tickets, boarding passes, and other documents so you can access them quickly and easily. With iCloud, you can ensure that these documents are available on any iCloud-enabled device.

- **Photos**—iCloud's Photo Stream functionality may be one of its best features. Using Photo Stream, the photos you take on your iPhone, iPad, or iPod touch are immediately uploaded to the cloud and then downloaded to other devices. Configuring a computer to use Photo Stream is especially useful because this automatically provides a backup of your photos. Be aware that the photos stay in the cloud for only 30 days. And you can store up to 1,000 photos at a time; when you reach 1,000, the oldest photos are removed to make room for new photos. For more permanent storage, you should use Photo Stream to automatically download them to a computer or other external storage.

- **Documents**—iCloud enables you to access any of your documents on iOS devices, Macs, and Windows PCs. These documents can be of a number of types, including Pages, Word, PDF, Excel, Numbers, Keynote, and PowerPoint.

You can also use iCloud to help locate and protect your iPhone through the Find My iPhone feature. In addition to locating your iPhone, you can lock it or even remotely wipe its memory if you've lost control of it.

Another useful function of iCloud is the ability to back up your iPhone so you can restore its information if something bad happens.

You'll learn about these features throughout this book (such as Photo Stream, which is covered in Chapter 15, "Working with Photos and Video You Take with Your iPhone"). The tasks in this chapter show you how to set up and configure the iCloud features you'll likely want to use.

Obtaining an iCloud Account

Of course, to use iCloud on your iPhone, you need to have an iCloud account. The good news is that you probably already have one. The other good news is that even if you don't, obtaining one is simple and free.

If you have any of the following accounts, you already have an iCloud account and are ready to start using iCloud and can skip ahead to the next section:

- **iTunes Store**—If you've ever shopped at the iTunes Store, you created an account with an Apple ID and password. You can use that Apple ID and password to access iCloud.

- **Apple Online Store**—As with the iTunes Store, if you made purchases from Apple's online store, you created an account with an Apple ID and password that also enables you to use iCloud.

- **MobileMe/.Mac**—If you used these previous iterations of Apple's online services, you can use the same login information to access your iCloud account.

- **Find My iPhone**—If you obtained a free Find My iPhone account, you can log in to iCloud using that Apple ID.

During the initial iPhone startup process, you were prompted to sign into or create an iCloud account. If you created one at that time, you are good to go and can move to the next section.

If you don't have an iCloud account, you can use your iPhone to create one by performing the following steps:

1. On the Home screen, tap Settings.

2. Swipe up the screen and tap iCloud.

3. Tap Get a Free Apple ID.

4. Provide the information required on the following screens; tap Next to move to the next screen after you've entered the required information. You start by entering your birthdate.

During the process, you'll be prompted to use an existing email address or to create a free iCloud email account. You can choose either option. The email address you use will become your iCloud username. If you create a new email account, you can use that account from any email app on any device, just like other email accounts you have.

You'll also create a password, enter a rescue email address (optional), set up security questions, and agree to license terms. When your account has been created, you're prompted to enter your password.

When you've provided all of the required information, you're prompted to allow iCloud to track the location of your iPhone.

5. Tap OK to activate Find My iPhone. You are ready to complete the configuration of your iCloud account, which is covered in the next section.

Multiple iCloud Accounts
You can have more than one iCloud account. However, you can have only one iCloud account active on your iPhone at the same time.

Setting Up and Logging In to Your iCloud Account

To be able to use an iCloud account on your iPhone, you need to first sign into your account and then enable the services you want to use and disable those that you don't want to use. After iCloud is set up on your iPhone, you rarely need to change your account settings. If you restore your iPhone at some point, you might need to revisit these steps to ensure iCloud remains set up as you want it.

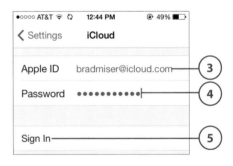

To get started, sign into your iCloud account—if you created your iCloud account on your iPhone, you don't need to perform these steps and can skip to the next task.

1. On the Home screen, tap Settings.

2. Tap iCloud.

3. Enter your Apple ID. If you see an account field instead of the Apple ID field, an iCloud account is already enabled on the iPhone. If it is your account, skip to the next section. If it isn't your account, swipe up the screen and tap Delete Account; tap Delete and continue with these steps.

4. Enter your Apple ID password.

5. Tap Sign In. You are logged in to your iCloud account.

6. At the prompt, tap either OK to allow iCloud to access your iPhone's location or Don't Allow if you don't want this to happen. You need to allow this for Find My iPhone, which enables you to locate your phone, to work. You're ready to configure the rest of iCloud's services.

Enabling iCloud to Keep Your Information in Sync

One of the best things about iCloud is that it helps you have the same email, contacts, calendars, reminders, bookmarks, notes, and passbook data on all your iCloud-enabled devices. You can choose to use iCloud syncing for any or all of these types of information by performing the following steps:

1. Move to the iCloud screen by tapping Settings, iCloud. Just below the account currently signed in are the iCloud data-syncing options. Each of these has a two-position switch. When green shows on a switch, it means that switch is turned on and the related data is synced to your iCloud account. For example, if Contacts shows green, your contact information is being stored on the cloud so you can have the same contacts and all your iCloud-enabled devices. By default, all these switches are in the on position.

2. If you don't want a specific type of data to be synced, tap its switch so that it moves to the left and is no longer green. The related data-syncing is disabled on your iPhone. When you disable syncing, you might be prompted as to whether to keep the information on your iPhone or delete it.

    If you choose Keep on My iPhone, the information remains on your iPhone but is no longer connected to the cloud; this means any changes you make will exist only on the iPhone. If you choose Delete from My iPhone, the information is erased (it is still available on the cloud, however).

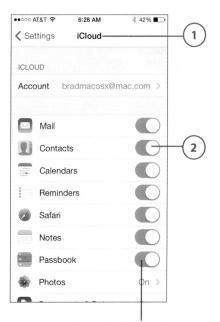

Green indicates the data is being synced to the cloud

Syncing Your Keychain

Apple was expected to add the ability to use iCloud to sync your keychain information, which is where passwords and other sensitive information is stored, shortly after this book was published. When this feature is added, you'll see a Keychain switch on the iCloud screen. A detailed explanation of how this feature works will be posted on this book's page at quepublishing.com as soon as it is available. Be sure to visit the site and register your book so you can access this and other additional information.

Configuring Photo Stream

Photo Stream is a really nice feature because it enables you to store your photos in your personal Internet storage space so they can be automatically available or downloaded to other devices. You can also share photos with others and access photos being shared with you. To configure Photo Stream, do the following:

1. On the iCloud Settings screen, tap Photos.

2. Ensure that the My Photo Stream switch is on (green). Any photos you take with the iPhone's camera are copied onto iCloud, and from there they are copied to your other devices on which the Photo Stream is enabled.

3. To be able to share your Photo Stream and to subscribe to other people's Photo Streams, set the Photo Sharing switch to on (green).

4. Tap iCloud.

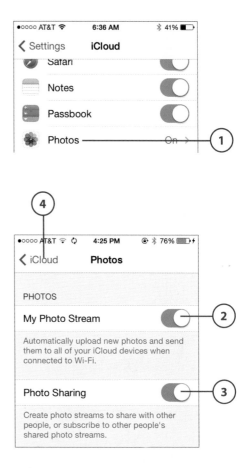

Configuring Documents and Data

You can store documents and other data in your iCloud storage space, which is useful for many things. For example, you can store a Pages document in the cloud and seamlessly work on the same document on your iPhone, an iPad, and a computer. To configure this function, do the following:

1. On the iCloud screen, tap Documents & Data.

2. Ensure the Documents & Data switch is in the on position (green) so that your documents and data are stored in the cloud.

3. If your cellular data plan has a limit on how much data you can use per month, you might want to set the Use Cellular Data to off (white). This prevents documents and data from being synced through your cellular network, which can use up a significant amount of your monthly data plan. If you have unlimited data or you don't use that many documents, leave this on (green).

4. Tap iCloud.

Enabling Find My iPhone and Choosing Where to Back Up

Find My iPhone enables you to locate and secure your iPhone if needed. And you can choose where you want to back up the information stored on your iPhone. To set up these areas, do the following:

1. If you didn't enable Find My iPhone when you logged in to your iCloud account, set the Find My iPhone switch to on (green); you'll need to touch the Touch ID button on an iPhone 5S or type your Apple ID password on other iPhone models to be able to activate this feature.

2. Tap Storage & Backup.

3. To have your iPhone's settings and other information backed up to your iCloud account, slide the switch next to iCloud Backup to on (green).

4. Tap OK. Be aware that when you use iCloud to back up your information, it is not backed up to your computer automatically (however, you can use iTunes to back it up on your computer manually).

5. Tap iCloud. Your iCloud account configuration is complete.

MORE ON ICLOUD BACK UP

In most cases, you'll want to back up your iPhone to your iCloud account. This is convenient because your content is backed up automatically whenever your iPhone can connect to the Internet via a Wi-Fi network (which is much of the time). The downside of this is that your iCloud account has limited space available (5GB by default), and if you use your iCloud to store lots of documents and other information, you can quickly reach this limit. You can buy more disk space by tapping Buy More Storage (this is labeled Change Storage Plan if you have already upgraded) and choosing to upgrade 20GB (25 total) or 50GB (55total). Fortunately, music and other content you obtain from the iTunes Store doesn't count against this limit, nor does your iTunes Match or Photo Stream content. You can start the backup process manually by moving to the Storage & Backup screen and tapping Back Up Now. The backup process starts and its status appears at the bottom of the screen.

Advanced Configuration of Your iCloud Account

Most of the time, you can use your iCloud account just fine if you only configure it as described in the previous section. However, there are a number of other configuration options that you might want to use at some point, and those are explained in this task.

1. Move to the iCloud Settings screen.

2. Tap your account.

3. If desired, change the description of the account to make it more distinctive in lists of accounts on your phone, such as in the Mail app.

4. Use the controls in the STORAGE PLAN section to increase the amount of storage your account has (or decrease it, if you have previously increased it).

5. Swipe up the screen.

6. Tap the account shown next to Mail.

7. If you want to change the name shown in the From field on messages you send, tap your name and edit it.

8. Tap Email.

9. Tap the email address that you want to be the default when you use your iCloud email. The addresses you see depend on how your account is configured. For example, if you have created email aliases (see the Go Further section at the end of these steps), you can choose an alias as your default email address.

10. Tap Mail.

11. On the ALLOW SENDING FROM list, set the switch to on (green) for any addresses that you want to allow sending email from, or turn it off if you want to prevent email from being sent from that address.

12. Swipe up the screen. You see the OUTGOING MAIL SERVER section. Here, you see and can configure information about the Simple Mail Transfer Protocol (SMTP) server your account uses to send email. In almost all cases, you leave this configured as it is by default (see the Go Further sidebar at the end of these steps for more information on SMTP).

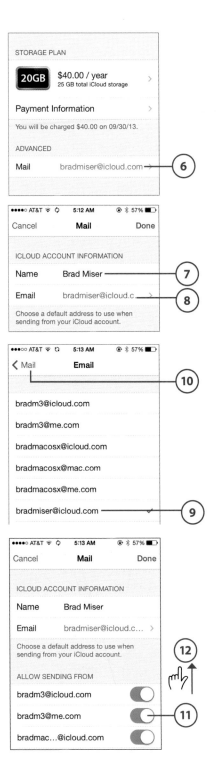

13. Tap Advanced. On this screen, you can configure where various types of email messages are stored.

14. Tap Drafts Mailbox.

15. To have drafts of your emails stored on the iPhone, tap Drafts in the ON MY IPHONE section, or to have them stored on the server, tap Inbox or one of the other folders in the ON THE SERVER section. The advantage of storing drafts on the server is that you can work on them from any locations that can access your account, such as an email app on a computer. If you save them on your iPhone, you can work on them only using the iPhone.

16. Tap Advanced.

17. Using the same process as in steps 15 and 16, set the location where you want send, deleted, and archived messages sent. Like drafts, you can have them stored on your iPhone or on the iCloud server.

18. Tap Deleted Mailbox if you want messages to move into that folder when you delete them or Archive mailbox if you prefer to have them moved there instead. The difference between these folders is that messages stay in the Archive folder whereas they are removed from the Deleted mailbox periodically.

19. Tap Remove.

20. Choose when you want deleted email to be removed from the server. The longer the timeframe, the more storage space on the server is used for deleted messages, but the longer you can recover those messages. If you choose to archive your messages, this doesn't really matter because you can always move back to your archive folder to retrieve deleted messages.

21. Tap Advanced.

22. Tap Mail.

23. Tap Done on the Mail screen.

24. Tap Done on the Account screen.

TWEAKING YOUR ICLOUD ACCOUNT

>>>Go Further

Here are some other things you might want to know about your iCloud account settings:

•The SMTP server is the one that sends email. In most cases, you just use the SMTP server configured for you automatically when you set up your iCloud account. However, if you have problems sending email, you might need to adjust the server's configuration—or you can even add another SMTP server, such as one available with one of your other accounts, so you can use that server when the iCloud SMTP is not available. To configure the SMTP servers, tap SMTP on the Mail screen. The Primary Server section displays the main SMTP server that is used to send messages. You should leave the primary server set to what it is. In the OTHER SMTP SERVERS section is the list of SMTP servers from the other email accounts on your iPhone (that use SMTP to send email). You can enable or disable these servers. To add a new SMTP server, tap Add Server and then enter the information for the server you want to add.

- One of the great features of iCloud is using email aliases. You can create alias addresses for specific purposes, such as avoiding spam or just to use an email address you prefer. Email sent to one of your aliases comes into your normal inbox, yet when you send email from an alias, it appears to be from that other address, even though all your aliases still relate to the same account. You can create email aliases for your iCloud account using the iCloud website. For more information on using your iCloud website and creating aliases, see my book *Sams Teach Yourself iCloud in 10 Minutes,* 2nd Edition.

- Secure/Multipurpose Internet Mail Extensions (S/MIME), which are at the bottom of the Advanced screen when you are configuring iCloud Mail, are a means to encrypt emails so that a key is required to be able to decrypt the information contained in them. To use S/MIME, you must install a certificate on your iPhone for any account that uses these extensions. Accounts that are generally available, such as iCloud, Gmail, and so on, are very unlikely to support these extensions. If you do have access to an account that supports S/MIME, you'll need the certificate, key, and configuration information from the account provider to be able to configure it on your iPhone.

>>>Go Further   ICLOUD IS EVERYWHERE

One of the great things about iCloud is that you can use it to sync content to many devices, including other iOS devices (iPod touches and iPads), Macs, and Windows PCs. Setting up iCloud on other iOS devices is just like setting it up on an iPhone (because they all run the same operating system). To set up iCloud on a Mac, open the iCloud pane of the System Preferences app, and then enter your iCloud account info; after you are logged in, you can set the type of information you want to sync between your Mac and the cloud. To set up iCloud on a Windows PC, you need to download and install the iCloud control panel, use it to log in to your account, and then configure the information you want to sync. For more information on using iCloud on iOS and other devices, see my book *Sams Teach Yourself iCloud in 10 Minutes,* 2nd Edition.

Setting Up Other Types of Accounts on Your iPhone

Many types of online accounts provide different services, including email, calendars, contacts, social networking, and so on. To use these accounts, you need to configure them on your iPhone. The process you use for most types of accounts is similar to the steps you used to set up your iCloud account. In this section, you'll learn how to configure Exchange, Google, Twitter, and Facebook accounts.

Configuring an Exchange Account

Microsoft Exchange is the most widely used system for corporate email. Your iPhone is compatible with Exchange, which is good news indeed. (You can even configure multiple Exchange accounts on your iPhone if you can't get by with just one.) You can sync Exchange email, contact, calendar, reminder, and notes information on your iPhone; this works similarly to synchronizing with your iPhone using an iCloud account.

Before you can use Exchange on your iPhone, the Exchange server for your account must be configured to support iOS devices. Almost all are these days, but if the following steps don't work, you'll need to contact the department that supports the Exchange system you use to verify that iOS devices are supported. If they are supported but the following steps don't work for you, ask for help from that department to get the account set up on your iPhone.

1. On the Home screen, tap Settings.

2. Tap Mail, Contacts, Calendars.

3. Tap Add Account.

4. Tap Exchange.

5. Enter your email address.

6. Enter your password.

7. Change the description of the account if you want to use something more specific than Exchange.

8. Tap Next. The information you've entered is verified. If it can't be, you see a dialog box saying so and you'll need to correct it. If it is, you see the types of information that you can sync via Exchange.

9. Slide the switch to off (white) for any of the information you don't want to be moved onto the iPhone. (If a switch is green, that type of information will be synced onto your iPhone.)

10. Tap Save. The account configuration is saved, and you move back to the Mail, Contacts, Calendars screen where your Exchange account is displayed. Under the account description is the information that is synced with the account, such as Mail, Contacts, Calendars.

Annoying Warnings

Sometimes, you might need to change your account's password if it gets reset. Because your iPhone won't be able to connect your account with the current password, you will see messages telling you the iPhone can't access your account. These can be quite annoying as you have to keep clearing them and they keep reappearing immediately. They might even get your Exchange account locked if the iPhone tries and fails to connect a certain number of times. If this happens, you can disable the account by turning off all the data options so your phone won't try to connect to the account. After you get a new password, update it on the account screen and then turn on the data options again. Or, use the technique my great acquisitions editor employs; when she encounters a password issue, she puts the iPhone in Airplane mode so it won't present annoying warnings while she updates the password.

Performing Advanced Configuration of an Exchange Account

Like other types of accounts, you can do some additional, but optional, configuration:

1. On the Mail, Contacts, Calendars screen, tap the Exchange account you want to configure.

2. Tap the account.

3. Use the Email, Server, Domain, Username, Password, and Description fields to make any changes needed. If the account is configured properly, you shouldn't need to change any of these. But, if you have problems with the account, you can update or verify the settings on this screen. The one field you might need to use regularly is the Password field. If your organization requires your password to be reset periodically, you'll need to enter the updated password in the Password field to be able to access your account. (See the sidebar "Annoying Warnings," on the previous page, for some tips related to this.)

4. Tap Advanced Settings.

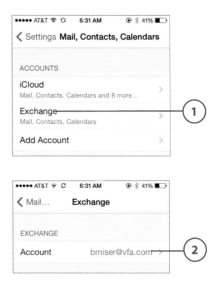

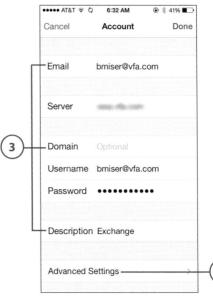

5. If necessary, you can change the status of the Secure Sockets Layer (SSL) setting. SSL is a means of encrypting data; most organizations use it, so this should be on (green).

6. Tap Deleted Mailbox to store messages you delete there or Archive Mailbox if you want to retain deleted messages. (See the sidebar "Tweaking Your iCloud Account" in the previous section for information about S/MIME.)

7. Tap Account.

8. Tap Done.

9. Tap the switch for the types of data to enable (green) or disable (white) syncing for that type.

10. Tap Mail Days to Sync.

•••• AT&T 🛜 🗘   6:32 AM   @ ⚡ 41% 🔋

⑦ ←Account **Advanced Settings**

Use SSL   ⑤

MOVE DISCARDED MESSAGES INTO:

⑥ ⌐Deleted Mailbox ✓
  └Archive Mailbox

S/MIME

S/MIME

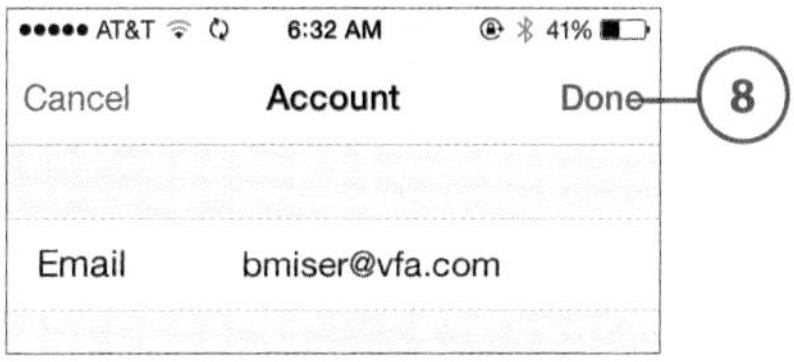

•••• AT&T 🛜 🗘   6:32 AM   @ ⚡ 41% 🔋

Cancel   **Account**   Done ⑧

Email   bmiser@vfa.com

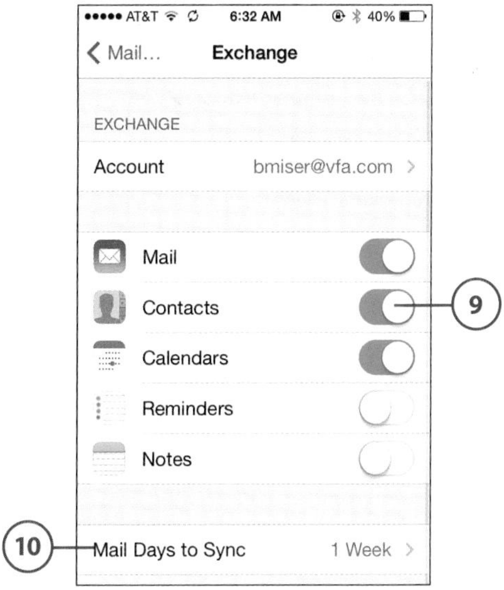

•••• AT&T 🛜 🗘   6:32 AM   @ ⚡ 40% 🔋

‹ Mail...   **Exchange**

EXCHANGE

Account   bmiser@vfa.com ›

✉ Mail

👤 Contacts ⑨

📅 Calendars

⁞ Reminders

🗒 Notes

⑩ Mail Days to Sync   1 Week ›

11. Tap the amount of time over which Exchange information should be synced. For example, to have one week of Exchange information on your iPhone, tap 1 Week.

12. Tap the return button, which is labeled with your email account's description.

13. Tap Mail. You start receiving information from your Exchange account according to your settings.

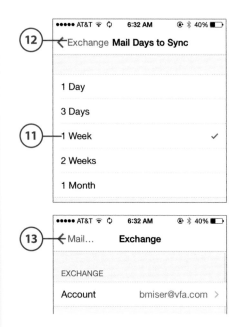

Configuring a Google Account

A Google account provides email, contacts, calendar, and note syncing that is similar to iCloud and Exchange. To set up a Google account on your iPhone, do the following:

1. On the Home screen, tap Settings.

2. Tap Mail, Contacts, Calendars.

3. Tap Add Account.

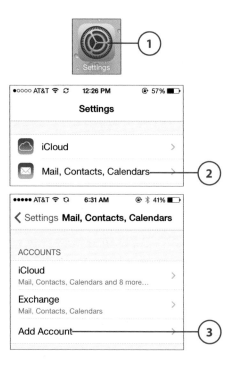

4. Tap Google.

5. Enter your name.

6. Enter your Google email address.

7. Enter your Google account password.

8. Change the default description, if you want to. This description appears on various lists of accounts, so you should use something easily recognizable.

9. Tap Next. If your account information is verified, you briefly see check marks next to each item and move to the account options screen. If there is a problem with the information you entered, you need to correct it before your account can be verified.

10. Enable the features of the account you want to access on the iPhone, which are Mail, Contacts, Calendars, and Notes. Do this by setting the switch for the feature to on (green) to add it to your iPhone or to off (white) if you do not want to include it on your iPhone.

11. Tap Save. The account is saved, and the data you enabled becomes available on your iPhone.

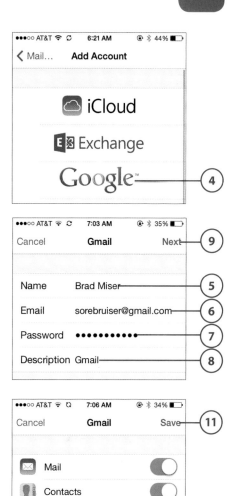

Advanced Google

Similar to iCloud and Exchange, a Google account has some settings you aren't likely to use, but it's good to know how to get to them in case you do. To access these settings, move to the Mail, Contacts, Calendars screen and tap your Google account. On the Gmail screen, you can change the types of data you are syncing. Tap Account, and then tap Advanced to move to those settings. Working with these is similar to iCloud and Exchange. For example, you can determine where messages are stored.

Configuring Other Types of Online Accounts

You can access many types of online accounts on your iPhone. These include accounts that are "built in," which include iCloud, Exchange, Google, Yahoo!, AOL, and Outlook.com. Setting up a Yahoo!, AOL, or Outlook.com account is similar to iCloud, Exchange, and Google. Just select the account type you want to use and provide the information for which you are prompted.

There are lots of other accounts you might want to use. An Email account included with an Internet access account, such as one from a cable Internet provider, is one example. Support for these accounts isn't built in to the iOS; however, you can usually set up such accounts on your iPhone fairly easily.

There are two basic ways to set up other types of accounts.

- Using iTunes Sync

- Manually

If you already have an account set up on your computer, you can use iTunes syncing to configure the account on your iPhone. This is the easiest and best method because you don't have to enter the account's information manually. Just include the account in the sync settings and sync the iPhone. The account becomes available for you to use. See Chapter 5, "Working with iTunes on Your Computer," for information on syncing your iPhone with iTunes.

If you don't already have the account configured on a computer or you don't want to use iTunes to sync it onto your iPhone, you can manually configure it with just a bit more work.

When you obtain an account, such as email accounts that are part of your Internet service, you should receive all the information you need to configure those accounts in an application on a computer, which is the same information you need to configure those accounts on your iPhone. If you don't have this information, visit the provider's website and look for information on configuring the account in an email application. You need to have this information to configure the account on the iPhone.

Setting Up an Account Manually

With the configuration information for the account in hand, you're ready to set it up:

1. Move to the Mail, Contacts, Calendars screen and tap Add Account.

2. Tap Other.

3. Tap the type of account you want to add. For example, to set up an email account, tap Add Mail Account.

4. Enter the information by filling in the fields you see. You will see different types of information for various kinds of accounts; you just need to enter the information you received from the account's provider.

5. Tap Next. If the iPhone can set up the account automatically, its information is verified and it is ready for you to use (if the account supports multiple types of information, you can enable or disable the types with which you want to work on your iPhone). If the iPhone can't set up the account automatically, you're prompted to enter additional information to complete the account configuration. When you're done, the account appears on the list of email accounts and is ready for you to use.

Multiple Accounts

There is no limit (that I have found so far) on the number of online accounts (even of the same type, such as Gmail) that you can access on your iPhone.

Configuring a Twitter Account

Twitter has become a popular way to communicate with others. Fortunately, your iPhone has Twitter integrated into its software, so you can tweet as a separate activity and can also tweet from within other applications, such as to share a webpage you are browsing with Safari. You can even tweet a great photo you just took with your iPhone.

To start tweeting, you need to install the Twitter application (if necessary—it might be installed by default). Then you must create an account if you don't have one or configure your existing Twitter account. After your Twitter account is configured, you can access it through the Twitter app or from many other apps.

To set up your Twitter account on your iPhone, perform the following steps:

1. Move to the Home screen and tap Settings.

2. Swipe up the screen and tap Twitter. If you see INSTALLED at the top of the screen, the Twitter app is installed on your iPhone and you can get right into your account. If not, tap INSTALL to install the app (downloading and installing apps is covered in Chapter 6, "Downloading Apps, Music, Movies, TV Shows, and More onto Your iPhone"); when the app is done installing, continue with these steps.

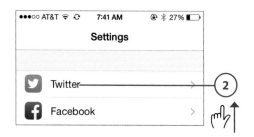

No Twitter Account?

If don't have a Twitter account, tap Create New Account and follow the onscreen instructions to create one. When you are done creating the new account, you're signed into it automatically, or you can follow the rest of these steps to sign into your account.

3. Type your Twitter username (everything after the @).

4. Type your Twitter password.

5. Tap Sign In. Your account information is verified and you sign into your account.

6. Tap Update Contacts. Twitter tries to match email addresses for your contacts with Twitter accounts. When it finds matches, it adds Twitter usernames to those contacts. When that process is complete, you are ready to access your Twitter account in the Twitter app and in many others on your iPhone.

Configuring a Facebook Account

Like Twitter, Facebook is one of the most popular social media channels you can use to keep informed about other people and inform them about you. Also like Twitter, Facebook is integrated into the iOS so you can share photos, messages, and such via your Facebook page, along with using the Facebook app.

To configure Facebook, perform the following steps:

1. Move to the Home screen and tap Settings.

2. If needed, swipe up the screen and tap Facebook. If you see INSTALLED at the top of the screen, the Facebook app is installed on your iPhone and you can get right into your account. If not, tap INSTALL to install the app (download and installing apps is covered in Chapter 6); when the app is done installing, continue with these steps.

No Facebook Account?

If don't have a Facebook account, tap Create New Account and follow the onscreen instructions to create one. When you are done creating the new account, you're signed into it automatically, or you can follow the rest of these steps to sign into your account.

---

3. Type your Facebook username.

4. Type your Facebook password.

5. Tap Sign In. Your account information is verified and you are signed into your account.

6. Tap Sign In.

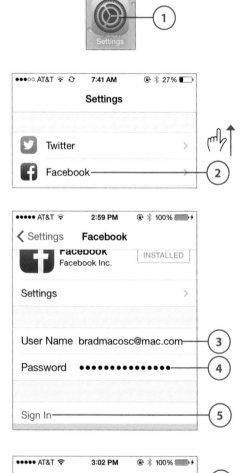

7. To prevent apps from accessing your Facebook information, slide their switches to the off position (white).

8. Tap Update All Contacts. Facebook attempts to match as much of your contact information with your friends as it can. When the process is complete, you are ready to access your Facebook account within the Facebook app or in any number of other apps.

More Facebook Settings

If you tap Settings on the Facebook Settings screen, you can do some additional configuration such as enabling or disabling sound and vibration for Facebook notifications. If you tap your name on that screen, you can change your password (which you might need to do from time to time).

Setting How and When Your Accounts Are Updated

The great thing about online accounts is that their information can be updated any time your iPhone can connect to the Internet. This means you have access to the latest information, such as new emails, changes to your calendars, and so on. There are three basic ways information gets updated:

- **Push**—When information is updated via Push, the server pushes (thus the name) updated information onto your iPhone whenever that information changes. For example, when you receive a new email, that email is immediately sent (or pushed) to your iPhone. Push provides you with the most current information all the time but uses a lot more battery than the other options.

Place icons in folders to keep your Home screens organized

Customize the layout of the icons on your Home screens by placing icons where you want them

Tap to personalize your iPhone to make it your own

Choose the image you want as wallpaper

7. To prevent apps from accessing your Facebook information, slide their switches to the off position (white).

8. Tap Update All Contacts. Facebook attempts to match as much of your contact information with your friends as it can. When the process is complete, you are ready to access your Facebook account within the Facebook app or in any number of other apps.

●●●●○ AT&T 📶	8:24 AM	✈ ✳ 82% 🔋
‹ Settings	**Facebook**	

Facebook
Facebook Inc.
INSTALLED

Settings >

Brad Miser >

ALLOW THESE APPS TO USE YOUR ACCOUNT

📅 Calendars ⬤ ⟵ 7

👤 Contacts ⬤

f Facebook ⬤

Update All Contacts ⟵ 8

More Facebook Settings

If you tap Settings on the Facebook Settings screen, you can do some additional configuration such as enabling or disabling sound and vibration for Facebook notifications. If you tap your name on that screen, you can change your password (which you might need to do from time to time).

Setting How and When Your Accounts Are Updated

The great thing about online accounts is that their information can be updated any time your iPhone can connect to the Internet. This means you have access to the latest information, such as new emails, changes to your calendars, and so on. There are three basic ways information gets updated:

- **Push**—When information is updated via Push, the server pushes (thus the name) updated information onto your iPhone whenever that information changes. For example, when you receive a new email, that email is immediately sent (or pushed) to your iPhone. Push provides you with the most current information all the time but uses a lot more battery than the other options.

- **Fetch**—When information is updated via fetch, your iPhone connects to the account and retrieves the updated information according to a schedule, such as every 15 minutes. Fetch doesn't keep your information quite as current as push does, but it uses much less battery than Push does.

- **Manual**—You can cause an app's information to be updated manually. This happens whenever you open or move into an app or by a manual refresh. For example, you can get new email by moving onto the Inboxes screen in the Mail app and swiping down from the top of the screen.

You can configure which method is used globally, and you can set the method for specific accounts. Some account types, such as iCloud and Exchange, support all three options while others might support only Fetch and Manual. The global option for updating is used unless you override it for individual accounts. For example, you might want your work account to be updated via Push so your information there is always current, while configuring Fetch on a personal account may frequently enough.

Configuring How New Data is Retrieved for Your Accounts

To configure how your information is updated, perform the following steps:

1. Move to the Mail, Contacts, Calendars screen.

2. Tap Fetch New Data.

3. To enable data to be pushed to your iPhone, slide the Push switch to on (green). To disable push to extend battery life, set it to off (white). This setting is global, meaning that if you disable Push here, it is disabled for all accounts even though you can still configure Push to be used for individual accounts, for example, if an account is set to use Push but Push is globally disabled, the account's setting is ignored and data is fetched instead.

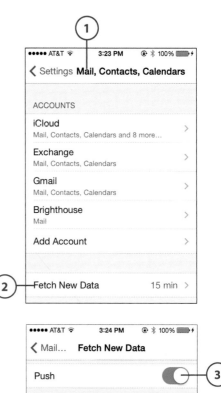

4. To change how an account's information is updated, tap it. The account's screen displays. The options on this screen depend on the kind of account it is. You always have Fetch and Manual; Push is displayed only for accounts that support it.

5. Tap the option you want to use for the account: Push, Fetch, or Manual. If you choose Manual, information is retrieved only when you manually start the process by opening the related app (such as Mail to fetch your email) or by using the refresh gesture, regardless of the global setting.

6. If you choose the Push option, choose the mailboxes whose information you want to be pushed by tapping them so they have a check mark; to prevent a mailbox's information from being pushed, tap it so that it doesn't have a check mark.

7. Tap Back.

8. Repeat steps 5-7 until you have set the update option for each account. (The current option is shown to the right of the account's name.)

9. Tap the amount of time when you want the iPhone to fetch data when Push is turned off and for those accounts that don't support Push; tap Manually if you want to manually check for information for fetch accounts or when Push is off. Information for your accounts is updated according to your settings.

It's Not All Good

WARNING: Editorial comment coming…I find Push, especially for email and other data that changes frequently, distracting and intrusive. One of the benefits of email is that you can use it when you choose to use it. With Push enabled for email and your iPhone configured to notify you each time you receive an email, you might find it distracting as emails come pouring in—and, worse, you might be tempted to pay attention to email when you should be paying attention to something else. (If you've ever been in a meeting where people are constantly checking and reading email on their mobile devices instead of paying attention to what's happening around them, you know what I mean.) I find setting most accounts to Fetch or Manual is best for me because I control when I deal with updates (such as new email) and don't have the distraction of new information coming in so frequently. Or you can set Fetch at a reasonable time, such as every 30 minutes. Email and other information are retrieved automatically but won't be so distracting. Do we really need a constant stream of email and other updates? Perhaps more importantly, not using Push makes your battery last much longer, as does a longer Fetch time.

>>>Go Further

TIPS FOR MANAGING YOUR ACCOUNTS

As you add and use accounts on your iPhone, keep the following points in mind:

- You can temporarily disable any data for any account by moving to the Mail, Contacts, Calendars screen and tapping that account. Set the switch for the data you don't want to use to off (white). You might be prompted to keep or delete that information; if you choose to keep it, the data remains on your iPhone but is disconnected from the account and is no longer be updated. If you delete it, you can always recover it again by simply turning that data back on. For example, suppose you are going on vacation and don't want to deal with work email, meeting notifications, and so on. Move to your work account and disable all its data. That data disappears from the related apps, meaning the account's mailboxes no longer appear in the Mail app. When you want to start using the account again, simply re-enable its data.

- If you want to completely remove an account from your iPhone, move to its configuration screen, swipe up the screen, and tap Delete Account. Tap Delete in the confirmation dialog box and the account is removed from your iPhone. (You can always sign into the account to start using it again.)

- You can have different notifications for certain aspects of an account, such as email. See Chapter 4, "Configuring an iPhone to Suit Your Preferences," for the details of configuring and using notifications.

- You can change how information is updated at any time, too. If your iPhone is running low on battery, disable Push and set Fetch to Manually so you can control when the updates happen. When your battery is charged again, you can re-enable Push or set a fetch schedule.

Place icons in folders to keep your Home screens organized

Customize the layout of the icons on your Home screens by placing icons where you want them

Tap to personalize your iPhone to make it your own

Choose the image you want as wallpaper

In this chapter, you learn how to make an iPhone into your iPhone. Topics include the following:

→ Customizing your Home screens
→ Working with the Settings app
→ Setting the screen's brightness and wallpaper
→ Setting text-related and format options
→ Choosing the sounds your iPhone makes
→ Setting up notifications and the Notification Center
→ Configuring the Control Center
→ Setting Do Not Disturb preferences
→ Setting Privacy and Location Services preferences
→ Setting Passcode, Fingerprint, and Auto-Lock preferences
→ Restricting access to content and apps

Configuring an iPhone to Suit Your Preferences

There are lots of ways that you can turn an iPhone into *your* iPhone so that it works, looks, and sounds the way you want it to. Some examples include changing how text appears on the screen, creating and using text shortcuts, choosing the sounds your iPhone uses, configuring the notifications your iPhone displays and plays to keep you informed about what's happening, and so on. One important customization that goes beyond just looks or sounds is to make your phone more secure by configuring and using a passcode/fingerprint and restricting access to content and apps.

To do most of this personalization of your iPhone, you use the Settings app, which you've seen several times in the previous chapters. This app is the starting place for almost all of the customization you'll do, not only of the iPhone's native software, but also of any apps you download and install.

You can also customize your Home screens, which is where this chapter begins.

Customizing Your Home Screens

The iPhone's Home screens are the starting point for anything you do because these screens contain the icons that you tap to access the apps and webpage icons that you want to use. You see and use the Home screens constantly, so it's a good idea to make them look the way you want them to.

In the background of the Lock screen and every Home screen is the wallpaper image. In the section called "Customizing the Wallpaper on the Home and Lock Screens," you learn how to configure your iPhone's wallpaper.

As you know, you can access apps and webpage icons on your Home screens by tapping them. The Home screens come configured with icons in default locations. You can change the location of these icons to be more convenient for you. As you install more apps and create your own webpage icons, it's a good idea to organize your Home screens so that you can quickly get to the items you use most frequently. You can move icons around the same screen, move icons between the pages of the Home screen, and organize icons within folders. You can even change the icons that appear on the Home screens' toolbar. You can also delete icons you no longer want.

Moving Icons Around Your Home Screens

You can move icons around on a Home screen, and you can move icons among screens to change the screen on which they are located.

1. Press the Touch ID/Home button to move to a Home screen.

2. Swipe to the left or right across the Home screen until the page containing an icon you want to move appears.

3. Tap and hold any icon. After a moment, the icons begin jiggling and you can then move icons on the Home screens. You might also see Delete buttons (an x) in the upper-left corner of some icons, which indicate that you can delete both the icon and app or the webpage link (more on this later in this section).

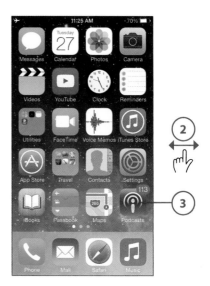

4. Tap and hold an icon you want to move; it becomes larger to show that you have selected it.

5. Drag the icon to a new location on the current screen; as you move the icon around the page, other icons separate and are reorganized to enable you to place the icon in its new location.

6. When the icon is in the location you want, lift your finger up. The icon is set in that place.

7. Tap and hold on an icon you want to move to a different page.

8. Drag the icon to the left edge of the screen to move it to a previous page or to the right edge of the screen to move it to a later page. As you reach the edge of the screen, you move to the desired page.

9. Drag the icon around on the new screen until it is in the location where you want to place it.

10. Lift your finger up. The icon is set in its new place.

11. Continue moving icons until you've placed them in the locations you want; then press the Touch ID/Home button. The icons are locked in their current positions, they stop jiggling, and the Delete buttons disappear.

Creating Folders to Organize Apps on Your Home Screens

You can place icons into folders to keep them organized and to make more icons available on the same page. To create a folder, do the following:

1. Move to the Home screen containing two icons you want to place in a folder.

2. Tap and hold an icon until they start jiggling; the Delete buttons appear.

3. Drag one icon on top of another one that you want to be in the new folder together.

4. When the first icon is on top of the second and a border appears around the second icon, lift your finger. The two icons are placed into a new folder, which is named based on the type of icons you place within it. The folder opens and you see its default name.

5. To edit the name, tap in the name field.

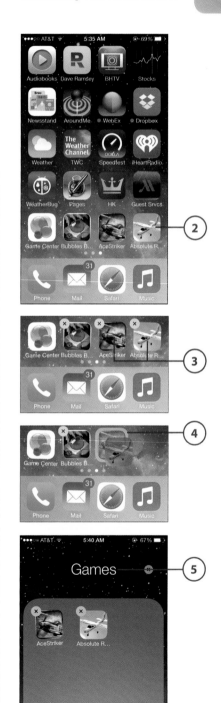

6. Edit the folder's name.

7. Tap Done.

8. If you're done organizing the Home screen, press the Touch ID/Home button. The icons stop jiggling.

Locating Folders

You can move a folder to a new location in the same way you can move any icon. Tap and hold an icon until the icons start jiggling. Drag the folder icon to where you want it to be.

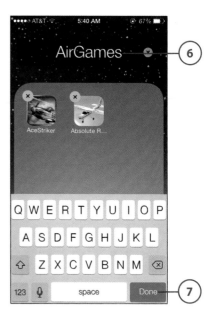

Placing Icons in Folders

You can add icons to an existing folder like so:

1. Move to the Home screen containing an icon you want to place in a folder.

2. Tap and hold an icon until the icons start jiggling and the Delete buttons appear.

3. Drag the icon you want to place into a folder on top of the folder's icon so that the folder's icon enlarges. (The icon doesn't have to be on the same Home screen page; you can drag an icon from one page and drop it on a folder on a different page.)

New folder containing two icons

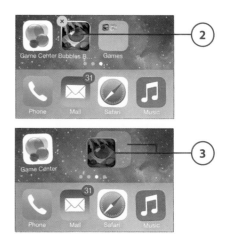

4. When the folder opens, lift up your finger. The icon is placed within the folder and you see its current location within the folder. (If you don't want to change the icon's location when you place it in the folder, lift up your finger as soon as the folder's icon enlarges; this places the icon in the folder but doesn't cause the folder to open. This is more efficient when you want to place multiple icons within a folder during the same time period.)

5. Drag the new icon to its location within the folder.

Removing Icons from Folders

To remove an icon from a folder, open the folder from which you want to remove the icon. Tap and hold an icon until it starts jiggling. Drag the icon you want to remove from inside the folder to outside the folder. When you cross the border of the folder, the folder closes and you can place the icon on a Home screen.

6. Tap outside the folder. The folder closes.

Folders and Badges

When you place an icon that has a badge (the red circle with a number in it that indicates the number of new items in the app) in a folder, the badge transfers to the folder so that you see it on the folder's icon. You still see the number of new items, but you can't really tell which of the apps in the folder is generating the badge. When you place more than one app with a badge in the same folder, the badge on the folder becomes the total number of new items for all the apps in the folder.

Configuring the Home Screen Toolbar

The toolbar on the bottom of the Home screen appears on every page. You can place any icons on the toolbar that you want, including folder icons.

1. Move to the Home screen containing an icon you want to place on the toolbar.

2. Tap and hold an icon until the icons start jiggling and the Delete buttons appear.

3. Drag an icon that is currently on the toolbar from the toolbar onto the Home screen. This creates an empty space on the toolbar.

4. Drag an icon or folder containing icons from the Home screen onto the toolbar.

5. Drag the icons on the toolbar around so they are in the order you want them to be.

6. Press the Touch ID/ Home button to set the icons in their current places.

Deleting Icons

You can delete icons from a Home screen to remove them from your iPhone. When you delete an app's icon, its data is also deleted and you won't be able to use the app anymore (of course, you can download it again if you change your mind). When you delete a webpage's icon (see Chapter 13, "Surfing the Web," for information on creating webpage icons), that bookmark is deleted.

1. Move to the Home screen containing an icon you want to delete.

2. Tap and hold an icon until the icons start jiggling and the Delete buttons appear.

3. Tap the icon's Delete button.

4. Tap Delete. If the icon was for an app, it and any associated data on your iPhone are deleted. If the icon was for a bookmark, the bookmark is deleted.

>>>Go Further

MORE ON ORGANIZING HOME SCREENS

Organizing your Home screens can make the use of your iPhone more efficient and make it more what you want it to be. Here are a few more things to keep in mind:

- You can place many icons in the same folder. When you add more than nine, any additional icons are placed on new pages within the folder. As you keep adding icons, pages keep being adding to the folder. You can swipe to the left or right within a folder to move amongst its pages, just as you can on the Home screen.

- To change a folder's name, move to a screen showing the folder. Tap and hold an icon until the icons jiggle. Tap the folder, and then tap the current name. Type the new name, tap Done, and tap outside the folder to close it. Press the Touch ID/Home button to save the new name.

- To delete a folder, remove all the icons from it. The folder is deleted as soon as you remove the last icon from it.

- You can delete only icons for things you've added to your iPhone, which are either apps you've installed or bookmarks to web pages you've added. You can't delete any of the default apps, which is why their icons don't have Delete buttons when you move into Edit mode. If you don't use some of these default icons, move them to pages of your Home screen that you don't use very often so they don't get in your way, or create a folder for unused icons and store them there, out of your way.

- You can also organize your iPhone's Home screens using iTunes on a computer. Move to the Sync screen in iTunes and click the Apps tab. You see thumbnails for each of your Home page screens. Using techniques similar to those you've learned in this section, you can move icons around, create folders, place icons in folders, and so on. When you sync the iPhone, the Home screens change accordingly. Refer to Chapter 5, "Working with iTunes on Your Computer," for information about using iTunes on a computer.

Working with the Settings App

If you've read previous chapters, you've already used the Settings app a couple of times. Aptly named, the Settings app is where you configure the many settings that change how your iPhone looks, sounds, and works. Most of the tasks in this chapter involve the Settings app. Rather than repeat the first couple of steps within each task, it is more efficient to show you how the app works so you can easily access the controls you need for each task.

1. On the Home screen, tap Settings. The Settings app opens. The app is organized in sections starting at the top with controls you use to enable, disable, or configure key functions of your iPhone including Airplane mode, Wi-Fi, and so on. The next set of tools configures notifications, the Control Center, and the Do No Disturb function. The third group includes General, Sounds, Wallpapers & Brightness, and Privacy. The remainder of the sections are the app settings you use to configure how specific apps work.

2. Swipe up or down the screen to get to the settings area you want to use.

3. Tap the area you want to configure, such as Sounds.

4. Use the resulting controls to configure that area. The changes you make take effect immediately.

5. When you're done, you can leave the Settings app where you are or tap the back button, which is always located in the upper-left corner of the screen, until you get back to the main Settings screen.

Chapter Shorthand

For almost all the tasks you read about in this chapter, you use the Settings app. The first step in these tasks is always to open the related settings area; you use the steps 1–3 to do this. These three steps are not repeated in each task. Instead, the tasks start with you selecting the settings area you need. So, when you see something like "Tap Wallpapers & Brightness," it means you should move into the Settings app, swipe up or down until you see the area you need (Wallpapers & Brightness for example), and then tap it. If you were previously using a different area in the Settings app, you need to tap the back button (step 5) to return to the main Settings screen and then find and tap the area you want to use.

Setting the Screen's Brightness and Wallpaper

Because you continually look at your iPhone's screen, it should be the right brightness level for your eyes. However, the screen is also a large user of battery power, so the less bright an iPhone's screen is, the longer its battery lasts. You have to find a good balance between viewing comfort and battery life. Fortunately, your iPhone has a brightness feature that automatically adjusts for current lighting conditions.

Wallpaper is the image you see "behind" the icons on your Home screens. Because you see this image so often, you might as well have an image that you want to see or that you believe makes using the Home screens easier and faster. You can use the iPhone's default wallpaper images, or you can use any photo stored on your iPhone. You can also set the wallpaper image you see on the iPhone's Lock screen (you can use the same image as on the Home screens or a different one).

Lots More to the Settings App

There's a lot more you can do with the Settings app than is explained in this chapter; here you learn about most of the "general" iPhone customization/configuration for which you can use the Settings app. You also learn how to use it to configure app- or function-specific settings throughout this book. For example, you learn how to use Settings to configure Internet access in Chapter 2, "Connecting Your iPhone to the Internet, Bluetooth Devices, and iPhones/iPods/iPads," and to configure email preferences in Chapter 9, "Sending, Receiving, and Managing Email."

Setting Your Screen's Brightness

To set the screen brightness, perform the following steps:

1. In the Settings app, tap Wallpapers & Brightness.

2. Drag the slider to the right to raise the base brightness or to the left to lower it. A brighter screen uses more power but is easier to see.

3. If you don't want to use the Auto-Brightness feature slide the switch to off (white) to disable this feature. The Auto-Brightness feature adjusts the screen brightness based on the lighting conditions in which you are using the iPhone. You'll get more battery life with Auto-Brightness on, but you might not be comfortable with the screen when you use the iPhone where there isn't a lot of ambient light. Try using your iPhone with this feature enabled to see whether the automatic adjustment bothers you. You can always set the brightness level manually, as described in step 2, if it does.

●●●○○ AT&T 🌐	5:43 AM	✻ 100% 🔋⚡

Settings

⚙️	General	>
🔊	Sounds	>
✺	Wallpapers & Brightness——→	①

Searching...	11:43 AM	82% 🔋

‹ Settings **Wallpapers & Brightness**

BRIGHTNESS ②

☀ ———————●——— ☀

Auto-Brightness ⬤ ③

A Faster Way

A faster way to adjust brightness is to swipe up from the bottom of the screen to open the Control Center. Use its Brightness slider, which also changes the Brightness slider in the Settings app, to set the brightness and then tap outside of the Control Center to close it.

Customizing the Wallpaper on the Home and Lock Screens

When you use the Home screens, you see wallpaper "behind" the icons on the screen. You also see wallpaper on the Lock screen (when your iPhone isn't asleep, that is). You can set the wallpaper in both of these places either by using the default wallpaper collection or by choosing any photo on your iPhone. To configure your wallpaper, perform the following steps:

1. In the Settings app, tap Wallpapers & Brightness.

2. Tap one of the images in the CHOOSE WALLPAPER section, which show the screens on which you can set wallpaper; the wallpaper you currently have set on these screens is shown in the thumbnails. On the resulting screen are two sections. The APPLE WALLPAPER section enables you to choose one of the default wallpaper images, and the PHOTOS section shows you the photos available in the Photos app. If you don't have any photos stored on your iPhone, you can only choose from the default images. To choose a default image, continue with step 3; to use one of your photos as wallpaper, skip to step 7.

3. Tap Dynamic if you want to use dynamic wallpaper or Stills if you want to use a static image. Dynamic wallpaper has motion (kind of like a screen saver on a computer). Stills are static images.

4. Swipe up and down the screen to browse the images available to you.

5. Tap the image you want to use as wallpaper.

6. Tap Set and skip to step 13.

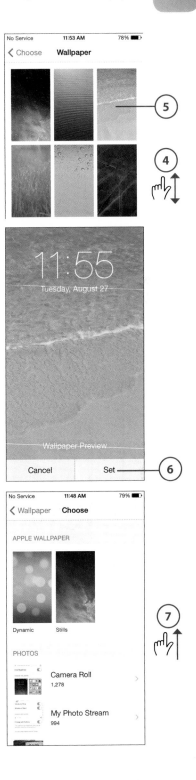

7. To use a photo as wallpaper, swipe up the screen to browse the sources of photos available to you; these include your Camera Roll, Photo Stream, albums, and so on.

Working with Photos

To learn how to work with the photos on your iPhone, see Chapter 15, "Working with Photos and Video You Take with Your iPhone."

8. Tap the source containing the photo you want to use.

9. Swipe up and down the selected source to browse its photos.

10. Tap the photo you want to use. The photo appears on the Move and Scale screen, which you can use to resize and move the image around.

11. Use your fingers to unpinch to zoom in or pinch to zoom out, and hold down and drag the photo around the screen until it appears how you want the wallpaper to look.

12. Tap Set.

13. Tap Set Lock Screen or Set Home Screen to apply the wallpaper to only one of those screens; tap Set Both to apply the same wallpaper in both locations. The next time you move to the screen you selected, you see the wallpaper you chose.

14. If you set the wallpaper in only one location, tap Choose to move back to the Choose screen and repeat steps 3–13 to set the wallpaper for the other screen.

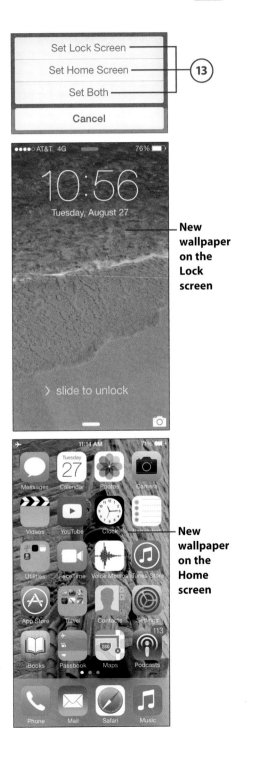

New wallpaper on the Lock screen

New wallpaper on the Home screen

Setting Text, Language, and Format Options

You'll be working with text in many apps on your iPhone. You can customize a number of text- and format-related options so text appears and behaves the way you want it to. You can also choose the language your iPhone uses to communicate to you.

Changing Text Size

To change the size of text in various apps, such as Mail, Messages, and so on, perform the following steps:

1. On the Settings screen, tap General.

2. Tap Text Size.

3. Drag the slider to the right to make text larger or to the left to make it smaller. Now, look at text in an app, such as Mail, to see whether it is the right size.

4. If the text isn't the right size, move back to the Settings app and repeat step 3 until it is the best size for you.

●●●●○ AT&T 🔇   5:54 AM   @ ✈ 97% ▭+

Settings

⚙   General ——————————————— ›   ①

🔊   Sounds   ›

✳   Wallpapers & Brightness   ›

✋   Privacy   ›

●●●●○ AT&T 🔇   5:55 AM   @ ✈ 98% ▭+

‹ Settings   **General**

Siri   ›

Spotlight Search   ›

Text Size——————————————— ›   ②

Accessibility   ›

●●●●○ AT&T 🔇   5:55 AM   @ ✈ 97% ▭+

‹ General   **Text Size**

Apps that support Dynamic Type will adjust to your preferred reading size below.

Drag the slider below

A   A   ③

Setting Keyboard Preferences

You use the iPhone's keyboard to input text in many apps, including Mail, Messages, and so on. A number of settings determine how the keyboard works.

1. On the Settings screen, tap General.

2. Swipe up the screen.

3. Tap Keyboard.

4. To prevent your iPhone from automatically capitalizing as you type, set Auto-Capitalization to off (white). The iPhone no longer changes the case of letters as you type them.

5. To disable the automatic spell checking/correction, set Auto-Correction to off (white). Your iPhone no longer automatically suggests corrections to what you type.

6. To disable the iPhone's Spell Checker, set the Check Spelling switch to off (white). You'll be on your own spelling-wise.

7. To disable the Caps Lock function, set the Enable Caps Lock to off (white). The Cap Locks function won't be available to you when you tap the Shift key twice.

8. To disable the shortcut that types a period followed by a space when you tap the spacebar twice, set the "." Shortcut switch to off (white). You must tap a period and the spacebar to type these characters when you end a sentence.

9. Tap Keyboards. This enables you to add more keyboards so that you can choose a specific language's keyboard when you are entering text.

10. Tap Add New Keyboard.

11. Swipe up and down the screen to browse the available keyboards.

12. Tap the keyboard you want to add.

13. Tap the keyboard you added in step 12.

14. Tap the software keyboard layout you want to use.

15. Tap the hardware keyboard layout you want to use.

16. Tap Keyboards.

17. Repeat steps 10–16 to add and configure additional keyboards.

Removing Keyboards

To delete a keyboard, move to the Keyboards Settings screen and swipe to the left on the keyboard you want to remove. Tap Delete. The keyboard is removed. (You can always add it again later.)

Creating and Working with Text Shortcuts

Text shortcuts are useful because you can use just a few letters to type a series of words. You type the shortcut, and it is replaced by the phrase with which it is associated. To configure your text shortcuts, do the following:

1. Move the Keyboard screen as described in steps 1–3 in the previous task.

2. Swipe up the screen until you see the SHORTCUTS section.

3. Review the current shortcuts.

4. To add a shortcut, tap Add New Shortcut.

5. Type the phrase for which you want to create a shortcut.

6. Type the shortcut you want to be replaced by the phrase you created in step 5.

7. Tap Save. If the shortcut doesn't contain any disallowed characters, it is created and you move back to the Shortcuts section where you see your new shortcut. If there is an error, you see an explanation of the error; you must correct it before you can create the shortcut.

8. Repeat steps 4–7 to create other text shortcuts.

Shortcuts to Shortcuts

To change a shortcut, tap it. Use the resulting screen to change the phrase or shortcut, and tap Save to update the shortcut. To remove a shortcut, swipe to the left on it and tap Delete. And, yes, you can create a phrase without a shortcut, but I don't really see much use for that!

Setting Language and Format Preferences

There are a number of formatting preferences you can set that determine how information is formatted in various apps. For example, you can choose how addresses are formatted by default by choosing the region whose format you want to follow.

1. On the Settings screen, tap General.

2. Swipe up the screen.

3. Tap International.

4. Tap Language.

5. Swipe up and down the screen to view the languages with which your iPhone can work. The current language is marked with a check mark.

6. Tap the language you want to use.

7. Tap Done. Your iPhone starts using the language you selected.

8. Tap Voice Control.

●●●●○ AT&T 📶 6:50 AM @ 🖅 100% 🔋⚡

Settings

⚙️ General ─────── ①

●●●●○ AT&T 📶 6:50 AM @ 🖅 100% 🔋⚡

‹ Settings **General**

Passcode Lock After 5 Minutes ›

Restrictions Off › ②

Date & Time ›

Keyboard ›

International ─────── ③

●●●●○ AT&T 📶 6:52 AM @ 🖅 100% 🔋⚡

‹ General **International**

④

Language English ›

●●●●○ AT&T 📶 7:03 AM @ 🖅 100% 🔋⚡

Cancel **Language** Done ─── ⑦

English ─────── ✓ ⑥

Français

Deutsch ⑤

日本語

Nederlands

Italiano

Language English › ⑧

Voice Control English ›

9. Swipe up and down the screen to view the languages you can use to speak to your iPhone (this is the language Siri uses; see Chapter 12, "Working with Siri," for details about Siri). The current language is marked with a check mark.

10. Tap the language you want to use.

11. Tap International. Your iPhone starts using the language you selected, and you move back to the International screen. (To configure keyboards, see the previous task.)

12. Tap Region Format.

13. Swipe up and down the regions available to you. The current region is marked with a check mark.

14. Tap the region whose formatting you want to use; if there are options within a region, you move to an additional screen and can tap the specific option you want to use.

15. Tap International. Your iPhone starts using the formatting associated with the region you selected.

16. Tap Calendar.

17. Tap the calendar you want your iPhone to use.

18. Tap International. You move back to the International screen. At the bottom of the screen are examples of the format options you have selected.

>>>Go Further

THE ACCESSIBLE iPHONE

If you tap the Accessibility option on the General setting screen, a large number of options you can configure to make your iPhone more accessible appear. You can enable VoiceOver to have the iPhone guide you through screens by speaking their contents. Zoom magnifies the entire screen, while Larger Type enables you to increase the size of the text displayed for easier reading. Invert Colors changes the screen from dark characters on a light background to light characters on a dark background. Speak Selection has the iPhone speak text you have selected, and Speak Auto-text has the iPhone speak corrections it suggests to you, such as auto-capitalizations. There are other options you can configure; explore this screen to find settings of interest to you.

Choosing the Sounds Your iPhone Makes

Sound is one important way your iPhone uses to communicate with you. You can configure the sounds the phone uses in two ways. One is by choosing the general sounds your iPhone makes, which is covered in this section. You can also configure sounds specific apps make when they notify you about certain events; this is covered in the next section.

To configure your iPhone's general sounds, do the following:

1. On the Settings screen, tap Sounds.

2. If you want your iPhone to also vibrate when it rings, set the Vibrate on Ring switch to on (green).

3. If you want your iPhone to vibrate when you have it muted, set the Vibrate on Silent switch to on (green).

4. Set the volume of the ringer and alert tones by dragging the slider to the left or right.

5. If you want to also be able to change this volume using the volume buttons on the side of the phone, set the Change with buttons switch to on (green).

6. Tap Ringtone. On the resulting screen, you can set the sound and vibration your iPhone uses when a call comes in.

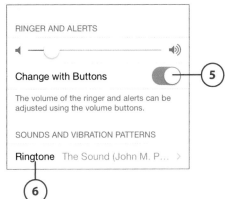

RINGER AND ALERTS

Change with Buttons — **5**

The volume of the ringer and alerts can be adjusted using the volume buttons.

SOUNDS AND VIBRATION PATTERNS

Ringtone   The Sound (John M. P... >

6

Individual Ringtones and Vibrations

The ringtone and vibration you set in steps 6–14 are the default or general settings. These are used for all callers except for people in your Contacts app for whom you've set specific ringtones or vibrations. In that case, the contact's specific ringtone and vibration are used instead of the defaults. See Chapter 7, "Managing Contacts," to learn how to configure ringtones and vibrations for contacts.

7. Swipe up and down the screen to see all the ringtones available to you. There are two sections of sounds on this screen: RINGTONES and ALERT TONES. These work in the same way; alert tones tend to be shorter sounds.

8. Tap a sound, and it plays.

9. Repeat steps 7 and 8 until you have selected the sound you want to have as your general ringtone.

10. If necessary, swipe down the screen so you see the Vibration section at the top.

11. Tap Vibration. A list of Standard and Custom vibrations available is displayed.

●●●●○ AT&T 🛜   7:33 AM   🔋 ◢ 100% ▭▸

‹ Sounds   **Ringtone**   Store

— **11**

Vibration   Quick ›   **7**

RINGTONES

(Don't Fear) The Reaper

Golden Age of Leather   **10**

Kryptonite

Oh Where Is My Cell Phone?

Sweet Home Alabama (Ringback)   **8**

The Ride of the Rohirrim

The Sound (John M. Perkins' Blues)

12. Swipe up and down the screen to see all the vibrations available.

13. Tap a vibration. It "plays" so you can feel it.

14. Repeat steps 12 and 13 until you've selected the general vibration you want to use; you can tap None at the bottom of the Vibration screen below the CUSTOM section if you don't want to have a general vibration.

15. Tap Ringtone.

16. Tap Sounds. The ringtone you selected is shown on the Sounds screen next to the Ringtone label.

17. Tap Text Tone.

18. Use steps 7–16 to set the sound and vibration used when you receive a new text. The process works the same as for ringtones, though the screens look a bit different. For example, the ALERT TONES section is at the top of the screen because you are more likely to want a short sound for new texts.

19. When you're done setting the Text tone, tap Sounds.

20. Using the same pattern as you did for ringtones and text tones, set the sound and vibrations for the rest of the events you see.

21. If you don't want your iPhone to make a sound when you lock it, slide the Lock Sounds switch to off (white). Your iPhone no longer makes this sound when you press the Sleep/Wake button to put it to sleep and lock it.

22. If you don't like the audible feedback when you tap keys on the iPhone's virtual keyboard, slide the Keyboard Clicks switch to off (white) to disable that sound. The keyboard is silent as you type on it.

23. Tap Settings. Your iPhone uses the sounds and vibrations you selected to notify you of events you want to be aware of.

•••••○ AT&T 🌐	7:59 AM	ⓐ ⚊ 100% 🔋➔	23
‹ Settings	**Sounds**		
Text Tone		Bell ›	
New Voicemail		Tri-tone ›	
New Mail		Ding ›	
Sent Mail		Swoosh ›	
Tweet		Tweet ›	20
Facebook Post		Swish ›	
Calendar Alerts		Alert ›	
Reminder Alerts		Update ›	
AirDrop		Typewriters ›	
Lock Sounds		⬤▬	21
Keyboard Clicks		⬤▬	22

SOUNDING OFF

>>>Go Further

Following are some other sound- and vibration-related pointers:

- You can tap the Store button on the Ringtone screen to move to the iTunes Store, where you can download ringtones to your iPhone. See Chapter 6, "Downloading Apps, Music, Movies, TV Shows, and More onto Your iPhone," for more information about downloading content from the iTunes Store.

- You can also create your own ringtones using an audio app on a computer, such as GarageBand. GarageBand enables you to move ringtones you create directly into iTunes. If you use a different app, you need to export the sound from that app and then add it to your iTunes Library. In either case, you can then sync the tones onto your iPhone. See Chapter 5 for information about syncing.

- You can create custom vibration patterns, too. On the Vibration screen, tap Create New Vibration. Tap the vibration pattern you want to create; when you're done tapping, tap Stop. Tap Record to start over if you don't like the one you created. When you're done, tap Save. Name the pattern and tap Save. The patterns you create are available in the CUSTOM section on the Vibration screen, so you can use them just like the iPhone's default patterns. To remove a custom pattern, swipe to the left on it and tap Delete.

Setting Up Notifications and the Notification Center

Many apps use notifications to communicate information to you, such as to inform you about new information, provide status updates, new email messages, new text messages, and so on. You can use the Notifications settings to enable or disable notifications and to configure them for specific apps. Configuring notifications is one of the most important ways to customize your iPhone so that it keeps you informed as much as you want it to without overwhelming you.

Understanding Notifications and the Notification Center

There are several types of notifications, which include badges, banners, alerts, vibrations, and sounds.

Number of new items in the app

Badges are the counters that appear on an app's icon to let you know how many new of something you have, such as email messages, texts, event invitations, and so on. You can enable or disable the badge for an app's icon.

Banner notification for a new email message

Banners are small messages that appear at the top of the screen when something happens, such as when you receive an email message. Banners contain the icon of the app from which they come, and they can show a preview (if you enable the preview setting). Banners are nice because they don't interfere with what you are doing. If you ignore a banner, after a few seconds, it disappears. If you tap a banner, you move into the app producing the banner. When you receive a new banner when one is visible on the screen, the first one rotates out of the way so the newest one is displayed. If you receive a lot of notifications at the same time, you see a summary of how many you have received.

Alerts are another means that apps use to communicate with you. There are alerts for many types of objects, such as texts, emails, reminders, missed call notifications, and so on. The differences between a banner and an alert are that alerts appear in the center of the screen and you must do something to make the alert go away, such as listen to or ignore a voice message. Some alerts have an Options button; tap this button to see and do actions related to the notification. Tap Close to ignore it.

Cellular Emergency Notifications

Depending on where you live and which provider you use, you might receive emergency notifications from government agencies for such things as weather emergencies, Amber Alerts (in the United States, these are issued when a child is abducted), and so on. These alerts appear on your iPhone when they are issued to keep you informed of such events. You can enable or disable certain of these notifications.

You should use alerts when you want to be sure to take action on the occurrence about which a reminder is being sent. For example, you might want to use alerts for calendar events so you have to respond to the notice that the event is coming up, such as the start of a meeting. Banners are better for those notifications that you want to be aware of but that you don't want to interrupt what you are doing, such as email messages. (If an alert appeared each time you received an email message, they could be very disruptive.)

Sounds are audible indicators that something has happened. For example, when something happens in the Game Center, you can be notified via a sound. Earlier in this chapter, you learned how to configure your iPhone's general sounds. You also can configure the sounds used for a specific app's notifications.

Vibrations are a physical indicator that something has happened. Like sounds, you can configure general vibrations, and you can also configure an app's vibration pattern for its notifications.

The Notification Center provides an overview of important information being managed in several different apps

The Notification Center enables you to access all your notifications on one screen. It can include information from apps, such as the current weather, and it collects notifications from each app and groups them together. As you learned in Chapter 1, "Getting Started with Your iPhone," swipe down from the top of the screen to reveal the Notification Center. You can configure a number of settings related to the Notification Center.

Setting Global Notification Preferences

Use the following steps to configure general notification settings:

1. On the Settings screen, tap Notification Center. The Notifications Center screen has a number of sections.

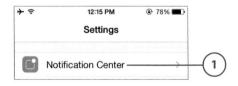

2. In the ACCESS ON LOCK SCREEN section, set the Notifications View switch to off (white) if you don't want the notification information to be available in the Notification Center when you view it from the Lock screen.

3. Set the Today View switch to off (white) if you don't want to see today's events in the Notification Center when you view it on the Lock screen; the Today tab no longer appears in the Notification Center.

4. In the TODAY VIEW section, enable or disable the various sections that are available on the Notification Center. Set the corresponding switch to off (white) if you don't want that section included or on (green) if you do. You can configure this setting for the Today Summary, Next Destination, Calendar Day View, Reminders, Stocks, and Tomorrow Summary.

5. In the NOTIFICATIONS VIEW section, choose Sort By Time if you want the notifications shown in the Notification Center to be organized based on the most recent information being toward the top of the screen and skip to step 12; tap Sort Manually if you want to set the order (from top to bottom) of how apps appear in the Notification Center.

6. Tap Edit to continue with the manual sorting.

Maintaining Order

You can set the order of the apps when either Manually or By Time is selected. The order you set persists when you switch between the two options, so you can change back and forth whenever you want without changing the order in which the apps are listed.

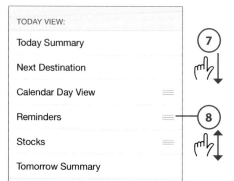

7. Swipe down the screen to move back to the TODAY VIEW section.

8. Drag items by their order button up and down to change the order in which they appear in the Notification Center.

9. Swipe up the screen to view the INCLUDE section.

10. Drag items by their order button up and down to change the order in which they appear on the Notification Center.

11. When you are done manually sorting the order, tap Done.

12. Configure each app's notification settings; the details of this are explained in the next task.

13. Swipe up the screen until you see the GOVERNMENT ALERTS section.

More Alerts

Depending on where you live, you might see a different set of alert options in the GOVERNMENT ALERTS section. You can enable or disable any of the alerts you see in this section as explained in steps 14 and 15.

14. If you don't want to receive AMBER alert notifications, set the AMBER Alerts switch to off (white).

15. If you don't want to receive other types of emergency alerts, set the Emergency Alerts switch to off (white).

Setting Notification Preferences for Specific Apps

You can configure which apps can send notifications and, if you allow notifications, which type. You can also configure other aspects of notifications, such as whether an app displays in the Notification Center, whether its notifications appear on the Lock screen, and so on. Apps support different notification options, and not all apps support all options. Some apps, such as Mail, support notification configuration by account (for example, you can set a different alert sound for new mail in each account). However, you can follow the same general steps to configure notifications for each app; you should explore all the options for the apps you use most often to ensure they work the best for you.

The following steps show how to configure Mail's notifications, which is a good example because it supports a lot of notification features; other apps might have fewer features or might be organized slightly differently. But, configuring the notifications for any app follows a similar pattern.

1. Continuing in the Notification Center screen from the previous task, swipe up to see the INCLUDE section. Here, you see each app on your iPhone that supports notifications. The INCLUDE sections shows apps whose notifications are currently shown in the Notification center, while those for which the Notification Center is disabled are shown in the DO NOT INCLUDE section.

2. Tap the app whose notifications you want to configure.

3. Tap Include.

4. Tap the number of items you want to be shown in the Notification Center.

5. Tap the back button, which is labeled with the name of the app you are configuring (Mail, in this example). If an app supports multiple accounts, you can configure the notifications for each account. If not, you see the notifications screen showing all the options for that app and you can skip to step 6.

6. Tap the account for which you want to configure notifications.

7. Choose the type of notification you want the app for the account to provide by tapping None, Banners, or Alerts. The selected alert type is the one whose name is enclosed in an oblong.

8. To display the app's badge, set the Badge App Icon switch to on (green); if you set it to off (white), the badge is not displayed when new email arrives.

9. Tap Alert Sound.

10. Use the resulting Alert Sound screen to choose the alert sound and vibration for new email messages to the account (refer to the section on setting general sound preferences earlier in this chapter for details).

11. Tap the back button located in the upper-left corner of the screen.

Installed App Not Shown?
You must have opened an app at least once for it to appear on the Notification Center screen.

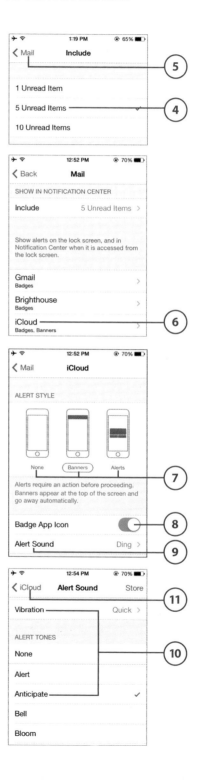

12. If you don't want the app's notifications for the account to appear in the Notification Center, set the Show in Notification Center switch to off (white) to disable this. When you set this switch to off (white), the app is placed in the DO NOT INCLUDE section on the Notification Center screen.

13. If you want the app's notifications for the account to appear on the Lock screen, slide the Show on Lock Screen switch to on (green); if you set it to off (white), you won't see notifications from the app for the account when your iPhone is locked.

14. If you don't want a preview to appear in the app's notifications, slide the Show Preview switch to off (white). For example, you might want to keep some types of messages private; to do so, disable the preview option for that account.

15. Tap the back button, which is located in the upper-left corner of the window and is labeled with the app you are configuring (Mail, in this example).

16. Configure notifications for the other accounts used in the app.

17. Configure notifications for VIP email.

18. Tap Back.

19. Repeat these steps for each app shown on the Notification Center screen. Certain apps might not have all the options shown in these steps, but the process to configure their notifications is similar. For example, some apps might have only the Show in Notification Center switch setting.

20. Tap Settings.

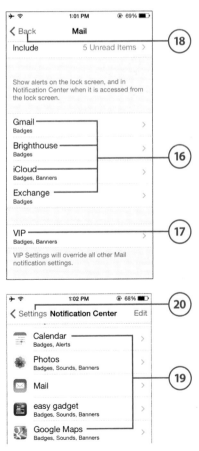

VIPs Are Special

Mail supports VIPs, which are people from whom email messages are treated specially, such as having a dedicated mailbox in the Mail app. You can apply specific notification settings to VIP messages using the VIP option. These override the notification settings for the email account to which messages from VIPs are sent.

Configuring the Control Center

As you learned in Chapter 1, the Control Center provides quick access to various settings, app controls, and even apps.

There are a couple of Control Center preferences you can set:

1. On the Settings screen, tap Control Center.

2. To be able to access the Control Center from the Lock screen, set the Access on Lock Screen switch to on (green).

3. To be able to access it when you are using an app, set the Access Within Apps switch to on (green).

4. Tap Settings.

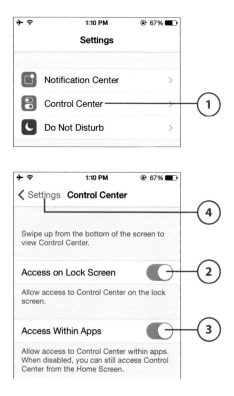

Setting Do Not Disturb Preferences

As you learned in Chapter 1, the Do Not Disturb feature enables you to temporarily silence notifications; you can also configure quiet times during which notifications are automatically silenced.

You can set an automatic Do Not Disturb schedule by performing the following steps:

1. On the Settings screen, tap Do Not Disturb.

2. To activate Do Not Disturb manually, set the Manual switch to on (green). (This is the same as activating it from the Control Center.)

3. To configure Do Not Disturb to activate automatically on a schedule, slide the Scheduled switch to on (green).

4. Tap the From and To box.

5. Tap From.

6. Swipe on the time selection wheels to select the hour and minute (AM or PM) when you want the Do Not Disturb period to start.

7. Tap To.

8. Swipe on the time selection wheels to set the hour and minute (AM or PM) when you want the Do Not Disturb period to end.

9. Tap Back.

10. Tap Allow Calls From.

11. Tap the option for whose calls should be allowed during the Do Not Disturb period. The options are Everyone, which doesn't prevent any calls; No One, which sends all calls to voicemail; Favorites, which allows calls from people on your Favorites lists to come through but all others go to voicemail; or one of your contact groups, which allows calls from anyone in the selected group to come through while all others go to voicemail.

12. Tap Back.

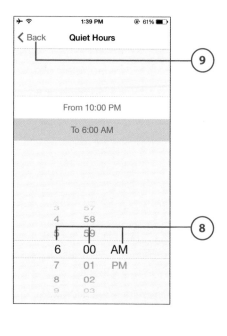

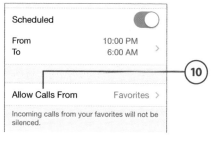

13. Set the Repeated Calls switch to on (green) if you want a second call from the same person within three minutes to be allowed through. This feature is based on the assumption that if a call is really important, someone will try again immediately.

14. If you want notifications to be silenced only when your phone is locked, tap Only while iPhone is locked. Tap Always if you want notifications to be silenced regardless of the Lock status.

15. Tap Settings. During the Do Not Disturb period, your iPhone is silent, except for any exceptions you configured. When the period ends, your iPhone resumes its normal notification activity.

✈ 📶	1:41 PM	61% 🔋

⟨ Settings **Do Not Disturb**

From	10:00 PM
To	6:00 AM ⟩

Allow Calls From	Favorites ⟩

Incoming calls from your favorites will not be silenced.

Repeated Calls	⬤

When enabled, a second call from the same person within three minutes will not be silenced.

SILENCE:

Always

Only while iPhone is locked ✓

Incoming calls and notifications will be silenced while iPhone is locked.

App Settings

Many apps include settings you can use to configure how the apps work or look. On the Settings screen, tap the app whose settings you want to configure and use the resulting screen to configure it's options. You'll be learning how to use many of the app settings in detail throughout this book.

Setting Privacy and Location Services Preferences

Using its GPS or network connection, your iPhone's Location Services feature can determine where the phone is. This is useful in many situations, such as in the Maps app when you want to generate directions. Lots of other apps use this capability, too, such as apps that provide you location-specific information (the Urban Spoon app uses it to determine the restaurants near you, for example). You can configure certain aspects of how these services work. And, if you don't want specific apps to be able to access your iPhone's current location, you can disable this feature for those apps. Of course, if you do, apps that rely on this capability won't work properly (they prompt you to allow access to this service as you try to use them).

To configure privacy settings, do the following:

1. Move to the Settings screen and tap Privacy.

2. Tap Location Services. Under the Location Services switch is a list of all the apps that have requested access to Location Services. When an app's switch is on (green), that app has permission to use Location Services. When an app's switch is off (white), it does not. Apps marked with a purple arrow have recently accessed your location; those that have done so within the past 24 hours are marked with a gray arrow. An outline arrow indicates that the app is using a geofence, which is a perimeter around a location that defines an area that is used to trigger some event, such as a reminder.

No Service for You!

During the setup process, you were prompted to enable Location Services. If you chose not to enable it at that time, you need to slide the Location Services switch to the on position (green) before you can perform step 3.

3. To prevent a specific app from using Location Services, tap its switch to turn it off (white) for that app. That app is no longer able to determine your location (if that is critical to what it does, it might no longer be useful).

4. To disable Location Services for all apps, set the Location Services switch to off (white); to leave it enabled, skip to step 6.

5. Tap Turn Off. No apps are able to identify your location; skip the rest of these steps because they don't apply when Location Services is disabled.

6. If necessary, swipe up the screen until you see Find My iPhone.

7. Tap Find My iPhone.

iCloud Required

To use the Find My iPhone service, you must have an iCloud account configured on your iPhone (refer to Chapter 3, "Setting Up iCloud and Other Online Accounts").

8. To allow your iPhone to be tracked so its location can be determined, ensure Find My iPhone is set to on (green).

9. To show an icon for your iPhone in the status bar at the top of the screen when you are tracking it on another device, set the Status Bar Icon to on (green). This puts an icon on your iPhone showing that it is being tracked. You might not want to display this in case someone has your iPhone who you might not want to know you are tracking it.

10. Tap Back.

11. Tap System Services.

12. Enable or disable Location Services for the System Services you see. As with apps, if you disable location services for a system function, it might not work properly.

13. Tap Back.

Frequent Locations

One of the System Services is Frequent Locations. This service tracks places you visit. This information is used to improve the performance of some apps. If you want to prevent this, tap Frequent Locations and then set the Frequent Locations switch to off (white). If you leave it enabled, you can enable information to be fed back to Apple to improve the Maps app by setting the Improve Maps switch to on (green). In the HISTORY section, you see the various locations this service is tracking. Tap a location to see it on a map. Tap Clear History and then tap Clear at the prompt to remove locations from the HISTORY list.

14. Tap Privacy. Next, allow or prevent apps from accessing data stored on your iPhone.

15. Tap the first app on the list; this example shows Contacts. A list of apps that have requested to use the app's data is displayed. If the requesting app is able to use the app's data, its switch is on (green).

16. Prevent a requesting app from accessing the app's data by setting its switch to off (white). That app is no longer able to use the data it requested (which can inhibit some of its functionality).

17. Repeat step 16 for each app you see that you want to prevent from accessing the data.

18. Tap Privacy.

19. Repeat steps 15–19 for each app on the list (if you want to, of course; most of time, you can just leave the permissions the way they are unless you want to block a specific app from using a certain kind of data).

20. When finished, tap Settings to return to the main Settings screen.

Advertising

At the bottom of the Privacy screen, you see the Advertising option. If you tap this, you can limit the tracking of ads you view by setting the Limit Ad Tracking switch to on (green). Typically, this tracking is used by advertisers to present ads that are related to ads you have viewed (the point being to make the ads more effective). You can reset the identifier used to identify you by tapping Reset Advertising Identifier and then tapping Reset.

	6:24 PM	@ 28%
❮ Settings	**Privacy**	
⌖ Location Services	On ❯	
👤 Contacts	❯	
📇 Calendars	❯	
☷ Reminders	❯	
🌸 Photos	❯	
❋ Bluetooth Sharing	❯	
🎤 Microphone	❯	

As applications request access to your data, they will be added in the categories above.

Setting Passcode, Fingerprint, and Auto-Lock Preferences

Your iPhone contains data you probably don't want others to access. You can require a passcode so your iPhone can't be unlocked without the proper passcode being entered. This gives you a measure of protection should you lose control of your phone. If you have an iPhone 5S, you can configure your fingerprints so that you can unlock your phone (by automatically entering the passcode) and enter your Apple ID password by touching the Touch ID/ Home button.

The Auto-Lock feature automatically locks your phone after a specific period of time. In combination with a passcode, this is a good way to protect the information on your iPhone.

Securing Your iPhone with Auto-Lock

To configure your phone so it locks automatically, perform the following steps.

1. On the Settings screen tap, General.

2. Swipe up the screen until you see Auto-Lock.

3. Tap Auto-Lock.

4. Tap the amount of idle time you want to pass before the iPhone automatically locks and goes to sleep. You can choose from 1 to 5 minutes; choose Never if you want to manually lock your iPhone. I recommend that you keep Auto-Lock set to a relatively small value to conserve your iPhone's battery and to make it more secure. Of course, the shorter you set this time to be, the more frequently you have to unlock it.

5. Tap General. You're ready to configure your passcode and fingerprints (iPhone 5S).

Configuring Your Passcode and Fingerprints (iPhone 5S)

To configure the passcode you have to enter to unlock your iPhone, perform the following steps:

1. On the Settings screen tap, General.

2. Swipe up the screen until you see Passcode & Fingerprint (iPhone 5S) or Passcode (other models).

3. Tap Passcode & Fingerprint (iPhone 5S) or Passcode (other models).

Already Have a Passcode?

If your iPhone already has a passcode set, when you perform step 3, you're prompted to enter your current passcode. When you enter it correctly, you move to the Passcode & Fingerprint (iPhone 5S) or Passcode (other models) screen and you can make changes to the current passcode, add new fingerprints, and so on. In this case, you can skip directly to step 7. If you want to change your current passcode, tap Change Passcode and follow steps 5 and 6 to change it. Then continue with step 7.

4. Tap Turn Passcode On.

5. Enter a four-digit passcode.

6. Reenter the passcode. If the two passcodes match, the passcode is set.

7. Tap Require Passcode.

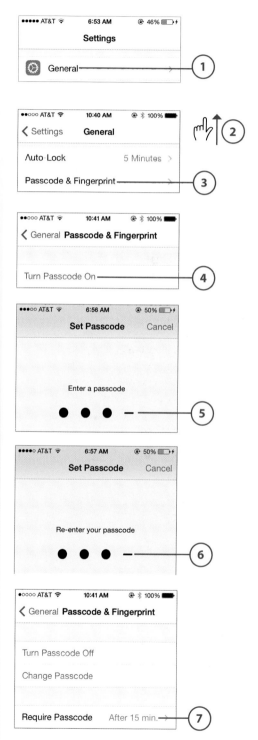

8. Tap the amount of time the iPhone is locked before the passcode takes effect. The shorter this time is, the more secure your iPhone is, but also the more times you'll have to enter the passcode if your iPhone locks frequently.

9. Tap Back.

Are You Complex?

By default, your passcode is a simple four-digit number. If you want to have a more complex (and more secure) passcode, set the Simple Passcode switch to off (white). You are prompted to create a new, complex passcode. The passcode field becomes more flexible, and you can enter text and numbers. This is more secure, especially if you use a code that is eight characters or longer that includes both letters and numbers. The steps to set a complex password are similar; the difference is that you use the keyboard to configure the passcode instead of just the numeric keypad.

10. If you have an iPhone 5S, tap Fingerprints and continue to step 11; if you have a different model, skip to step 23.

11. Tap Add a fingerprint. You see the Place Your Finger screen.

12. Touch the finger you want to be able to use to unlock your phone and enter your Apple ID password to the Touch ID/Home button, but don't press the button. An image of a fingerprint appears.

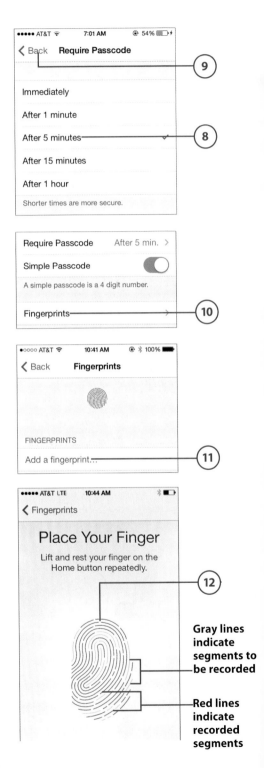

Gray lines indicate segments to be recorded

Red lines indicate recorded segments

13. Leave your finger on the Touch ID/Home button until you feel the phone vibrate, which indicates part of your fingerprint has been recorded and you see some segments turn red. The parts of your fingerprints that are recorded are indicated by the red segments, gray segments are not recorded yet.

14. Take your finger off the Touch ID/Home button and touch that button again, adjusting your finger on the button to record other parts that currently show gray lines instead of read ones. Another segment of your fingerprint is recorded.

15. Repeat step 14 until all the segments are red. You are prompted to change your grip so you can record more of your fingerprint.

16. Repeat step 14, again placing other areas of your finger to fill in more gray lines with red ones. When the entire fingerprint is covered in red lines, you see the Success screen.

17. Tap Continue. The fingerprint is recorded and you move back to the Fingerprints screen. You see the fingerprint that has been recorded.

18. Repeat steps 11 through 17 to record up to five fingerprints. These can be yours or someone else's if you want to allow that person to access your iPhone.

19. Tap the Passcode Unlock switch so it is on (green) to be able to use your fingerprint to unlock your phone.

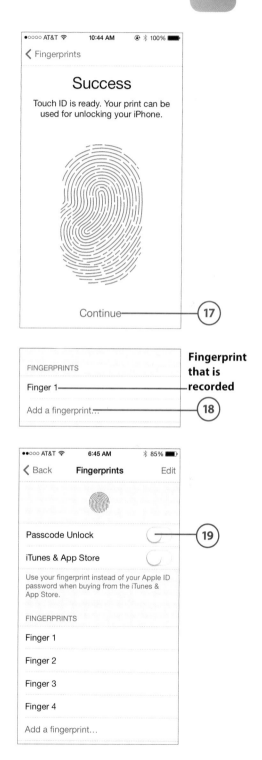

Fingerprint that is recorded

20. If you want to also be able to enter your Apple ID password by touching your finger to the Touch ID/Home button, set the iTunes & App Store switch to on (green).

21. Enter your Apple ID password and tap OK.

22. Tap Back.

23. To allow Voice Dial to work when your phone is locked, ensure that the Voice Dial switch is on (green). If off (white), you won't be able to use Voice Dial from the Lock screen. (Voice Dial enables you to make calls by speaking even if you don't use Siri.)

24. If you want to prevent Siri from working when your iPhone is locked, set the Siri switch to the off (white) position. If you leave Siri enabled, your phone is less secure because it can be used to some degree even when it is locked.

25. To prevent the information in the Passbook app from being accessed while the iPhone is locked, set the Passbook switch to the off (white) position. You have to unlock the iPhone to use the Passbook app. This is not convenient because the Passbook is designed to be readily accessible and it's a lot faster to tap your iPhone to use Passbook information then it is to have to unlock your iPhone, but it is more secure.

26. To prevent being able to reply to an incoming call or FaceTime request with a text message when the iPhone is locked, set the Reply with Message switch to off (white).

27. If you want the iPhone to automatically erase all your data after an incorrect passcode has been entered 10 times, tap the Erase Data switch.

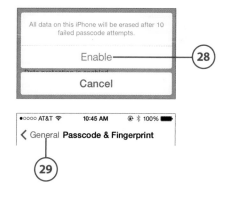

Automatic Erase

When you have enabled the Erase Data function and you enter an incorrect passcode when unlocking your iPhone, you see a counter showing the number of unsuccessful attempts. When this reaches 10, all the data on your iPhone will be erased on the next unsuccessful attempt.

28. Tap Enable. The status of Erase Data becomes on (green). Should you or anyone else be unable to enter the correct passcode on the eleventh try, your data (basically any changes you've made to the contents of the iPhone) will be erased.

29. Tap General to return to the Settings screen.

Making Changes

Any time you want to make changes to your passcode and fingerprint (iPhone 5S) settings, move back to the Passcode & Fingerprint (iPhone 5S) or Passcode (other models) screen. Before you can move back to this screen, you must enter your current passcode at the prompt. After you enter your current passcode, you move to the Passcode & Fingerprint (iPhone 5S) or Passcode (other models) screen. To disable the passcode, tap Turn Passcode Off, tap Turn Off, and enter the passcode. To change your passcode, tap Change Passcode. You then enter your current passcode and enter your new passcode twice. You return to the Passcode Lock screen, and the new passcode takes effect. You can change the other settings similar to how you set them initially as described in these steps. For example, you can add new fingerprints. To remove a fingerprint, move to the Fingerprints screen, swipe to the left on the fingerprint you want to remove, and tap Delete.

Setting Restrictions for Content and Apps

You can restrict the access to specific content and apps on your phone. Suppose you let other people borrow your iPhone but don't want them to use certain apps or to see data you'd rather keep to yourself. You can enable a restriction to prevent someone from accessing these areas without entering the restriction code. You can also restrict the use of apps movies, music, and other content based on the age rating that the app or other content has.

To restrict access to content or apps, perform the following steps:

1. On the Settings screen, tap General.

2. Swipe up the screen until you see Restrictions.

3. Tap Restrictions.

4. Tap Enable Restrictions.

5. Create a restrictions passcode. You have to enter this passcode to change the content restrictions or to be able to access restricted content.

6. Reenter your restrictions passcode. You return to the Restrictions screen, and the ALLOW buttons are enabled.

Dueling Passcodes

There are two passcodes: the Lock passcode and the Restrictions passcode. Each controls access to its respective functions. Limiting access to content and apps likely means you will be letting someone else use your phone, so he needs to have the Lock passcode. You should use different Unlock and Restrictions passcodes because if they are the same, anyone who can use your iPhone has the Lock passcode and can also change the restrictions, which defeats the purpose of having a Restrictions passcode.

7. In the ALLOW section, set the switch next to each function you want to disable to off (white). For example, to prevent web browsing, set the Safari switch to off (white); the Safari icon is removed from the Home screen and can't be used. With the other controls, you can prevent access to the Camera, FaceTime, iTunes Store, and so on.

8. Swipe up to see the ALLOWED CONTENT section.

9. Tap Ratings For.

10. Tap the country whose rating system you want to use for content on your iPhone.

Whose Ratings?

The country you select in step 10 determines the options you see in the remaining steps because the restrictions available depend on the location you select. The steps show the United States rating systems; if you select a different country, you see rating options for that country instead.

11. Tap Restrictions.

12. Tap Music & Podcasts.

13. To prevent content tagged as explicit in the iTunes Store from being played, set the Explicit switch to off (white). Explicit content will not be available in the Music or Podcasts app.

14. Tap Restrictions.

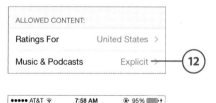

15. Tap Movies.

16. Tap the highest rating of movies that you want to be playable (for example, tap PG-13 to prevent R and NC-17 movies from playing); tap Allow All Movies to allow any movie to be played; or tap Don't Allow Movies to prevent any movie content from playing. Prevented movie ratings are high-lighted in red.

17. Tap Restrictions.

18. Tap TV Shows and use the result-ing screen to set the highest rating of TV shows that you want to be playable (for example, tap TV-14 to prevent TV-MA shows from playing); tap Allow All TV Shows to allow any show to be played; or tap Don't Allow TV Shows to prevent any TV con-tent from playing. Prevented ratings are highlighted in red. Tap Restrictions to return to the Restrictions screen.

19. Use the Books option to enable or disable access to sexually explicit books.

20. Tap Apps and set the highest rating of app that you want to be available (for example, tap 12+ to prevent 17+ applications from working); tap Allow All Apps to allow any application to be used; or tap Don't Allow Apps to prevent all applications. Tap Restrictions to return to the Restrictions screen.

21. Use the Siri option to restrict explicit language for searching the Web.

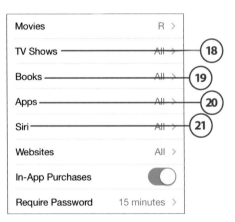

22. Use the Websites option to control the websites that can be accessed. The options are to limit sites with adult content or to allow only specific websites to be visited. When you select this option, you can create a list of sites and only those sites can be visited.

23. To prevent purchases from being made within apps, slide the In-App Purchases switch to off (white). Purchases can't be made from within apps. This is a good way to prevent unintended purchases, particularly when someone else is using your iPhone.

24. Tap Require Password.

Movies	R >
TV Shows	All >
Books	All >
Apps	All >
Siri	All >
Websites	All >
In-App Purchases	
Require Password	15 minutes >

Where's My Good Stuff?

When you change content restriction settings, such as allowing explicit content after it was prevented, you might have to resync your iPhone for those changes to take effect. For example, if you prevent R-rated movies from playing and then allow them to play again, you might need to resync your movie content for those movies to appear on the iPhone.

25. Tap Immediately if you want a password to be required for every purchase, or 15 minutes if you don't want a password to be required for each purchase within a 15-minute window.

26. Tap Restrictions.

27. Swipe up the screen until you see the Privacy section.

28. Tap Location Services.

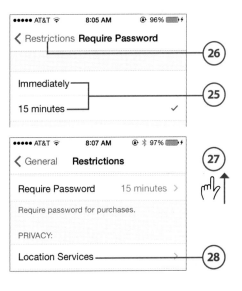

••••• AT&T 🤖   8:05 AM   ⓐ 96% 🔋⚡
‹ Restrictions **Require Password**

Immediately
15 minutes ✓

••••• AT&T 🤖   8:07 AM   ⓐ 🅰 97% 🔋⚡
‹ General **Restrictions**

Require Password   15 minutes >
Require password for purchases.

PRIVACY:

Location Services

29. To prevent changes from being made to Location Services, tap Don't Allow Changes. This disables the Location Services controls that you learned about earlier and locks them in their current states.

30. Tap Restrictions.

31. Tap Contacts.

32. Tap Don't Allow Changes if you want to prevent new apps from accessing your Contacts and lock the current permissions as they are (preventing any changes to apps that are currently allowed to access this information).

33. Tap Restrictions.

34. Use the rest of the settings in the Privacy section to determine whether new apps can access information stored in each area and whether they should be locked in their current states. For example, you can prevent new apps from accessing your calendars or photos.

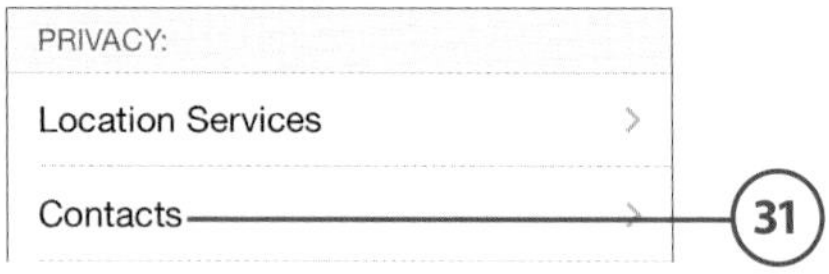

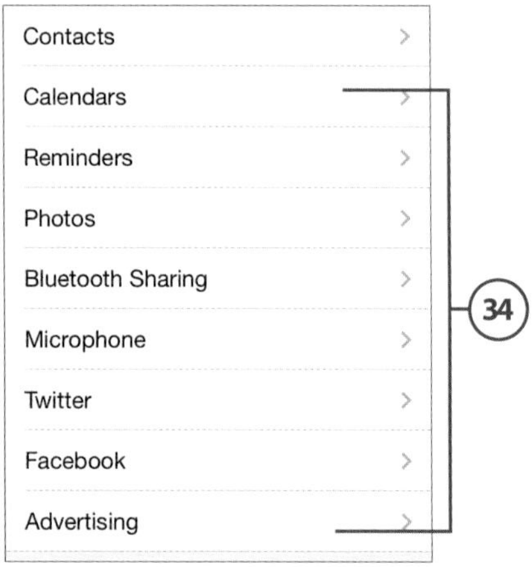

•••• AT&T 🛜 8:07 AM ⊕ ∗ 97% ▭▸⚡

❮ Restrictions **Contacts**

Allow Changes ✓

Don't Allow Changes

Disallowing changes locks the settings shown below and prevents new apps from using your contacts.

StreetPilot

Applications that have requested access to your contacts will appear here.

PRIVACY:

Location Services ›

Contacts ›

•••• AT&T 🛜 8:25 AM ⊕ ∗ 100% ▭▸⚡

❮ Restrictions **Contacts**

Allow Changes ✓

Don't Allow Changes

Disallowing changes locks the settings shown below and prevents new apps from using your contacts.

StreetPilot

Applications that have requested access to your contacts will appear here.

Contacts ›

Calendars ›

Reminders ›

Photos ›

Bluetooth Sharing ›

Microphone ›

Twitter ›

Facebook ›

Advertising ›

35. Swipe up the screen.

36. Tap Accounts.

37. To prevent accounts for email, calendars, or contacts from being created or changed, tap Don't Allow Changes.

38. Tap Restrictions.

39. In a similar way, allow or prevent changes related to cellular data use, background app refreshing, and the volume limit.

40. To prevent multiplayer games in the Game Center, set the Multiplayer Games switch to off (white). Users will no longer be able to play games against other people.

41. To prevent new friends from being added in the Game Center, set the Adding Friends switch to off (white). Players will be restricted to the friends already allowed.

42. Tap General to return to the General page of the Settings app.

Removing Restrictions

To remove all restrictions, move to the Restrictions screen (your passcode is required) and tap Disable Restrictions. Enter your passcode, and the restrictions are removed.

ALLOW CHANGES:

Accounts

Cellular Data Use

•••• AT&T 🤶 8:08 AM @ ∗ 97%

‹ Restrictions **Accounts**

Allow Changes ✓

Don't Allow Changes

Disallowing changes prevents adding, removing, or modifying accounts in Mail, Contacts, Calendars.

‹ General **Restrictions**

Facebook

Advertising

ALLOW CHANGES:

Accounts

Cellular Data Use

Background App Refresh

Volume Limit

GAME CENTER:

Multiplayer Games

Adding Friends

Sync the content of your
iTunes Library, such as
your music, to enjoy it on
your iPhone

iTunes is a good
partner for your
iPhone

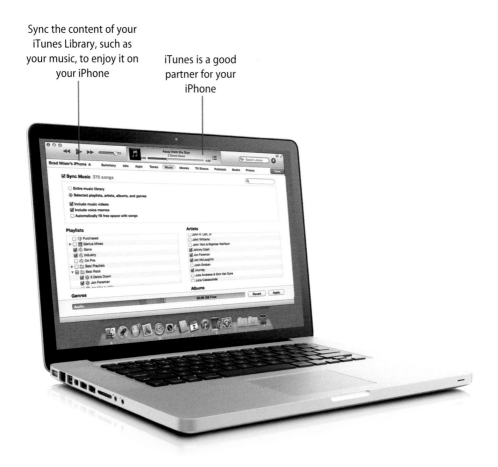

In this chapter, you learn how the iTunes app on a computer is useful for your iPhone. Topics include the following:

→ Preparing music on audio CDs for your iPhone
→ Using iTunes to download movies, music, books, and more from the iTunes Store
→ Synchronizing content on your computer with your iPhone
→ Working with iTunes Match

5

Working with iTunes on Your Computer

iTunes is a great application you can use to store, organize, and enjoy all sorts of music, movies, TV shows, podcasts, and other types of digital content. You can also access the iTunes Store from within iTunes so you can seamlessly shop for and download new content from the store's vast selection. iTunes enables you to create, organize, and manage your digital media, enabling you to quickly access and enjoy anything in your digital library.

The reason this chapter exists, however, is that iTunes is also useful as a partner to your iPhone. You can use iTunes on your computer to manage your iPhone's operating system software (iOS). You can also use the sync process to move any content in your iTunes Library onto your iPhone so you can listen to, watch, or read it there.

You'll definitely want to be able to use iTunes to restore your iPhone's software should that become necessary to solve a problem (doing this is explained later in this chapter).

In addition to restoring your iPhone's software, how much you'll use iTunes to manage the content on your iPhone depends mostly on the type of content you have.

If you download all your music, movies, books, and so on from the iTunes Store, then you don't need to use iTunes to move that content onto your iPhone because you can do that directly on the iPhone using the iTunes app (this is covered in Chapter 6, "Downloading Apps, Music, Movies, TV Shows, and More onto Your iPhone"). Likewise, if you use streaming apps, such as Pandora or iHeartRadio, to listen to music or watch video, you don't need iTunes because that content moves directly from the Internet onto your phone.

If you have music on audio CDs, you can use iTunes to convert that music into a format compatible with your iPhone so you can listen to it with the Music app on your phone. (You can move music from iTunes onto your iPhone through the sync process or via iTunes Match, both of which are explained in this chapter.) If you have content on DVD, such as movies or TV shows, that you want to watch on your iPhone, you'll need to first store that content in iTunes and then use the sync process to move it onto the iPhone.

If you have a Windows PC, iTunes might not be installed on your computer (iTunes is automatically installed on Macs). To download and install iTunes on a Windows PC, go to http://www.apple.com/itunes/download/ and click the Download Now button. Follow the onscreen instructions to complete the installation.

This Is Not an iTunes Book

iTunes is a very powerful and useful application. It can do lots of things, and only the key iPhone-related features of iTunes are described in this book. To learn how to use iTunes more fully, see my book *iTunes and iCloud for iPhone, iPad,& iPod touch Absolute Beginner's Guide* on www.quepublishing.com.

Converting Music on Audio CDs for Your iPhone

iTunes enables you to convert music on an audio CD into an iPhone-compatible format and store the converted music in your iTunes Library on your computer. After that's done, you can move the music onto your iPhone by syncing it or by using iTunes Match.

To get started, configure iTunes to convert the music on audio CDs into files stored on your computer; you only need to do this when you first get started or if you want to change how the conversion process works at a later time. After iTunes is configured, importing CDs into your iTunes Library is a snap.

Setting Up iTunes to Import Audio CDs

There are a few import preferences you should set for iTunes:

1. Launch iTunes by double-clicking its application icon, selecting it on the Windows Start menu, or clicking it on the Mac's Dock.

2. On a Windows PC, hold down the Alt key (so the iTunes menu bar appears) and select Edit, Preferences; on a Mac, select iTunes, Preferences. The Preferences dialog box appears.

3. Click the General tab.

4. On the When you insert a CD menu, select Import CD and Eject.

5. Click Import Settings.

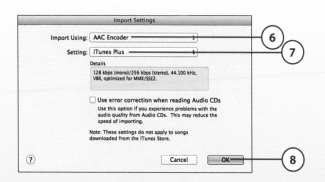

6. On the Import Using drop-down menu, select AAC Encoder.

7. On the Setting drop-down menu, select iTunes Plus.

8. Click OK.

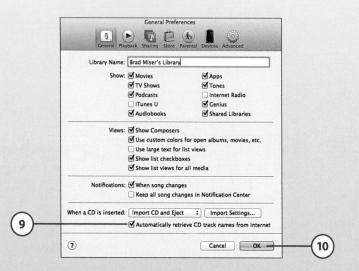

9. Check Automatically retrieve CD track names from Internet.

10. Click OK. You're ready to start importing your CDs.

Importing Audio CDs to the iTunes Library

When you've configured iTunes as described in the previous task, importing music from your audio CDs is a snap:

1. Launch iTunes by double-clicking its application icon, selecting it on the Windows Start menu, or clicking it on the Mac's Dock.

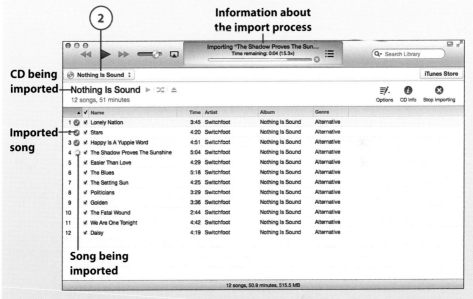

2

Information about the import process

CD being imported

Imported song

Song being imported

2. Insert the CD you want to import into the computer. iTunes connects to the Internet and identifies the CD. When that's done, the import process starts. As songs are imported, they are marked with a check mark. The process is done at several times faster than playback speed, so importing a typical CD requires only a few minutes. When the process finishes, iTunes plays an alert sound and ejects the disc. The songs on the disc are in your iTunes Library, and you can use iTunes to listen to them, put them in playlists, move them onto your iPhone, and so on.

3. Insert the next CD you want to import. After it has been ejected, insert the next CD and so on until you've added all the CDs you want to have in your iTunes Library.

No Duplicates, Please

After you import a CD into your iTunes Library, you won't likely ever need to use it again on your computer. So after you import all your CDs, change the iTunes On CD Insert setting to Ask to Import CD so that you don't accidentally import multiple copies of the same CD in the rare case you do insert a CD into your computer again. (Don't worry, though—if you leave the setting as is, iTunes prompts you the next time you insert the CD to see if you want to replace the previous version.)

ADDING DVD CONTENT TO ITUNES

Adding movies and TV shows that you have on DVD to your iTunes Library is a bit more complicated because iTunes can't import that content directly. You need another application to convert the DVD content into a digital format. Many of these are available for Mac and Windows PCs—just do a web search to find and download the application you want to use. Most offer multiple format options; if you are going to move the content onto your iPhone, you need to choose a compatible format when you convert the content. After you've set up the import application, you convert (also called *encode* or *rip*) the DVD content into the iPhone-compatible format. When that is done, you can add the converted content to your iTunes Library on a Windows PC by pressing the Alt key (so the iTunes menu appears), selecting File, selecting Add File to Library, moving to and selecting the converted content, and clicking Open. You can do the same on a Mac by selecting File, selecting Add to Library, moving to and selecting the converted file, and clicking OK. After the converted content has been added to your iTunes Library, you can watch it in iTunes or move it onto your iPhone through the sync process (which is explained later in this chapter).

Using iTunes to Download Movies, Music, Books, and More from the iTunes Store

The iTunes Store has a large selection of music, movies, TV shows, books, and other content that you can preview, purchase or rent, and download to your iTunes Library. You can listen to or watch that content in iTunes on a computer, and you can do the same on an iPhone.

No Sync Required—Most of the Time

For almost all the content you download from the iTunes Store, you don't need to sync your iPhone with iTunes because you can always download that content directly onto your iPhone. As you learn in Chapter 6, you can configure your iPhone so that all the content you download from the Store on any device is automatically downloaded to your iPhone, too. The exception to this is rented movies; rented movies can exist on only one device at a time. So, if you rent a movie in iTunes on a computer, you must use the sync process to move that rented movie onto your iPhone.

To download content from the iTunes Store, you must have an iTunes Store account, also known as an Apple ID. (You can preview content without an Apple ID.) If you have an AIM/AOL screen name, you can also use that to sign into the store. (You have to provide credit card information to use an AIM/AOL account to make purchases.) You can sign into your account within iTunes and begin shopping for and downloading content.

Obtaining an iTunes Store Account (Apple ID)

An account with the iTunes Store enables you to purchase or rent music, movies, TV shows, apps, ringtones, books, and other content that is then downloaded to your iTunes Library. From there, you can move it onto your iPhone (you can set up your phone so this happens without iTunes on your computer, as explained in Chapter 6). Even if you don't intend to purchase movies, books, or other content from the iTunes Store, you still need an account to download and install free apps for your iPhone.

If you already have an Apple ID, you don't need to create another one to use the iTunes Store—if some form of payment isn't associated with your current account, you need to add that to be able to download any content that isn't free (your'e prompted to provide the required information when it is needed). If you have a current Apple ID, you can just sign into that account by skipping to the next section.

To create a new Apple ID, perform the following steps:

1. Open iTunes.

2. Click iTunes Store. You connect to the Internet and move into the iTunes Store.

3. Click Sign In. The Sign In dialog box appears.

No Sign In Button?

If you see an Apple ID instead of the Sign In button, an Apple ID is already signed into the iTunes Store. If the current account is yours, you can skip the rest of these steps and the next task as well. If the current account isn't yours and you are using a Mac, select Store, Sign Out. If you are using a Windows PC, open the iTunes menu (located in the upper-left corner of the window), select iTunes Store, and then select Sign Out. Then return to step 3 and click Sign In.

4. Click Create Apple ID. You move to the first screen in the account creation process.

5. Read the information and follow the onscreen instructions to create an Apple ID. After you complete the steps, you receive your Apple ID and password and are ready to sign into your new account in iTunes.

Signing Into the iTunes Store

The first step to use the iTunes Store is to sign into your account. iTunes remembers your account, so unless you sign out (as described in the "No Sign In Button" sidebar) you need to sign in only once.

1. Open iTunes.

2. Click iTunes Store. You connect to the Internet and move into the iTunes Store.

3. Click Sign In. The Sign In dialog box appears.

4. Enter your Apple ID and password.

5. Click Sign In. You are logged in to your iTunes Store account.

The account currently signed into the iTunes Store

One Login to Rule Them All

You can use the same Apple ID in the iTunes Store, for an iCloud account, and in the Apple online store. When you get an Apple ID via the iTunes Store, you can just use your iCloud account email address as the login. Although iCloud is free, you need to provide payment information to use your Apple ID in the iTunes Store. You don't have to use just one account, though. For example, if you want to share iTunes content with your family, you can get one Apple ID for shopping in the iTunes Store but get a different Apple ID for your personal iCloud account.

Shopping in the iTunes Store

When you are signed into your iTunes account, using the iTunes Store is simple because it is integrated into iTunes and it uses an interface that is intuitive and easy to use.

Here are three general steps to download iTunes Store content to your iTunes Library:

- **Find the content of interest to you**—There are a couple of ways to do this:

  One way to find content is by browsing. Just about every graphic and almost all the text you see are linked to either categories of content or to specific content. You can browse the store just by clicking around. For example, you can click the Music link to browse music or click any of the other links you see on the Home page to browse some other type of content. There are numerous ways to browse, but all of them involve just clicking around. If you don't have something specific in mind, browsing is a great way to discover, preview, and purchase content.

  Another way is to search for specific content. This is useful when you know something about the content you want, such as the artist, because it gets you to that content very quickly. Steps to search are provided shortly.

- **Preview the content**—You can listen to portions of songs, watch trailers for movies, read information, and so on to get a good idea of whether the content is something you want to have in your Library. If it is, you can move to the next step. If not, keep performing steps 1 and 2 until you find what you are looking for.

- **Download the content**—This involves clicking the appropriate button. If the content has a cost, you see that cost in the button. If there are options, such as High Definition (HD) and Standard Definition (SD) versions of a movie, you see a button for each option. Some content is free, in which case it has a Free button. Whichever path you take, the content is downloaded to your computer and becomes available in your iTunes Library.

A quick example of searching for content to download from the iTunes Store will show you how easy shopping in the Store is:

1. Click the iTunes Store button. iTunes connects to the iTunes Store, and the Home page displays.

2. Click in the Search Store bar.

3. Type the information for which you want to search. You can perform a general search by typing a small amount of text, such as "3 doors down," which finds all the content by that group. Make the search more specific by combining text phrases, such as "3 doors down time of my life." As you type, iTunes tries to complete your search; if you want to use one of the terms it recommends, click it. If not, keep typing until you've entered all of the search term.

4. Press the Enter key on your computer's keyboard. Items that meet your search criteria display in the lower parts of the window. The results are organized into logical collections based on the type of content for which you searched. For example, when you search for music, you see albums, songs, and music videos. You see different kinds of information for each type of content available in the store.

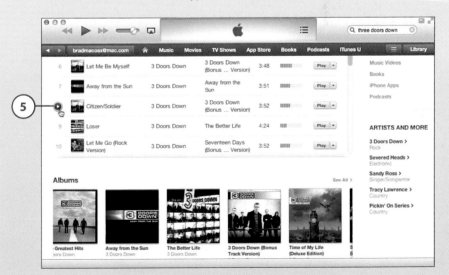

5. To preview music, move the pointer over it and click the Play button that appears; where it appears depends on what you hover over. When you hover over a song, the Play button replaces the track number; when you hover over a video, the Play button appears in the lower-right corner of the thumbnail. After you click the button, a preview plays. The length of the preview depends on the specific content you are previewing. For example, when you preview most songs, the preview lasts 90 seconds.

6. If you select video, watch the video in the preview window that appears.

7. When you want to purchase and download content, click its *buy* button. This button can include different information depending on the content you are viewing. It always shows the price of the content. It can also describe what you are buying. For example, when you browse a TV show, one *buy* button enables you to purchase the entire season, whereas you can use the *buy* buttons next to each episode to purchase one episode at a time.

8. If prompted, enter your account's information and click Buy—or just click the Buy button depending on the prompt that displays. The content you purchase is downloaded to your computer and added to your iTunes Library.

Buy Now!

If you check the Don't ask me or Remember check box in the various prompts you see when you purchase items, in the future when you click the Buy or Rent button, content is purchased or rented immediately. This is convenient but also doesn't give you a chance to reconsider.

9. Click the Library button to return to your iTunes Library.

10. Choose Music on the Source menu.

11. Click the Playlists button.

12. Click the Purchased playlist to see content you've downloaded from the iTunes Store. You can listen to or watch this content, put it in other playlists, move it onto your iPhone, and so on.

More Than Buy

If you click the downward-facing arrow to the right of the *buy* buttons in the iTunes Store, a menu with various commands appears; commands on this menu include Gift, which enables you to give the content to someone; share via Facebook; and so on. One useful option enables you to add content to your wish list, which is much like a shopping cart where you can store content you might be interested in purchasing at a later time; after you add content to your wish list, you can move back to it by clicking the My Wish List item on the Quick Links section of the iTunes Store home page. From your wish list, you can preview or purchase content.

>>>Go Further
ORGANIZING YOUR ITUNES CONTENT

As you build up your iTunes Library, you'll end up with a lot of content of all types. It's a good idea to organize your content to make it easier to find, and much easier to move onto your iPhone through the sync process. You can use playlists to manually place content into your own collections, sorted in just the way you want. With a smart playlist, you can define a set of criteria (such as a specific artist) and iTunes collects the associated content into a group automatically. You can also use folders to group your playlists to keep those organized, too. Playlists and folders make configuring and syncing content using iTunes easier and also makes finding and using that content on your phone easier. My book *iTunes and iCloud for iPhone, iPad, & iPod touch Absolute Beginner's Guide* provides the details on how to accomplish these tasks. You can find this book on www.quepublishing.com.

Synchronizing Content on Your Computer with Your iPhone

iTunes communicates with your iPhone for a number of purposes. Configuring some aspects of how your iPhone works and copying or moving content from your iTunes Library onto your iPhone so you can use that content in your iPhone's apps are just a few of the ways iTunes interacts with your iPhone. This is called *syncing* because you are synchronizing the content of your iPhone with your iTunes Library. You can determine the kind of data that is copied or moved to your iPhone by configuring the various sync settings available in iTunes. Each of these has its own tab with controls that are appropriate for that tab. The sync tabs available are:

- **Summary**—Use this tab to configure some aspects of how your iPhone works, such as if you can sync wirelessly.

- **Info**—This tab enables you to sync contacts, calendars, email accounts, and other information on your iPhone. If you keep this information in an online account, such as iCloud or Exchange, you don't need to include these in the sync process. However, this can be useful to sync content that is only stored on your computer.

- **Apps**—Use this tab to add apps to or remove them from your iPhone. You can also organize your Home screens on this tab.

- **Tones**—With this tab, you can choose the custom ring and alert tones available on your iPhone.

- **Music**—Use this tab to copy music onto your iPhone (if you use iTunes Match, which is covered later in this chapter, you can ignore this tab).

- **Movies**—You can copy movies onto your iPhone so you can watch them in the Videos app. You can also move rented movies from the computer onto your iPhone (unlike other content, rented movies can exist on only one device at a time).

- **TV Shows**—Here, you can choose which series, and which episodes of those series, are available on your phone.

- **Podcasts**—This tab enables you to select the podcasts you want to copy from the computer onto the iPhone. If you use the Podcasts app on the iPhone, you won't need to use this tab (see Chapter 16, "Using Other Cool iPhone Apps," for information about the Podcasts app).

- **Books**—Use this tab to copy ebooks, PDFs, and audiobooks onto your iPhone.

- **Photos**—This tab enables you to copy photos from your desktop or a photo app (such as iPhoto or Photoshop Elements) onto your phone.

- **On This iPhone**—Using this tab, you can browse the current contents on your iPhone.

Understanding the Sync Process

The general steps to sync your iPhone follow:

1. **Connect your iPhone** to your computer using its USB cable (after it's configured, you can sync wirelessly, too).

Show Some Trust

The first time you connect your iPhone to a computer, you're prompted (on the iPhone) to trust the computer. Or you might see the prompt on your computer. You must indicate that you trust the device in one of those places to be able to sync. If you don't, you won't be able to sync it and will see the prompt again the next time you connect it to your computer.

2. Open iTunes, if it doesn't open automatically.

3. Click the iPhone button in the upper-right corner of the iTunes window. If your computer can communicate with more than one device, this button is labeled X Devices, where X is the number of devices it is communicating with. Click this button and then select your iPhone on the resulting menu. You see the tabs of the sync screen.

4. Click the tab for the area you want to configure.

5. Use the tab's controls to configure that aspect of the sync process, such as what content you want to move or sync.

6. Repeat steps 4 and 5 for each tab.

7. Click Apply (if you haven't changed any settings, you see the Sync button instead). The iPhone is synced according to your settings.

8. To move back to your iTunes Library, click Done.

Although each tab has different controls, the process you follow to configure them is the same. Because it is a bit different from the others, the detailed steps to configure the Summary settings are listed next.

Configuring Summary Sync Settings

The Summary tab is where you configure how certain aspects of your iPhone work, and you can also use it to maintain your iPhone's software. To configure the summary sync settings, do the following:

1. Click the Summary tab.

2. If you have an iCloud account configured and want to back up your iPhone on the cloud, click the iCloud radio button.

3. If you want to back up to your computer, click This computer.

4. If you back up to your computer and want to protect the backup of your iPhone's data (used to restore your iPhone) with encryption, check Encrypt iPhone backup, create and verify a password, and click Set Password; this password will be required to restore the backed-up information onto the iPhone.

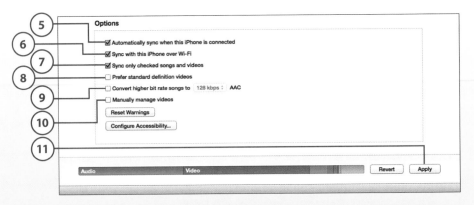

5. Check the Automatically sync when this iPhone is connected check box if you want the sync process to start automatically when you connect the iPhone to your computer.

6. Check Sync with this iPhone over Wi-Fi if you want to be able to sync your iPhone via a Wi-Fi network. This is useful because you don't have to physically connect your iPhone to your computer to sync it. You can enable this option and still have the option to connect your iPhone to your computer using the USB cable to sync.

7. If you don't want content that you have configured iTunes to ignore to be moved onto the iPhone, check the Sync only checked songs and videos check box. (You configure iTunes to ignore content by unchecking the check boxes next to songs or other content you want to be skipped; enabling this sync setting mirrors those selections and unchecked items won't be moved onto your iPhone.)

8. If you want to include only the standard definition of I ID video, check the Prefer standard definition videos check box; this saves space because the HD versions are larger files.

9. To cause iTunes to convert songs that have been encoded so they are high quality (larger file sizes) to files that have smaller sizes (so more content fits onto the iPhone), check the Convert higher bit rate songs to check box and select the conversion you want to use, such as 128kbps, on the menu. (You aren't likely to hear the difference when playing this content with your iPhone.) This is useful to save some storage space on your iPhone if you've included audio encoded to a higher quality setting . If you've imported audio from CD using the settings earlier in the chapter, or downloaded it from the iTunes Store, you don't need to set this because your content is already using an efficient format.

10. If you check the Manually manage music and videos check box, you can place content on the iPhone by dragging movies and other video content onto the iPhone in addition to moving it via the sync process. (If you are using iTunes Match, this check box is just Manually manage videos because you manage all your music through iTunes Match.)

11. To apply the settings to your iPhone and sync it now, click Apply. If you are also going to configure other settings, you can skip this step and wait until you have configured the other tabs.

Backing Up Isn't Hard to Do

Like other data, you should back up the contents of your iPhone so you don't lose data if something happens to your iPhone. The backup process occurs automatically (both the iCloud and computer options), so you don't need to do anything. However, you can also back up your iPhone manually by clicking the Back Up Now button, which backs up your content on your computer regardless of the backup option you have selected. So, you can choose to back up your iPhone to iCloud and periodically also back it up on your computer to be extra safe.

Syncing Content onto Your iPhone

As mentioned previously, the process to configure each tab of the Sync screen is similar. Walking through the details for one tab (the following steps show the Music tab) will help you understand what you need to do to configure the other tabs (the controls you have change for each tab, but using them is similar using those on the Music tab). To configure the music you want on your iPhone, perform the following steps:

1. Click the Music tab.

2. Check the Sync Music check box.

3. If you have enough room on the iPhone to store all the music content you have in your Library, check the Entire music library radio button. Unless you have a small amount of music and other content in your Library, you'll probably need to check the Selected playlists, artists, albums, and genres radio button instead; this enables you to select specific music to move onto the iPhone. The rest of these steps assume this option is selected. When you select it, the Playlists, Artists, Albums, and Genres selection tools appear.

4. Check Include music videos if you want music videos in your collection to be moved onto the iPhone.

5. Check Include voice memos if you use the Voice Memos or another app to record audio notes and want those memos to be included in the sync.

6. If you want any free space on the iPhone to be filled with music that iTunes selects, check the Automatically fill free space with songs check box.

7. To include a playlist in the sync so that all the items that playlist contains are moved onto the iPhone, check the check box next to it on the Playlists list.

8. To expand or collapse a folder to see or hide the playlists it contains, click its triangle.

9. To copy all the items within a folder of playlists onto the iPhone, check the folder's check box.

10. To copy all the songs by specific artists onto the iPhone, check the artist's name on the Artists list.

11. Click the check box next to each genre whose contents you want to copy onto the iPhone. For example, to move all the music in the Rock genre, check its check box.

12. Check the check boxes for albums you want to copy onto the iPhone.

Scrolling, Scrolling, Scrolling

Each section on the Music tab has its own scroll bar that you can use to browse the content in that section. You can also use the iTunes scroll bar to move up and down the tab, which you might need to do to see all its contents.

13. To apply the settings to your iPhone and sync it now, click Apply. The music you selected is available on your iPhone. If you are also going to sync other content, you can skip this step and wait until you have configured the other sync tabs.

Genres	Albums
☐ Christmas	☐ BlackHawk - Blackhawk
☐ Classical	☐ BlackHawk - BlackHawk: Greatest Hits
☑ Country	☐ Blake Lewis - Blake Lewis - EP
☐ Dance	☐ Blue Merle - Every Ship Must Sail Away - Single
☐ Disney	☑ Blue Öyster Cult - Don't Fear the Reaper - The Best of Blue Öyster Cult
☐ Easy Listening	☑ Blue Öyster Cult - Some Enchanted Evening
☐ Folk	☑ Blue Öyster Cult - Workshop of the Telescopes: The Best of Blue Öyster...
☐ Gospel & Religious	☑ Bob Dylan - Must Be Santa - Single of the Week
☐ Holiday	☑ Bob Seger - Greatest Hits
☐ Inspirational	☑ Boston - Boston
☐ Instrumental	☑ Boston - Greatest Hits
☑ Jazz	☐ Boyz II Men - II
☐ New Age	☐ Brad Fiedel - The Terminator - The Definitive Edition
☐ Novelty	☐ Brainy Baby Brainy Baby: Classical Tunes
☐ Pop	☐ Brian McKnight - The Most Wonderful Time Of The Year - Discovery Do...
☑ R&B	☐ Brian Setzer - Christmas Rocks: The Best-Of Collection
☐ Religious	☑ Bruce Springsteen - Born in the U.S.A.
☑ Rock	☑ Bruce Springsteen - Born to Run
☐ Singer/Songwriter	☑ Bruce Springsteen & The E Street Band - Bruce Springsteen & the E Str...
☐ Soundtrack	☐ The Byrds - The Byrds: Greatest Hits
☐ Vocal	☐ Cale Parks - To Swift Mars EP

(11)   (12)   (13)

Audio   17.24 GB Free   Revert   Apply

ITUNES STORE ONLY?

>>>Go Further

If all the content you want to move onto the iPhone came from the iTunes Store, you don't need to sync. You can download this content directly to your iPhone at any time using the iTunes app (without paying for it again), and you can configure your iPhone so any new music, app, or book purchases you make on any device download to the iPhone automatically. These tasks are covered in Chapter 6. (Remember that the exception to this is rented movies, which can live on only one device at a time; this means you must sync with iTunes to move a rented movie onto your iPhone.)

Keeping Your iPhone in Sync

Following are some additional points to ponder when it comes to keeping your iPhone in sync:

Audio   Video   Revert   Apply

Use this gauge to see if your iPhone has enough room for the content you've selected to sync

- As you select content to sync onto your iPhone, the Capacity gauge at the bottom of the screen is updated to show you exactly how much of your iPhone's storage the current sync settings will use. The gauge is segmented by type of content, including audio, video, photos, and so on. If you have more content selected than will fit, the gauge is full and a warning icon is displayed. You'll need to remove content from the sync to be sure of the content that will be moved onto the iPhone (if you sync anyway, some of the content won't be moved onto the iPhone or the sync process won't finish).

  If there's enough space on the iPhone for the content you've selected, the sync process continues until all the content has been copied or moved onto the phone. If you've selected more content than there is room for on the iPhone, a warning dialog box explaining how much content you selected versus how much space is available displays. (You can tell this is a problem before the sync process begins if a warning icon appears to the right of Capacity gauge.)

  If you have selected too much content, you need to decrease the amount of content you are syncing and perform the sync again by clicking Apply.

- Not having enough space on the iPhone to complete the sync is just one type of warning you might see during the sync process. If you've included content that can't be synced for some reason, such as a movie that isn't in the correct format, you also see a warning. Or if you want to sync content from more than five iTunes Store accounts, that content won't be synced onto the iPhone. In most cases, the sync process continues but the content with the problem is not copied onto the iPhone. Just click OK to clear any warnings and cause the sync process to continue. You can also get more detail about the issue in the warning dialog box.

- The sync process can work in the background so you can use iTunes for other things while your iPhone is being synced.

- When the sync is complete, the iPhone sync is complete message appears in the Information area at the top of the iTunes window.

- When you've made changes to the sync settings, the Apply button appears at the bottom of the screen. Clicking this saves your current settings and starts the sync process. When the process completes, the button becomes the Sync button. When you click this button, the sync process starts using the current settings; even though the settings are the same, different content can be involved, such as new songs being added to a smart playlist.

- If you decide you don't want to use changes you've made to the sync settings, click Revert. Any changes you have made are discarded and the prior sync settings are restored.

- To exit the sync screen, click the Done button. If you've made changes to the settings but haven't synced, you are prompted to Apply the settings and sync—or you can choose Don't Apply, which discards the changes.
- If you've configured automatic syncing, the sync process starts as soon as you connect your iPhone to your computer.
- Don't disconnect your iPhone during the sync process because it might not complete correctly.
- You can sync your iPhone with more than one iTunes Library, but you can sync the same type of content, such as Music, with only one computer at a time.
- If you configured Wi-Fi syncing, you can use the sync screen whenever your iPhone and computer are on the same network. This works just like when your phone is connected to the computer with a USB cable, except the phone isn't charged as it is when connected with the cable.

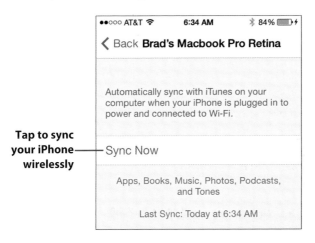

Tap to sync your iPhone wirelessly

- With Wi-Fi syncing enabled, you can start the sync process on the iPhone. Move to the Settings app, tap General, tap iTunes Wi-Fi Sync, and tap Sync Now. If you have synced the phone with more than one computer, tap the computer with which you want to sync and then tap Sync Now. The sync process occurs using the current settings. You can also change the sync settings when you are syncing over Wi-Fi, too; just select the iPhone as you do when it is connected with a cable and configure the sync in the same way as when it is connected to the computer. If you don't see your iPhone in iTunes, make sure your iPhone is on the same Wi-Fi network as the computer, or connect it to your computer using the USB cable and ensure that the Sync with this iPhone over Wi-Fi is enabled in the Summary tab.

KEEPING ITUNES CURRENT

Apple updates iTunes regularly to correct issues, add features, and so on. You can configure iTunes so that it notifies you when updates are available. On a Windows PC, open the iTunes Preferences dialog box, click the General tab, check the Check for new software updates automatically check box, and click OK; when updates are available, you're prompted to download and install them. On a Mac, open the System Preferences app and click Software Update. Then check the Automatically check for updates, Download newly available updates in the background, and Install system data files and security updates check boxes and close the System Preferences app. When an iTunes update is available, you're prompted to allow OS X to install it.

Working with iTunes Match

iTunes Match enables you to download and play any music in your iTunes Library on your iPhone. And you can add more than one Library to iTunes Match; for example, you can have your work and home computers both using iTunes Match. The music in your iTunes Library is either matched with music available in the iTunes Store or uploaded to the cloud if it isn't available in the store. Thus, all your music is always available on the cloud.

If you have music in your iTunes Library you didn't get from the iTunes Store, such as audio CDs you imported, iTunes Match enables you to access that music without the sync process. This is great as you don't have to think about syncing content because you always have the music you want to hear at any point in time; you see all the music content in your iTunes Library on your iPhone. If music isn't currently stored on your iPhone, you just tap it and when the music starts to download, it also starts to play.

If you don't have any music that didn't come from the iTunes Store, you don't need to use iTunes Match because you can download that music to your phone at any time. If all the music in your iTunes Library can fit on your phone (along with the other content you want there), again, you don't need iTunes Match because you can sync all your music is on the phone already.

If you want to use iTunes Match, you must pay for the service; the cost is currently $24.99 per year in the United States (it might have a different price in other areas). (And, if you configure your iPhone to use iTunes Match, the Music tab in the iTunes sync window contains only a check box to indicate whether you want your voice memos synced. All your music is already available to you on your iPhone so there is no need to sync it.)

To use iTunes Match, you need to add the service to your Apple ID. Then configure each of your iTunes Libraries on your computers, your iPhone, and other iOS devices to use it.

Subscribing to iTunes Match

To start using iTunes Match, you need to add the service to your iCloud account. As mentioned previously, this requires paying a fee. To set up iTunes Match, perform the following steps:

1. Choose Store, Turn On iTunes Match.

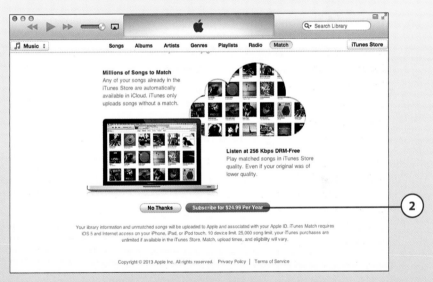

2. Click Subscribe for $24.99 Per Year (in the United States; other locations may require a different fee).

3. Follow the onscreen instructions to complete the subscription process. You'll need to sign into your account and agree to the fee.

It's Not All Good

iTunes was going through some development when this book was being written. Additionally, the Mavericks operating system for Macs hadn't been released yet. This means there might be some differences in the details of how iTunes looks and works than you see in this chapter.

Configuring iTunes Match on Your Computer

To enable iTunes Match on any computer (you don't need to do this on the same computer you used to subscribe to iTunes Match), do the following:

1. Choose Store, Turn On iTunes Match.

2. Click Add This Computer.

3. Enter your Apple ID password.

4. Click Add This Computer.

iTunes Match starts by identifying all the music in your iTunes Library that is available in the iTunes Store. This content becomes available to download on your iPhone immediately.

After that is done, iTunes Match begins uploading music that is in your iTunes Library but that isn't in the iTunes Store to your cloud. If you have a lot of this type of music, this process can take a while; however, you can use iTunes for other tasks as iTunes Match works in the background. As music is uploaded, it becomes available for downloading on your iPhone.

All the music in this library is available for downloading to an iOS device

When the process is complete, all your music is available on the cloud.

iTunes Match automatically keeps the music in your cloud in sync with your iTunes Library. For example, if you add music from a new CD, it will be uploaded to or matched in the cloud automatically.

Configuring iTunes Match on Your iPhone

After you've enabled iTunes match on one or more computers, set up your iPhone to use it:

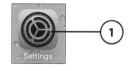

1. Tap Settings.

2. Tap Music.

3. Slide the iTunes Match switch so that it is on (green).

●●○○○ AT&T 🗢	7:21 AM	⚡ 99% 🔋+
Settings		
Ⓐ iTunes & App Store		>
🎵 Music		>

●●●○○ AT&T 🗢	7:21 AM	⚡ 99% 🔋+
‹ Settings	**Music**	
EQ		Off >
Volume Limit		Off >
Lyrics & Podcast Info		🔘
Group By Album Artist		🔘
Show All Music		🔘

All music that has been downloaded or that is stored in iCloud will be shown.

iTunes Match	🔘

Store all your music in the cloud with iTunes Match. **Learn more...**

4. Tap Enable at the prompt.

5. If you want all the music available to you to be shown in the iPhone, slide the Show All Music switch to on (green); if you set it to off (white), only music that has been downloaded to the iPhone is shown.

The music content of your iPhone becomes what is available via iTunes Match. See Chapter 14, "Finding and Listening to Music," for the steps to listen to music provided through iTunes Match.

Gotta Be Connected

iTunes Match works by streaming (downloading) music from the cloud to your iPhone. When you play music, it is downloaded to the iPhone and remains there until replaced by other music. However, you can download music not currently stored on your iPhone only when it is connected to a Wi-Fi or cellular network. So, make sure you have all the music downloaded that you want to listen to if you are going to be without a network connection for a while (such as when you are using the iPhone in Airplane mode).

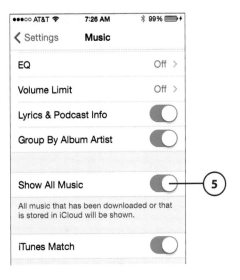

Use the iTunes Store app to load up your phone with great music, movies, TV shows, and more

Use the App Store app to download and install cool and useful apps on your iPhone

In this chapter, you learn how to add apps, music, TV shows, and other content onto your iPhone. Topics include the following:

→ Configuring store settings
→ Using the App Store app to find and install iPhone apps
→ Using the iTunes Store app to download music, ringtones, movies, and TV shows
→ Downloading apps or iTunes Store content you've purchased previously

Downloading Apps, Music, Movies, TV Shows, and More onto Your iPhone

One of Apple's marketing campaigns for the iPhone stated that if you want to do something with an iPhone, there is an app for it. That was quite a claim, but it also was, and continues to be, pretty accurate. Your iPhone is a powerful device and supports a full suite of programming tools. That's a good thing because this capability has unleashed the creativity of developers around the world, and thousands of apps are available now. You can use the App Store app to download and install any of these apps on your iPhone.

Along with all these great apps, there is also lots of music, movies, TV shows, ebooks, audiobooks, and much more content available to enjoy on your iPhone. Using the iTunes Store app, you can easily browse and search for content and then download it to your iPhone with just a couple of taps.

A benefit of using the App Store and iTunes Store apps is that anything you download once can be downloaded again at no cost. If you happen to lose some of your content, you can simply download it again. Or, when you upgrade your iPhone, you can re-download content you've previously purchased onto it at no cost (you can do the same thing on any of your other iOS devices, too).

Another nice thing about using the iTunes and Apps Stores is that you can configure downloads to any of your devices to be automatically downloaded to your iPhone, too, which is where we start this chapter.

Configuring Store Settings

You'll likely be accessing the iTunes Store using more than one device, such as a computer, an iPad, and of course, your iPhone. You can configure your iPhone so that music, apps, and books that you download from any of your devices are automatically downloaded to your phone as well. For example, if you purchase an album on your iPad, that same album can be immediately downloaded to your iPhone, too. You can also have any updates to apps installed on your iPhone downloaded and installed automatically.

Configuring Automatic Store Downloads

To have content you purchase from the iTunes Store be automatically downloaded to your iPhone, perform the following steps:

1. Tap Settings.

2. Tap iTunes & App Stores.

3. To show all the music you've purchased from the iTunes Store on your iPhone, even if it is not currently stored on your phone, set the Music switch to on (green). This enables you to access the music from the store at any time.

4. To show all videos you've downloaded from the store on your phone even if they aren't currently stored there, set the Videos switch to on (green).

5. If you have added iTunes Match to your Apple ID account and haven't already configured it on your iPhone, set the iTunes Match switch to on (green) and tap Enable to activate it on the phone. (iTunes Match is explained in Chapter 5, "Working with iTunes on Your Computer.")

6. Slide the switches to on (green) for the types of content you want to be downloaded to your iPhone automatically; the options are Music, Apps, Books, and Updates, which causes any updates to apps on your iPhone to be downloaded and installed automatically.

7. If you don't have an unlimited data plan, you might want to set the Use Cellular Data to off (white) so content is downloaded only when you are on a Wi-Fi network. If this is enabled (green), content is downloaded to your iPhone when you are using a cellular network, which can consume significant amounts of your data plan. If you exceed your data plan allowance, the overage can be quite expensive, so you need to be careful about allowing cellular downloads.

After you've completed these steps, any content you enabled in step 6 is downloaded to your iPhone automatically when it is purchased on any of your devices (content you've purchased before you configured the Store settings is not downloaded automatically, but as you learn at the end of this chapter, you can manually download that content at any time).

Apple ID

To work with your Apple ID, tap the account shown at the top of the iTunes & App Store screen. On the resulting prompt, you can view your Apple ID, sign out of your account, or reset your password. If you sign out of your account, the Store screen only has the Sign In button. Tap this and sign into the Apple ID you want to configure.

Using the App Store App to Find and Install iPhone Apps

You might think that with thousands of apps available it might be difficult to find and download apps on your iPhone. The good news is that the App Store app enables you to quickly and easily browse and search for apps, view information about them, and then download and install them on your iPhone with just a few taps.

When you use the App Store app, you can find apps to download using any of the following options:

- **Categories**—This link shows you various categories of apps that you can browse.

- **Featured**—This button takes you to apps featured in the iTunes Store. This screen organizes apps in several categories. New & Noteworthy shows you apps that are new (and noteworthy I suppose) to the store. What's Hot lists apps that are the most popular downloads. Various collections of apps are available, such as apps for your commute.

- **Top Charts**—This takes you to lists of the top iPhone apps. This screen has three sections: Paid shows you the top apps for which you have to pay a license fee; Free shows you a similar list containing only free apps; and Top Grossing shows the apps that have been downloaded the most (rather than those that have made the most money).

- **Near Me**—This option shows apps that are popular near your current location.

- **Search**—This button enables you to search for apps. You can search by name, developer, and other keywords.

- **Updates**—Through this, you can get to the Purchased screen, which enables you to find and download apps you have previously downloaded to your iPhone or other device and shows you the update status of your apps on your iPhone (this topic is covered in the last section of this chapter).

Finding and downloading any kind of app follows this same pattern:

1. **Find the app you are interested in.** You can use the options described previously, find apps by browsing for them, or use the search option to find a specific app quickly and easily.

2. **Evaluate the app.** The information screen for apps provides lots of information that you can use to decide whether you want to download an app (or not). The information available includes a text description, screenshots, ratings and reviews of other users, and so on.

3. **Download and install the app.**

The following sections provide detailed examples for each of these steps.

Searching for Apps

If you know something about an app, such as its name, its developer, or just about anything else, you can quickly search the App Store to find the app. Here's how to search for an app:

1. Move to the Home screen and tap App Store.

2. Tap Search.

3. Tap in the Search box.

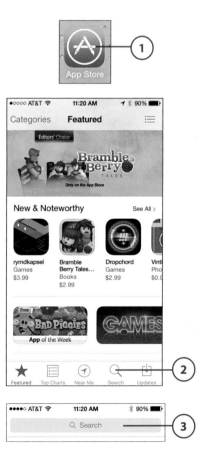

4. Type a search term. This can be the name of someone associated with the app, its title, its developer, or even a topic. As you type, the app suggests searches that are related to what you are typing.

5. Tap the search you want to perform. The apps that meet your search term appear.

6. Swipe on the screen to review the apps that resulted from your search.

7. If none of the apps are what you are looking for, tap the x in the Search box and repeat steps 4–6.

8. When you find an app of interest to you, tap it. You move to the app's information screen.

9. Use the information on the information screen to evaluate the app and decide if it's what you are looking for; this is explained in the task called "Evaluating Apps."

Browsing for Apps

If you don't know of a specific app you want, you can browse the App Store. To browse, you can tap any graphics or links you see in the App Store app. There are a number of ways to start the browsing process: Categories, Featured, Top Charts, or Near Me. When you select one of these options, you can then browse apps associated with or organized by the option you selected. The following steps show you how to browse for apps by category; the other options are similar:

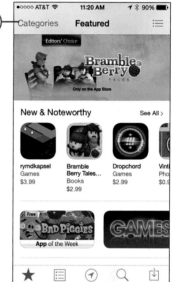

1. Move to the Home screen and tap App Store. At the bottom of the App Store screen, you see the buttons you can use to choose a method to find apps.

2. Tap Categories.

3. Swipe up and down the screen to browse the list until you see a category of interest.

4. Tap a category in which you are interested.

5. If the category has subcategories, swipe up and down the screen to browse the subcategories; if you moved directly to apps, skip to step 7.

6. Tap a subcategory in which you are interested.

7. Swipe up and down to browse the groupings of apps, such as New, What's Hot, and so on.

8. Swipe left and right on a grouping to browse the apps it contains.

See All, Know All

To browse all the apps in a grouping, tap See All. You see all the apps in that grouping; swipe up and down the screen to browse the list. Tap an app to see its information.

9. Tap an app in which you are interested. You move to that app's information screen.

10. Use the information on the information screen to evaluate the app; this is explained in the next task, "Evaluating Apps."

Evaluating Apps

The App Store provides lots of information about apps that you can use to evaluate an app to decide whether it is worth downloading. When you move to an app's information screen, you can evaluate it using the following steps:

1. Tap the Details tab.

2. Review the name, average user rating, and cost (displayed in the app's download button).

3. To read a description, swipe up on the screen.

4. Read the description; you will probably have to swipe up on the screen to read all of it. If not all of the description is displayed, tap More.

5. Read the Information section to find out the version, file size, rating, and other specifics.

But Wait, There's More

If you continue to swipe up the screen, you see additional sections, such as Version History, Developer Info, and so on. If you really want to get into the details, you can tap each of these to get even more information.

6. Swipe down on the screen to view screenshots of the app shown above the description.

7. Look at the app's screenshots. If the app is horizontally-oriented, rotate the iPhone so the screenshots make sense. (Note that the screen you view doesn't reorient like most screens do, but at least the screenshots themselves look better.)

8. Swipe on the screenshots to see them all.

9. Tap Reviews. (If you've rotated the iPhone, you'll need to move it back to the vertical orientation.)

10. Read the user reviews for the app; you'll have to swipe up to see them all. You should have all the information you need about the app to be able to decide if it is worth your time and cost, if any, to download it.

Make Your Voice Known

After you have used an app, you can add your own review by moving back to its Reviews tab and tapping Write a Review. You move to the Write a Review screen where you have to enter your iTunes Store account information before you can write and submit a review.

Downloading Apps

Downloading and installing apps is about as easy as things get, as you can see:

1. Move to the information screen for the app you want to download.

2. To download the app, tap FREE if it is a free app or tap the price to download the app if it has a license fee. The button then becomes INSTALL if it is a free app or BUY if it has a license fee.

3. Tap INSTALL or BUY. Depending on how long its been since you signed into your Apple ID, you might be prompted to sign in to start the download. If you have recently signed into your account, you can skip the next step because the app starts downloading immediately.

4. If you are using an iPhone 5S, touch the Touch ID /Home button at the prompt; if you are using another model, type your Apple ID password and tap OK.

   You see the progress of the process.

   When the process is complete, the status information is replaced by the Open button. This indicates the app has been downloaded and installed. (Its icon appears on the next available spot on your Home screens.) Tap Open to launch the app.

   You don't have to wait for apps to download. You can start the process and then use your iPhone normally as the download occurs in the background.

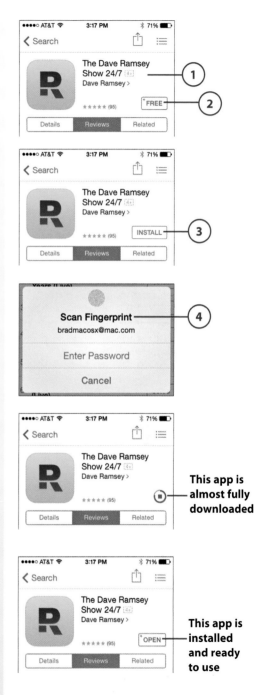

This app is almost fully downloaded

This app is installed and ready to use

Adding Apps to the Wish List

The Wish List is a nice tool you can use to collect apps in which you might be interested; this works similarly to a shopping cart on a retail website. You can collect apps on your Wish List and then go back and easily locate them again. The Wish List can be used only for apps that have a license fee, which makes sense since you can just download any free apps you are interested in.

To add an app to your Wish List, do the following:

1. Move to the information screen for the app that you want to add to your Wish List.

2. Tap the Action button.

3. Tap Add to Wish List. The app is added to your Wish List.

Using Your Wish List

To work with your Wish List, do the following:

1. Tap the Wish List button.

2. To move to an app's Information screen, tap it.

3. To download an app, tap its price button.

4. To remove apps from the list, tap Edit.

5. Tap the apps you want to remove to select them.

6. Tap Delete.

7. Tap Done to close the Wish List.

Deleting Wish List Apps

You can also remove an app from the list by swiping to the left on it and tapping Delete.

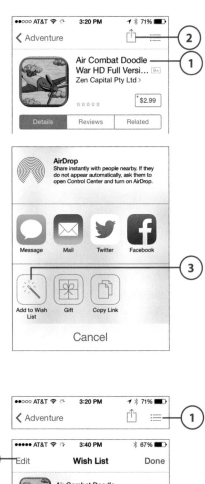

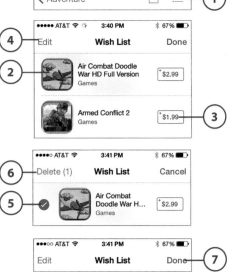

>>>Go Further

MORE ON APPS

As you use the App Store app to install apps on your iPhone, keep the following hints handy:

- Like other software, apps are updated regularly to fix problems, add features, or make other changes. If you set the iTunes & App Store Updates setting to on (green) as described earlier in this chapter, updates to your apps happen automatically in the background. Your apps are always current and so you don't have to update them manually. (More information on updating apps is in Chapter 17, "Maintaining and Protecting Your iPhone and Solving Problems.")

- If you see the Download button (which is a cloud with a downward-pointing arrow), that means you have already downloaded the app but it is not currently installed on your iPhone. Tap the button to download and install it.

- To let someone else know about the app, tap the Action button and then tap how you want to let him know; the options are AirDrop, Message, Mail, Twitter, and Facebook.

- Apps can work in the background to keep their information current, such as weather and stocks. To configure this, open the Settings app, tap General, and tap Background App Refresh. Set Background App Refresh to on (green). To enable an app to work in the background, set its switch to on (green). To disable background activity for an app, set its switch to off (white).

- To give the app to someone, tap the Action button and tap Gift.

- To send the link to the app to someone, tap Copy Link and then past the link into an email message or other location where you want to use it.

- To see apps that are related to the one you are evaluating, tap the Related tab and browse the resulting screen.

- If you want to report a problem you're having with an app, move to the app's Reviews tab and tap App Support. You move to the developer's website and can get information and help with the app.

- The next time you sync your iPhone (by connecting it to your computer or via a Wi-Fi network), the apps you've added using the App Store app will be copied into your iTunes Library.

- Tap an app's icon on the Home screen to launch it.

- After you install an app, move to the Settings screen and look for the app's icon. If it is there, the app has additional settings you can use to configure the way it works. Tap the app's icon and use its settings screen to configure it.

- To remove an app you have installed, tap and hold on its icon on the Home screen. When the icons starting jiggling, raise your finger. Tap the Delete button (x). Confirm the deletion at the prompt that appears, and the app will be deleted. (Any data stored in the app is also deleted, so be careful.) As you see in the last section of this chapter, you can download the app again at any time—but your data might not be restored when you do.

Using the iTunes Store App to Download Music, Ringtones, Movies, and TV Shows

You can use the iPhone's iTunes Store app to download audio and video content from the iTunes Store directly onto your iPhone. You can listen to music you download in the Music app, watch movies and TV shows in the Videos app, use tones for ringtones and alert tones, and so on.

Using the iTunes Store app involves the following general steps:

- **Find the content you are interested in**—Like the App Store app, there are a number of ways to do this. You can search for specific content, or you can browse for content by type, which includes the following (to get to some of these, such as Tones, tap the More button and then tap the category):

  - Music enables you to download music.

  - Movies takes you to the movies in the iTunes Store so you can browse, preview, and download them.

  - TV Shows does the same for TV programming.

  - Audiobooks enables you to download audiobooks to listen to.

  - Tones enables you to purchase ringtones and alert tones that you can use as various sounds on your iPhone.

  - Genius shows you recommendations based on content you have previously downloaded that you might also be interested in.

- **Preview the content**—You can sample content before you download it. For example, you can listen to a preview of songs (typically 90 seconds' worth), watch movie trailers, listen to tones, and so on.

- **Download the content**—After you download content to your iPhone, it becomes available in the related app.

In the following tasks, you see examples of each of these steps.

Searching for iTunes Store Content

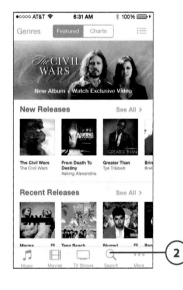

When you know something about the content you want, searching is a good way to find it because it is easy and fast. Also, when you search, your results can include multiple types of content. For example, searching on a title can yield an album, a movie, a song, and an audiobook. Here's how to search in the store:

1. On the iPhone's Home screen, tap iTunes Store. You move to the iTunes Store app. At the bottom of the screen, you choose how you want to look for content by tapping one of the buttons on the iTunes Store toolbar.

2. Tap Search.

3. Tap in the Search box.

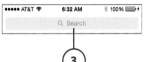

4. Type a search criterion, such as an artist's name, a movie title, or even a general topic (for example, a franchise, such as *Star Trek*). As you type, content that matches your search appears under the Search bar.

5. When you see something of interest on the results list, tap it. For example, tap an artist's name or a more general topic. A list of content related to your search appears. If there are multiple types of content associated with the search, you see tabs at the top of the screen showing you the available types.

6. Swipe up, down, right, and left to browse the search results, which are organized into categories, such as Movies, Albums, Songs, Ringtones, Music Videos, and so on.

7. To limit the results to a specific type of content, tap the related tab. For example, to see the movies related to what you searched for, tap Movies.

8. Swipe on the screen to browse the list of results for the type of content you selected.

9. When you see something of interest, tap it. You see the Information screen for that content.

10. Use the Information screen to preview and explore the content. Details are provided later in this chapter in the task titled, "Previewing iTunes Store Content."

Stop the Search!

To clear a search, tap the Clear button (x) in the Search bar.

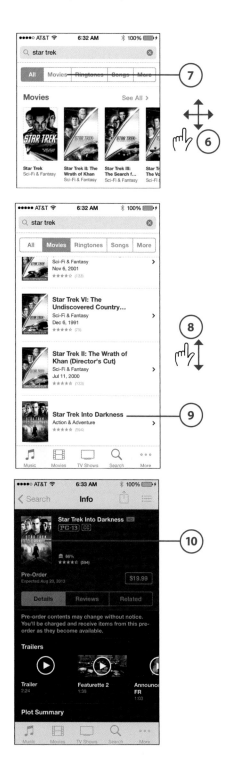

Browsing for iTunes Store Content

Even though browsing isn't as efficient as searching, it is a good way to discover content you might not know about. And sometimes you can get to specific content by browsing almost as quickly as searching. The details of browsing depend on the type of content for which you are looking. The following example shows browsing music to demonstrate the general process:

1. On the iPhone's Home screen, tap iTunes Store. You move to the iTunes Store app. At the bottom of the screen, you can choose how you want to look for content by tapping one of the buttons on the iTunes Store toolbar.

2. Tap Music. You move to the Music Home page. At the top of the screen, you see options you can use to browse: Genres, Featured (the default), and Charts.

3. Swipe the screen to browse the current contents. The rest of these steps show browsing by genre. The steps for using the other browse options are similar.

4. Tap Genres. You see the list of genres.

5. Tap the genre you want to explore.

6. Swipe the screen to browse the contents being displayed.

7. Tap something of interest to see more detail. Tap the See All link for a category to see all the items in that category.

8. Swipe the results to browse them.

9. Tap an item for which you'd like to see more detail.

10. Use the Information screen to preview and explore the content. Details are provided in the task "Previewing iTunes Store Content."

But Wait, There's More

You can access additional categories of content by tapping the More button. On the More screen, you see Audiobooks, Tones, and Genius. Tap Audiobooks to browse audiobooks you can download and listen to. Tap Tones to download sound snippets from songs or special effects to use as ringtones or alert tones. Tap Genius to see recommended content based on content you have downloaded or content related to content you have downloaded.

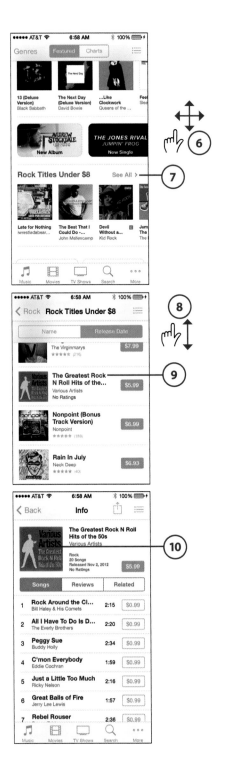

Previewing iTunes Store Content

You can use the Information screen to explore content in which you are interested. This screen looks a bit different for various kinds of content, such as a movie versus an album. However, the general features of this screen are similar, so the following steps showing an album's Information screen will get you started:

1. Move to the Information screen for content you might want to download.

2. Review the summary information at the top of the screen.

3. On the Songs tab (this is called Details for some other types of content), tap More.

4. Read the detailed description/ notes.

5. Swipe up the screen to see the list of songs.

6. Tap the Reviews tab.

7. Swipe up and down the screen to read all the review information. At the top, you see an overview of the reviews, indicated by the star ratings. Toward the bottom of the screen, you can read the individual reviews.

8. Tap Songs.

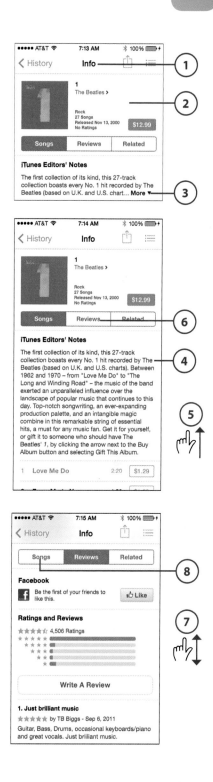

9. To preview a track, tap it. A short preview plays. While it's playing, the track's number is replaced by the Stop button, which you can tap to stop the preview.

10. Continue previewing the content until you are ready to make a decision to download it—or not.

Previewing Video

When you preview video content, such as watching a trailer for a movie, it plays in a video player that works much like the Videos app (the Videos app is covered in Chapter 16, "Using Other Cool iPhone Apps").

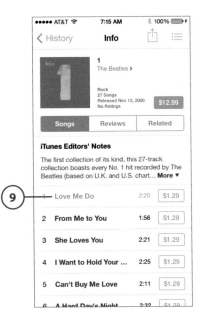

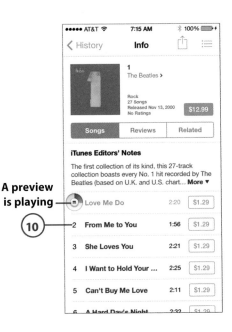

A preview is playing

Downloading iTunes Store Content

Like downloading apps, downloading movies, tones, songs, albums, and so on is just a tap away:

1. Move to the Information screen for content you want to download.

2. Tap the appropriate buy button, which shows the price of the item. For example, to buy an album, tap its buy button. To buy a song, tap its price button instead. Likewise, you can buy a movie by tapping its price button (some movies are offered in different formats, and each one has its own price button). The button changes to show what you are buying.

3. Tap the Buy button again, such as BUY ALBUM. If it's been a while since you signed into your Apple ID, you're prompted to sign into your account. If you recently signed in, the download starts without you signing in and you can skip step 4.

4. If you are using an iPhone 5S, at the prompt, touch the Touch ID/Home button. If you are using a different model, enter the password for your Apple ID and tap OK.

   The badge on the More button updates to show you how many items are being downloaded to the iPhone. The download process starts and you can continue to shop in the store or move into a different app; the download process occurs in the background. If you want to, you can monitor the download process by continuing with these steps.

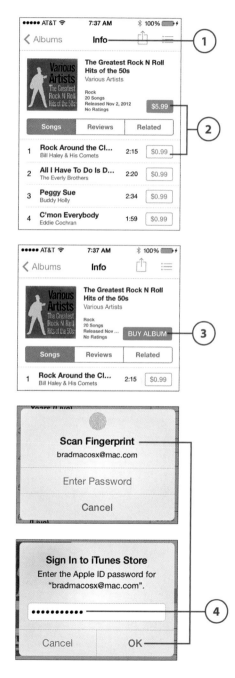

5. Tap More.

6. Tap Downloads. You move to the Downloads screen, which displays the progress of the tracks you are purchasing.

When the process is complete, the Downloads screen becomes empty. This indicates that the content you purchased has been added to the iPhone and is ready for you to listen to or watch in the related app.

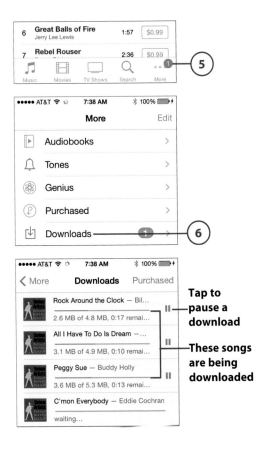

Tap to pause a download

These songs are being downloaded

Using Your iTunes Store History List

As you are looking at content in the iTunes Store, you'll likely encounter music, movies, and so on that you are interested in but are not sure you want to download. It would be a pain to get back to content via searching or browsing. Fortunately, you can use the History List to go back to content you have previewed.

To add content to your History List, preview it. This can be done by listening to a song on an album, watching a movie trailer, and so forth. Just looking at an item's Information screen is not sufficient; you need to preview it for it to be added to your History List.

When you preview content, such as watching a movie's trailer, it is added to your History List

To work with your History List, do the following:

1. Tap the History button.

2. Tap the category you want to see. For example, tap Previews to see the content you have previewed. (Tap Wish List to see your Wish List or Radio to see iTunes Radio content to which you've listened.)

3. Swipe the screen to browse the list of items.

4. To move to an item's Information screen, tap it.

5. To buy an item, tap it's price button and then tap its BUY button.

6. If you've purchased something on this list, tap PLAY to play it.

7. To clear your list, tap Clear and then tap Clear History.

8. To close the list, tap Done.

>>>Go Further

SHOPPING LIKE A PRO

Here are a few more pointers to make your iTunes Store experience even better:

- **Preorder** —You can order content that isn't released yet, such as movies, or a full season of a TV show that is in a current season. When the content you have preordered becomes available, it is downloaded to your iPhone automatically.

- **Renting**—You can rent movies, too. This is less expensive than buying them, but it comes with limitations. You can keep a rented movie for only 30 days. And, after you start watching it, it will play for a 24-hour period (48 hours in some locations). When either of these time periods is up, the rented movie is deleted from your iPhone automatically.

- **Customizing the iTunes Store app toolbar**—You can place any four buttons on the iTunes Store app toolbar by customizing it (the More button is always visible on the toolbar). To change the buttons displayed, tap More and then tap Edit. Drag the buttons you want to place on the bar from the upper part of the screen, and drop them on the toolbar at the location you want them to appear. You can also drag icons around the toolbar to change their locations. When the toolbar is what you want it to be, tap Done.

- **Add Your Own Review**—To add your own review of an item, move to its Reviews tab and tap Write a Review. Complete the resulting form to record your feedback.

- **Related**—Tap the Related tab to see content that is "related to" the content you are exploring. This shows you other content that was purchased by the same people who downloaded the content you are considering.

- **Move from Song to Album**—When you browse a list of songs, tap a song twice to move to the Information screen for the album from which that the song comes.

- **Pausing Downloads**—You can tap the Pause button for items being downloaded to temporarily stop the download process. For example, if you are leaving the area covered by the Wi-Fi network you are using, you might want to delay completion of a download until you return so it isn't completed over the cellular data network.

- **Share and Share Alike**—Tap the Action button at the top of iTunes screens to share the content you are exploring. You can share by email, message, Twitter, and Facebook. The messages you send contain a link to the item. You can also share via AirDrop or tap Copy Link to copy the item's link to the Clipboard, from where you can paste into other areas such as a document. Tap Gift to give the content to someone else.

- **The Next Time You Sync**—The next time you sync after purchasing audio and video from the iTunes Store on the iPhone, that audio and video is moved into your iTunes Library. If you've created any smart playlists with live updating enabled and the new audio and video matches that playlist's criteria, the new audio and video become part of those playlists automatically.
- **Automatic Downloads**—If you have other iOS devices or iTunes on your computers configured to automatically download iTunes Store purchases, the content is downloaded to those locations, too.

Downloading Apps or iTunes Store Content You've Purchased Previously

You can download any content you've purchased from the App or iTunes Stores again without paying a fee (rented movies are an exception because you can download those only once and have to pay for them again to download them again). For example, you might download an app, decide that you don't want it any more, delete it, and then change your mind and want it again. (Of course, this doesn't really apply to free apps since you can always download those at no cost.)

Downloading Previously Purchased App Store Apps

To download apps you previously purchased, perform the following steps:

1. Tap the App Store icon to open the app.

2. Move to the Information screen for the app you want to download again.

3. Tap the Download button. The app is downloaded and installed on your iPhone. When the process is complete, the OPEN button appears.

Downloading Previously Purchased iTunes Content

To download music, movies, or other content you previously downloaded, perform the following steps:

1. Open the iTunes Store app.

2. Tap More.

3. Tap Purchased.

4. Tap Music, Movies, or TV Shows. The rest of these steps show downloading music, but the steps to download other content are similar.

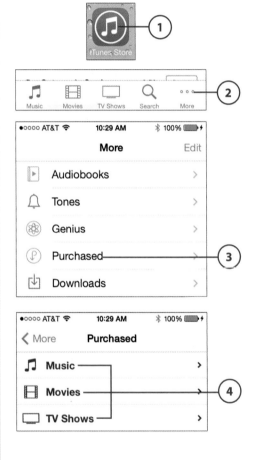

5. Tap Not on This iPhone. The list shows all the music you've purchased from the iTunes Store but that is not currently stored on your iPhone. At the top of the screen are the number of songs you've purchased that aren't on the iPhone and the number of recent purchases. (You can tap either of these to browse those lists of content.) Below this are all the artists associated with content you haven't downloaded to the iPhone as well as the number of tracks for each artist.

6. Swipe up and down to browse the list.

7. Tap the artist whose music you want to download. A list of content for that artist, organized into categories such as albums or songs, is displayed.

8. Tap the Download button for the content you want to download or tap the Download All button to download all the content shown.

9. If prompted and you are using an iPhone 5S, touch the Touch ID/ Home button; if you are using a different model, enter your Apple ID password and tap OK. The content is downloaded to your iPhone. When that process is complete, you can watch or listen to it in the related app.

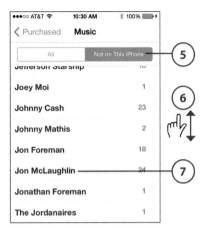

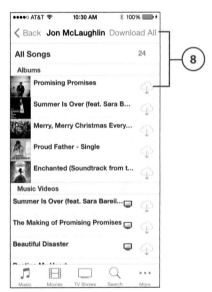

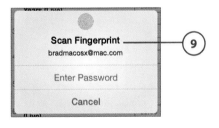

Tap here to work with your contact information

Use Settings to configure how contacts are displayed

Use your contact information in many apps

In this chapter, you learn how to ensure that your iPhone has the contact information you need when you need it. Topics include the following:

→ Setting your contacts preferences
→ Creating contacts on your iPhone
→ Working with contacts on your iPhone
→ Managing contacts on your iPhone

Managing Contacts

Contact information, including names, phone numbers, email addresses, and physical addresses, is useful to have on your iPhone. For example, when you send email, it's much easier to select the appropriate email addresses by tapping the recipients' names rather than having to remember them and type them in. When you want to call someone, you don't need to remember a phone number; instead, just tap the name of the person you want to call. Likewise, you might want to see a contact's address on a map in the Maps app.

The Contacts app enables you to do all these things plus much more. This app makes using your contact information seamless. You can access contact information directly in the Contacts app and take action on it (such as placing a call), or you can use your contact information within other apps, such as Mail, Phone, Safari, and so on.

To use contact information, it first must be stored in the Contacts app. You can add this information to your iPhone via syncing with a computer or via iCloud, Exchange, and other similar accounts; by capturing it when you perform tasks (such as reading email); or by entering information manually. And, you'll need to manage your contact information over time, such as adding to it, updating it, and so on.

Setting Your Contacts Preferences

Before you start using the Contacts app, you should set your preferences for contact information. You can determine how contacts are sorted and displayed, if or how names are shortened on various screens, your contact information, and which account should be the default for contact information.

To configure your contacts settings, perform the following steps:

1. On the Home screen, tap Settings.

2. Swipe up the screen until you see Mail, Contacts, Calendars.

3. Tap Mail, Contacts, Calendars.

4. Swipe up the screen until you see the Contacts section.

5. Tap Sort Order.

6. To have contacts sorted by first name and then last name, tap First, Last.

7. To have contacts sorted by last name and then first name, tap Last, First.

8. Tap Mail.

9. Tap Display Order.

10. To show contacts in the format *first name, last name,* tap First, Last.

11. To show contacts in the format *last name, first name,* tap Last, First.

12. Tap Mail.

13. Tap Short Name. If enabled, short names are displayed for your contacts in various locations instead of full names (for example, showing only a person's first name on an email message). You can choose whether short names are used and if they are, what form they take. Short names are useful because more contact information can be displayed in a smaller area , and they look "friendlier."

14. To use short names, tap the Short Name switch to move it to the on position (green); if the switch is already green, skip this step.

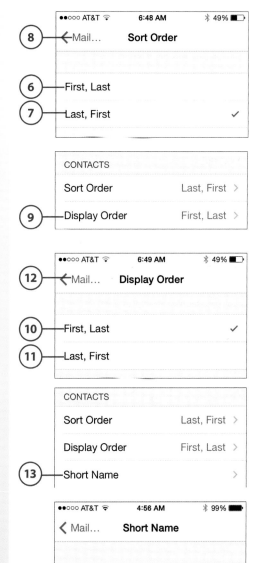

15. Tap the format of short name you want to use. You can choose from a combination of initial and name or just first or last name. The selected format is marked with a check mark.

16. If you want nicknames for contacts used for the short name, set the Prefer Nicknames switch to on, which is indicated by it being green.

17. Tap Mail.

18. Tap My Info.

19. Browse or search the All Contacts screen (to learn different ways to browse this screen, jump ahead to the section called "Using the Contacts App" and then come back here).

20. Tap your name. This tells the Contacts app your contact information, which it can insert for you in various places; your contact information is indicated by the label "me" next to the alphabetical index. You return to the Mail, Contacts, Calendars screen where your name appears next to My Info.

21. To determine the default account for your contacts, tap Default Account. (You see this option only if you are syncing contacts with at least two accounts.)

22. Tap the account in which you want new contacts to be created by default.

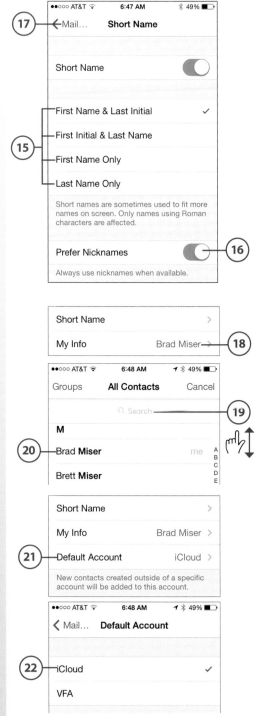

Creating Contacts on Your iPhone

You can create new contacts on an iPhone in a number of ways. You can start with some information, such as the email address on a message you receive, and create a contact from it, or you can create a contact manually "from scratch." In this section, you learn how to create a new contact starting with information in an email message and a map. You also learn how to create a new contact manually "from scratch."

Creating New Contacts from Email

When you receive an email, you can easily create a contact to capture the email address. (To learn how to work with the Mail app, see Chapter 9, "Sending, Receiving, and Managing Email.")

1. On the Home screen, tap Mail.

2. Use the Mail app to read an email message (see Chapter 9 for details).

3. Tap the email address with which you want to create a new contact. The Info screen appears—the label of the screen depends on the type of email address you tapped. For example, if you tapped the address from which the email was sent, the screen is labeled Sender. You see as much information as your iPhone could discern from the email address, which is typically the sender's name and email address.

4. Tap Create New Contact. The New Contact screen appears. The name and email address are added to the new contact. The email address is labeled with iPhone's best guess, such as other or home.

5. Use the New Contact screen to enter more contact information and save the new contact. This works just like when you create a new contact manually, except that you already have some information—in this case, a name and an email address. For details on adding and changing more information for the contact, see "Creating Contacts Manually," later in this chapter.

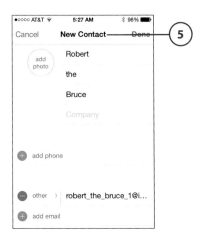

Creating New Contacts from a Map

When you view a location on a map in the Maps app, you can create a contact with that location's information.

1. On the Home screen, tap Maps.

2. Find a location by typing information in the Search bar.

3. Tap the Info bar for the location.

4. Swipe up the screen.

5. Tap Create New Contact. The New Contact screen appears, and the iPhone adds as much information as it can based on the location, such as name, phone number, address, website, and so on.

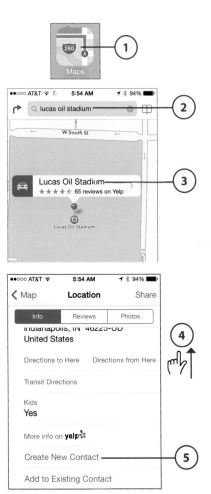

6. Use the New Contact screen to configure the new contact. This works just like when you create a new contact manually, except that you already have information for the new contact—in this case, the location name (if it has one), phone number, and so on. See "Creating Contacts Manually," next for details.

●●○○○ AT&T   5:54 AM   ✈ ✱ 94% ▬

Cancel   **New Contact**━━━━━ ~~Done~~   ⑥

add photo

First

Last

Lucas Oil Stadium

⊖   Phone 〉   +1 (317) 262-8600

⊕   add phone

MORE ON CREATING CONTACTS FROM APPS

It's useful to be able to create contact information by starting with some information in an app. Keep these points in mind:

- The two examples in this section were only some of the apps from which you can create contacts. You can start a contact in just about any app you use to communicate with people, such as Messages, Phone, and so on. The steps to start a contact in these apps are similar to those for Mail and Maps. Tap the person for whom you want to create a contact, and then tap Create New Contact. The Contacts app fills in as much of the information as it can, and you can complete the rest yourself.

- You can add more contact information to an existing contact. You can do this by tapping Add to Existing Contact instead of Create New Contact. You then search for and select the contact to which you want to add the additional information. After it's saved, that information is associated with the contact. For example, suppose you have created a contact for a company but all you have is its phone number. You can quickly add the address to the contact by using the Maps app to look it up and then add the address to the company's existing contact information by tapping Add to Existing Contact.

Creating Contacts Manually

Most of the time, you'll want to get the information for a new contact from an app, as the previous examples have shown, or through the sync process, such as contacts stored in your Exchange account. If these aren't available, you can also start a contact from scratch and add all the information you need to it. Also, you use the same steps to add information to an existing contact that you do to create a new one, so even if you don't start from scratch often, you do need to know how to do so.

The following steps show creating a new contact containing just some of the common information you will want to have; however, there are a lot more fields you can add if needed. Often, you'll create a new contact with only a few bits of information and add to it over time.

1. On the Home screen, tap Contacts. (If you don't see the Contacts app on the Home screen, tap the Utilities folder to open it and you should see the app's icon.) The All Contacts screen displays.

   If you see the Groups screen, tap Done to move to the All Contacts screen.

   If you have only one account for contact information, you should see its contact list, and you are ready to create a new contact.

2. Tap the Add button. The New Contact screen appears with empty fields for lots of the information you can include. (You can add more data fields as needed using the add field command.)

   One of the most interesting things to store for your contacts is a photo. To associate a photo with a contact, that photo has to be stored on the iPhone. Although you can also use the iPhoto's camera to take a photo to use.

(See Chapter 15, "Working with Photos and Video You Take with Your iPhone," for the info you need to use the iPhone's Camera app to take photos and the Photos app to work with your photos.)

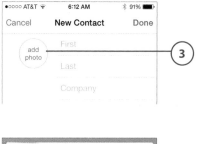

3. To associate a photo with the contact, tap add photo. You can choose a photo already on your phone or take a new photo. These steps show using an existing photo. See the "Taking Photos" note for the steps to take a new photo.

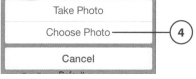

4. Tap Choose Photo.

5. Use the Camera app to move to, select, and configure the photo you want to associate with the contact (see Chapter 15 for help with the Camera app).

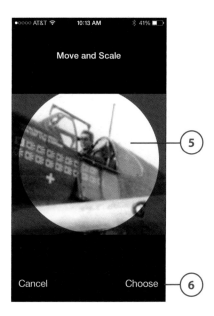

6. Tap Choose. You return to the New Contact screen where the photo you selected is displayed.

7. Tap in the First field and enter the contact's first name; if you are creating a contact for an organization only, leave this field empty. (The Display Order preference you set earlier determines whether the First or Last field appears at the top of the screen. It doesn't really matter because the fields are so close that you always see them at the same time.)

8. Tap in the Last field and enter the contact's last name (except if you are creating a contact for an organization, in which case, leave this field empty).

9. Enter the organization, such as a company, with which you want to associate the contact, if any.

10. To add a phone number, tap add phone. A new phone field appears along with the keypad.

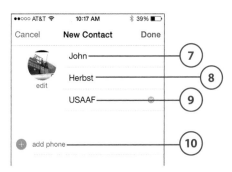

Taking Photos

To take a new photo for a contact, tap Take Photo in step 4 instead of Choose Photo. The Take Picture screen appears. Use the iPhone's camera to capture the photo you want to associate with the new contact (taking photos is covered in Chapter 15, "Working with Photos and Video You Take with Your iPhone"). Use the Move and Scale screen to adjust the photo so it is what you want to use. Then, tap Use Photo. The photo is pasted into the image well on the New Contact screen.

11. Use the keypad to enter the contact's phone number, including any prefixes you need to dial it, such as area code, country code, and so on. The app formats the number for you as you enter it. Note that the information for a contact is labeled because you can have more than one of the same type. For example, you might have a work and a mobile phone number.

12. Tap the label for the phone number, such as home, to change it to another label. The Label screen appears.

13. Swipe up and down the label screen to see all the options available.

14. Tap the label you want to apply to the number, such as iPhone. That label is applied and you move back to the New Contact screen.

15. Repeat steps 10–14 to add more phone numbers to the contact.

16. Swipe up the screen until you see add email.

17. Tap add email. The keyboard appears.

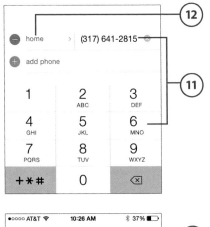

18. Type the contact's email address.

19. Tap the label for the email address to change it.

20. Tap the label you want to apply to the email address. You move back to the New Contact screen.

21. Repeat steps 17–20 to add more email addresses.

22. Swipe up the screen until you see Ringtone.

23. Tap Ringtone. The list of ringtones and alert tones available on your iPhone appears.

24. Swipe up and down the list to see all of the tones available.

25. Tap the ringtone you want to play when the contact calls you. When you tap a ringtone, it plays so you can experiment to find the one that best relates to the contact. You can choose any ringtone stored on your iPhone or an alert tone. Setting a specific ringtone helps you identify a caller without looking at the phone.

26. Tap Done. You return to the New Contact screen, where the tone you selected appears.

You've probably noticed that the Contacts app leads you through creating each type of information you want to capture. You can choose to enter any or all of the default information on the New Contact screen.

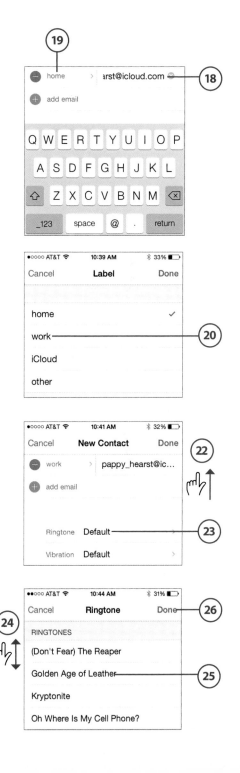

27. Using the pattern you have learned in the previous steps, move to the next item you want to set and tap it.

28. Use the resulting screens to enter the information you want to store, apply a label, and so on. After you've done a couple of the fields, it is easy to do the rest because the same pattern is used throughout. To move from field to field, tap in the field you want to move to and then either configure that field or tap Done. You can set a vibration when the contact calls and a tone and vibration for text messages, URLs, addresses, birthday, dates, related names, notes, and so on.

29. When you've added all the information you want to capture, tap Done. The New Contact screen closes and the new contact is created and ready for you to use in the Contacts and other apps. It is also moved onto other devices with which your contact information is synced.

A new contact

CREATING CONTACTS EXPANDED

Contacts are useful in many ways so you should make sure you have all the contact information you need. Here are a few points to ponder:

- You can (and should) sync contacts on multiple devices (computers and other iOS devices) by using iCloud, Exchange, Gmail, or other similar accounts to store your contact information on the cloud from where all these devices can access it. Refer to Chapter 3, "Setting Up iCloud and Other Online Accounts," for the details of setting up an account through which you can sync your contacts. You can also sync contacts with a computer (Mac or Windows PC) via iTunes; refer to Chapter 5, "Working with iTunes on Your Computer," to learn how to configure iTunes contact syncing.

- By the way, syncing your contacts works in both directions. Any new contacts you create or any changes you make to existing contact information on your iPhone move back to your other devices through the sync process. The bottom line is that you always have the same contact information available no matter which device you are using, which is a very good thing indeed.

- To remove a field in which you've entered information, tap the red circle with a dash in it next to the field and then tap Delete. If you haven't entered information into a field, just ignore it because empty fields don't appear on the contact screen.

- The address format on the contact screens are determined by the country you associate with the address. If the current country isn't the one you want, tap it and select the country in which the address is located before you enter any information because the fields appropriate for that country's addresses will then appear on the screen.

- If you want to add a type of information that doesn't appear on the New Contact screen, swipe up the screen and tap add field. A list of additional fields you can add displays. Tap a field to add it; for example, tap Nickname to add a nickname for the contact. Then enter the information for that new field.

- When you add more fields to contact information, those fields appear in the appropriate context on the Info screen. For example, if you add a nickname, it is placed at the top of the screen with the other "name" information. If you add an address, it appears with the other address information.

Working with Contacts on Your iPhone

There are many ways to use contact information. The first step is always finding the contact information you need, typically by using the Contacts app. Whether you access it directly or through another app (such as Mail), it works the same way. Then, you select the information you want to use or the action you want to perform.

Using the Contacts App

You can access your contact information directly in the Contacts app. For example, you can search or browse for a contact and then view the detailed information for the contact in which you are interested.

1. On the Home screen, tap Contacts. The contacts screen displays with the contacts listed in the view and sort format you selected when you set your Contact preferences (refer to the task, "Setting Your Contacts Preferences," at the beginning of this chapter).

The title of the screen depends on what you have selected to view; if All Contacts appears, you are browsing all your contact information. If Contacts appears, you are browsing only some of your contact information based on the contact groups you have to elected to view; you learn how to change the groups of contacts you are viewing shortly. (If the Groups screen appears, tap Done. You move back to the Contacts screen.)

You can find a contact to view by browsing (step 2), using the index (step 3), or searching (step 4). You can use combinations of these, too, such as first using the index to get to the right area and then browsing to find the contact in which you are interested.

2. Swipe up or down to scroll the screen to browse for contact information; flick your finger up or down to browse rapidly.

3. Tap the index to jump to contact information organized by the first letter of the selected format (last name or first name).

4. Use the Search tool to search for a specific contact; tap in the tool, type the name (last, first, or company), and then tap the contact you want to view on the results list.

5. To view a contact's information, tap the contact you want to see.

6. Swipe up and down the screen to view all the contact's information.

7. Tap the data or icons on the screen to perform actions, including the following:

- **Phone numbers**—Tap a phone number to dial it.

- **Email addresses**—Tap an email address to create a new message to it.

- **URLs**—Tap a URL to open Safari and move to the associated website.

- **Addresses**—Tap an address to show it in the Maps app.

- **FaceTime**—Tap FaceTime to start a FaceTime call with the contact.

- **Text**—Tap Send Message and choose the phone number or email address to which you want to send a text message.

- **Share Contact**—Tap the Share Contact button. The Share Contact Using menu appears. To share the contact via email, tap Mail; to share it via a text, tap Message; or to share it using AirDrop, tap AirDrop. Then use the associated app to complete the task. For example, when you choose Mail, a new email message is created with the contact added as a vCard (virtual address card). Recipients of the email can add the contact information to their own contact applications by importing the vCard.

- **Favorites**—Tap Add to Favorites and choose the phone number or email address you want to designate as a favorite. You can use this in the associated app to do something faster. For example, if it's the Phone app, you can tap the Favorites tab to see your favorite contacts and quickly dial one by tapping it. You can add multiple items (such as phone numbers) as favorites for one contact.

8. To return to the Contacts list without performing an action, tap Contacts.

>>>Go Further

MAKE CONTACT

When working with your contacts, keep the following points in mind:

- **Last known contact**—The Contacts app remembers where you last were and takes you back there whenever you move into the app. For example, if you view a contact's details and then switch to a different app and then back to Contacts, you return to the screen you were last viewing. To move to the contacts screen, tap the Contacts button in the upper-left corner of the screen.

- **Groups**—In a contact app on a computer, such as Contacts on a Mac, contacts can be organized into groups, which in turn can be stored in an online account, such as iCloud. When you sync, the groups of contacts move onto the iPhone along with the contacts. You can limit the contacts you browse or search; tap Groups on the contacts screen.

The Groups screen displays the accounts (such as iCloud or Exchange) with which you are syncing contact information; under each account are the groups of contacts stored in that account. If a group has a check mark next to it, its contacts are displayed on the Contacts screen. To hide a group's contacts, tap it so that the check mark disappears. To hide or show all of a group's contacts, tap the All *account*, where *account* is the name of the account in which those contacts are stored. Tap Show All Contacts or Hide All Contacts to show or hide all the groups and contacts; then tap each group whose contacts you want to show on the contacts screen.

Tap Done to move back to the contacts screen.

- **Speaking of contacts**—You can use Siri to speak commands to work with contacts, too. You can get information about contacts by asking for it, such as "What is William Wallace's work phone number?" If you want to see all of a contact's information, you can say "Show me William Wallace." When Siri displays contact information, you can tap it to take action, such as tapping a phone number to call it. (See Chapter 12, "Working with Siri," for more on using Siri.)

It's Not All Good

When you create a new contact, it is associated with the account you designated as the default in the Contacts settings and is stored at the account level (not in any of your groups). You can't create groups in the Contacts app, nor can you change the group with which contacts are associated. You have to use a contacts app on a computer to manage groups and then sync your iPhone (which happens automatically when you use an online account, such as iCloud) to see the changes you make to group information.

Accessing Contacts from Other Apps

You can also access contact information while you are using a different app. For example, you can use a contact's email address when you create an email message. When you perform such actions, you use the Contacts app to find and select the information you want to use. The following example shows using contact information to send an email message, and using your contact information in other apps (such as Phone or Messages) is similar.

1. Open the app from which you want to access contact information (this example uses Mail).

2. Tap the New Message button.

3. In the To: field, tap the Add button.

4. Search, browse, or use the index to find the contact whose information you want to use.

5. Tap the contact whose information you want to use.

If the contact has only one type of the relevant information (such as a single email address, if you started in the Mail app), you immediately move back to the app and the appropriate information is entered. You can move directly to step 7.

6. If the contact has multiple entries of the type you are trying to use, tap the information you want to use—in this case, the email address. The information is copied to the app.

7. Complete the task you are doing, such as sending an email message.

```
●oooo AT&T 🔋 ⟳      9:39 AM        ⟱ 98% ▰▰▸
              Choose a contact to mail
❮ Contacts

         🖼️     Wyatt Earp
                "Lawdawg"
                Dodge City Marshall

    work
    tombstone_lawman@me.com────── ⑥

    home
    lawdawg@law.com

    other
    sorebruiser@gmail.com
```

```
●●ooo AT&T 🔋 ⟳      9:39 AM        ⟱ 98% ▰▰▸
 Cancel      New Message      Send

 To: Wyatt Earp,────────────────── ⊕

 Cc/Bcc, From: bradmiser@icloud.com

 Subject: ────────────────────── ⑦



 Sent from my iPhone
```

The email address from the Contacts app

Managing Your Contacts on Your iPhone

When you sync contacts with an iCloud, Exchange, or other accounts (or with a contact application via iTunes on a computer), the changes go both ways. For example, when you change a contact on the iPhone, the synced contact manager application, such as Outlook, makes the changes for those contacts on your computer. Likewise, when you change contact information in a contact manager on your computer, those changes move to the iPhone. If you add a new contact in a contact manager, it moves to the iPhone, and vice versa. You can also change contacts manually.

Updating Contact Information

You can change any information for an existing contact, such as adding new email addresses, deleting outdated information, and so on.

1. View the contact's Info screen.

2. Tap Edit. The Info screen moves into Edit mode, and you see Unlock buttons.

3. Tap current information to change it; you can change a field's label by tapping it, or you can change the data for the field by tapping the information you want to change. Use the resulting tools, such as the phone number entry keypad, to make changes to the information. These tools work just like when you create a new contact (refer to "Creating Contacts Manually," earlier in this chapter).

4. To add more fields, tap the add button in that section, such as add phone; then, select a label for the new field and complete its information. This also works just like when you add a field to a contact you create manually.

5. To remove a field from the contact, tap its Unlock button.

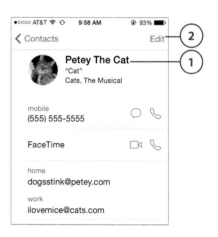

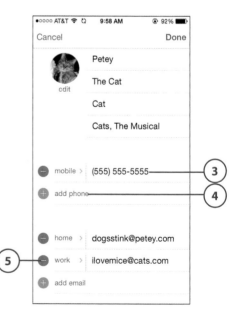

6. Tap Delete. The information is removed from the contact.

7. To change the contact's photo, tap the current photo, or the word *edit* under the current photo, and use the resulting menu and tools to select a new photo, take a new photo, or edit the existing one.

8. When you finish making changes, tap Done. Your changes are saved, and you move out of Edit mode.

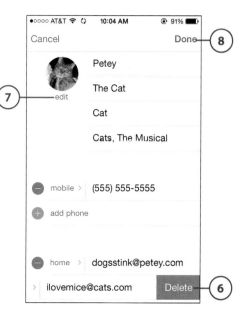

No Tones or Vibes?

If you leave the default tones or vibration patterns set for a contact, you won't see those fields when you view the contact. However, when you edit a contact, all the fields you need to add these to a contact become available.

Adding Information to an Existing Contact While Using Your iPhone

As you use your iPhone, you'll encounter information related to a contact but that isn't part of that contact's information. For example, a contact might send you an email from a different address than the one you have stored for her. When this happens, you can easily add the new information to an existing contact. Just tap the information to select it (such as in an email address), and then tap Add to Contacts (or Add to Existing Contact, if you already have some contact info for that person) on the screen that holds the info you want to add. For example, to add an email address, tap the name or email address in the email message and then tap Add to Existing Contact. Then select the contact to which you want to add the information.

Deleting Contacts

To get rid of contacts, you can delete them from the Contacts app.

1. Find and view the contact you want to delete.

2. Tap Edit.

3. Swipe to the bottom of the Info screen.

4. Tap Delete Contact.

5. Tap Delete Contact again to confirm the deletion. The app deletes the contact, and you return to the contacts screen.

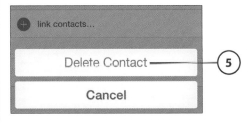

LINKING CONTACTS

When you edit a contact, the Linked Contacts section appears at the bottom of the screen. You can use this to combine contacts. For example, if you end up with two contacts for the same person, you can link them to combine their information into one contact. Or, you might want to link multiple people to a company. When you link contacts, information from all the linked contacts appears on one contact, which is the contact from which you start the link process.

To link a contact, edit it and tap link contacts. Find and tap the contact to which you want to link the one you are editing. That contact's information displays. Tap Link.

The information from the second contact is linked to the first. You can repeat this as many times as you want. The contact to which the others are linked is known as the *unified contact* (or card).

And you have to have the group within which a contact is stored displayed to be able to link it.

You can change how the information for the unified contact is displayed by viewing the unified contact and tapping one of the linked contacts. Then tap the command you want to use, such as Use This Photo For Unified Card, which displays the contact image for the contact on which you tapped for the unified contact.

To unlink contacts, edit the linked contact, tap the Unlock button next to a linked contact, and tap Unlink. The contact information is separated as it was before you linked them.

Tap to make FaceTime calls.

Tap to configure Phone and FaceTime settings

Tap to make calls, listen to voicemail, and more

In this chapter, you explore all the cell phone and FaceTime functionality that your iPhone has to offer. The topics include the following:

→ Setting phone preferences
→ Making voice calls
→ Managing in-process voice calls
→ Receiving voice calls
→ Managing voice calls
→ Using visual voicemail
→ Communicating with FaceTime

Communicating with the Phone and FaceTime Apps

Although it's also a lot of other great things, such as a music player, web browser, email tool, and such, there's a reason the word *phone* is in *iPhone*. It's a feature-rich cell phone that includes some amazing features, two of which are visual voicemail and FaceTime. Other useful features include a speakerphone, conference calling, and easy-to-use onscreen controls. Plus your iPhone's phone functions are integrated with its other features. For example, when using the Maps application, you might find a location, such as a business, that you're interested in contacting. You can call that location just by tapping the number you want to call directly from the Maps screen. No need to fumble around switching to phone mode and dialing the number manually. The iPhone makes your mobile phone use quicker, easier, and smarter in so many ways, as you'll see in the pages that follow.

Setting Phone Preferences

Before jumping into making voice calls, take a few minutes to configure your iPhone's phone functions to work the way you want them to. You can set your phone's sounds, such as ringtones, and notifications so that you always know what is happening with phone activity. You can also configure some other less visible settings to further tweak how the phone works.

Setting Phone Sounds and Notifications

Of course, we all know that your ringtone is the most important phone setting, and you'll want to make sure your iPhone's ringtones are just right. Use the iPhone's Sounds settings to configure custom or standard ringtones and other phone-related sounds, including the new voicemail sound. These are explained in Chapter 4, "Configuring an iPhone to Suit Your Preferences."

You can also set ringtones for specific contacts; you have different ringtones for different people so you can know who is calling just by the ringtone (configuring contacts is explained in Chapter 7, "Managing Contacts").

You'll also want to configure notifications for the Phone app. These include alerts, the app's badge, and so on. Configuring notifications are also explained in Chapter 4.

Configuring Phone Settings

There are a number of settings you can use to configure the way the phone functions work.

1. On the Home screen, tap Settings.

2. Swipe up the screen.

3. Tap Phone. You move to the Phone screen. (Your number is shown at the top of the screen in case you ever forget it. And, yes, I have forgotten my own number.)

4. To see the images associated with contacts on the Favorites list, set the Contact Photos in Favorites switch to on (green). (You learn about your Favorites list a little later in this chapter.) A small image showing the contact's photo appears next to each favorite on the list. If you set this to off (white), you see only names on the Favorites list.

5. To create a custom text reply that a caller sees if you choose to send the text rather than answer a call, tap Respond with Text. (More on this later in this chapter.) If you just want to use the default messages such as, "I'll call you later," skip to step 9. On the Respond with Text screen, you see the three default text responses that are available.

6. To replace one of the default responses, tap it and type a custom reply. Custom replies are shown in a darker text, while the defaults are shown in the lighter text.

7. To remove a custom reply, tap its delete button. It is replaced with a default reply.

8. When you're done customizing replies, tap Phone.

9. To forward your calls to another number, tap Call Forwarding; if you don't want to forward calls, skip to step 14.

10. Turn Call Forwarding on (green). The Forwarding To screen appears.

●●●●● AT&T 🔶	10:28 AM	🔋 64% ▪️
‹ Settings	**Phone**

My Number   +1 (   ) ▨▨ ▨▨▨   ›

Contact Photos in Favorites ⚪️ ——④

CALLS

Respond with Text ————————→ ⑤

●●●●○ AT&T 🔶	11:09 AM	🔋 63% ▪️
‹ Phone **Respond with Text**	——⑧

CAN'T TALK RIGHT NOW...

I'll call you later.

I'm on my way. ——⑥

On another call, will call you back ASAP ⊗ ——⑦

These quick responses will be available when you respond to an incoming call with a text. Change them to say anything you like.

CALLS

Respond with Text   ›

Call Forwarding———————→ ⑨

●●●●○ AT&T 🔶	11:10 AM	🔋 62% ▪️
‹ Phone **Call Forwarding**	

Call Forwarding   ⚪️ ——⑩

For the First Time

The first time you turn on Call Forwarding, you move immediately to the Forwarding To screen. After you've forwarded your calls to another number at least once, the next time you enable call forwarding, the iPhone assumes you'll use that number again. To change the current number, tap Forward to on the Call Forwarding screen.

11. Enter the number to which you want to forward calls. Include the number's area code, and country code, if applicable. You can use the special symbols located in the lower-left corner of the keypad to enter pauses and such.

12. Tap Back. The number is saved, and you return to the Call Forwarding screen. The number to which your iPhone forwards calls shows next to the Forward to text. The forward icon appears at the top of the screen.

13. Tap Phone.

14. To disable call waiting, tap Call Waiting; the Call Waiting screen appears. To leave Call Waiting active, skip to step 17.

15. To disable call waiting, turn Call Waiting off (white). When call waiting is turned off and you receive a second call while you're already on another call, the second call immediately goes to voicemail.

16. Tap Phone.

17. To hide your information when you make calls, tap Show My Caller ID; to leave it showing, skip to step 20.

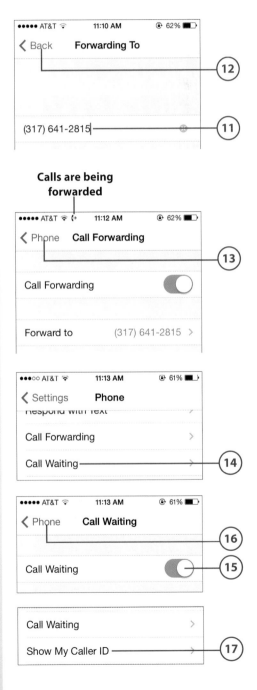

18.   Turn Show My Caller ID off (white) and your information won't be transmitted when you make a call.

19.   Tap Phone.

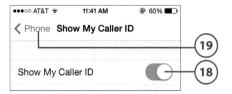

Blocking Calls

To block calls, tap Blocked. Tap Add New and choose the contact whose calls (messages and FaceTime requests, too) you want to block. Tap Add New again to block more contacts; then tap Phone. The step-by-step instructions to block calls are in Chapter 17, "Maintaining and Protecting Your iPhone and Solving Problems."

20.   Enable the Dial Assist feature if you want the correct country code to be added to numbers in your country when dialing those numbers from outside your country or if you want the correct area codes to be added when you dial a local number. For example, if you live in the United States and don't want the correct prefixes added to U.S. phone numbers when you dial them from outside the United States, turn Dial Assist off (white). You now have to add any prefixes manually when dialing a U.S. number from outside the United States. (This step is specific to the iPhone in the United States with service provided by AT&T. If you have a different provider, this function might perform a different action.)

21.   Tap Settings.

>>>Go Further

OTHER PHONE SETTINGS

TTY devices enable hearing-impaired people to use a telephone. To use TTY with your iPhone, you need an adapter to connect your iPhone to a TTY device. You also need to turn on TTY support by turning TTY on (green).

The Change Voicemail Password command enables you to reset your voicemail password; this is covered at the end of this chapter.

Your iPhone uses a subscriber identity module (SIM) card to store certain data about your phone; the SIM PIN setting enables you to associate a personal ID number (PIN) with the SIM card in an iPhone. You can remove this card from your iPhone and install it in other phones that support these cards to use your account with a different phone. If you set a PIN, that PIN is required to use the card in a different phone.

The AT&T Services option (when your iPhone is supported by AT&T in U.S. markets) enables you to get information about your account. When you send a request for information, you receive the answer via a text message. If you use a different provider, there is a command specific to your provider here.

Making Voice Calls

There are a number of ways to make calls with your iPhone; after a call is in progress, you can manage it in the same way no matter how you started it.

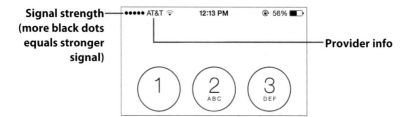

You can tell you are able to make a call or receive calls when you see your provider's information at the top of the screen along with strength of the signal your phone is receiving. As long as you see at least one dark dot, you should be good to go. More dots are better because they mean you have a stronger signal, meaning the call quality will be better.

With a reasonably strong signal, you are ready to make calls.

Which Network?

When you leave the coverage area for your provider and move into an area that is covered by another provider that supports roaming, your iPhone automatically connects to the other provider's network. When you are roaming, you see a different provider near the signal strength indicator at the top of the screen. For example, if AT&T is your provider and you travel to Toronto, Canada, the provider becomes Rogers instead of AT&T, which indicates you are roaming. (In some cases, your provider might send you a text message explaining the change in networks, including information about roaming charges.) Although the connection is automatic, you need to be very aware of roaming charges, which can be significant depending on where you use your iPhone and what your default network is. Before you travel outside of your default network's coverage, check with that network to determine the roaming rates that apply to where you are going. Also, see if there is a discounted roaming plan for that location. If you don't do this before you leave, you might get a nasty surprise when the bill arrives showing substantial roaming charges.

Dialing with the Keypad

The most obvious way to make a call is to dial the number.

1. On the Home screen, tap Phone. The Phone apps opens.

2. If you don't see the keypad, tap Keypad.

3. Tap numbers on the keypad to dial the number you want to call. If you dial a number associated with one or more contacts, you see the contact's name and the type of number you've dialed just under the number. (If you make a mistake in the number you are dialing, tap the Delete button to edit it.)

4. Tap Call. The app dials the number, and the Call screen appears.

5. Use the Call screen to manage the call; see "Managing In-Process Voice Calls" later in this chapter for the details.

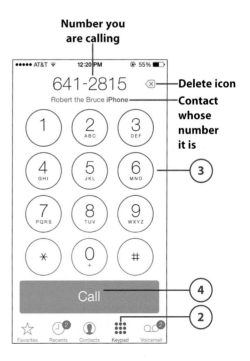

Number you are calling

Delete icon

Contact whose number it is

Dialing with Contacts

As you saw in Chapter 7, the Contacts app is a complete contact manager so you can store various kinds of phone numbers for people and organizations. To make a call using a contact, follow these steps.

1. On the Home screen, tap Phone.

2. Tap Contacts.

3. Browse the list, search it, or use the index to find the contact you want to call. (Refer to Chapter 7 for information about using the Contacts app.)

4. Tap the contact you want to call.

5. Tap the number you want to dial. The app dials the number, and the Call screen appears.

6. Use the Call screen to manage the call; see "Managing In-Process Voice Calls" later in this chapter for the details.

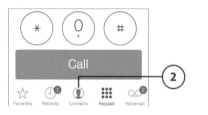

Dialing with Favorites

You can save contacts and phone numbers as favorites to make dialing them even simpler. (You learn how to save favorites in various locations later in this chapter. You can learn how to make a contact into a favorite in Chapter 7.)

1. On the Home screen, tap Phone.

2. Tap the Favorites button.

3. Browse the list until you see the favorite you want to call.

4. Tap the favorite you want to call; to place a voice call, tap a phone number (if you tap a FaceTime contact, a FaceTime call is placed instead). The app dials the number, and the Call screen appears.

5. Use the Call screen to manage the call; see "Managing In-Process Voice Calls" later in this chapter for the details.

Nobody's Perfect

If your iPhone can't complete the call for some reason, such as not having a strong enough signal, the Call Failed screen appears. Tap Call Back to try again or tap Done to give up. When you tap Done, you return to the screen from which you came.

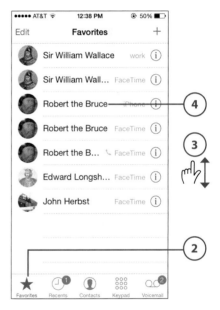

Dialing with Recents

As you make, receive, or miss calls, your iPhone keeps tracks of all the numbers for you on the Recents list. You can use the recent list to make calls.

1. On the Home screen, tap Phone.

2. Tap Recents.

3. Tap all to see all calls.

Info on the Recents Screen

If you have a contact on your iPhone associated with a phone number, you see the person's name and the label for the number (such as mobile). If you don't have a contact for a number, you see the number itself. If a contact or number has more than one call associated with it, you see the number of recent calls in parentheses next to the name or number. If you initiated a call, you see the phone icon under the contact's name next to the contact's label.

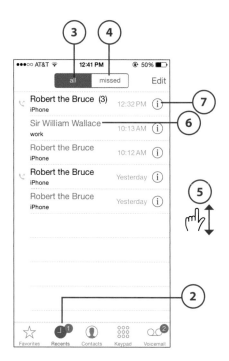

4. Tap missed to see only calls you missed.

5. If necessary, browse the list of calls.

6. To call the number associated with a recent call, tap the title of the call, such as a person's name. The app dials the number, and the Call screen appears. Skip to step 10.

7. To get more information about a recent call, tap its Info button. The Info screen appears.

8. Read the information about the call. For example, if the call is related to someone in your Contacts list, you see detailed information for that contact. The numbers associated with the call are highlighted in red if they were missed or in blue if the call went through. If there are multiple recent calls, you see information for each call, such as its status (Canceled or Outgoing Call, for example) and time.

9. Tap a number on the Info screen. The app dials the number, and the Call screen appears.

10. Use the Call screen to manage the call; see "Managing In-Process Voice Calls" later in this chapter for the details.

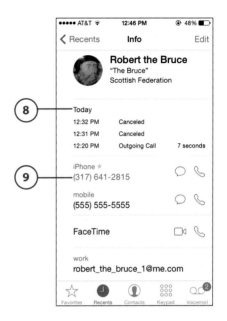

Going Back

To return to the Recents screen without making a call, tap Recents.

Managing In-Process Voice Calls

When you place a call, there are several ways to manage it. The most obvious is to place your iPhone next to your ear and use your iPhone like any other phone you've ever used. As you place your iPhone next to your ear, the controls on its screen becomes disabled so you don't accidentally tap onscreen buttons with the side of your face or your ear. When you take your iPhone away from your ear, the Call screen appears again and the Phone app's controls become active again.

When you are in a call, press the Volume buttons on the left side of the iPhone to increase or decrease its volume. Some of the other things you can do while on a call might not be so obvious, as you'll learn in the next few tasks.

Following are some of the buttons on the Call screen that you can use to manage an active call:

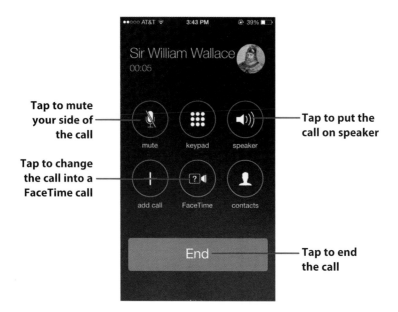

Tap to mute your side of the call

Tap to change the call into a FaceTime call

Tap to put the call on speaker

Tap to end the call

- To mute your side of the call, tap mute. You can hear the person on the other side of the call, but he can't hear anything on your side.

- Tap speaker to use the iPhone's speakers to hear the call. You can speak with the phone held away from your face, too.

- Tap FaceTime to convert the voice call into a FaceTime call (more on FaceTime later in this chapter).

- When you're done with the call, tap End.

Contact Photos on the Call Screen

If someone in your contacts calls you, or you call her, the photo associated with the contact appears on the screen. Depending on how the image was captured, it either appears as a small icon at the top of the screen or fills the entire screen as wallpaper.

Entering Numbers During a Call

You often need to enter numbers during a call, such as to log in to a voice mail system, access an account, and so on.

1. Place a call using any of the methods you've learned so far.

2. Tap Keypad.

3. Tap the numbers.

4. When you're done, tap Hide. You return to the Call screen.

Making Conference Calls

Your iPhone makes it easy to talk to multiple people at the same time. You can have two separate calls going on at any point in time. You can even create conference calls by merging them together. Not all cell providers support conference calling, though. If yours doesn't, you won't be able to perform the steps in this section.

1. Place a call using any of the methods you've learned so far.

2. Tap add call.

3. Tap the button you want to use to place the next call. Tap Favorites to call a favorite, tap Recents to use the Recents list, tap Contacts to place the call via contacts, or tap Keypad to dial the number. These work just as they do when you start a new call.

4. Place the call using the option you selected in step 3. Doing so places the first call on hold and moves you back to the Call screen while the Phone app makes the second call. The first call's information appears at the top of the screen, including the word HOLD so you know the call is on hold. The app displays the second call just below that, and it is currently the active call.

Similar but Different

If you tap contacts instead of add call, you move directly into the Contacts screen. This might save you one screen tap if the person you want to add to the call is in your contacts list.

5. Talk to the second person you called; the first remains on hold.

6. To switch to the first call, tap it on the list or tap swap. This places the second call on hold and moves it to the top of the call list, while the first call becomes active again.

7. To join the calls so all parties can hear you and each other, tap merge calls. The iPhone combines the two calls, and you see a single entry at the top of the screen to reflect this.

Merging Calls

As you merge calls, your iPhone attempts to display the names of the callers at the top of the Call screen. As the text increases, your iPhone scrolls it so you can read it. Eventually, the iPhone replaces the names with the word Conference.

Number of Callers

Your provider and the specific technology of the network you use can limit the number of callers you place in a conference call. When you reach the limit, the add call button is disabled.

8. To add another call, repeat steps 2–7. Each time you merge calls, the second line becomes free so you can add more calls.

9. To manage a conference call, tap the Info button at the top of the screen.

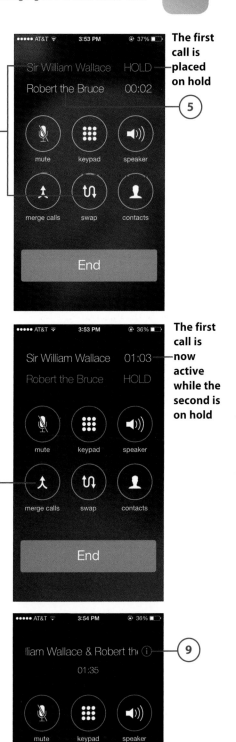

The first call is placed on hold

The first call is now active while the second is on hold

10. To speak with one of the callers privately, tap Private. Doing so places the conference call on hold and returns you to the Call screen showing information about the active call. You can merge the calls again by tapping merge calls.

11. To remove a caller from the call, tap End. The app disconnects the caller from the conference call. You return to the Call screen and see information about the active call.

12. To move back to the Call screen, tap Back. You move to the Call screen and can continue working with the call, such as adding more people to it.

13. To end the call for all callers, tap End.

It's Not All Good

When you have multiple calls combined into one, depending on your provider, the minutes for each call can continue to count individually. So if you've joined three people into one call, each minute of the call may count as three minutes against your calling plan. Before you use this feature, check with your provider to determine what policies govern conference calling for your account.

Using Another App During a Voice Call

If your provider's technology supports it, you can use your iPhone for other tasks while you are on a call. When you are in a call, press the Touch ID/Home button once to move to the Home screen and then tap a different app (placing the call in speaker mode is the most convenient for this). Or, you can press the Touch ID/Home button twice and use the Multitasking screen to move into a different app. The call remains active and you see the active call information in a green bar at the top of the screen. You can perform other tasks, such as looking up information, sending emails, and so on. You can continue to talk to the other person just like when the Call screen is showing. To return to the call, tap the green bar.

Tap to return to the call

A call is active, and you can use other apps while still talking

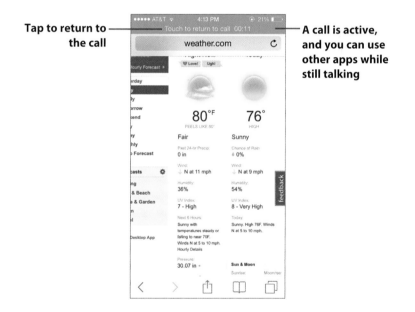

Receiving Voice Calls

Receiving calls on your iPhone enables you to access the same great tools you can use when you make calls, plus a few more for good measure.

Answering Calls

When your iPhone rings, it's time to answer the call—or not. If you configured the ringer to ring, you hear your default ringtone or the one associated with the caller's contact information when a call comes in. If vibrate is turned on, your iPhone vibrates whether the ringer is on or not. And if those two ways aren't enough, a message appears on iPhone's screen to show you information about the incoming call. If the number is in your Contacts app, you see the contact with which the number is associated, the label for the number, and the contact's image if there is one. If the number isn't in your contacts, you see the number only.

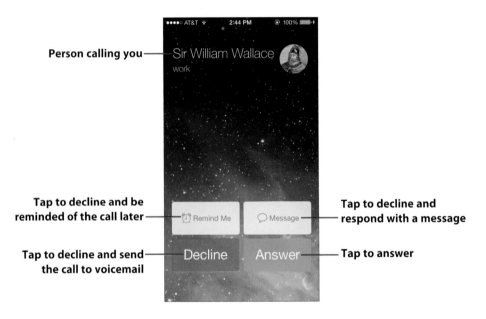

Person calling you — Sir William Wallace — work

Tap to decline and be reminded of the call later — Remind Me

Tap to decline and respond with a message — Message

Tap to decline and send the call to voicemail — Decline

Answer — Tap to answer

Wallpaper

In some cases, the contact's image becomes wallpaper behind the call screen. This happens when you take a photo with the iPhone's camera and use that as the contact's image. It also happens when you use a larger image for a contact. If the contact's image is relatively small, you see a small icon and your current Home screen wallpaper in the background.

EarPods

If you are wearing your EarPods when a call comes in, press the center part of the switch on the right earbud cable to answer the call. Press it again to hang up. You can press the upper part or lower part of the switch to change a call's volume while it is active.

If your iPhone is locked when a call comes in, swipe the slider to the right to answer it.

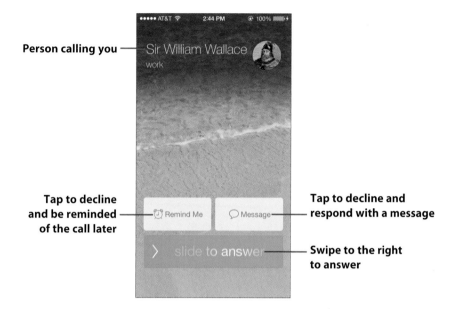

Person calling you

Tap to decline and be reminded of the call later

Tap to decline and respond with a message

Swipe to the right to answer

When you receive a call, you have the following options:

- **Answer**—Tap Answer (if the iPhone is unlocked) or swipe the slider to the right (if the iPhone is locked) to take the call (you don't have to unlock the phone to answer a call). You move to the Call screen and can work with the call just like calls you place. For example, you can add a call, merge calls, place the call on hold, end the call, and so on.

- **Decline**—If you tap Decline (when the iPhone is unlocked), the Phone app immediately routes the call to voicemail. You can also decline a call by quickly pressing the Sleep/Wake button twice.

- **Silence the ringer**—To silence the ringer without sending the call directly to voicemail, press the Sleep/Wake button once or press either volume button. The call continues to come in, and you can answer it even though you shut off the ringer.

- **Respond with a message**—Tap Message to send the call to voicemail and send a message back in response. You can tap one of the default messages (earlier in the chapter, you learned how to configure these messages), or you can tap Custom to create a unique message. Of course, the device making the call must be capable of receiving messages for this to be useful.

- **Decline the call but be reminded later**—Tap Remind Me and the call is sent to voicemail. Tap In 1 hour, When I leave, or When I get home to set the timeframe in which you want to be reminded. A reminder is created in the Reminders app to call back the person who called you, and it is set to alert you at the time you select.

Silencio!

To mute your iPhone's ringer, slide the Mute switch located above the Volume switch toward the back so the orange line appears. The Mute icon (a bell with a slash through it) appears on the screen to let you know you turned off the ringer. To turn it back on again, slide the switch forward. The bell icon appears on the screen to show you the ringer is active again. To set the ringer's volume, use the Volume controls (assuming that setting is enabled) when you aren't in a call and aren't listening to an app, such as the Music app.

Answering Calls During a Call

As you saw earlier, your iPhone can manage multiple calls at the same time. If you are on a call and another call comes in, you have a number of ways to respond.

- **Decline incoming call**—Tap Decline Incoming Call to send the incoming call directly to voicemail.

- **Place the first call on hold and answer the incoming call**—Tap Answer Hold Current Call to place the current call on hold and answer the incoming one. After you do this, you can manage the two calls just as when you called two numbers from your iPhone. For example, you can place the second call on hold and move back to the first one, merge the calls, add more calls, and so on.

- **End the first call and answer the incoming call**—Tap Answer End Current Call to terminate the active call and answer the incoming call.

Auto-Mute

If you are listening to music or video when a call comes in, the app providing the audio, such as the Music app, automatically pauses. When the call ends, the music or video picks up right where it left off.

Managing Voice Calls

You've already learned most of what you need to know to use your iPhone's cell phone functions. In the following sections, you learn the rest.

Clearing Recent Calls

Previously in this chapter, you learned about the Recents tool that tracks call activity on your iPhone. As you read, this list shows both completed and missed calls; you can view all calls by tapping the all tab or only missed calls by tapping missed. On either tab, missed calls are always in red, and you see the number of missed calls in the badge on the Recents tab since you last looked at the list. You also see how you can get more detail about a call, whether it was missed or made.

Over time, you'll build a large Recents list, which you can easily clear.

1. Tap Phone.

2. Tap Recents.

3. Tap Edit.

4. To clear the entire list, tap Clear; to delete a specific recent call, skip to step 6.

5. Tap Clear All Recents. The Recents list is reset.

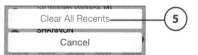

Delete Faster

On the Recents screen, you can delete an individual recent item by swiping to the left on it and tapping Delete.

6. Tap a recent item's unlock button.

7. Tap Delete. The recent item is deleted.

8. When you are done managing your recent calls, tap Done.

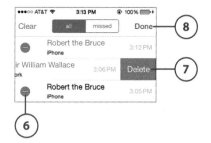

Adding Calling Information to Favorites

Earlier you learned how simple it is to place calls to someone on your favorites list. There are a number of ways to add people to this list, including adding someone who has called you.

1. Move to the Recents list.

2. Tap the Info button for the person you want to add to your favorites list. The Info screen appears. If the number is associated with a contact, you see that contact's information.

3. Swipe up to move to the bottom of the screen.

Make Contact First

To make someone a favorite, he needs to be a contact in the Contacts app. Refer to Chapter 7 to learn how to make someone who has called you into a contact.

---

4. Tap Add to Favorites. If the person has multiple numbers associated with his contact information, you see each available number. Numbers that are already set as favorites are marked with a blue star. You also see email addresses, which you can set as favorites for FaceTime conversations. If the person has only one piece of contact information, such as a single phone number or email, you skip directly to step 6.

5. Tap the number or email address you want to add as a favorite.

6. If you tap a phone number, tap Voice Call to add the number for voice calls or tap FaceTime to set it as a favorite for FaceTime calls.

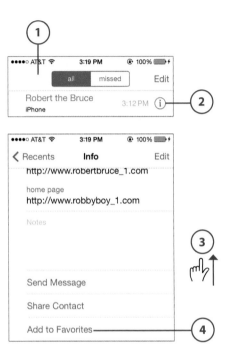

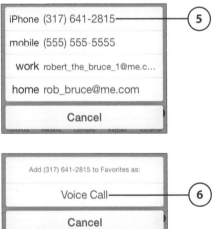

I Have No Choice!

When you tap a phone number that has already been designated as a favorite for Voice or FaceTime, you won't see that as an option in step 6. For example, the number shown in the figure has already been tagged as a FaceTime favorite so I don't see that option on the menu.

7. Repeat steps 4 and 5 if you want to add the contact's other numbers to the favorites list. Any numbers or email addresses that are set as favorites are highlighted in blue and marked with a blue star. If all the numbers and email addresses are assigned as favorites, the Add to Favorites button disappears.

Using the iPhones Headset for Calls

Your iPhone includes an EarPod headset with a microphone on one of its cords. The mic includes a button in the center of the switch on the right side of the EarPod's cable that you can use to do the following:

- **Answer**—Press the mic button once to answer a call.

- **End a call**—Press the mic button while you are on a call to end it.

- **Decline a call**—Press and hold the mic button for about two seconds. Two beeps sound when you release the button to let you know that your iPhone sent the call to voicemail.

- **Put a current call on hold and switch to an incoming call**—Press the mic button once and then press again.

- **End a current call on hold and switch to an incoming call**—Press the mic button once and hold for about two seconds. Release the button and you hear two beeps to let you know you ended the first call. The incoming call is ready for you.

- **Activate Siri**—Press and hold the mic button until you hear the Siri chime. This is useful when you want to make a call to someone without looking or touching your phone.

Oh, That Ringing in My Ears

When you have headphones plugged into your iPhone and you receive a call, the ringtone plays on both the iPhone's speaker (unless the ringer is muted, of course) and through the headphones.

Using Visual Voicemail

Visual voicemail just might be the best of your iPhone's many great features. No more wading through long, uninteresting voicemails to get to one in which you are interested. You simply jump to the message you want to hear. And because voicemails are stored on your iPhone, you don't need to log in to hear them. If that isn't enough for you, you can also jump to any point within a voicemail to hear just that part.

Recording a Greeting

The first time you access voicemail, you are prompted to record a voicemail greeting. Follow the onscreen instructions to do so.

You can also record a new greeting at any time.

1. Move to the Phone screen and tap Voicemail.

2. Tap Greeting.

3. To use a default greeting that provides only the iPhone's phone number, tap Default and skip to step 10.

4. To record a custom greeting, tap Custom. If you have previously used a custom greeting, it is loaded into the editor. You can replace it by continuing with these steps.

5. Tap Record. Recording begins.

6. Speak your greeting. As you record your message, the red area of the timeline indicates (relatively) how long your message is.

7. When you're done, tap Stop.

No Visual Voicemail?

If your voicemail password isn't stored on your iPhone when you tap Voicemail, your phone dials into your voicemail. If that happens, you need to reset your voicemail password. Follow your provider's instructions to reset the password. When you have the new password, open the Phone Settings screen, tap Change Voicemail Password, enter the reset password, create a new password, and re-enter your new password. (You need to tap Done after each time you enter a password.)

8. Tap Play to hear your greeting.

9. If you aren't satisfied, drag the Playhead to the beginning and repeat steps 5–8 to record a new message.

Adding to a Custom Message

To add onto an existing greeting, drag the playhead to where you want to start recording and tap Record. Tap Stop when you're done.

10. When you are happy with your greeting, tap Save. The Phone app saves the greeting as the active greeting and returns you to the Voicemail screen.

Change Greeting

To switch between the default and the current custom greeting, move to the Greeting screen, tap the greeting you want to use (which is marked with a check mark), and tap Save. When you choose Custom, you use the custom greeting you most recently saved.

Listening to and Managing Voicemails

Unless you turned off the voicemail sound, you hear the sound you selected each time a caller leaves a voicemail for you. In the badge on the Phone icon and on the Voicemail button on the Phone screen (unless you've disabled the badge), you also see the number of new voicemails you have. (New is defined as those voicemails to which you haven't listened.)

If you receive a voicemail while your iPhone is locked, you see a message on the screen alerting you that your iPhone received a voicemail (unless you have disabled these notifications from appearing on the Lock screen). (It also indicates a missed call, which is usually the case when a call ends up in the voicemail.) Swipe to the right on the notification to jump to the Voicemail screen so that you can work with the message.

Missing Password

If something happens to the password stored on your iPhone for your voicemail, such as if you restore the iPhone, you are prompted to enter your password before you can access your voicemail. Do so at the prompt and tap OK. The iPhone logs you in to voicemail, and you won't have to enter your password again (unless something happens to it again of course).

And in yet another scenario, if you are using your iPhone when a message is left, you see a notification (either a banner or an alert unless you have turned off notifications for the Phone app) that enables you to ignore the new message or to listen to it.

Contacts or Numbers?

Like phone calls, if a contact is associated with a number from which you've received a voicemail, you see the contact's name associated with the voicemail message. If no contact exists for the number, you see the number only.

Finding and Listening to Voicemails

Working with voicemails is simple and quick.

1. Move into the Phone app and tap Voicemail (if you tapped a new voicemail banner or the Listen button on an alert, you jump directly to the associated voicemail).

2. Swipe up and down the screen to browse the list of voicemails. Voicemails you haven't listened to are marked with a blue circle.

3. To listen to a new voicemail, tap it. You see the timeline bar and commands and the message starts to play.

4. To pause a message, tap its Pause button.

5. To hear the message on your iPhone's speaker, tap Speaker.

6. To move to a specific point in a message, drag the Playhead to the point at which you want to listen.

Moving Ahead or Behind

You can also drag the Playhead while a message is playing to rewind or fast-forward it. This is also helpful when you want to listen to specific information without hearing the whole message again.

7. Tap the Play button.

8. To call back the person who left the message, tap Call Back.

9. To delete the message, tap Delete.

10. To get more information about a message, tap its Info button. The Info screen appears. If the person who left the message is on your contacts list, you see her contact information. The number associated with the message is highlighted in blue.

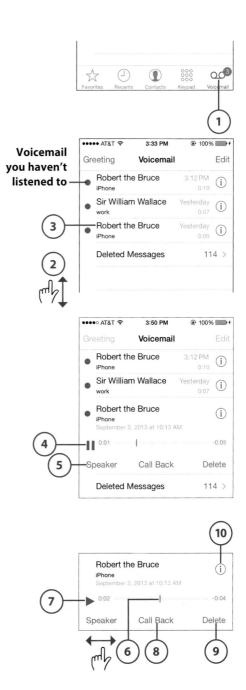

Voicemail you haven't listened to

11. Swipe up or down the screen to review the caller's information.

12. Tap Voicemail.

13. To listen to a message you have listened to before (one that doesn't have a blue dot), tap the message and then tap the Play button. It begins to play.

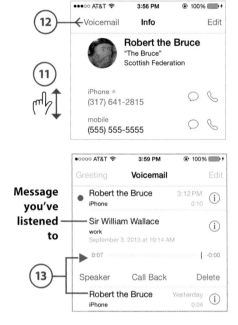

Deleting Messages

To delete a voicemail message that isn't the active message, tap it so it becomes the active message and then tap Delete.

Listening to and Managing Deleted Voicemails

When you delete messages, they are moved to the Deleted Message folder. You can work with deleted messages as follows.

1. Move to the Voicemail screen.

2. If necessary, swipe up the screen until you see the Deleted Messages option.

3. Tap Deleted Messages.

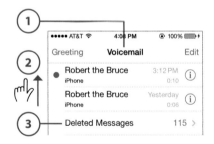

What's Missed?

In case you're wondering, your iPhone considers any call you didn't answer as a missed call. So if someone calls and leaves a message, that call is included in the counts of both missed calls and new voicemails. If the caller leaves a message, you see an alert informing you that you have a new voicemail and showing who it is from (if available). If you don't answer and the caller doesn't leave a message, it's counted only as a missed call and you see an alert showing a missed call along with the caller's identification (if available).

4. Swipe up or down the screen to browse all the deleted messages.

5. Tap a message to listen to it.

6. Tap the Play button. You can use the other playback tools just like you can with undeleted messages.

7. Tap Undelete to restore the deleted message. The iPhone restores the message to the Voicemail screen.

8. To remove all deleted messages permanently, tap Clear All. (If this is disabled, close the open message by tapping it.)

9. Tap Clear All at the prompt. The iPhone erases the deleted messages and returns you to the Deleted screen.

10. To return to the Voicemail screen, tap Voicemail.

Lost/Forgot Your Password?

If you have to restore your iPhone or it loses your voicemail password for some other reason and you can't remember it, you need to have the password reset to access your voicemail on the iPhone. For most cell phone providers, this involves calling the customer support number and accessing an automated system that sends a new password to you via a text message. For AT&T, which is one of the iPhone provider's in the United States, call 611 on your iPhone and follow the prompts to reset your password (which you receive via a text). Whatever provider you use, it's a good idea to know how to reset your voicemail password just in case.

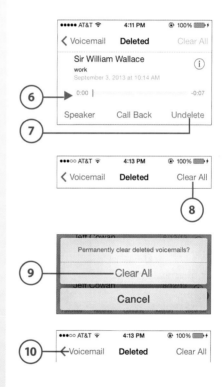

Communicating with FaceTime

FaceTime enables you to see, as well as hear, people with whom you want to communicate. This feature exemplifies what's great about the iPhone; it takes complex technology and makes it simple. FaceTime works great, but there are two conditions that have to be true for you and the people you want some FaceTime with. To be able to see each other, both sides have to use a device that has the required cameras (this includes iPhone 4s and newer, iPod touches third generation and newer, iPad 2s and newer, and Macs running Snow Leopard and newer), and have FaceTime enabled (via the settings on an iOS device as you saw earlier or via the FaceTime application on a Mac). And each device has to be able to communicate over a network; an iPhone or iPad can use a cellular data network (if that setting is enabled) or a Wi-Fi network. When these conditions are true, making and receiving FaceTime calls are simple tasks.

In addition to making video FaceTime calls, you can also make audio-only FaceTime calls. These work similarly to making a voice call except the minutes don't count against your voice plan when you use a Wi-Fi network (if you are making the call over the cellular network, the data does count against your data plan so be careful about this).

Configuring FaceTime Settings

FaceTime is a great way to use your iPhone to hear and see someone else. Like the phone function, there are a few FaceTime settings you should configure. You can connect with other FaceTime users via your phone number, an email address, or your Apple ID.

1. Move to the Settings screen.

2. Tap FaceTime.

3. If the FaceTime status is off (white), tap the FaceTime switch to turn it on (green).

4. To use your Apple ID for FaceTime calls, tap Use your Apple ID for FaceTime. If you already see your Apple ID, it means you are signed in already and can skip to step 7. (If you don't sign in to an Apple ID, you can still use FaceTime but it is always via your phone number.)

5. Enter your Apple ID password. (If you haven't recorded your Apple ID in another app on your iPhone, such as by registering your iCloud account, you need to enter your Apple ID along with the password.)

6. Tap Sign In.

7. Configure the email addresses you want people to use to contact you for FaceTime sessions by tapping them to enable each address (enabled addresses are marked with a check mark) or to disable addresses (these don't have a check mark). (If you don't have any email addresses configured on your iPhone, you are prompted to enter email addresses.)

Managing Addresses

You can add more email addresses at any time by tapping Add Another Email and following the onscreen prompts to add and confirm the new addresses. To remove an address from FaceTime, tap its info button (i) and then tap Remove This Email.

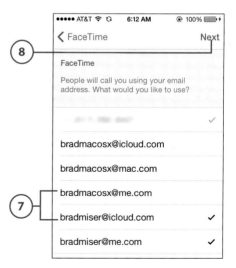

8. Tap Next. The information you entered is verified. If a problem is detected, you must correct it.

9. If necessary, swipe up the screen until you see the CALLER ID section.

10. Tap the phone number or email address by which you will be identified to the other caller during a FaceTime call.

11. Tap Settings.

Blocking FaceTime

If you tap Blocked at the bottom of the FaceTime Settings screen, you can block people from making calls, sending messages, or making FaceTime requests to your iPhone. Tap Add New and then tap the contact you want to block.

Making FaceTime Calls

FaceTime is a great way to communicate with someone because you can hear and see him. Because iPhones have cameras facing each way, it's also easy to show something to the person you are talking with. You make FaceTime calls starting from the FaceTime, Contacts, or Phone apps. No matter which way to start a FaceTime session, you manage it in the same way.

Careful

If your iPhone is connected to a Wi-Fi network, you can make all the FaceTime calls you want because you have unlimited data. However, if you are using the cellular data network, be aware that FaceTime calls may use data under your data plan. If you have a limited plan, it's a good idea to use FaceTime primarily when you are connected to a Wi-Fi network. (Refer to Chapter 2, "Connecting Your iPhone to the Internet, Bluetooth Devices, and iPhones/iPods/iPads," for information on connecting to Wi-Fi networks.)

To start a FaceTime call from the Contacts app, do the following:

1. Use the Contacts app to open the contact with whom you want to chat (refer to Chapter 7 for information about using the Contacts app).

Playing Favorites

If you've set a FaceTime contact as a favorite, you can open the Phone app, tap Favorites, and tap the FaceTime favorite to start the FaceTime session.

2. To place an audio-only FaceTime call, tap the FaceTime audio button. (The rest of these steps show a FaceTime video call, but a FaceTime audio-only is very similar to voice calls described earlier in this chapter.)

3. Tap the contact's FaceTime video button. The iPhone attempts to make a FaceTime connection. You hear the FaceTime "chirping" and see status information on the screen while the call is attempted. When the connection is complete, you hear a different tone and see the other person in the large window and a preview of what he is seeing (whatever your iPhone's front-side camera is pointing at—mostly likely your face) in the small window. If the person you are trying to FaceTime with isn't available for FaceTime for some reason (perhaps he doesn't have a FaceTime-capable device or is not connected to the Internet), you see a message saying that the person you are calling is unavailable for FaceTime and the call terminates.

Failing FaceTime

If a FaceTime request fails, you can't really tell the reason why. It can be a technical issue, such as none of the contact information you have is FaceTime-enabled, the person is not signed into a device, or the person might have declined the request. If you repeatedly have trouble connecting with someone, contact him to make sure he has a FaceTime-capable device and that you are using the correct FaceTime contact information.

4. After the call is accepted, manage the call as described in the "Managing FaceTime Calls" task.

Transforming a Call

You can transform a voice call into a FaceTime session by tapping the FaceTime button on the Call screen. When you transform a call into a FaceTime session, the minutes no longer count against the minutes in your calling plan because all communication happens over the Wi-Fi network or your cellular data plan if you enabled that option and aren't connected to a Wi-Fi network. (The voice call you started from automatically terminates when the switch is made.)

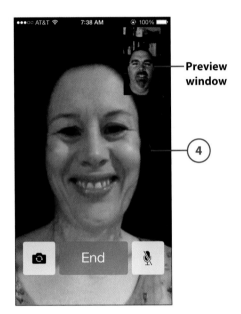

Preview window

4

Other Ways to FaceTime

To use the FaceTime app to start a call, tap the FaceTime icon on the Home screen. Tap Favorites to start the session by tapping a favorite, Recents to use your Recents list to do so, or Contacts to select a contact. These options work just like they do when you place a voice call.

You can also place a FaceTime call using Siri by activating Siri and saying "FaceTime *name*" where *name* is the name of the person with whom you want to FaceTime. If there are multiple options for that contact, you must tell Siri which you want to use. After you've made a selection, Siri starts the FaceTime call.

Receiving FaceTime Calls

When someone tries to FaceTime with you, you see the incoming FaceTime request screen message showing who is trying to connect with you and the image you are currently broadcasting. Swipe to the right on the green bar to accept the request and start the call. Manage the call as described in the "Managing FaceTime Calls" task.

Tap Remind Me to decline the FaceTime request and create a reminder or Message to decline the request and send a message. These options work just as they do for a voice call (you have the same custom message options). You can also press the Sleep/Wake button to decline the request.

However you decline the FaceTime request, the person trying to call you receives a message that you're not available (and a message if you choose that option). She can't tell whether there is a technical issue or if you simply declined to take the call.

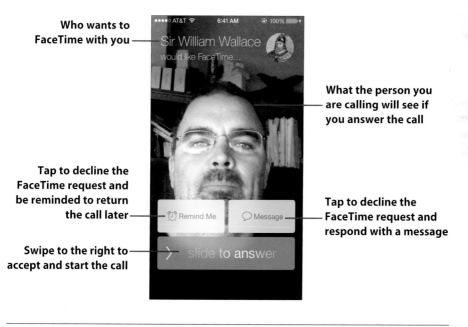

Who wants to FaceTime with you — *Sir William Wallace would like FaceTime...*

What the person you are calling will see if you answer the call

Tap to decline the FaceTime request and be reminded to return the call later — *Remind Me*

Tap to decline the FaceTime request and respond with a message — *Message*

Swipe to the right to accept and start the call — *slide to answer*

Tracking FaceTime Calls

FaceTime calls are tracked just as voice calls are. Open the FaceTime app and tap Recents. On the Recents list, FaceTime calls are marked with the video camera icon. FaceTime audio-only calls are marked with a telephone receiver icon. FaceTime calls that didn't go through are in red and are treated as missed calls. You can do the same tasks with recent FaceTime calls that you can with recent voice calls.

Managing FaceTime Calls

During a FaceTime call (regardless of who placed the call initially), you can do the following:

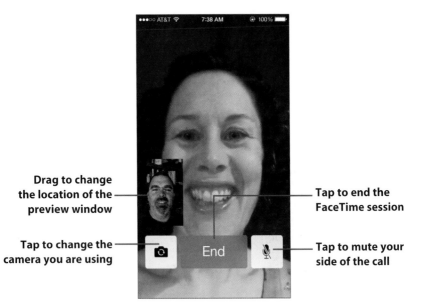

Drag to change the location of the preview window

Tap to change the camera you are using

Tap to end the FaceTime session

Tap to mute your side of the call

- Drag the preview window, which shows the image that the other person is seeing, around the screen to change its location. It "snaps" into place in the closest corner when you lift your finger up.

- Move your iPhone and change the angle you are holding it to change the images you are broadcasting to the other person. Use the preview window to see what the other person is seeing.

- Tap Mute to mute your side of the conversation. Your audio is muted and you see the Mute icon in the preview window. Video continues to be broadcast so the other person can still see you.

- To use the camera on the backside of the iPhone, tap the Change Camera button. The other person now sees whatever you have the camera on the back of the iPhone pointed at. If the other person changes her camera, you see what her backside camera is pointing at.

- After a few moments, the controls disappear. Tap the screen to make them reappear.

- Rotate your iPhone to change the orientation to horizontal. This affects what the other person sees (as reflected in your preview), but you continue to see the other person in her iPhone's current orientation.

- Tap End to end the FaceTime call.

FaceTime Break

Just like when you are in a voice call, you can move into and use other apps (if your provider's technology supports this functionality). You see the green FaceTime in progress bar at the top of the screen. The audio part of the session continues, but the other person sees a still image with a camera icon and the word "Paused." As soon as you move back into the FaceTime session, the video resumes. Likewise, if the other person moves out of the Phone app, you'll see the Paused icon.

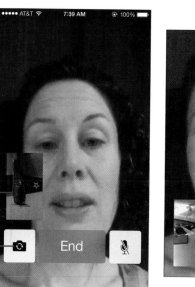
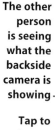

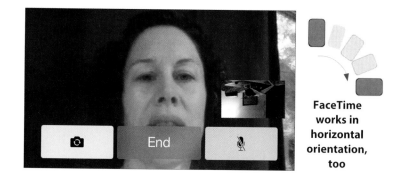

The other person is seeing what the backside camera is showing

Tap to change the camera you are using

Tap the screen to make the controls reappear

FaceTime works in horizontal orientation, too

Tap to
configure
email
settings

Tap to use email

In this chapter, you explore all the email functionality that your iPhone has to offer. Topics include the following:

→ Configuring email accounts
→ Setting Mail app preferences
→ Working with email
→ Managing email

Sending, Receiving, and Managing Email

For most of us, email is an important way we communicate with others, both in our professional and personal lives. Fortunately, your iPhone has great email tools so you can work with email no matter where you are. Of course, you need to be connected to the Internet through a Wi-Fi or cellular data connection to send or receive email—although you can read downloaded messages, reply to messages, and compose messages when you aren't connected.

To use email on your iPhone, you use the Mail app. This app has lots of great features that help you really take advantage of email from all your accounts. Before jumping into the app, you need to have email accounts configured on your iPhone; there are also a number of email-related settings that you should configure to tailor how the Mail app works to suit your preferences.

Configuring Email Accounts

Before you can start using an iPhone for email, you have to configure the email accounts you want to access with it. The iPhone supports many kinds of email accounts, including iCloud, Exchange, Gmail, and so on. In fact, you can configure any kind of email account on your iPhone. Setting up the most common types of email accounts is covered in Chapter 3, "Setting Up iCloud and Other Online Accounts," so if you haven't done that already, go back to that chapter and get your accounts set up.

Setting Mail App Preferences

Your iPhone includes a number of settings that determine certain aspects of how the Mail app works. For example, you can determine how many lines of emails appear as a preview when you are viewing a list of emails. Or, you can determine whether you want Mail to organize your email in threads.

Configure Mail's settings by performing the following steps:

1. Tap Settings on the Home screen.

2. Swipe up the screen.

3. Tap Mail, Contacts, Calendars.

4. Swipe up the screen until you see the Mail section.

5. Tap Preview.

Change Text Size

To change the size of text used in the Mail app, open the Settings app, tap General, and tap Text Size. Drag the slider to set the size of the text you want to use. This changes the text size in Mail and other apps that support Dynamic Type.

6. Tap the number of lines you want to display for each email when you view the Inbox and in other locations, such as alerts. This preview enables you to get the gist of an email without opening it. More lines give you a better gist but take up more space on the screen so you see fewer messages without swiping.

7. Tap Mail.

8. Slide the Show To/Cc Label switch to on (green) to always see the To and Cc labels in email headers. (With this disabled, you can still view this information for an email by tapping Details on the New Message screen.)

9. Tap Flag Style.

10. Tap Color to use a colored circle to flag messages, or tap Shape to use the flag shape to flag them. Flagging messages marks messages that you want to know are important or that need your attention.

11. Tap Mail.

12. If you don't want to confirm your action when you delete messages, slide the Ask Before Deleting switch to off (white). When you delete a message, it immediately goes into the trash. If this switch is on (green), you have to tap Delete in a prompt before a message you are deleting is moved into the Trash.

13. If you want images in HTML email messages to be displayed automatically when you read messages, slide the Load Remote Images switch to on (green). If you disable this, you can manually load images in a message. If you receive a lot of spam, you should disable this so that you won't see images in which you might not be interested.

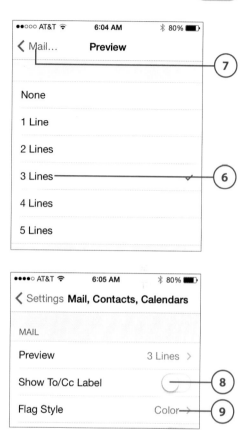

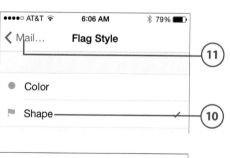

14. If you don't want Mail to organize your messages by thread (which means grouping them based on their subject so you see all the messages on a single topic on the same screen), disable this feature by sliding the Organize By Thread switch to off (white).

15. If you want to receive a blind copy of each email you send, slide the Always Bcc Myself switch to on (green). Each time you send a message, you'll also receive a copy of it but your address will not be shown to the message's other recipients.

16. Tap Increase Quote Level.

17. If you don't want Mail to automatically indent current content (quoted content) when you reply or forward email, slide the switch to off (white). Generally, you should leave this enabled so it is easier for the recipients to tell when you have added content versus what is quoted content.

18. Tap Mail.

19. Tap Signature to configure default signatures that are automatically added to new email messages you create.

20. To use the same signature for email you send from any account, tap All Accounts; to use a different signature for each account, tap Per Account. If you selected All Accounts, you see one signature box. If you selected Per Account, you see a signature box for each account. If you have only one account, you don't see this option, and should skip to step 22.

21. Tap in the signature box you want to configure.

22. Type the signature you want to use. You can enter whatever text you want to use as a signature.

No Signatures, Please

If you don't want any text automatically appended to your messages, choose the All Accounts option and then delete all the text in the signature box.

23. If you selected the Per Account option in step 20, create a signature for each account.

24. Tap Mail.

25. Tap Default Account.

26. Tap the account you want to be your default. The default account is used as the From address for emails you create as new messages in Mail—you can change the From address on a new message to be that of any of your accounts. It is also the one used when you send email from other apps, such as when you email photos, videos, and so on.

27. Tap Mail. The configuration is complete and you are ready to start using email.

Email Notifications and Sounds

Because you will probably have a lot of email activity and will likely want to be aware of it, be sure you configure the notifications for the Mail app. These include whether unread messages are shown in the Notification Center, the type of alerts, whether the badge appears on the Mail icon, whether the preview is shown, the alert sound, and whether new messages are shown on the Lock screen. For a detailed explanation of configuring notifications, refer to Chapter 4, "Configuring an iPhone to Suit Your Preferences."

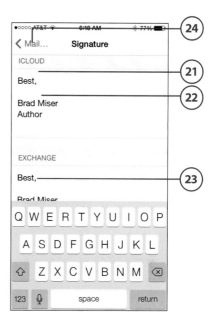

Working with Email

With your email accounts and settings configured, you're ready to start using your iPhone for email. To do this, you use the iPhone's Mail app, which offers lots of great features and is ideally suited for working with email on your iPhone. The Mail app offers a consolidated Inbox, so you can view email from all your accounts at the same time. Also, the Mail app organizes your email into threads (assuming you didn't disable this, of course), which makes following a conversation convenient.

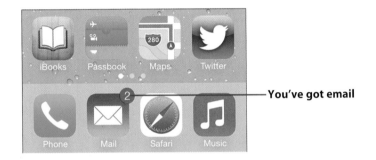

You've got email

When you move to a Home screen, you see the number of new email messages you have in the badge on the Mail app's icon (if you haven't disabled it); tap the icon to move to the app. Even if you don't have any new email, the Mail icon still leads you to the Mail app. Other ways Mail notifies you of new messages include by displaying alerts and the new mail sound. (You determine which of these options is used for each email account by configuring its notifications as explained in the prior note.)

The Mail app enables you to receive and read email for all the email accounts configured on your iPhone. The Mailboxes screen is the top-level screen in the app and is organized into two sections.

The Inboxes section shows the Inbox for each account along with one Inbox for people designated as VIPs (more on this later); next to each Inbox the number of new emails received in that account is shown. (A new message is simply one you haven't viewed yet.) At the top of the section is All Inboxes, which shows the total number of new messages to all accounts; when you tap this, the integrated Inbox containing email from all your accounts is displayed.

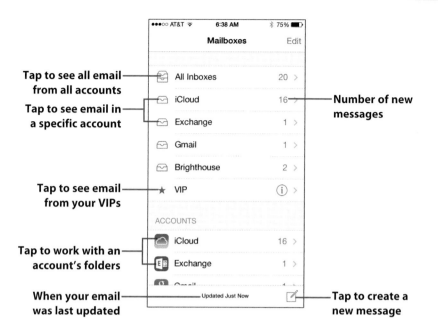

Tap to see all email from all accounts

Tap to see email in a specific account

Number of new messages

Tap to see email from your VIPs

Tap to work with an account's folders

When your email was last updated

Tap to create a new message

The Accounts section shows each email account with another counter for new messages. The difference between these sections is that the Inbox options take you to just the Inbox for one or all of your accounts, whereas the Account option takes you to all the folders under that account.

If you have only one email address configured, you don't see the Mailboxes screen. Instead, you just see the Inbox and other folders for your email account.

About Assumptions

The steps in this section assume you have more than one email account configured and are actively receiving email from those accounts on your iPhone. If you have only one email account active, your Mailboxes screen contains that account's folders instead of what appears in these figures. Similarly, if you disable the Organize by Thread setting, you won't see messages in threads as these figures show. Instead, you work with each message individually.

Receiving and Reading Email

To read email you have received, perform the following steps:

1. On the Home screen, tap Mail. The Mail application opens. If the Mailboxes screen isn't showing, tap the back button in the upper-left corner of the screen until you reach the Mailboxes screen.

2. To read messages, tap the Inbox that contains messages you want to read, or tap All Inboxes to see all your messages. Various icons indicate the status of each message, if it is part of a thread, if it has attachments, and so on. At the top of the screen is the Search tool you can use to find specific messages.

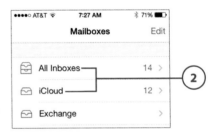

3. Swipe up or down the screen to browse the messages.

4. If a message you are interested in is in a thread, tap it. You can tell a message is part of a thread by double right-facing arrows along the right side of the screen—single messages have only one arrow. (If it isn't part of a thread, skip to step 6.)

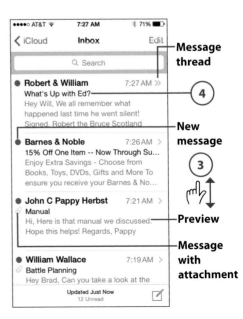

5. Swipe up or down the screen to browse the messages in the thread.

6. To read a message, tap it. As soon as you open a message, it's marked as read and the new mail counter reduces by one. You see the message screen with the address information, including who the message is from and who it was sent to, at the top. Under that the message's subject along with time and date it was sent are displayed. Below that is the body of the message. If the message has an attachment or is a reply to another message, the attachment or quoted text appears toward the bottom of the screen.

7. Swipe up and down the screen to read the entire message, if it doesn't all fit on one screen.

Standard Motions Apply

You can use the standard finger motions on email messages, such as unpinching or tapping to zoom, swiping directions to scroll, and so on. You can also rotate the phone to change the orientation of messages from vertical to horizontal; this makes it easier to type for some people.

Number of messages in the thread

Message thread

Title of thread

Messages in the thread

Quoted message

8. If the message contains an attachment, swipe up the screen to get to the end of the message. If an attachment hasn't been downloaded yet, it starts to download automatically (unless it is a large file). If the attachment hasn't been downloaded yet, which is indicated by a downward-facing arrow in the attachment icon, tap it to download it into the message. When an attachment finishes downloading, its icon changes to represent the type of file it is. If the icon remains generic, it might be of a type the iPhone can't display.

9. Tap the attachment icon to view it.

10. Scroll the document by swiping up, down, left, or right on the screen.

11. Unpinch or double-tap to zoom in.

12. Pinch or double-tap to zoom out.

13. To see the available actions for the attachment, tap the Action button.

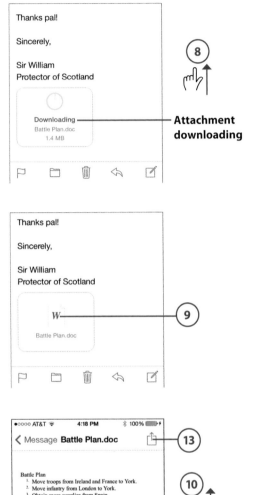

Attachment downloading

14. Swipe to the left or right to see all the available actions.

15. Tap the action you want to take, such as opening the attachment in a different app, printing it, sharing it via email, and so on. Tap Cancel to return to the attachment if you don't want to do any of these. If you open the attachment in an app, work with the attachment in that app. To return to the email, move back into Mail.

16. Tap Message.

17. To view information for an email address, such as who sent the message, tap it. The Info screen appears; its title tells you how the person relates to the message. For example, if you tapped the email address in the From field, the screen title is Sender. You see the person's email address along with actions you might want to perform, such as adding her to your VIP list if the person is in your Contacts app or create a contact if she isn't.

18. Tap Message.

19. To read the next message in the current Inbox, tap the down arrow.

20. To move to a previous message in the current Inbox, tap the up arrow.

21. To move back to see the entire Inbox, tap Inbox.

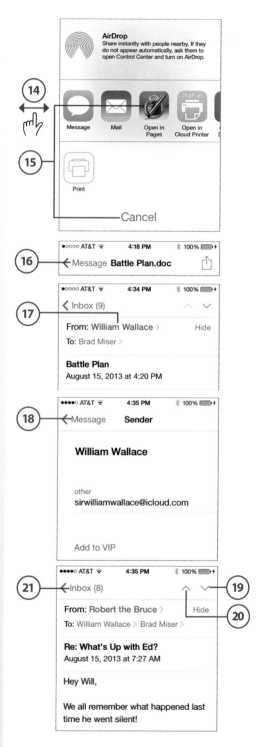

MORE ON RECEIVING AND READING EMAIL

Check out these additional pointers for working with email you receive:

- You can move directly into a new email message by tapping its alert notification; when you receive a notification on the Lock screen, swipe to the left on it to move to the message after you unlock your iPhone. You receive alerts no matter what app you are using, so this makes getting to new email fast and convenient.

- If more messages are available than are downloaded, tap the Load More Messages link. The additional messages download to the inbox you are viewing.

- You can change the amount of detail you see at the top of the message screen by tapping More to show all of the detail, such as the entire list of recipients, or Hide to collapse that information. Even with the detail hidden, you always see who the message is from and at least one recipient.

- How Mail treats the names of people you see in the Mail app depends on the Short Name setting within the Contacts settings (to move there, open the Settings app; tap Mail, Contacts, Calendars; and swipe up the screen until you see the Contacts section). For example, if Short Name is enabled and the First Name Only option is selected (as is the case in the figures in this section), you see only people's first names in the To, Cc, and Bcc lists. Refer to Chapter 7, "Managing Contacts," for information about configuring the Contacts settings.

- The Mail app identifies a thread by its subject and sender. As replies are made, the messages continue to be categorized by subject because Re: is appended to it. It even remains in the thread if the initial subject continues to be in the message but other words are added. If you happen to receive email messages with the same subjects but from different senders, the Mail app places them in separate threads. It also separates messages into different threads if you receive multiple messages from the same sender with the same words with minor differences in the subject (for example, one subject includes punctuation and another does not include it).

- If you enabled the Show To/Cc Label setting, a small "To" or "Cc" is displayed next to each message's title on a list of messages where the email address in the message's To or Cc field is associated with one of your email addresses. When you see To, it means one of your addresses is included on the message's To list. Likewise, when you see Cc, one of your addresses was included on the Cc list for the message.

- To change the status of a message back to Unread, tap the Flag button at the bottom of the screen and tap Mark as Unread. The message is marked with a blue dot again as if you'd never read it.

- If a message includes a photo, Mail displays the photo in the body of the email message. You can zoom in or out and scroll to view it just as you can for photos in other apps.

- If you tap a PDF attachment in a message and the iBooks app is installed on your iPhone, you're prompted to select Quick Look or Open in iBooks. If you select Quick Look, the document will be opened within Mail. If you select Open in iBooks, the document will be moved into the iBooks app where you can read it using the powerful features it offers for reading ebooks and other documents. See Chapter 16, "Using Other Cool iPhone Apps," for information about using iBooks.

- Mail can receive HTML-formatted email that behaves like a webpage. When you tap a link (usually blue text, but it can also be photos and other graphics) in such an email, Safari opens and takes you to the link's source. You then use Safari to view the webpage. See Chapter 13, "Surfing the Web," for information about Safari.

- Some emails, especially HTML messages, are large and don't immediately download in their entirety. When you open a message that hasn't been fully downloaded, you see a message stating that this is the case. Tap the link to download the rest of the message.

- If you have other apps with which an attachment is compatible, you can open the attachment in that app. For example, if you have Pages installed on your iPhone and are viewing a Word document, you can tap the Action button in the upper-right corner of the screen and tap Open in Pages to open the document in the Pages app. You can get the same options by tapping and holding down on the attachment's icon until the Action menu appears.

Emailing by Speaking

Using Siri, you can speak to create new email messages and to reply to messages. You can also dictate into messages you are writing. See Chapter 12, "Working with Siri," for information on using Siri.

Sending Email

You can send email from any of your accounts. Follow these steps for a basic walk-through of composing and sending a new email message:

1. Tap the New Mail button on any Mail screen. A new email message is created. If you tap the New Mail button while you are on the Mailboxes screen or the Inboxes screen, the From address is the one for the account you set as your default; otherwise, the From address is the email account associated with the Inbox you are in. Your signature is placed at the bottom of the message's body.

2. To type a recipient's email address, tap the To field and type in the address. As you type, Mail attempts to find matching addresses in your Contacts list, or in emails you've sent or received, and displays the matches it finds. To select one of those addresses, tap it. Mail enters the rest of the address for you. Or, just keep entering information until the address is complete.

3. To address the email using your contacts, tap the Add button.

4. Use the Contacts app to find and select the contact to whom you want to address the message. (Refer to Chapter 7, "Managing Contacts," for the details about working with contacts.) When you tap a contact with one email address, that address is pasted into the To field and you return to the New Message window. When you tap a contact with more than one email address, you move to the Info screen, which shows all available addresses; tap the address to which you want to send the message.

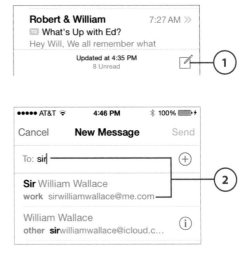

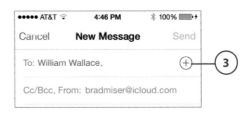

5. Repeat steps 2–4 to add all the recipients to the message.

6. Tap the Cc/Bcc, From line. The Cc and Bcc lines expand.

Removing Addresses

To remove an address, tap it so it is highlighted in a darker shade of blue; then tap the Delete button on the iPhone's keyboard.

7. Follow the same procedures from steps 2–4 to add recipients to the Cc field.

8. Follow the same procedures from steps 2–4 to add recipients to the Bcc field.

9. To change the account from which the email is sent, tap the From field; if the correct account is shown, skip to step 11. The account wheel appears at the bottom of the screen.

10. Swipe up or down the wheel until the From address you want to use is shown between the lines.

11. Tap in the Subject line. The account wheel closes.

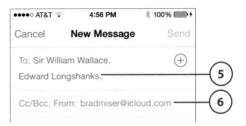

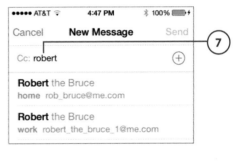

12. Type the subject of the message.

13. Tap in the body, and type the body of the message above your signature. Mail uses the iOS's text tools, attempts to correct spelling, and makes suggestions to complete words. To accept a proposed change, tap the spacebar when the suggestion appears on the screen; to ignore a correction, tap the *x* in the suggestion box. You can also use the copy and paste feature to move text around, and you can edit text using the spell checker and other text tools. (Refer to Chapter 1, "Getting Started with Your iPhone," for the details of working with text.)

14. To make the keyboard larger, rotate the iPhone clockwise or counterclockwise.

15. When you finish the message, tap Send. The progress of the send process is shown at the bottom of the screen; when the message has been sent, you hear the send mail sound you configured, which confirms that the message has been sent.

Write Now, Send Later

If you want to save a message you are creating without sending it, tap Cancel. A prompt appears; select Save Draft to save the message; if you don't want the message, tap Delete Draft instead. When you want to work on a draft message again, tap and hold down the New Message button. After a moment, you see your most recent draft messages; tap the draft message you want to work on. You can make changes to the message and then send it or save it as a draft again. (You can also move into the Drafts folder to select and work with draft messages; moving to this folder is covered later in this chapter.)

Replying to Email

Email is all about communication, and Mail makes it simple to reply to messages.

1. Open the message you want to reply to.

2. Tap the action button.

3. Tap Reply to reply to only the sender or, if there was more than one recipient, tap Reply All to reply to everyone who received the original message. The Re: screen appears showing a new message. Mail pastes the contents of the original message at the bottom of the body of the new message below your signature. The original content is in blue and is marked with a vertical line along the left side of the screen.

4. Use the message tools to add or change the To, Cc, or Bcc recipients.

5. Write your response.

6. Tap Send. Mail sends your reply.

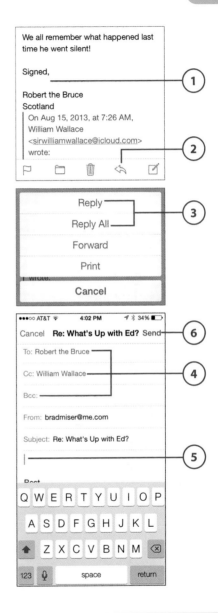

Sending Email from All the Right Places

You can send email from a number of places on your iPhone. For example, you can share a photo with someone by viewing the photo, tapping the action button, and then tapping Mail. Or you can tap a contact's email address to send an email from your contacts list. For yet another example, you can share a YouTube video. In all cases, the iPhone uses Mail to create a new message that includes the appropriate content, such as a photo or link; you use Mail's tools to complete and send the email.

Print from Your iPhone

If you need to print a message, tap the action button and tap Print. To learn about printing from your iPhone, refer to Chapter 1.

Forwarding Emails

When you receive an email you think others should see, you can forward it to them.

1. Read the message you want to forward.

2. Tap the action button.

3. Tap Forward.

4. If the message includes attachments, tap Include at the prompt if you also want to forward the attachments, or tap Don't Include if you don't want them included. The Forward screen appears. Mail pastes the contents of the message you are forwarding at the bottom of the message below your signature and attaches the files if you elected to include them.

5. Address the forwarded message using the same tools you use when you create a new message.

6. Type your commentary about the message above your signature.

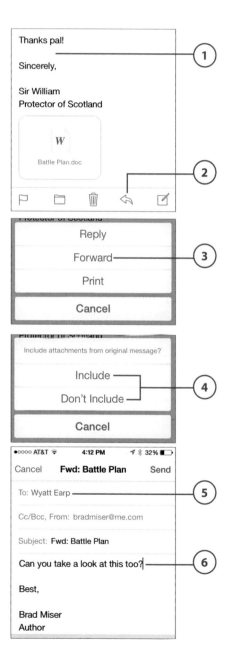

7. Swipe up the screen to see the forwarded content. Forwarded content is in blue and is marked with a vertical line along the left side of the screen.

8. Edit the forwarded content as needed, such as to remove unwanted content.

9. Tap Send. Mail forwards the message.

●○○○○ AT&T 📶　　　4:12 PM　　　🛫 ❋ 32% 🔋

Cancel　　**Fwd: Battle Plan**　　Send ── 9

Date: August 15, 2013 at 4:20:27 PM EDT

To: Brad Miser
<bradmiser@me.com>

Subject: Battle Plan

Hey Brad,

Can you take a look at the attached doc and let me know what you think ── 8
about it please?

Large Messages

Some emails, especially HTML messages, are so large that they don't immediately download in their entirety. When you forward a message whose content or attachments haven't fully downloaded, Mail prompts you to download the "missing" content before forwarding. If you choose not to download the content or attachments, Mail forwards only the downloaded part of the message.

Managing Email

Following are some ways you can manage your email. You can check for new messages, see the status of messages, delete messages, and organize messages using the folders associated with your email accounts.

Including a Photo or Video in a Message

To add a photo or video to a message, tap twice in the body. Swipe to the left on the resulting toolbar until you see the Insert Photo or Video command, and then tap it. Use the Photos app (see Chapter 15, "Working with Photos and Video You Take with Your iPhone," for information about this app) to move to and select the photo or video you want to attach. Tap Choose. The photo or video you selected is attached to the message.

Checking for New Email

To manually retrieve messages, swipe down from the top of the Inbox screen. The screen "stretches" down and when you lift your finger, the Mail app checks for and downloads new messages.

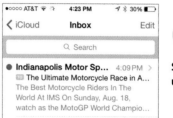

Swipe down to update your email

Mail also retrieves messages whenever you move into the app or into any Inbox or all your Inboxes. Of course, it also retrieves messages according to the option you selected. It downloads new messages immediately when they arrive in your account if Push is enabled or automatically at defined intervals if you've set Fetch to get new email periodically. (Refer to Chapter 3, "Setting Up iCloud and Other Online Accounts," for an explanation of these options and how to set them.)

How many unread messages you have in the current Inbox

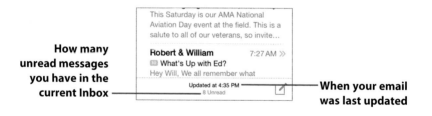

When your email was last updated

The bottom of the Mailboxes or Inbox screen always shows the status of the most recent check.

Understanding the Statuses of Email

When you view an Inbox or a message thread, you see icons next to each message to indicate its status (except for messages that you've read but not done anything else with, which aren't marked with an icon).

Message you've forwarded
Message to which you've replied
Unread message
Message from a VIP
Message you've flagged
Message with attachments

Deleting Email from the Message Screen

To delete a message while viewing it, tap the Trash button. If you enabled the warning preference, confirm the deletion and the message is deleted. If you disabled the confirmation prompt, the message is deleted immediately.

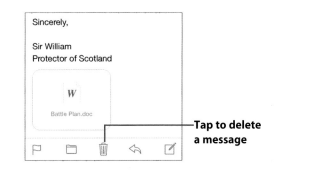

Tap to delete a message

Dumpster Diving

As long as an account's trash hasn't been emptied (Chapter 3 has tasks to show how to configure when this happens), you can work with a message you've deleted by moving to the account's screen and opening its Trash folder.

Deleting Email from the Inbox

You can also delete email by selecting multiple messages on an Inbox screen, which is a more efficient way to get rid of multiple messages.

1. Move to the Inbox screen showing messages you want to delete.

2. Tap Edit. A selection circle appears next to each message, and actions appear at the bottom of the screen.

3. Select the message(s) you want to delete by tapping its selection circles. As you select each message, its selection circle is marked with a check mark. At the top of the screen, you see how many messages you have selected.

4. Tap Trash. Mail deletes the selected messages and exits Edit mode. (If you enabled the warning prompt, you have to confirm the deletion.)

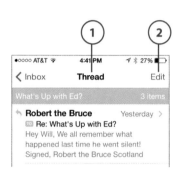

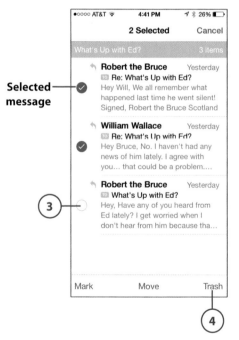

Selected message

More Inbox Tricks

While you are on an Inbox screen showing messages, swipe to the left across a message or a thread. The More and Trash buttons appear. Tap the Trash button to delete the message or all the messages in the thread. Tap the More button to see a list of commands, which are Reply, Forward, Flag, Mark as Unread, Move to Junk, Move Message, and Cancel. Tap the action you want to take on the email message.

Organizing Email from the Message Screen

You can have various folders to organize email, and you can move messages among these folders. For example, you can recover a message from the Trash by moving it from the Trash folder back to the Inbox.

1. Open a message you want to move to a different folder.

2. Tap the Mailboxes button. The Mailboxes screen appears. At the top of this screen is the message you are moving. Under that are the mailboxes available under the current account.

Move to Other Accounts

If you want to move a message to a folder under a different account, tap Accounts in the upper-left corner of the screen. Tap the account to which you want to move the message (not all accounts will be available; if an account is grayed out, you can't move a message to it). Then tap the mailbox into which you want to move the message.

3. Tap the mailbox to which you want to move the message. The message moves to that mailbox, and you move to the next message in the list you were viewing.

Makin' Mailboxes

You can create a new mailbox to organize your email. Move to the Mailboxes screen and tap the account on which you want to create a new mailbox. Tap Edit, and then tap New Mailbox. Type the name of the new mailbox. Tap the Mailbox Location and then choose where you want the new mailbox located (for example, you can place the new mailbox inside an existing one). Tap Save. You can then store messages in the new mailbox.

Organizing Email from the Inbox

Like deleting messages, organizing email from the Inbox can be made more efficient by creating folders to use when organizing your messages.

1. Move to an Inbox screen showing email you want to move to a folder.

2. Tap Edit. A selection circle appears next to each message. Buttons appear at the bottom of the screen.

3. Select the messages you want to move by tapping their selection circles. As you select each message, its selection circle is marked with a check mark.

4. Tap Move.

5. Tap the folder into which you want to place the messages. They are moved into that folder, and you return to the previous screen, which is no longer in Edit mode.

Picking at Threads

When you select a thread, you select all the messages in that thread. Whatever action you select is taken on all the thread's messages at the same time.

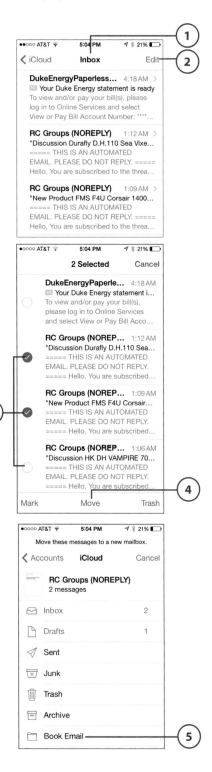

Viewing Messages in a Mailbox

You can open a mailbox within an account to work with the message it contains. For example, you might want to open the Trash mailbox to recover a deleted message.

1. Move to the Mailboxes screen.

2. Tap the account containing the folders and messages you want to view. You see all the account's folders.

3. Tap the folder containing the messages you want to view. You see the messages it contains. In some cases, this can take a few moments if that folder's messages haven't been downloaded.

4. Tap a message or thread to view it, tap Edit, and select messages to perform an action such as moving them to another folder.

Changing Mailboxes

You can change the mailboxes that appear on the Mailboxes screen. Move to the Mailboxes screen and tap Edit. To cause a mailbox to appear, tap it so that it has a check mark. To hide a mailbox, tap its check mark so that it just shows an empty circle. For example, you can show your Drafts mailbox to make draft messages easier to get to. Drag the Order button for mailboxes up or down the screen to change the order in which mailboxes appear. Tap Add Mailbox to add a mailbox not shown to the list. Tap Done to save your changes.

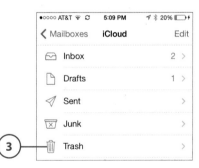

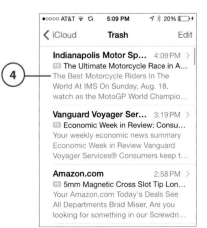

Saving Images Attached to Email

Email is a great way to share photos. When you receive a message that includes photos, you can save them on your iPhone.

1. Move to the message screen of an email that contains one or more photos or images.

2. Tap the action button.

3. Tap Save *X* Images, where *X* is the number of images attached to the message. (If there is only one image, the command is just Save Image.) The images are saved in the Camera Roll album in the Photos application. (See Chapter 15, "Working with Photos and Video You Take with Your iPhone," for help working with the Photos app.)

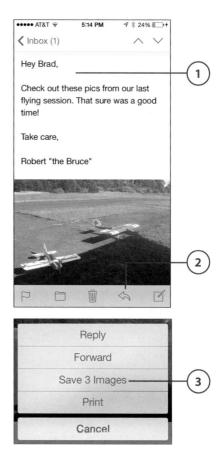

Searching Your Email

As you accumulate email, you might want to find specific messages. Mail's Search tool can help you do this.

1. Move to the screen you want to search, such as an account's Inbox or a folder's screen.

2. Swipe down to move to the top of the screen.

3. Tap in the Search tool.

4. Enter the text for which you want to search. As you type, Mail first searches the messages in the current location and then searches other mailboxes. The messages that meet your search are shown above the keyboard.

5. When you complete your search term, tap Search. The keyboard closes and you see all the messages that met your search. The top part of the list shows the messages in the current mailbox, while the messages in other locations are shown in the Other Mailboxes section.

6. Work with the messages you found, such as tapping a message to read it.

7. To limit the results to only those messages in the current location, tap Current Mailbox.

8. To show all messages that were found again, tap All Mailboxes.

9. To clear a search and exit Search mode, tap Cancel.

10. To clear a search but remain in Search mode, tap the Clear button.

It's Not All Good

The Mail app doesn't include any spam tools (however, if you use an account that features a junk mail/spam tool, it will act on mail sent to your iPhone, too—see the next note). If you enable an already-spammed address, all the spam is going to come right to your iPhone, which can be a nuisance.

The best thing to do is to keep your important addresses from being spammed. Consider using a "sacrificial" email account when you shop and post messages, and in the other places where you're likely to get spammed. If you do get spammed, you can stop using the sacrificial account and create another one to take its place. Or you can delete the sacrificial account from your iPhone and continue to use it on your computer where you likely have spam tools in place.

Dealing with Junk

If an account you use, such as iCloud or Gmail, has some spam/junk tools in place, it might send mail it deems as spam into its Junk folder. You can open the Junk folder under an account to see the messages that are placed there. You can also manually move messages there by moving into the Edit move, selecting the messages you want to send to junk, tapping Mark, and tapping Move to Junk.

Working with VIPs

The VIP feature enables you to indicate specific people as your VIPs. When a VIP sends you email, it is marked with a star icon and goes into the special VIP mailbox so you can access these important messages easily.

Designating VIPs

To designate someone as a VIP, perform the following steps:

1. View information about the person you want to be a VIP by tapping his name in the To or Cc fields as you learned earlier in the chapter.

2. On the Info screen, tap Add to VIP. The person is designated as a VIP and any email from that person receives the VIP treatment.

Accessing VIP Email

To work with VIP email, do the following:

1. Move to the Mailboxes screen.

2. Tap VIP.

3. Work with the VIP messages you see.

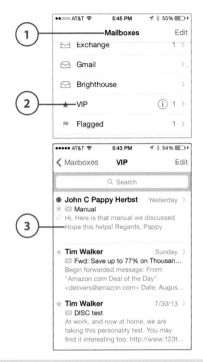

MORE ON VIPS

Here are a few more very important tidbits on VIPs:

- Messages from VIPs are marked with the star icon no matter in which mailbox you see the messages.

- To see the list of your current VIPs, move to the Mailboxes screen and tap the Info button (i) for the VIP mailbox. You see everyone currently designated as a VIP. Tap Add VIP to add more people to the list.

- To return a VIP to normal status, view his information and tap Remove from VIP.

>>>Go Further

Flagging Messages

You might want to flag messages to indicate they are important. Open the message you want to flag, and tap the Flag button in the lower-left corner of the window. Tap Flag. The message is marked with a flag, or orange dot if you selected that option, shown on the message's screen and in mailboxes where it appears. You can also choose the Flagged mailbox to see all your flagged messages (this appears only when you have flagged at least one message). To remove a flag, view the message, tap the flag button, and tap Unflag.

Tap to send and receive text messages, photos, video, and more

Tap to configure Messages

In this chapter, you'll explore the texting and messaging functionality your iPhone has to offer. The topics include the following:

→ Preparing Messages for messaging
→ Sending messages
→ Receiving, reading, and replying to messages
→ Working with messages

Sending, Receiving, and Managing Texts and iMessages

You can use the iPhone's Messages app to send, receive, and converse; you can also send and receive images, videos, links, and so on with this app. You can maintain any number of conversations with other people at the same time, and your iPhone lets you know whenever you receive a new message via audible and visible notifications you configure. In addition to conversations with other people, many organizations use text messaging to send important updates, such as airlines communicating flight status changes. You might find messaging to be one of the most used functions of your iPhone.

The Messages app can send and receive text messages via your cell network based on telephone numbers—this is the texting function that almost all cell phones support. Using this option, you can send text messages to and receive messages from anyone who has a cell phone capable of text messaging.

You can also use iMessages within the Messages app to send and receive messages via an email account to and from other iOS devices (iOS 5 or newer) or Macs (running OS X Lion or newer). This is especially useful when your cell phone account has a limit on the number of texts you can send via your cell account; when you use iMessages for texting, there is no limit on the amount of data you can send and so you incur no additional costs for your messages. This is also really useful because you can send messages to and receive messages from iPod touch, iPad (some models), and Mac users since those devices don't have cell phone capability.

Preparing Messages for Messaging

Like most of the apps described in this book, there are settings for the Messages app you can configure to choose how the app works for you. For example, you can configure iMessages so you can communicate via email addresses, configure how standard text messages are managed, and so on. You can also choose to block messages from specific people.

Setting Your Texts and iMessages Preferences

Perform the following steps to set up Messages on your IPhone:

1. Move to the Settings app and tap Messages.

2. Set the iMessage switch to on (green).

3. Tap Use your Apple ID for iMessage.

Already Signed In to Your Apple ID?

If you have signed in to your Apple ID on your iPhone, such as to sign in to your iCloud account, you might move directly to the sign in screen, in which case you skip step 3.

●○○○○ AT&T 📶	6:20 AM 100% 🔋✦
Settings	
📞 Phone	>
💬 Messages	→ ①

●●●●● AT&T 📶	6:20 AM 100% 🔋✦
‹ Settings **Messages**	
iMessage	②
iMessages can be sent between iPhone, iPad, iPod touch, and Mac. Learn More...	

●●●●● AT&T 📶 ☀	6:29 AM 100% 🔋✦
‹ iCloud **Messages**	
iMessage	◯
Waiting for activation...	
Use your Apple ID for iMessage	③

4. Type your Apple ID password and tap Sign In.

Dedicated Apple ID

If you don't want to use your current Apple ID for messages, you can create a new one for that purpose by tapping Create Apple ID instead of signing in to your existing Apple ID.

5. To prevent an email address from being available for messages, tap it so it doesn't have a check mark; to enable an address so it can be used for messages, tap it so it does have a check mark.

6. Tap Next. The addresses you selected are activated for iMessages.

Verify and Notify

When you enable email addresses for iMessages, you might have to confirm the email addresses you enabled by responding to an email message to those addresses (the first time you enable them for iMessages). You also receive notifications on other devices informing you that the addresses have been enabled for iMessages on your iPhone.

7. To notify others when you read their messages, slide the Send Read Receipts switch to on (green). Be aware that receipts apply only to iMessages (not texts sent over a cellular network).

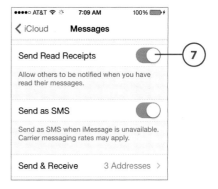

8. To send texts via your cellular network when iMessage is unavailable, slide the Send as SMS switch to on (green). If your cellular account has a limit on the number of texts you can send, you might want to leave this set to off (white) so you use iMessage only when you are texting. If your account has unlimited texting, you should set this to on.

9. Tap Send & Receive. At the top of the iMessage screen, you see the Apple ID via which you'll send and receive iMessages. In the center part of the screen are the phone number and email addresses that can be used with the Messages app.

10. Tap an address so it has a check mark to enable it for iMessages, or tap it so it doesn't have one to disable it.

11. Swipe up the screen until you can see the START NEW NOTIFICATIONS FROM section.

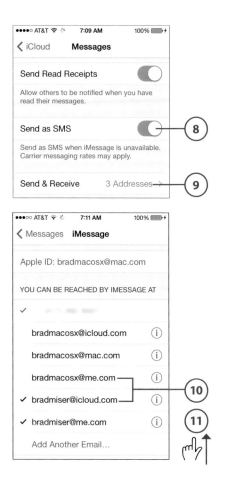

Removing and Adding Addresses

To remove an address from iMessage, tap its Info button (i) and then tap Remove This Email. Tap Remove Email Address at the prompt, and you are no longer be able to use that address for iMessage. You can add more email addresses for iMessage messages by tapping Add Another Email. Enter the email address you want to add. When the address is verified, you see it on the list of options for messaging. If you use an email that is not associated with your Apple ID, a verification email is sent to that address. You need to click the link in that email to be able to use the address with the Messages app.

12. Tap the phone number or email address you want to be used by default when you start a new text conversation.

13. Tap Messages.

14. Swipe up the screen so you see the SMS/MMS section. This is where you configure settings for texts you send and receive via your cellular phone connection.

15. If you don't want to allow photos and videos to be included in your messages, set the MMS Messaging switch to off (white). You won't be able to include images or videos with your messages. You might want to disable this option if your provider charges more for these types of messages—or if you simply don't want to deal with anything but text in your messages.

16. To keep messages you send to a group of people organized by the group, set the Group Messaging switch to on (green). When enabled, replies you receive to messages you send to groups (meaning more than one person) are shown on a group message screen where each reply from everyone is included on the same screen. If this is off (white), when someone replies to a message sent to a group, the message is separated out as if the original message was just to that person. (The steps in this chapter assume this is on.)

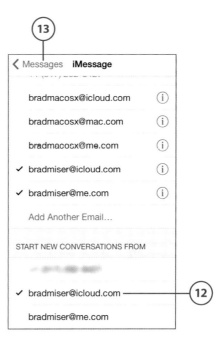

17. To add a subject field to your messages, set the Show Subject Field switch to on (green). This divides text messages into two sections; the upper section is for a subject, and you type your message in the lower section. This is not a common way to text, so you can just leave this off. (The steps in this chapter assume this setting is off.)

18. To display the number of characters you've written compared to the number allowed (such as 59/160), enable the Character Count setting by setting its switch to on (green). When it is off, you don't see a character count for messages you send.

19. Tap Settings. You're ready to send and receive messages.

(19)

●●○○○ AT&T 📶	7:22 AM	100% 🔋
‹ iCloud	**Messages**	

read their messages.

Send as SMS ⬤

Send as SMS when iMessage is unavailable. Carrier messaging rates may apply.

Send & Receive   3 Addresses ›

SMS/MMS

MMS Messaging ⬤

Group Messaging ⬤

Show Subject Field ◯ —— (17)

Character Count ⬤ —— (18)

Blocking People from Messaging or Texting You

To block a phone number or email address from sending you a message, you need to have a contact configured with that information. Refer to Chapter 7, "Managing Contacts," for the steps to create contacts. Creating a contact from a message you receive is especially useful for this purpose. When you start receiving messages from someone you want to block, use a message to create a contact. Then use the following steps to block that contact from sending messages to you:

1. Tap Messages in the Settings app.

2. Swipe up the Messages screen.

3. Tap Blocked.

4. Tap Add New.

5. Use the Contacts app to find and select the person you want to block. (Note that contacts without email addresses or phone numbers that don't have the potential to send messages to you are grayed out and cannot be selected.)

6. Tap the contact you want to block. You return to the Blocked screen and see the contact on your Blocked list. Any messages from the contact, as long as they come from an email address or phone number included in his contact information, won't be sent to your iPhone.

7. Repeat steps 4–6 to block more people.

8. Tap Messages when you're done blocking people.

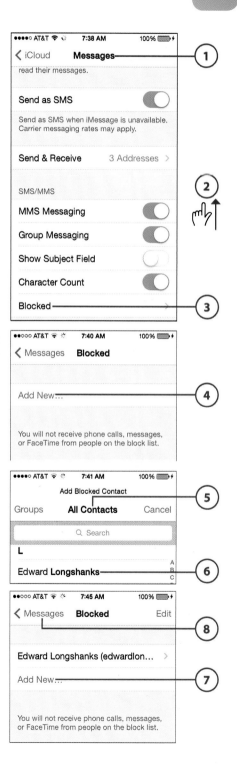

Unblocking People from Messaging or Texting You

To unblock someone, do the following:

1. Tap Messages in the Settings app.

2. Swipe up the Messages screen.

3. Tap Blocked.

4. Swipe to the left on the person you want to allow to send messages to you again.

5. Tap Unblock. The person is removed from your Blocked list, and you will again receive any messages she sends.

6. When you're done unblocking people, tap Messages.

MORE ON MESSAGES CONFIGURATION

Following are a few more Messages configuration tidbits for your consideration:

- You can use only one Apple ID for iMessages at a time. To change the account you are using, move to the iMessage screen by tapping Send & Receive on the Messages Settings screen. Then tap the Apple ID shown. Tap Sign Out. You can then sign in to a different Apple ID.

- SMS stands for Short Message Service, which is what text messages use. MMS stands for Multimedia Messaging Service, which adds the ability to include multimedia elements (photos, video, sound, and so on) in text messages. All text devices and accounts support SMS, but they don't all support MMS.

- Text messages are really intended for small amounts of text. For SMS messages, which are the type the Messages app sends via a cellular network, you should keep the number of characters to 160 or fewer. Enabling the Character Count feature makes this limit more obvious and enables you to easily see how many characters are in each message you create. This limitation does not apply to messages sent via an iMessage.

- You should also configure the notifications the Messages app uses to communicate with you. You can configure the alert styles (none, banners, or alerts), badges on the icon to show you the number of new messages, sounds and vibrations when you receive messages, and so on. Messages also supports repeated alerts, which by default is to send you two notifications for each message you receive but don't read. Configuring notifications is explained in detail in Chapter 4, "Configuring an iPhone to Suit Your Preferences."

Sending Messages

You can use the Messages app to send messages to people using a cell phone number (as long as the device receiving it can receive text messages) or an email address that has been registered for iMessages. If the recipient has both a cell number and iMessage-enabled email address, the Messages app assumes you want to use iMessages for the message.

When you send a message to more than one person and at least one of those people can use only the cellular network, all the messages are sent via the cellular network and not as an iMessage.

More on Mixed Recipients

If one of a message's recipients has an email address that isn't iMessages-enabled (and doesn't have a phone number), the message to that recipient is sent as an email message. The recipient receives the email message in an email app on his phone or computer instead of through the Messages app.

Whether messages are sent via a cellular network or iMessages isn't terribly important, but there are some differences. If your cellular account has a limit on the number of texts you can send, you should use iMessage when you can because those messages won't count against your limit. Also, when you use iMessage, you don't have to worry about a limit on the number of characters in a message. When you send a message via a cellular network, your messages might be limited to 160 characters.

Creating and Sending Messages

You can send text messages by entering a number or email address manually or by selecting a contact from your contacts list.

1. On the Home screen, tap Messages.

2. Tap New Message. If you haven't used the Messages app before, you can skip this step because you move directly to the compose message screen.

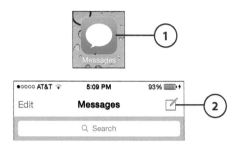

3. Type the recipient's name, email address, or phone number. As you type, the app attempts to match what you type with a saved contact. You see the available information, such as phone numbers and email addresses, for the contact. Phone numbers or addresses in blue indicate the recipient is registered for iMessages and your message will be sent via that means. When you see a phone number in green, the message will be sent as a text message over the cellular network. If a number or email address is black, you haven't sent any messages to it yet; you can tap it to attempt to send a message.

4. Tap the phone number or email address to which you want to send the message. The contact's name is inserted into the To field. Or, if the information you want to use doesn't appear, just type the complete phone number (as you would dial it to make a call to that number) or email address.

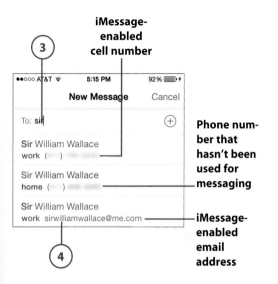

iMessage-enabled cell number

Phone number that hasn't been used for messaging

iMessage-enabled email address

Straight to the Source

You can tap the Add button (+) in the To field to use the Contacts app to select a contact to whom you want to address the message.

5. If you want to send the message to more than one recipient, tap in the space between the current recipient and the + button and use steps 3 and 4 to enter the other recipients' information, either by selecting contacts or by entering phone numbers or email addresses. As you add recipients, they appear in the To field. (If you addressed the message to a number or email address that matches a number in your contacts, the contact's name replaces the number in the To field. If not, the number or email address remains as you entered it.)

Change Your Mind?

To remove a contact or phone number from the To box, tap it once so it becomes highlighted in blue and then tap the Delete key on the keyboard.

6. Tap in the Message bar, which is labeled iMessage if you selected an email address or Text Message if you selected a cell phone. The cursor moves into it.

7. Type the message you want to send in the Message bar.

8. Tap Send. The Send status bar appears as the message is sent; when the process is complete, you hear the message sent sound and the status bar disappears.

If the message is addressed to iMessage recipients, your message appears in a blue bubble in a section labeled iMessage. If the person to whom you sent the message enabled his read receipt setting, you see when he reads your message.

If you sent the message to a cell phone, you see your message in a green bubble. If the message is sent to a cell phone or includes a cell phone recipient, it appears in a section labeled Text Message.

When you send a message, you see a new conversation screen if the message was not sent to someone or a group of people with whom you were previously messaging. If you have previously sent messages to the same recipient or recipients, you move back to the existing conversation screen and your new message is added to that conversation instead.

If you've addressed the message to only one person, that person's name appears at the top of the screen. If the message is going to more than one recipient, the title of the screen is Group MMS (assuming MMS is enabled) or just Group if it is an iMessage conversation.

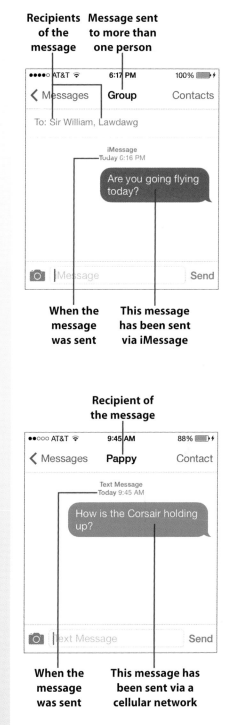

Recipients of the message

Message sent to more than one person

When the message was sent

This message has been sent via iMessage

Recipient of the message

When the message was sent

This message has been sent via a cellular network

TEXT ON

Following are some additional points to help you take your texting to the next level (where is the next level, anyway?):

- **iMessage or Cell**—If the recipient has an iOS device or Mac that has been enabled for iMessage, text messages are sent via iMessage when possible even if you choose the recipient's phone number (assuming you have an iMessages-enabled email address for that contact).

- **Group Messaging**—If you've enabled the Group Messaging setting, when you include more than one recipient, the title of the new screen becomes Group to indicate you are sending a group message. If all the recipients use the current version of the Messages app and have also enabled this setting, any messages sent in reply are grouped on one screen. If that isn't true, the messages are treated as if the Group Messaging setting is off.

- **No Group Messaging**—When you address a message to more than one person with Group Messaging disabled, it is sent to each person but becomes a separate conversation from that point on. If one or more of the recipients replies to the message, only you see the responses. In other words, replies to your messages are sent only to you, not to all the people to whom you sent the original message.

- **Larger Keyboard**—Like other areas where you type, you can rotate the iPhone to be horizontal where the keyboard is larger as is each key. This can make texting easier, faster, and more accurate.

- **Limits**—When you've enabled the Show Character Count setting, you see the number of characters in a message compared to the standard maximum number allowed for SMS messages (those sent via the cellular network), which is 160. The Messages app won't prevent you from sending messages with more than 160 characters, but it is a good idea to limit your messages to 160 or fewer. Not only is this good practice, but some devices will break up messages with more than 160 characters into multiple parts, which can disrupt what your message was intended to convey. (This doesn't apply to iMessages because its messages don't have a character limit.)

Receiving, Reading, and Replying to Messages

Text messaging is about communication, so when you send messages you expect to receive responses. And people can send new messages to you. The Messages app keeps messages grouped as a conversation consisting of messages you send and replies you receive.

Receiving Messages

When you aren't currently using the Messages screen in the Messages app and receive a new message (as a new conversation or as a new message in an ongoing conversation), you see, hear, and feel the notifications you have configured for the Messages app. (Refer to Chapter 4 to configure your message notifications.)

Swipe to the right on the notification to move into the Messages app to read the entire message

Message alert notification on the Lock screen

If you are on the Messages screen in the Messages app when a new message comes in, you hear and feel the new message notification but the alert does not appear.

New message received while using the Messages app

If a message is from someone to whom you have previously sent a message or received a message from and you haven't deleted all the messages to or from those recipients (no matter how long it has been since a message was added to that conversation), the new message is appended to an ongoing conversation and that conversation moves to the top of the list. If there isn't an existing message to or from the people involved in a new message, a new conversation is started and the message appears at the top of the list.

Speaking of Texting

Using Siri to hear and speak text messages is extremely useful. Check out Chapter 12, "Working with Siri," for examples showing how you can take advantage of this great feature.

Reading Messages

You can get to new messages you receive by doing any of the following:

Tap an alert to read a new message

- Tap the alert notification. You move into the message's conversation in the Messages app.

- Swipe to the right on a message notification when it appears on the Lock screen.

Conversations with new messages are marked with a blue dot

Tap a conversation with a new message to read the new message

- Open the Messages app and tap the conversation containing a new message; these conversations appear at the top of the Messages list and are marked with a blue circle. The conversation opens and you see the new message.

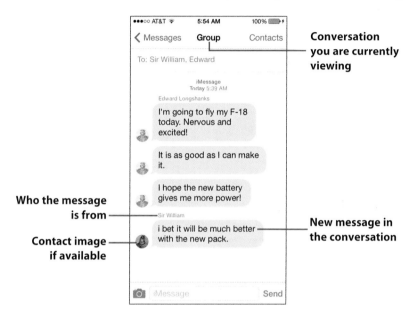

- If you receive a new message in a conversation that you are currently viewing, you immediately see the new message.

However you get to a message, you see the new message in either an existing conversation or a new conversation. The newest messages appear at the bottom of the screen.

Messages sent to you are on the left side of the screen and appear in a gray bubble. Just above the bubble is the name of the person sending the message; if you have an image for the contact, that image appears next to the bubble.

What's in a Name?

The Messages app displays names according to your Short Name settings for Contacts. For example, if you have the Short Name setting enabled and First Name Only selected, you see only the sender's first name. If you have the Prefer Nickname setting enabled and the sender has a nickname on her contact, the message is labeled with the nickname. Refer to Chapter 7 for information about configuring your contacts.

Replying to Messages

To reply to a message, read the message and do the following:

1. Read the most recent message.

2. Tap in the Message bar.

3. Type your reply.

4. Tap Send. (If the message will be sent via the cellular network, the Send button is green; if it will be sent via iMessage, it is blue.) The message is sent, and your message is added to the conversation. Messages you send are on the right side of the screen in a blue bubble if they were sent via iMessage or a green bubble if they were sent via the cellular network.

Mix and Match

The Messages app can switch between types of messages. For example, if you have an iMessages conversation going but can't access the iMessage service for some reason, the app can send messages as a cellular text. It can switch the other way, too. The app tries to send iMessages first if it can but chooses whichever method it can to get the messages through. (If you disabled the Send as SMS option, messages are only sent via iMessage.)

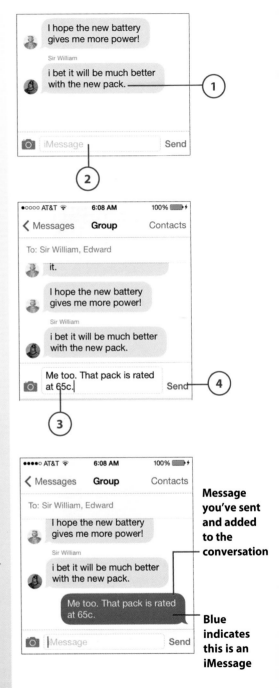

Message you've sent and added to the conversation

Blue indicates this is an iMessage

Having a Messages Conversation

Messaging is all about the back-and-forth communication with one or more people. You've already learned the skills you need so put them all together. You can start a new conversation by sending a message to one or more people with whom you don't have an ongoing conversation. Or, you can add to a conversation already underway.

Your message has been delivered

Your message has been read

The recipient is composing a response

1. Send a new message to a person or add a new message to an existing conversation. You see when your message has been delivered. If you sent the message to an individual person via iMessages and he has enabled his Read Receipt setting, you see when he has read your message and you see a people as he is composing a response. (If you are conversing with more than one person, the person doesn't have her Read Receipt setting enabled, or the conversation is happening via the cellular network, you don't see either of these.)

Seen But Not Read

Don't take the Read status too literally. All it means is that the conversation to which your message was added has been viewed. Of course, the Messages app can't know whether the recipient actually read the message.

As the recipient composes a response, you see a bubble on the screen where the new message will be when it is sent (again, only if it is an iMessage with a single individual). Of course, you don't have to remain on the conversation's screen waiting for a response. You can move to a different conversation or a different app. When the response comes in, you are notified per your notification settings.

2. Read the response.

3. Send your next message.

4. Repeat these steps as long as you want. Messages and conversations remain in the Messages app until you remove them, so you can have conversations that span long periods of time.

The iMessage Will Be With You...Always

Messages that are sent with iMessage move with you from device to device, so they appear on every device configured to use your iMessage account. Because of this, you can start a conversation on your iPhone while you are on the move and pick it up on your iPad or Mac later.

Working with Messages

As you send and receive messages, the interaction you have with each person or group becomes a separate conversation. A conversation consists of all the messages that have gone back and forth. You manage your conversations from the Messages screen.

Managing Messages Conversations

Use the Messages application to manage your messages.

1. On the Home screen, tap Messages.

   The Messages screen showing conversations you have going appears. Conversations containing new messages appear at the top of the list. The name of the conversation is the name of the person or people associated with it, or it might be labeled as Group if the app can't display the names. If a contact can't be associated with the person, you see the phone number or email address you are conversing with instead of a name.

Information Messages

Many organizations use messages to keep you informed. Examples are airlines that send flight status information, retailers who use messages to keep you informed about shipping, and so on. These messages are identified by a set of numbers that don't look like a phone number. You can't send a response to such messages; they are one-way only.

2. Swipe up and down the list to see all the conversations.

3. Tap a conversation you want to read or reply to. The conversation screen appears; the name of the screen is the person with whom you are conversing, her number if she isn't in your contacts list, or Group if the message includes multiple recipients.

If you have the badge enabled, you see the number of new messages on the Messages icon

Number of new messages in all conversations

Day or time of most recent message

Conversations with new messages

Who else is involved in the conversation

See the Time of Every Message

To see the time or date associated with every message the conversation being displayed, swipe to the left and hold your finger down on the screen. The messages shift to the left and the date or time of each message appears along the right side of the screen.

If a conversation involves only one other person, you see that person's name here instead of Group, and the To field is hidden

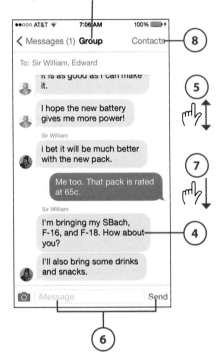

4. Read the new messages in the conversation. Your messages are on the right side of the screen in green (cell network) or blue (iMessage), whereas the other people's messages are on the left in gray. Messages are organized so the newest message is at the bottom of the screen.

5. Swipe up and down the conversation screen to see all the messages it contains.

6. To add a new message to the conversation, tap in the Message bar, type your message, and tap Send.

7. Swipe down the screen. As the screen scrolls down, you move back in time in the conversation.

8. To call or email the people in the conversation, or just to see their contact information, tap Contacts; this is Contact if only one other person is involved in the conversation. (You can also tap a name showing in the To section.) The people involved are shown along with icons for actions you can take.

9. To place a voice call or audio-only FaceTime call, tap the phone icon. If the person has a phone number configured, you're prompted to choose Voice Call or FaceTime Audio. When you make a choice, that call is placed. If the person only has an email address, an audio-only FaceTime call is placed. You move into the Phone or FaceTime app and use that app to complete the call. Move to the Home screen and tap Messages to return to the Messages app. (See Chapter 8, Communicating with the Phone and FaceTime Apps," for the details about these apps.)

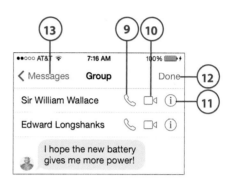

10. To place a FaceTime call, tap the video icon. You move into the FaceTime app to complete the call. When you're done, move to the Home screen and tap Messages to return to the Messages app.

11. To view the person's contact information, tap the info button.

12. When you're done with the contact information, tap Done.

13. When you're finished working with the conversation, tap Messages. You return to the Messages screen.

>>>Go Further

TEXT SHORTCUTS

You might find yourself using a lot of shorthand when you text to save time and taps. Sometimes shorthand is well understood, and sometimes it isn't. You can speed up text creation and reduce the number of taps required by configuring text shortcuts. Text shortcuts are better than shorthand because full words are used but you only have to tap the shortcut. You can create shortcuts for the phrases you use most often. For example, you might use the phrase "check this out" in your messages from time to time. You can create a shortcut—something like "cto"—and type that shortcut instead of the phrase. To set up your shortcuts, open the Settings app, tap General, and tap Keyboard. Swipe up the screen until you see the SHORTCUTS section. Tap Add New Shortcut. Type the phrase for which you are creating a shortcut in the Phrase box. Type the shortcut in the Shortcut box, and then tap Save. To enter the phrase, just type the shortcut you created and tap space. The phrase corresponding to the shortcut is entered. You can have as many shortcuts as you want, and they are available everywhere you type text.

Adding Images and Video to Conversations

You can include any image, photo, or video stored on your iPhone in a text conversation, or you can take a photo or video to include in a message. This is a great way to share photos and videos.

Limitations, Limitations

Not all cell carriers support MMS messages (the type that can contain images and video), and the size of messages can be limited. Check with your carrier for more information about what is supported and whether there are additional charges for using MMS messages. If you're using iMessages, you don't have this potential limit. Also be sure your recipient can receive MMS messages before sending one.

1. Move into the conversation with the person to whom you want to send a photo, or start a new conversation with that person.

2. Tap the Camera button.

3. To capture a new photo or video, tap Take Photo or Video and move to step 8; to send a photo or video already stored on your iPhone, tap Choose Existing.

4. Tap the source containing the photos you want to send. (For more information about viewing sources of photos, see Chapter 15, "Working with Photos and Video You Take with Your iPhone.")

5. Swipe up or down the screen until you see the photo you want to send.

6. Tap the photo you want to send.

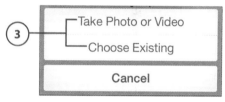

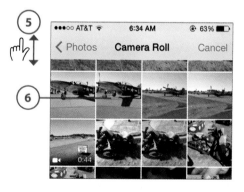

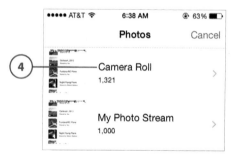

7. Tap Choose. You move back to the conversation and see the image in the Send box; move to step 10.

8. Take the photo or video you want to send. (For more information about taking photos or videos, see Chapter 15.)

9. Tap Use Photo.

10. Type the message you want to send with the photo or video. (You can just tap Send without adding a message.)

11. Tap Send. The message and photo or video are sent.

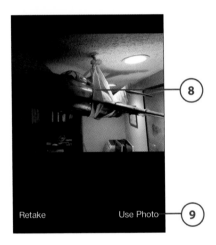

This Isn't Houston, but There Is a Problem

If a message you try to send is undeliverable or has some other problem, it is marked with an exclamation point inside a red circle. Tap that icon and tap Try Again to attempt to resend the message.

Sharing with Messages

You can share all sorts of information via Messages from many apps, such as Safari, Contacts, Maps, and so on. From the app containing the information you want to share, tap the Action button. Then tap Messages. The information with which you are working is automatically added to a new message. Use the Messages app to complete and send the message.

Working with Images or Video You Receive in Messages

When you receive a photo or video, it appears in a thumbnail along with the accompanying message.

To copy the photo or video and paste it into another app, tap and hold on it; when the Copy command appears, tap it. To forward it to someone else, tap and hold on the image. On the resulting menu, tap More. Tap the forward button located in the bottom-right corner of the screen. Complete the New Message that appears to send the photo along with a message.

To view a photo or video, tap it. You see the photo or video at full size.

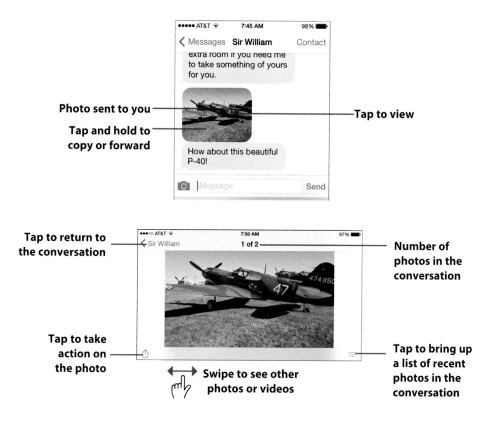

If there is more than one photo or video in the conversation, you see the number of them at the top of the screen. Swipe to the left or right to move through the available photos. You can rotate the phone, zoom, and swipe around the photo just like viewing photos in the Photos app. You can watch a video in the same way, too.

Tap the list button to see a list of the recent photos in the conversation. Tap a photo on the list to view it.

Tap the Action button to share the photo with others via a message, email, tweet, Facebook post, and so on.

To move back to the conversation, tap the Back button (which is labeled according to the people involved with the conversation).

Deleting Messages and Conversations

Old text conversations never die, nor do they fade away. All the messages you receive from a person or that involve the same group of people stay in the conversation. Over time, you can build up a lot of messages in one conversation. And you can end up with lots of conversations.

Long Conversation?

When a conversation gets very long, the Messages app won't display all its messages. It keeps the more current messages visible on the conversation screen. To see earlier messages, swipe down on the screen to move to the top and tap Load Earlier Messages.

When a conversation gets too long or if you just want to remove messages from a conversation, take these steps:

1. Move to a conversation containing an abundance of messages.

2. Tap and hold on a message you want to delete.

3. Tap More. The message on which you tapped is marked with a check mark to show it is selected.

Delete Them All!

To delete the whole conversation, instead of performing step 4, tap Delete All, which appears in the upper-left corner of the screen. Tap Delete Conversation. The conversation and all its messages are deleted.

4. Tap other messages you want to delete. They are marked with a check mark to show you have selected them.

5. Tap the Trash can icon.

6. Tap Delete X Messages, where X is the number of messages you have selected. The messages are deleted and you return to the conversation.

Pass It On

If you want to send one or more messages to someone else, perform steps 1–3. Tap the Forward button that appears in the lower-right corner of the screen. A new message is created and the messages you selected are pasted into it. Select or enter the recipients to whom you want to send the messages, and tap Send.

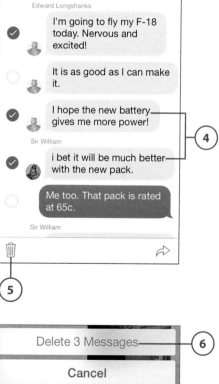

Deleting Conversations

If a conversation's time has come, you can delete it.

1. Move to the Messages screen.

2. Swipe to the left on the conversation you want to delete.

3. Tap Delete. The conversation and all the messages it contains are deleted.

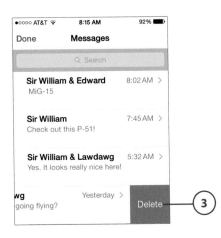

TEXTING LINGO

>>>Go Further

People frequently use shorthand when they text. Here is some of the more common shorthand you might see. This list is extremely short, but there are many websites dedicated to providing this type of information if you are interested. One that boasts of being the largest list of text message acronyms is www.netlingo.com/acronyms.php.

- FWIW—For What It's Worth
- LOL—Laughing Out Loud
- ROTFL—Rolling On the Floor Laughing
- CU—See You (later)
- PO—Peace Out
- IMHO—In My Humble Opinion
- TY—Thank You
- RU—Are You
- BRB—Be Right Back
- CM—Call Me
- DND—Do Not Disturb

- EOM—End of Message
- FSR—For Some Reason
- G2G —Got to Go
- IDK—I Don't Know
- IKR—I Know, Right?
- ILU—I Love You
- NM or NVM—Never Mind
- OMG—Oh My God
- OTP—On The Phone
- P911—Parent Alert
- PLZ—Please

Go here to figure out
where and when you're
supposed to be

Use this app
to remind
yourself of…
anything

Tap to configure
calendar and
reminder settings

In this chapter, you explore all the calendar and reminder functionality your iPhone has to offer. Topics include the following:

→ Setting calendar, reminder, and time preferences
→ Working with calendars
→ Working with reminders

11

Managing Calendars and Reminders

When it comes to time management, your iPhone is definitely your friend. Using the iPhone's Calendar app, you can view calendars that have been synchronized among all your devices, such as computers, iPads, and so on. Of course, you can also make changes to your calendars on your iPhone and then sync them with your other devices so you have consistent information no matter which device you happen to be using at any time. The Reminders app ensures you don't forget tasks or anything else you want to remember. Before jumping into these great apps, take some time to configure them to work the way you want.

Setting Calendar, Reminder, and Time Preferences

There are a few time, date, reminders and calendar settings you should configure before you start using your iPhone to manage your calendars and time. The first step in configuring all these settings is to tap the Settings icon on the Home page; you move to the Settings screen and can continue with the steps in each task.

Setting Your Calendar Preferences

Use the calendar settings to configure the Calendar app to your preferences:

1. On the Settings screen, tap Mail, Contacts, Calendars.

2. Swipe up until you see the Calendars section.

3. To be alerted when you receive event invitations, ensure that the New Invitation Alerts switch is set to the on position (green); if you don't want these notifications, set the switch to off (white).

4. Tap Time Zone Support.

5. Set the Time Zone Support switch to off (white) to have the iPhone automatically display meeting and event times on its calendars based on the iPhone's current time zone (you learn how the iPhone gets its time zone in the next task), and then skip to step 10. To have events shown according to a time zone you configure, set the Time Zone Support switch to on (green) and move to the next step.

6. Tap Time Zone.

7. Type the name of the city you want to use to set the time zone. As you type, cities that match your search are shown.

8. When the city you want to use appears on the list, tap it. You move back to the Time Zone Support screen, and the city you selected is shown.

9. Tap Mail.

10. To set the period of time over which past events are synced, tap Sync.

••••○ AT&T 🛜   5:57 AM   95% 🔋
‹ Mail... **Time Zone Support**

Time Zone Support

Time Zone   San Francisco ›

Time Zone Support always shows event dates and times in the time zone selected for calendars.

When off, events will display according to the time zone of your current location.

••○○ AT&T 🛜   5:57 AM   94% 🔋
‹ Back   **Time Zone**

🔍 las

Las Vegas, U.S.A.

••○○ AT&T 🛜   5:57 AM   95% 🔋
‹ Mail... **Time Zone Support**

Time Zone Support

Time Zone   Las Vegas ›

Time Zone Support always shows event dates and times in the time zone selected for calendars.

When off, events will display according to the time zone of your current location.

CALENDARS

New Invitation Alerts

Time Zone Support   Off ›

Sync   Events 3 Months Back

11. Tap the amount of time you want events to be synced; tap All Events to have all events synced, regardless of their age. If you select one of the time periods shown, such as Events 3 Months Back, only events that occurred within the past three months will be shown on your calendars.

12. Tap Mail.

13. Tap Default Alert Times.

14. Tap the item for which you want to set a default alert time, such as Birthdays.

15. Tap the alert time you want to be the default for the type of item you tapped in step 14. For example, if you tap Birthdays and then tap 1 week before, you're alerted one week before any birthdays on your calendar. (These settings are just the defaults; you can change the alerts for specific events by editing them in the Calendar app, as you learn later in this chapter.)

16. Tap Back.

17. Set the default alert times for the other items using steps 14–16.

18. Tap Mail.

19. Tap Start Week On.

20. Tap the day of the week you want to be first.

21. Tap Mail.

22. Tap Default Calendar. The list of all calendars configured on your iPhone appears. If you currently have only one calendar configured on your phone, this option doesn't appear and you can skip to step 25.

23. Tap the calendar you want to be the default, meaning the one that is selected automatically when you create new events. You can change this to any calendar for a specific event you create or change.

24. Tap Mail.

25. If you share your calendars with other people, slide the Shared Calendar Alerts switch to the on (green) position if you want to be alerted when changes, such as a new event being added, occur to a shared calendar.

Default Alert Times   >

Start Week On ———————————   **19**

●●●○○ AT&T 🜂   5:59 AM   93% ▰▸

21 ‹ Mail...   **Start Week On**

Sunday (United States default) ———— ✓   **20**

Monday

Tuesday

Start Week On   Sunday (United S... ›

Default Calendar   Brad's_Calendar →   **22**

New events created outside of a specific calendar will default to this calendar.

●●●●○ AT&T 🜂   5:59 AM   93% ▰▸

24 ‹ Mail...   **Default Calendar**

EXCHANGE

● Calendar

● tripit

GMAIL

● sorebruiser@gmail.com

ICLOUD

23 ● Brad's_Calendar   ✓

● Home

Default Calendar   Brad's_Calendar ›

New events created outside of a specific calendar will default to this calendar.

Shared Calendar Alerts   ⬤———   **25**

When enabled, you will be notified about new, modified, or deleted shared events.

>>>Go Further

MORE ON TIME ZONE SUPPORT

The Time Zone Support feature can be a bit confusing. If Time Zone Support is on, the iPhone displays event times according to the time zone you select on the Time Zone Support screen. When Time Zone Support is off, the time zone used for calendars is the iPhone's current time zone, which is set automatically based on your cellular network or your manual setting. This means that when you change time zones (automatically or manually), the times for calendar events shift accordingly.

For example, suppose Indianapolis (which is in the Eastern time zone) is the iPhone's current time zone. If you enable Time Zone Support and then set San Francisco as the time zone, the events on your calendars will be shown according to the Pacific time zone because that is San Francisco's time zone rather than Eastern time (Indianapolis's time zone).

In other words, when Time Zone Support is on, the dates and times for events become fixed based on the time zone you select for Time Zone support. If you change the time zone the iPhone is on, no change to the dates and times for events is shown on the calendar because they remain set according to the time zone you selected in the Time Zone Support. Therefore, an event's actual start time might not be accurately reflected for the iPhone's current time zone because it is based on the fixed Time Zone Support city.

In any case, you need to be aware of the time zone you are using on your calendars (the one you select if Time Zone Support is on or the time zone of your current location if it is off) and the time zone with which events are associated. With some calendar applications (such as Calendar on a Mac), you can associate an event with a specific time zone when you schedule it. This is helpful because the event should be shown according to the iPhone's current time zone even when Time Zone Support is on.

Setting Your Time and Date Preferences

The time and date settings are among the most important on your iPhone. Here's how to configure them:

1. On the Home screen, tap Settings.

2. Tap General.

3. Swipe up the screen.

4. Tap Date & Time.

5. To have the iPhone display time on a 24-hour clock, slide the 24-Hour Time switch to the on (green) position. The iPhone displays and tracks time using a 24-hour scale. To use a 12-hour clock, slide the slider to the off (white) position.

6. If you don't want the iPhone to set its time and date automatically using its cellular network time (in other words, you want to manage your iPhone's time and date manually), slide the Set Automatically switch to the off (white) position. Two additional options appear; follow steps 7–15 to use those options, or skip to the next section if you leave the Set Automatically switch in the on (green) position.

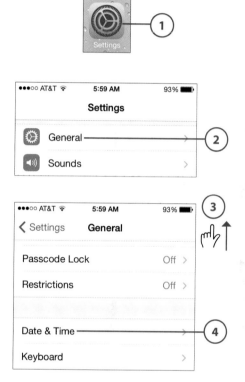

Auto Time

In most situations, you should allow your iPhone to set the time and date automatically. This is less work for you and also ensures that your iPhone is always using an accurate time even as you travel among different time zones. However, there can be occasions (rare though they are) during which your iPhone can't pull the correct time information from a cell network, so you should know how to set the time manually.

7. Tap Time Zone.

8. Type the name of the city you want to use to set the time zone. As you type, the Settings app lists the cities that match your search. If the specific city you want doesn't appear on the list, search for one that is in the same time zone as the city you want to use to set the iPhone's time zone.

9. When the city you want to use appears on the list, tap it. You move back to the Date & Time screen, which shows the city you selected in the Time Zone field.

10. Tap the current date and time. Controls to enable you to change this date and time appear.

11. Swipe up or down on the date wheel until the date you want to set as the current date appears in the center.

12. Swipe up or down on the hour wheel until the correct hour is shown.

13. Scroll and select the current minute in the same way.

14. Swipe up or down on the hour wheel to select AM or PM.

15. Tap General. The iPhone's date and time are set according to your preferences.

Setting Your Reminder Preferences

The Reminders app is a useful tool to help you remember "stuff." Configure the way it works as follows:

1. On the Settings screen, tap Reminders.

2. Tap Sync.

3. Tap how far back you want reminders to be kept on your lists of reminders (when you complete a reminder, it disappears from the active lists regardless of this setting).

4. Tap Reminders.

5. Tap Default List.

6. Tap the reminder list you want to be the default. Each account can have multiple lists associated with it, such as your task list in Outlook and a reminder list stored through your iCloud account. You can set one of these to be the default, which means that when you create reminders not associated with a specific list, they are added to the default list. (As you learn later in this chapter, the Reminders app can manage multiple lists of reminders for you.)

Notifications

The Calendar and Reminders apps can communicate with you in various ways, such as displaying alerts or banners, indicating when and how many invitations you've received and so on. Configuring notifications to suit your preferences will make these apps even more valuable. Configuring notifications is explained in the section called "Setting Up Notifications and the Notification Center" in Chapter 4, "Configuring an iPhone to Suit Your Preferences."

Working with Calendars

The Calendar app helps you manage your calendars; you'll notice I wrote *calendars* rather than *calendar*. That's because you can have multiple calendars in the app at the same time. To use the most cliché example, you might have a calendar for work and one for your personal life. Or, you might want a calendar for your travel plans and then share that calendar with people who care about your location.

In most cases, you start by adding existing calendar information from an Exchange, iCloud, or similar account or by using iTunes to sync your calendars with a calendar application on your computer. From there, you can view your calendars, add or change events, and much more directly in the Calendar app. Any changes you make in the Calendar app are automatically made in all the locations that use calendars from the same account, or you can manually sync calendar information via iTunes on your computer.

The best option for storing your calendar information is using online accounts (iCloud, Exchange, Google, and so on) because you can easily access that information from many devices, and your calendars are kept in sync automatically. To learn how to configure an online account for calendar information, refer to Chapter 3, "Setting Up iCloud and Other Online Accounts."

Viewing Calendars and Events

You use the Calendar app to view and work with your calendars, and you can choose how you view them, such as by month, week, or day.

To get into your calendars, move to the Home screen and tap Calendar (which shows the current day and date in its icon). The most recent screen you were viewing appears. There are three basic modes you use in the app. The one in which you'll spend most of your time in the app displays your calendars in various views, such as showing a month or a week and day. Another mode is the Calendars tool that enables you to choose and edit the calendar information that is displayed. The third mode is your Inbox, which you use to work with event invitations you receive.

 The badge indicates how many invitations to events you have received

Configuring Calendars

To configure the calendar information you see in the app, perform the following steps:

1. Tap Calendars. If you don't see this at the bottom of the screen, you are already on the Calendars screen (look for "Calendars" at the top of the screen), in which case you can skip this step. Or, you might have only one calendar on your iPhone and you don't need to set which calendar to display. In that case, you can skip to the next set of tasks.

   The Calendars screen displays the calendars available, organized by the account from which they come, such as ICLOUD, EXCHANGE, GMAIL, and so on. Under each account, the individual calendars are provided by the account. By default, all your calendars are displayed, which is indicated by the check marks next to the calendars' names.

2. Tap a calendar with a check mark to hide it. The check mark disappears and the calendar is hidden. (The calendar is still there, you just won't see it when you are viewing calendars.)

3. To show a calendar again, tap its name. It is marked with a check mark and appears when you are viewing calendars.

4. Tap the info button to see or change a calendar's information settings (not all types of calendars support this function).

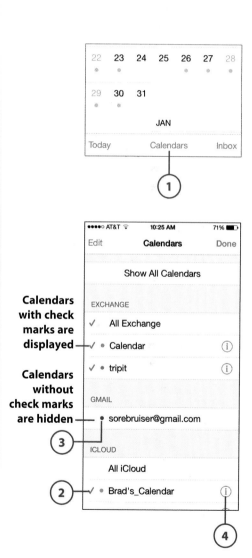

Calendars with check marks are displayed

Calendars without check marks are hidden

5. Change the name of the calendar if you want to.

6. Tap the color you want events on the calendar to appear in.

7. Tap Done.

8. Edit other calendars as needed.

9. Tap Done. The app moves into viewing mode, and the calendars you enabled are displayed.

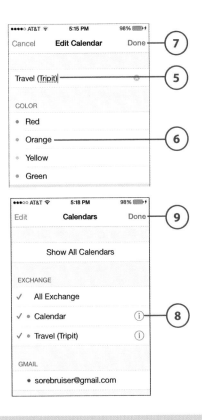

ALL OR NOTHING

You can make all your calendars visible by tapping the Show All Calendars button at the top of the screen; tap Hide All Calendars to do the opposite. After all the calendars are shown or hidden, you can tap individual calendars to show or hide them. You can show all the calendars from the same account by tapping the All command at the top of each account's calendar list, such as All Exchange to show all your Exchange calendars. Tap this again to hide all the account's calendars.

Another Way to Edit

You can also edit a calendar by tapping Edit at the upper-left of the Calendars screen and then tapping the calendar you want to edit. When you are done editing calendars, tap Done.

Navigating Calendars

The Calendar app uses a hierarchy of detail to display your calendars. The lowest level of detail, but longest timeframe displayed, is the year view. Next is the month view, which shows more detail but covers a shorter timeframe. This is followed by the week/day view; showing the highest level of detail is the event view.

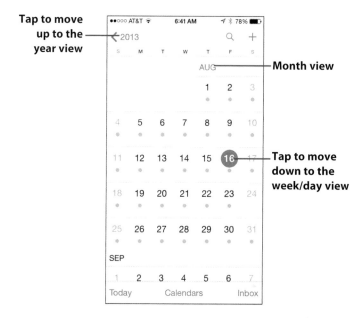

Tap to move up to the year view

Month view

Tap to move down to the week/day view

To move down in the hierarchy, you tap something on the view you are seeing. For example, to change from the month view to the week/day view, you tap the day in which you are interested. That day and the week it is in appear using the week/day view.

To move up in the hierarchy, you tap the back link, which is always located in the upper-left corner of the screen. This is labeled to indicate where you will move when you tap it. For example, if you are in the month view, this link is labeled with the month's year, indicating that when you tap the link, you'll see that year. Likewise, when you are viewing the week/day view, the link has the name of the month that week is in.

To move to the year view so you are set up for the next task, keep tapping the link in the upper-left corner of the screen until it disappears (which happens when you are in the year view).

Viewing Calendars

You can view your calendars from the year level all the way down to the day/week view. It's easy to move among the levels to get to the time period you want to see. Here's how:

1. Starting at the year view, swipe up and down until you see the year in which you are interested. (If you aren't in the year view, keep tapping the back button located in the upper-left corner of the screen until the back button disappears.)

2. Tap the month in which you are interested. The days in that month display, and days with events are marked with a dot.

3. Swipe up and down the screen to view different months.

4. To see the detail for a date, tap it. On the resulting screen, just below the Back button, which is labeled with the current month, are the days in the week in focus. The date in focus is highlighted with a black circle. Below this area is the detail for the day in focus showing the events on that date.

Today Is the Day

To quickly move to the current day, tap Today, located at the bottom of the screen.

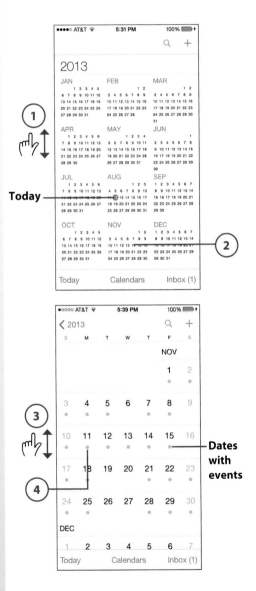

5. Swipe to the left or right on the dates or date being displayed to change the date for which detailed information is being shown.

6. Swipe up or down on the date detail to browse all its events.

7. Tap an event to view its detail.

8. Swipe up and down the screen to see all of the event's information.

9. Tap Edited by to see contact information for the person who last edited the event.

10. Tap Day to move back to the week/day view.

11. Tap the Month link to move back to the month view.

12. To view your calendars in the multiday view, rotate your iPhone so it is horizontal. You can do this while in the week/day view or the month view.

13. Swipe left or right to change the dates being displayed.

14. Swipe up or down to change the time of day being displayed.

15. Tap an event to see its detail.

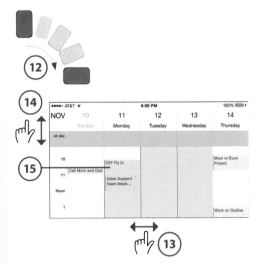

Adding Events to a Calendar

There are a number of ways you can add events to your calendar. You can create an event in an app on a computer, website, or other device and sync that event onto the iPhone through an online account or by syncing with iTunes on a computer. You can also manually create events in the Calendar app on the iPhone. Your events can include a lot of detail. You can choose to just create the basic information on your iPhone while you are on the move and complete it later from a computer or other device, or you can fill in all the details directly in the Calendar app.

1. Tap the Add button, which appears in the upper-right corner of any of the views when your phone is vertical. The initial date information is taken from the date currently being displayed, so you can save a little time if you view the date of the event before tapping the Add button.

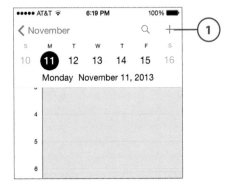

2. Tap in the Title field and type the title of the event.

3. Tap the Location bar and type the location of the event.

4. To set the event to last all day, set the All-day switch to the on position (green); to set a specific start and end time, leave this in the off (white) position.

5. To set a timeframe for the event, tap Starts. The date and time tool appears.

6. Swipe up or down on the date wheel until the date on which the event starts appears in the center.

7. Swipe up or down on the hour wheel until the event's starting hour is shown. (If you are configuring an all-day event, this step doesn't apply.)

8. Scroll and select the starting minute in the same way. (If you are configuring an all-day event, this step doesn't apply.)

9. Swipe up or down on the hour wheel to select AM or PM. (If you are configuring an all-day event, this step doesn't apply.)

10. Tap Ends.

11. Use the date and time tool to set the ending date and time for the event; these work the same way as for the start date and time.

12. Tap Ends. The date and time tool closes.

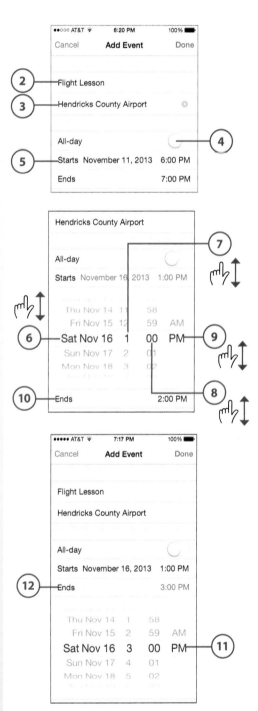

13. To make the event repeat, tap Repeat and follow steps 14–19. (For a nonrepeating event, skip to step 20.)

14. Tap the frequency with which you want the event repeated, such as Every Day, Every Week, and so on.

No Change Needed

If you don't make a change to one of the settings, such as on the Repeat screen, you need to tap the Add Event link to get back to the Add Event screen.

15. Tap End Repeat to set a time at which the event stops repeating.

16. To have the event repeat ad infinitum, tap Never and skip to step 19.

17. To set an end to the repetition, tap On Date.

18. Use the date tool to set the date for the last repeated event.

19. Tap Add Event.

20. To invite others to the event, tap Invitees; if you don't want to invite someone else, skip to step 23.

21. Enter the email addresses for each person you want to invite; as you type, the app tries to identify people who match what you are typing. You can tap a person to add him to the event. You can also use the Add button to choose people from your Contacts.

22. Tap Add Event.

23. To set an alert for the event, tap Alert; if you want to use the default alert, skip to the step 25.

24. Tap when you want to see an alert for the event.

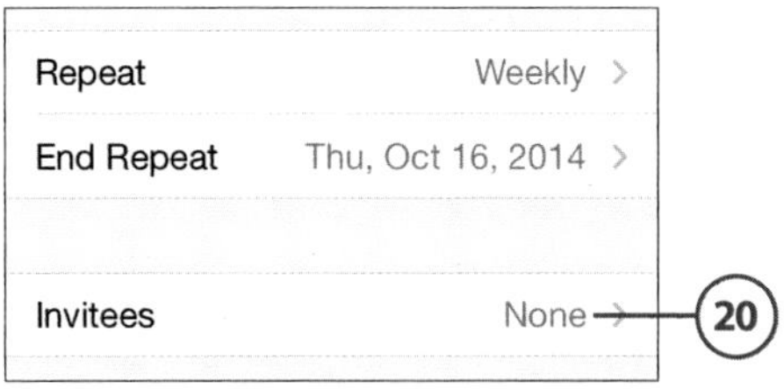

Repeat	Weekly >
End Repeat	Thu, Oct 16, 2014 >
Invitees	None → 20

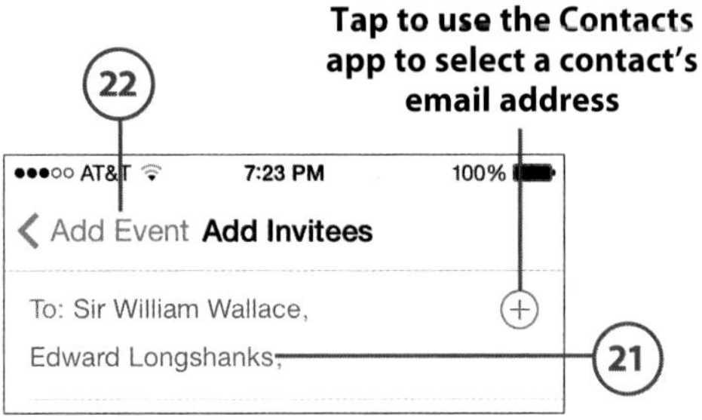

Tap to use the Contacts app to select a contact's email address

●●●○○ AT&T 📶 7:23 PM 100%

‹ Add Event **Add Invitees**

To: Sir William Wallace, Edward Longshanks; ⊕ 21

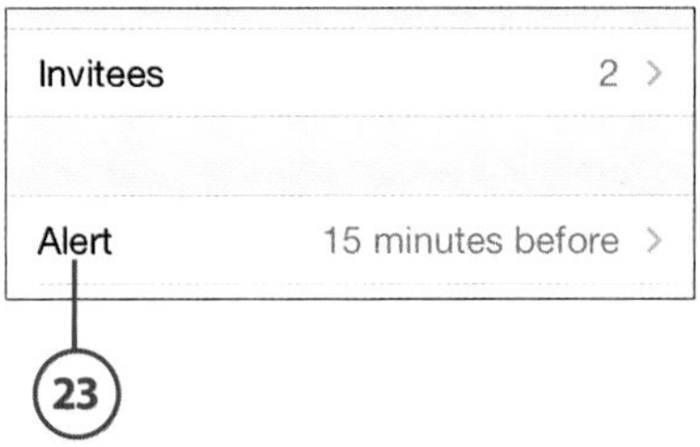

| Invitees | 2 > |
| Alert | 15 minutes before > |

23

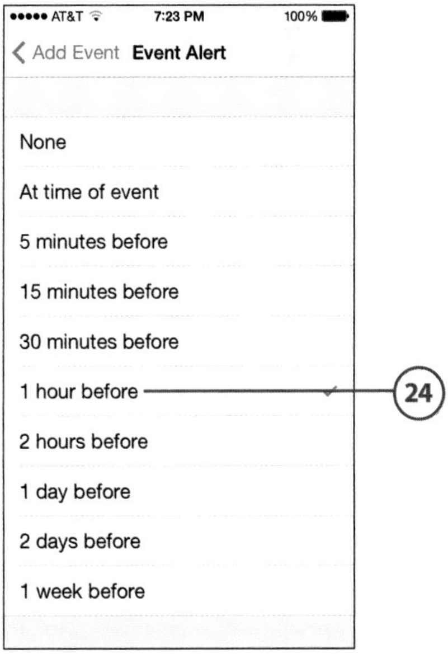

●●●●● AT&T 📶 7:23 PM 100%

‹ Add Event **Event Alert**

None
At time of event
5 minutes before
15 minutes before
30 minutes before
1 hour before ✓ 24
2 hours before
1 day before
2 days before
1 week before

25. To set a second alert, tap Second Alert.

26. Tap when you want to see a second alert for the event.

27. To change the calendar with which the event is associated, tap Calendar (to leave the current calendar selected, skip to step 29).

28. Tap the calendar with which the event should be associated.

29. To indicate your availability during this event, tap Show As.

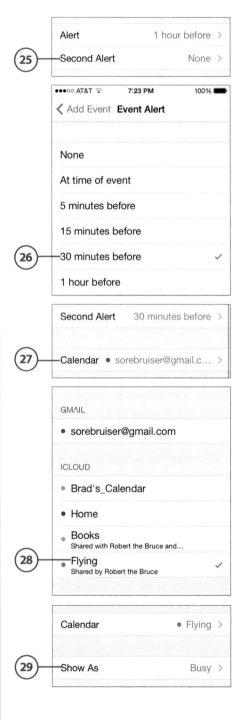

30. Tap the availability status you want to indicate during the event.

31. To enter a URL associated with the event, tap in the URL field and type the URL.

32. Tap Notes and type information you want to associate with the event.

33. Tap Done. The event is added to the calendar you selected, and invitations are sent to the email addresses you entered. Any alarms trigger according to your settings.

New event on the calendar

Searching Calendars

You can search for events to locate specific ones quickly and easily. Here's how:

1. Tap the Search tool. A list of all your events displays.

2. Tap in the Search box.

3. Type your search term. The events shown below the Search bar become limited to those that contain your search term.

4. Swipe up or down the list to review the results.

5. Tap an event to see its detail.

6. Swipe up or down the event's screen to review its information.

7. Tap Back to return to the results.

8. Continue reviewing the results until you get the information for which you were searching.

9. Tap Done to exit the search mode or the Clear button to clear the search but remain in search mode.

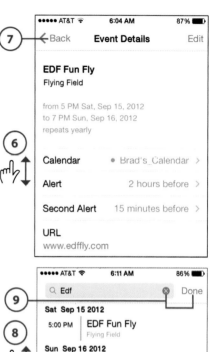

Working with Invitations

When someone invites you to an event, you receive an invitation notification in the Calendar app. You can accept these invitations, at which point the event is added to your calendar. You can tentatively accept, in which case the event is added to your calendar with a tentative status, or you can decline the event if you don't want it added to your calendar.

1. Tap the Calendar app icon when you see the badge on the app's icon indicating how many invitations you've received but not dealt with.

Invitation Notifications

You can use the Notification settings to configure how the Calendar app informs you about invitations you receive. Refer to Chapter 4 for details. You can move to an invitation directly from the related notification.

2. Tap Inbox (the number in parenthesis is the number of invitations you have received).

3. If you have multiple invitations, swipe up and down the screen to browse them.

4. If you see enough information about the event to be able to make a decision about it, tap the Accept, Decline, or Maybe button. The event is added to your calendar if you tap Accept or Maybe. If you tap Decline, it is not added.

5. Tap an invitation to see its detail.

6. Swipe up and down the Event Details screen to see all its details.

7. To choose the calendar on which the event should be shown, tap Calendar, and on the resulting screen, tap the calendar on which you want to store the event. Tap the back button located in the upper-left corner of the screen to return to the Event Details screen.

8. View details about whom the invitation is from and other attendees (if there are any) by tapping their areas. You move to detail screens for each. Tap the back button located in the upper-left corner of those screens to return to the Event Details screen.

9. If you want to change the event's alarm, tap Alert and use the resulting Alert screen to choose an alert.

10. To set your availability during the event, tap Show As and then tap your status during the event; in most cases, you will tap Busy so others who want to schedule time with you will see that you aren't available.

11. To see how the proposed event relates to other events on the same date, tap Show in Calendar. The date on which the event is being proposed displays, which can help you decide whether you want to accept it.

12. Indicate what you want to do with the event by tapping Accept, Maybe, or Decline. If you tap Accept or Maybe, the event is added to the calendar with the status you indicated. If you tap Decline, the event is not placed on a calendar, and the recipient receives a notice that you have declined.

    After you make a decision, you move to the Inbox. Any events you have accepted, indicated maybe, or declined disappear from the list of events. Events that you have accepted from another device, such as from a computer, are shown with an OK button.

13. Tap OK to clear events you've dealt with on other devices.

14. If you've dealt with all the invitations you have received, the Inbox closes; if you don't want to deal with all the invitations at the moment, tap Done to close the Inbox. You move to the calendar. If you accepted or indicated maybe, the event is added to your calendar.

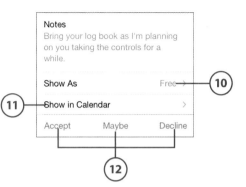

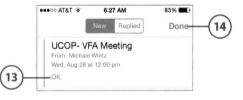

Sharing Calendars

You can share your calendars with other people to enable them to both see and change your calendar, according to the permissions you provide. If you set the View & Edit permission, the person is able to both see and change the calendar. If you set someone's permission to View Only, she can see, but not change, the calendar.

1. Move to the Calendars screen. Calendars you are sharing are indicated by the Shared with name, text just under the calendar name, where *name* is the name of the person with whom you are sharing the calendar.

2. To see who is currently sharing a calendar, or to share a calendar, tap the Info button for the calendar to be shared. If the calendar is currently being shared, the SHARED WITH section appears on the Edit Calendar screen, which contains the names of and permissions granted to the people who are sharing the calendar. The status of each person's acceptance is shown under his name (Accepted, Pending, or Declined).

3. To share a calendar with someone else (whether it is currently shared or not), tap Add Person.

4. Type and select the person's email address, and then tap Add. You return to the Edit Calendar screen, and see the person you added on the SHARED WITH list. The status next to each invitee's name is Pending until he accepts or rejects your invitation.

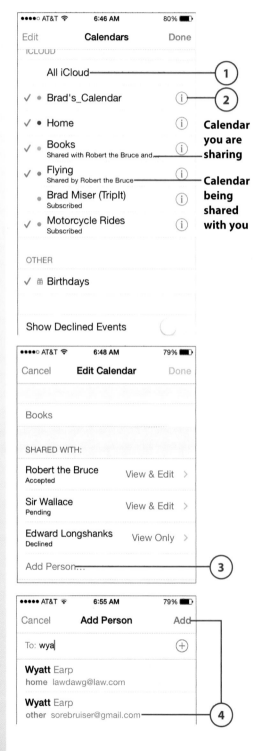

5. If you don't want the person to be able to change the calendar, tap View & Edit.

6. Slide the Allow Editing switch to off (white); the person will be able to view but not change the calendar.

7. When you're done configuring the calendar, tap Done.

●●●●● AT&T 🗢	6:55 AM	79% ▪▬▶
Cancel	**Edit Calendar**	Done

Books

SHARED WITH:

Robert the Bruce
Accepted   View & Edit >

Edward Longshanks
Declined   View Only >

Wyatt Earp
Pending   View & Edit ⟶ ⑤

●●●●○ AT&T 🗢	6:55 AM	79% ▪▬▶

‹ Edit Calendar **Wyatt Earp**

Wyatt Earp
sorebruiser@gmail.com   >

Allow Editing   ⬤ ⟶ ⑥

Allow this person to make changes to the calendar.

●●●●● AT&T 🗢	6:55 AM	79% ▪▬▶
Cancel	**Edit Calendar**	Done ⟶ ⑦

Managing Calendars, Events, and Invitations

Following are some more points about the Calendar app you might find helpful:

- When viewing the week/day view, the current date is highlighted in a red circle at the top of the screen. You can move to the current day by tapping Today at the bottom of the screen.

- You can see today's events at any time by swiping down from the top of the screen to open the Notification Center. On the Today tab is a summary of your events for the day. Swipe up and down on the Calendar section to see the entire day's events.

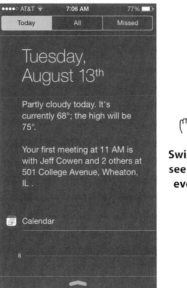

Swipe to
see your
events

- When an event's alarm goes off, an onscreen notification appears (according to the notification settings for the Calendar app) and the calendar event sound you've selected plays. When a banner notification appears, you see the event's name and location. You can tap the event to view its details or ignore it and it moves off the screen after a few moments. When an alert notification appears, the event's title, location (if one is set), and time appear. You have to take some action. You can tap OK to dismiss the alert or tap Options to see additional choices. On the Options dialog box, tap Snooze to snooze the alarm, View Event to see its details, or Close to dismiss the alarm.

Alert style event notification

- If you've invited people to an event, open its detail screen. On the Event Details screen, the statuses of the various meeting invitees appear. You see sections for each status, such as Accepted, No Reply, and so on. Tap the section showing who was invited; the Invitees screen displays and lists each invitee. Next to each name is an icon indicating the person's status for the event—for example, if the person hasn't replied, a ? icon is displayed; if he has accepted, a check mark is displayed, and so on. You can tap a person's name to see her contact information.

- If an event gets canceled after you accept it or indicated maybe, you receive a notification in your Inbox that displays a strikethrough through the event's title. Tap Delete to remove the event from your calendar.

- You can review invitations to which you've responded by moving into the Inbox and tapping the Replied tab. On this tab, you see the various invitations you've received grouped by the email address to which they were sent. Tap an invitation to see its detail. Tap Done to close the Inbox.

- Siri is useful for working with calendars, especially for creating events. See Chapter 12, "Working with Siri," for detailed information about using Siri.

- You can publish a calendar by making it public. When you do this, anyone who can access the shared calendar on the Web can view, but not change, the published calendar. To make a calendar public, move to its Edit Calendar screen and slide the Public Calendar switch to on (green). The calendar is published. Tap Share Link. Then tap mail to send the link via email, tap Message to send it via the Messages app, or tap Copy to copy the link so you can paste elsewhere. Tap AirDrop to share the link that way. The link can be clicked to view your calendar or, if the person uses a compatible application, to subscribe to it so it appears in her calendar application.

Telling Time

Your iPhone is also handy for knowing what time it is. The time is displayed at the top of many screens (it is hidden when an app uses the full screen or when an app's controls are hidden). It also appears on the Lock screen. To get the time quickly while your iPhone is locked, just press the Home or Sleep/Wake button. The Lock screen appears and displays the time and date. Who needs a watch when you have an iPhone?

Working with Reminders

The Reminders app does just what it sounds like it does, which is to remind you about things. The things it reminds you about are up to you; these might be to-do items/tasks, thoughts you want to be reminded to follow up on later, and so on. Reminders are also useful for lists of things you need to get or want to remember to think about later. Just as you can have multiple calendars to manage your events, you can have multiple lists for your reminders.

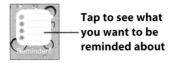

Tap to see what you want to be reminded about

When you open the Reminders app by tapping its icon on the Home screen, you might see the screen showing all the reminder lists you have available. To move to a specific list of reminders, tap it.

When you open the Reminders app, you might see a specific list of reminders. To move from a reminder list to the screen showing the list of your reminder lists, tap the stack of lists at the bottom of the screen.

You can see how easily you can move between these two views. There are a couple of other views you can use, too (as you learn in a bit), but you'll likely spend most of your time on these two.

Name of reminder list

Number of active reminders on this list

Reminder lists

Tap to open a list

Reminder list

Reminders

Complete radio button

Tap to move back to the list of reminder lists

Creating Reminders

You can manually create reminders by performing the following steps:

1. Tap the Reminders icon on the Home screen.

2. If you see a reminder list instead of the list of reminder lists, skip this step. If you see the list of your reminders lists, tap the list on which you want to create a new reminder.

3. Tap in an open reminder space. The keyboard appears.

4. Type the reminder.

5. To create more reminders, tap the return button on the keyboard.

6. Create the next reminder.

7. Repeat steps 5 and 6 until you've created all the reminders you want.

8. Tap Done. You can stop here if you only want basic information in the reminder, which is just the reminder's text (the app won't actually remind you unless you configure the reminder for a specific date and time). Continue these steps to fully configure a reminder.

9. Tap the reminder you want to configure.

10. Tap the info button.

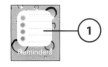
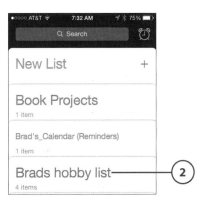
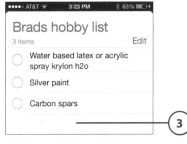
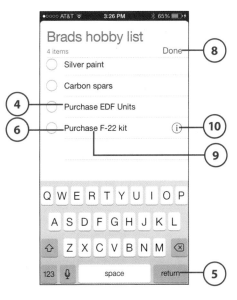

11. Slide the Remind me on a day switch to on (green) to set a specific date and time on which you want to be reminded; if you don't want the reminder to be time based, skip to step 16 instead.

12. Tap Alarm.

13. Use the date and time tool to set a time for the reminder; these work just like they do when you create an event (see "Adding Events to a Calendar," earlier in this chapter).

14. To have the reminder repeated, tap Repeat, and on the resulting screen tap the repeat interval.

15. If you configured the reminder to repeat, tap End Repeat (this appears only when you have set a reminder to repeat). Use the tools on the End Repeat screen to set the end of the repeating event, and tap Done (this works just like setting the Repeat).

16. Slide the Remind me at a location switch to on (green) to set the reminder to be activated based on you leaving or arriving at a location; if you don't want to set this, skip to step 20.

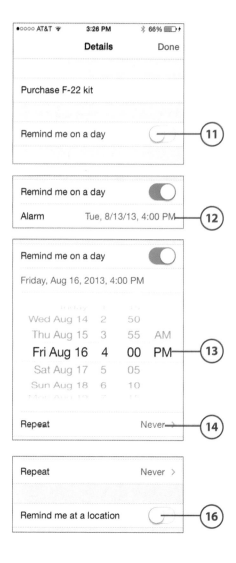

Location Services Required

If you haven't enabled Location Services on your iPhone and for the Reminders app specifically, you're prompted to do so the first time you enable the Remind me at a location feature. You only have to do this the first time or after you disable the required Location Services.

17. Tap Location.

18. Tap Current Location, tap one of the addresses that appear on the list, or enter an address to associate the reminder with one of those locations.

19. Tap When I arrive to be reminded when you arrive at the location you selected, or tap When I leave to be reminded when you leave the location you selected.

20. Drag the circle to be larger or smaller to change the distance from the location at which the reminder is triggered. As you drag, the distance appears.

21. Tap Details.

Location and Time Interactions

If you set both a date/time reminder and a location reminder, you're reminded at the earliest event, such as the time passing or the change in location you set.

22. Tap the priority you want to associate with the reminder.

23. Tap List.

24. Tap the list on which you want to store the reminder (reminder lists are organized by the accounts from which they come).

25. Tap Notes.

26. Type notes you want to associate with the reminder.

27. Tap Done. The reminder is complete and you return to the reminder list, where you see the reminder you created including the alert time and location and notes.

Arriving: 5312 Michael Ct Brown...

Priority None ! **!!** !!!

List RC Projects >

Notes

No shipping charge until 9/15

Organizing Reminders with Lists

You can keep multiple lists of reminders for different purposes. Following are some tips to help you with your lists:

- The title of the current list is shown at the top of the list screen.

Reminder list —— RC Projects

1 item Edit

!! Purchase F-22 kit
8/16/13, 4:00 PM
Arriving: IN ...
No shipping charge until 9/15

Swipe down to change lists

New reminder

- To move between your lists, swipe down from the top of the screen. The list of your lists appears. Tap the list you want to view; the list and the reminders it contains appear.

New List + —— Tap to create a new list

Book Projects
No items

Brad's_Calendar (Reminders)
1 item

The number of reminders on a list ——

Brads hobby list —— Tap the list you want to view
5 items

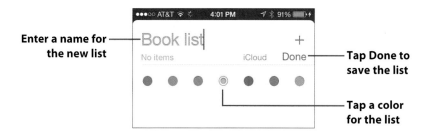

Enter a name for the new list

Tap Done to save the list

Tap a color for the list

- To create a new list, tap New List. Tap the account on which you want to store the list, such as Exchange or iCloud. Type the new list's name. Tap the color you want to associate with the list, and then tap Done. You can then assign reminders to the new list.

- To change a list, move to its screen and tap Edit. Change the list's name and color if needed, and tap Done.

- To delete a list, tap Edit while on its screen. Tap Delete List and confirm this is what you want to do at the prompt. The list and all the reminders it contains are deleted.

Managing Reminders

When you have reminders set up, you can manage them using some of the tips in the following list:

- When a reminder's Remind Me time or location event occurs, you see an alert according to the notification setting for the Reminders app. If it is a banner, you can tap it to view the reminder's details or ignore it. If it is an alert, you must dismiss it or view the reminder's details.

- To mark a reminder as complete, tap its radio button. The next time you move back to the list, the reminder doesn't appear (it is moved onto your Completed list).

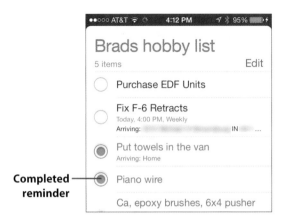

* To see your completed reminders, tap Show Completed, located at the bottom of the screen. All the reminders on the list appear. Those whose radio buttons are filled with the list's color are complete. Tap Hide Completed, also located at the bottom of the screen, to show only active reminders again.

* To see your reminders organized by date instead of by list, move to the Lists screen and tap the alarm clock icon located in the upper-right corner of the screen. The Scheduled screen shows your reminders based on the time and date with which they are associated.

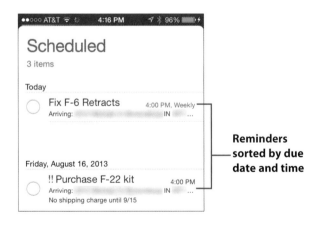

- To change or delete a reminder, tap it. Edit its text if needed. Tap the Information button to change its other details. Tap Done when you've made all the changes you want to make.

- To delete a reminder, swipe across it to the left and tap Delete.

>>Go Further

DO MORE WITH TIME—THE CLOCK APP

The Clock app is quite useful. It has four modes. World Clock enables you to set clocks for various time zones so you can get the time anywhere in the world with just a glance. Alarm enables you to configure time-based alarms. Stopwatch enables you to time events just as with a physical stopwatch. Timer enables you to set a time, and the app will countdown from that time and send an alarm when it is done. The Clock app is easy to get to also; just swipe up from the bottom of the screen to open the Control Center and then tap the Clock icon.

Speak to Siri to send and hear messages, create events and reminders, make calls, and much more

Go here to set up Siri

Dictate text input instead of typing

In this chapter, you'll learn about all the great things you can do with your iPhone by speaking to it. Topics include the following:

→ Setting up Siri
→ Understanding Siri's personality
→ Learning how to use Siri by example

Working with Siri

Siri gives you the ability to talk to your iPhone to control it and to dictate text. Siri also works with lots of iPhone apps—this feature enables you to accomplish many tasks by speaking instead of using your fingers on the iPhone's screen. For example, you can hear, create, and send text messages; reply to emails; make phone and FaceTime calls; create and manage events and reminders; and much more. Using dictation, you can speak text into any supported app instead of typing.

Siri is a great way to use your iPhone, especially when you are working in handsfree mode.

One especially good thing about Siri is that you don't have to train it to work with your voice; you can speak to it normally and Siri does a great job understanding what you say. Also, you don't have to use any specific kind of phrases when you have Siri do your bidding. Simply talk to Siri like you talk to people (well, you probably won't be ordering other people around like you do Siri, but you get the idea).

Because Siri works so well and quickly, you might not realize that your iPhone has to be connected to the Internet for Siri and dictation to work. That's because the words you speak are sent over the Internet, transcribed into text, and then sent back to your iPhone. If your iPhone isn't connected to the Internet, this can't happen, and if you try to use it, Siri reports that it can't complete its tasks. Because your iPhone is likely to be connected to the Internet most of the time (via Wi-Fi or a cellular network), this really isn't much of a limitation—but it is one you need to be aware of.

To start using Siri, configure it on your iPhone. Then, start speaking to your phone and be prepared to be amazed by how well it listens! You'll find many examples in this chapter to get you going with specific tasks; from there, you can explore to learn what else Siri can do for you.

Setting Up Siri

Before you can speak to Siri, perform the following steps to configure it:

1. Tap Settings.

2. Tap General.

3. Tap Siri.

4. If the Siri switch is off (white), slide it to on (green). If the switch is already on, skip to step 6.

5. Tap Enable Siri.

6. Tap Language.

7. Swipe up and down the screen to see all the languages Siri can use.

8. Tap the language you want to use to speak to Siri.

9. Tap Siri.

10. Tap Voice Gender. Not all languages support this feature; if you don't see it, the language you selected in step 8 does not and you can skip to step 13.

11. Tap the gender of the voice you want Siri to use to speak to you.

12. Tap Siri.

Siri sends information like your voice input, contacts, and location to Apple to process your requests.

Enable Siri — (5)

Cancel

●●●●● AT&T 🤶 6:58 AM ✳ 100% 🔋➕

❮ General   **Siri**

Siri

Siri helps you get things done just by asking. You can make a phone call, send a message, dictate a note, or even find a restaurant. About Siri and Privacy…

Language   English (United States)→ — (6)

●●●●● AT&T 🤶 6:58 AM ✳ 100% 🔋➕

❮ Siri   **Language** — (9)

Chinese (Cantonese - Hong Kong)

Chinese (Mandarin - China)

Chinese (Mandarin - Taiwan) — (7)

English (Australia)

English (Canada)

English (United Kingdom)

English (United States) — ✓ — (8)

Language   English (United States) ❯

Voice Gender   Female→ — (10)

●●●○○ AT&T 🤶 6:59 AM ✳ 100% 🔋➕

❮ Siri   **Voice Gender** — (12)

Male

Female — ✓ — (11)

13. Tap Voice Feedback. Siri provides you with audible confirmation when you speak to it. For example, when you tell it to create a reminder, Siri speaks the reminder it thinks you told it to create so you know what it is doing without having to look at the screen.

14. If you always want Siri to hear voice feedback, tap Always. If you only want voice feedback when you are operating in handsfree mode, such as when you are using the iPhone's EarPods or a Bluetooth headset, tap Handsfree Only. If you choose Handsfree Only, when you aren't using a headset, you will see Siri's feedback on the screen, which is typically faster than the voice feedback.

15. Tap Siri.

16. Tap My Info.

17. Use the Contacts app to find and tap your information. Siri often uses your name when it speaks to you; this tells Siri what name to use when it addresses you, among other things.

18. If you want Siri to activate when you raise the phone to your ear (like you would to talk on the phone), slide the Raise to Speak switch to the on position (green). As long as you aren't on a phone call, you can activate Siri by lifting the phone to your ear. Whether this is on or not, you can always activate Siri by pressing and holding the Touch ID/Home button or by pressing and holding the middle button on the EarPod controls.

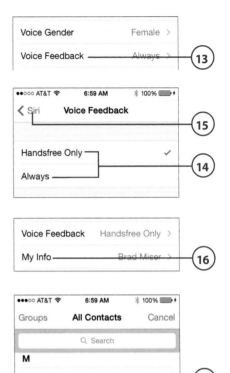

Understanding Siri's Personality

Siri's personality is pretty simple because it follows a consistent pattern when you use it, and it always prompts you for input and direction when needed.

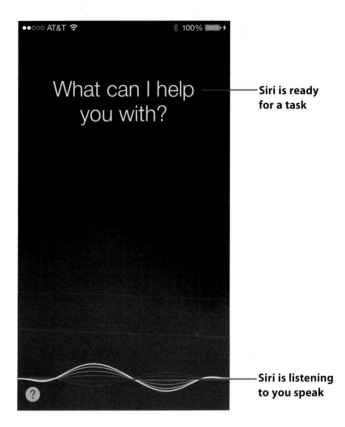

Siri is ready for a task

Siri is listening to you speak

Activate Siri by pressing and holding the Touch ID/Home button, pressing and holding the center part of the buttons on the EarPods, or lifting the iPhone to your ear (if you've enabled that setting) until you hear the Siri chime. (If Siri is already active, tap the Microphone icon.) This puts Siri in "listening" mode and the "What can I help you with?" text appears along with a line at the bottom of the screen that shows when Siri is hearing you. This screen indicates Siri is ready for your command.

Speak your command or ask a question. As you speak, the line at the bottom of the screen oscillates to show you that Siri is hearing your input. When you stop speaking, Siri goes into processing mode; the line is replaced by a rotating circle to show you that Siri is thinking.

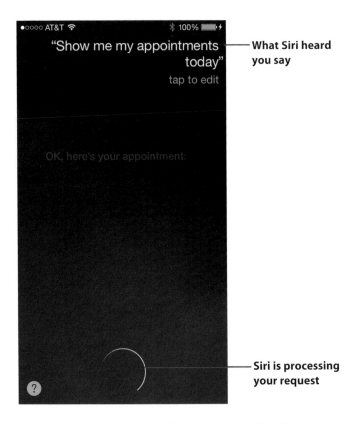

"Show me my appointments today"

tap to edit

What Siri heard you say

OK, here's your appointment:

Siri is processing your request

After Siri interprets what you've said, it provides two kinds of feedback to confirm what it heard: it displays what it heard on the screen and provides audible feedback to you (unless you've set it for Handsfree Only and aren't using a headset). Siri then tries to do what it thinks you've asked and shows you the outcome.

If it needs more input from you, you're prompted to provide it and Siri moves into "listening" mode automatically. If Siri asks you to confirm what it is doing or to make a selection, do so. Siri completes the action and displays what it has done; it also audibly confirms the result unless you've selected Handsfree Only and aren't using a headset.

If you want Siri to do more for you, tap the Microphone icon and speak your command. If you want to work with the object Siri created for you in its associated app, tap the object Siri presents.

When you're done with Siri, you can lock the iPhone or tap the Touch ID/ Home button to do something else.

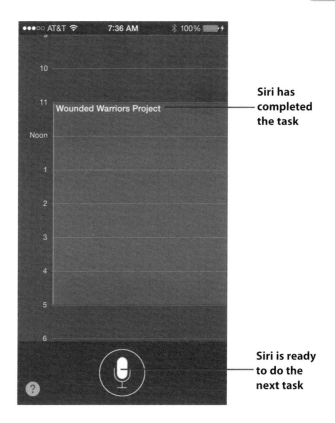

Siri has completed the task

Siri is ready to do the next task

Siri uses this pattern for all the tasks it does, but often Siri needs to get more information from you, such as when there are multiple contacts that match the command you've given. Siri prompts you for what it needs to complete the work. Generally, the more specific you make your initial command, the fewer steps you have to work through to complete it. For example, if you say "Meet Will at the park," Siri may require several prompts to get you to tell it who Will is and what time you want to meet him at the park. If you say "Meet William Wallace at the park on 10/17 at 10 am," Siri will likely be able to complete the task in one step.

Siri is amazingly flexible in how you can speak to it and the accuracy with which it interprets spoken input. However, using Siri effectively requires a bit of practice to learn the most efficient and effective ways to provide commands based on how you speak and what you want Siri to do. In many cases, Siri is a very good way to accomplish tasks, while for others, it might actually slow you down.

The best way to learn how and when Siri can help you is to try it—a lot. You find a number of examples in the rest of this chapter to get started. Don't be timid about trying Siri. You can't really hurt anything by trying it—as long as you pay attention to Siri's feedback so you can stop a task if it is going awry. For example, Siri might misinterpret a command and start doing something you don't want it to do, such as placing a call you didn't intend to make. You can always abort tasks Siri starts as long as you are paying attention and stop the task before it is completed.

Siri is amazing, but it does have some limitations, as all technology does. There are some things it seems like it should be able to do but might not be able to do. The list of what Siri can't do is getting shorter all the time, so make sure you try the tasks for which you might want to use Siri.

Following are some other Siri tidbits:

- If Siri doesn't automatically quit "listen" mode after you've finished speaking, tap the oscillating line. This stops "listen" mode and Siri starts processing your request. You need to do this more often when you are in a noisy environment because Siri might not be able to accurately discern the sound of you speaking versus the ambient background noise.

- If you are having trouble with Siri understanding commands, speak a bit more slowly and make sure you firmly end your words. If you tend to have a very short pause between words, Siri might run them all together, making them into something that doesn't make sense or that you didn't intend.

- However, you can't pause too long between words or sentences because Siri interprets pauses to mean that you are done speaking and goes into processing mode. Practicing with Siri will help you develop a good balance between speed and clarity.

- If Siri doesn't understand what you want, or if you ask it a general question, it will often perform a web search for you. Siri takes what it thinks you are looking for and does a search. You then see the results page for the search Siri performed but have to manually open and read the results by tapping the listing you want to see. It opens in the Safari app.

- When Siri presents information to you on the screen, such as events it has created, you can often tap that information to move into the app with which it is associated. For example, when you tap an event, you move into the Calendar app. For more complicated items, such as creating an event that has a lot of detail, use the following pattern to work with Siri. Use Siri to create the basic information, such as the event's title, time, and date, and when Siri creates it, tap it to move into the associated app to add more detail using that app's tools, such as inviting people to an event, changing the calendar it's associated with, and so on.

- When Siri needs direction from you, it presents your options on the screen, such as Yes, Cancel, Confirm, lists of names, and so on. You can speak these items or tap them to select them.

- Siri is very useful for some tasks, such as creating reminders, responding to text messages, and so on, but not so useful for others, such as inputting search criteria, because it can take longer to use Siri than to just type your input.

- Siri is not so good at editing text you dictate. In many cases, your only option is to replace the text you've dictated to change it. For short text blocks, such as text messages or tweets, this can be fine, but for longer blocks of text, you have to use the virtual keyboard to make changes to just portions of text. You can use Siri to quickly dictate blocks of text and then edit the text using the iPhone's text editing tools.

- To use Siri effectively, you should experiment with it by trying to say different commands or similar commands in different ways. For example, when creating events, you can include more information in your initial command to reduce the number of steps because Siri doesn't have to ask you for more information. Saying "Meet with Wyatt Earp at 10am on 11/3 in my office" requires fewer steps than saying "Meet with Wyatt Earp" because you've given Siri all the information it needs to complete the task. How you speak impacts the sort of commands that will work best for you. It can take a little practice to make Siri work effectively for you and to learn when Siri actually helps you complete tasks you want to do versus just being a cool way to accomplish them. Sometimes, experimentation leads you to unexpected, but very useful, results.

- Lots of apps support Siri commands, but over time, we can expect even more apps to be able to accept Siri control. As the apps you use get updated, keep your eyes out for any that add Siri support so you can start speaking to them as well.

- When Siri can't complete a task that it thinks it should be able to do, it usually responds with the "I can't connect to the network right now," or "Sorry, I don't know what you mean." This indicates that your iPhone isn't connected to the Internet, the Siri server is not responding, or Siri just isn't able to complete the command for some other reason. If your iPhone is connected to the Internet, try the command again.

- When Siri can't complete a task that it knows it can't do, it will respond by telling you so. Occasionally, you can get Siri to complete the task by rephrasing it, but typically you have to use an app directly to get it done.

- If you have a passcode set to protect your iPhone's data (which you should), Siri might not be able to complete some tasks because the phone is locked. If that happens, simply unlock your phone and continue with what you were doing.

- Siri sees all and knows all (well, not really, but it sometimes seems that way). If you want to be enlightened, try asking Siri questions. Some examples are "What is the best phone?," "Will you marry me?," "What is the meaning of life?," "Tell me a joke," etc. Some of the answers are pretty funny, and you don't always get the same ones so Siri can keep amusing you. I've heard it even has responses if you curse at it, though I haven't tried that particular option.

Learning How to Use Siri by Example

As mentioned, the best way to learn about Siri is to use it. Following are a number of tasks for which Siri is really helpful. Try these to get some experience with Siri and then explore on your own to make Siri work at its best for you.

Using Siri to Make Voice Calls

You can use Siri to make calls by speaking. This is especially useful when you are using your iPhone in handsfree mode.

1. Activate Siri by pressing and holding the Touch ID/Home button.

2. Say "Call *name numberlabel*," where *name* is the person you want to call and *numberlabel* is the label of the specific number you want to call, such as Home, Work, iPhone, and so on. Siri identifies the contact you named. If the contact has only one number or you were specific about which number you want to call, Siri

places the call and you move into the Phone app. If you weren't specific about the number you want to call (you simply said "Call *name*") and the person has multiple numbers, you see a list of the numbers while Siri lists the numbers available and asks you which number to use.

Siri has found multiple numbers for Wyatt

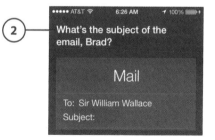

3. Speak the label for the number you want to call, or tap it. Siri dials the number for you and you move to the Phone app as if you had dialed the number yourself.

Placing FaceTime Calls

You can also use Siri to make FaceTime calls by saying "FaceTime *name*."

Composing New Email with Siri

To create email with Siri, do the following:

1. Activate Siri by pressing and holding the Touch ID/Home button.

2. Say "Send email to *name*," where *name* is the person you want to email. Siri creates a new email addressed to the name you spoke. (If the recipient has more than one email address, Siri prompts you to choose the address you want to use.) Next, Siri asks you for the subject of the email.

More Than One Recipient?

To send an email to more than one recipient, say "and" between each name as in, "Send email to William Wallace and Edward Longshanks." Siri adds each address before and after the "and."

3. Speak the subject of the email. Siri prompts you for the body of the message.

4. Speak the body of the email. As you speak, you can include punctuation; for example, to end a sentence, say the word "period" or to end a question, say the words "question mark." When Siri completes the email, it displays the message on the screen and prompts you to send it.

5. Say "send" to send the email or "cancel" to delete it. If you say "send," Siri sends the message, confirms it will be sent, and plays the sent mail sound when it is.

ANOTHER WAY TO ACTIVATE SIRI

If you are using the iPhone's EarPods, you can activate Siri by pressing and holding the center button of the control on the right EarPod's wire. When you've held the button long enough, you hear Siri's activation chime and are ready to speak your command.

Replying to Emails with Siri

You can also use Siri to speak replies to emails you've read. Here's how:

1. Open the message to which you want to reply.

2. Activate Siri by pressing and holding the Touch ID/Home button.

3. Say "reply." Siri prompts you for what you want your reply to say.

4. Complete and send the reply; this works just like when you create a new message.

Having Messages Read to You

The Messages app is among the best to use with Siri because you can speak just about any task you would normally do with messages. Especially useful is Siri's ability to read new messages to you. When you receive new text messages, do the following to have Siri read them to you:

1. When you receive a text notification, activate Siri by pressing and holding the Touch ID/Home button.

2. Speak the command "Read text messages." Siri reads all the new text messages you've received, announcing the sender before reading each message. You have the option to reply (covered in the next task) or have Siri read the message again.

   Siri only reads new text messages to you when you aren't on the Messages screen. If you've already read all your messages and you aren't in the Messages app, when you speak the command "Read text messages," Siri tells you that you have no new messages.

Siri is reading a text message

Reading Old Messages

To read an old message, move back to the conversation containing the message you want to hear. Activate Siri and say the command "Read text message." Siri reads the most recent text message to you.

DOING MORE IN EMAIL WITH SIRI

Following are some other ways to use Siri for email:

- If you tell Siri to "Read email," Siri tells you how many emails are in your Inboxes and starts reading the time and date of the most recent email message followed by the subject and sender of the message. Siri then does the same for the next email until it has read through all of them. You can tap an email message to read it yourself, but Siri can't read the content of email messages to you.

- To edit a message you have composed using the keyboard, tap it. It opens in the Mail app and you can change and send it from there.

- To edit an email Siri created, say "Change." Siri prompts you to change the subject, change the message, cancel it, or send it. If you choose one of the change options, you can replace the subject or the body of the message. To change just some of the subject or body or to change the recipients, tap the message and edit it in the Mail app.

- You can start a new and completely blank email by saying "New email." Siri prompts you for the recipients, subject, and body.

- You can address a new email and add the subject with one statement, such as "Send email to William Wallace about flying."

- You can retrieve your email at any time by activating Siri and saying "Check email." Siri checks for new email and then announces how many emails you have received since the oldest message in your Inboxes was received.

- You can determine if you have emails from a specific person by asking something like, "Any email from William Wallace?" Siri's reply includes the number of emails in your Inboxes from William and displays them on the screen. Tap an email to read it.

- You can forward an email you are reading by saying "Forward this email" and then following Siri's lead to complete the process.

Replying to Messages with Siri

You can also use Siri to speak replies to messages you've received. Here's how:

1. Listen to a message.

2. At the prompt, say "Reply." Siri prepares a reply to the message.

3. Speak your reply. Siri displays your reply.

4. At the prompt, say "Send" to send it, "Cancel" to delete it, or "Change" to replace it. If you send the message, Siri confirms it was sent.

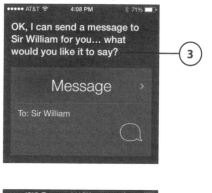

Sending New Messages with Siri

1. Activate Siri by pressing and holding the Touch ID/Home button.

2. Say "Send text to *name*," where *name* is the person you want to text. Siri confirms your command and prepares to hear your text message.

3. Speak your message. Siri listens and then prepares your message.

4. If you want to send the message, say "Send." Siri sends the message.

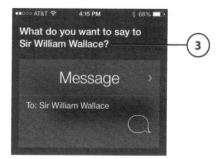

DOING MORE TEXTING WITH SIRI

Following are some other ways to use Siri with messaging:

- If you say "Change" when you are creating a message, Siri prompts you with four options, which are Cancel, Change, Review, and Send. If you say "Review," Siri reads your message back to you. If you say "Cancel," Siri stops the process and deletes the message.

- To send a text message to more than one recipient, say "and" between each name, as in, "Send text to William Wallace and Edward Longshanks."

- You can speak punctuation, such as "period" or "question mark" to add it to your message.

- You can tap buttons that Siri presents on the screen, such as Send or Cancel, to take those actions on the message you are working on.

- Messages you receive or send via Siri are stored in the Messages app just like messages you receive or send by tapping and typing.

- You can dictate into a text message you start in the Messages app (you learn about dictating later in this chapter).

Using Siri to Create Events

Siri is useful for capturing meetings and other events you want to add to your calendars. To create an event by speaking, do the following steps:

1. Activate Siri by pressing and holding the Touch ID/Home button.

2. Speak the event you want to create. There are a number of variations in what you can say. Examples include "Set up a meeting with William Wallace on Friday at 10 am," "Doctor appt on Thursday at 1 pm," "Meet Edward at 2 pm on October 20," "Meet Tim at the park on Saturday at 3 pm," and so on. Siri is pretty flexible about what you say. Like all tasks, Siri provides a confirmation of what you asked. If you have any conflicts with the event you are setting up, Siri lets you know about them.

Invitees

If you include the name of someone for whom you have an email address, Siri automatically sends invitations. If you include a name that matches more than one contact, Siri prompts you to choose the contact you want to invite. If the name doesn't match a contact, Siri enters the name but doesn't send an invitation.

3. Say "Confirm" if you don't have any conflicts or "Yes" if you do and you still want to have the appointment confirmed; you can also tap Confirm. Siri adds the event to your calendar. Say "Cancel" to cancel the event.

4. To add more information to an event Siri has created for you, tap it on the confirmation screen. You move into the Calendar app and can edit the event just like events you create within the app.

Using Siri to Create Reminders

Using Siri to create reminders is one of the most useful things you can do with Siri, assuming you find reminders useful of course. Here's how:

1. Activate Siri by pressing and holding the Touch ID/Home button.

2. Speak the reminder you want to create. There are lots of ways to do this. Examples include "Remind me to buy the F-15 at Banana Hobby," "Remind me to finish chapter 10 at 10 am on Saturday," "Remind me to buy milk when I leave home," and so on. Siri provides a confirmation of what you asked. If you didn't mention a time or date when you want to be reminded, Siri prompts you to provide the details of when you want to be reminded.

3. Speak the date and time when you want to be reminded. If you included a date and time in your original reminder request, you skip this step. Siri shows you the reminder it is going to create.

4. To create the reminder, say "Yes" or "Confirm," or to prevent it from being created, say "Cancel." If you confirmed the reminder, Siri adds it to your reminders.

5. To add detail to the reminder, tap it. You move into the Reminders app and can add more information to the reminder as you can when you create one manually.

GOING FURTHER WITH SIRI TO MANAGE TIME

>>>Go Further

Following are some other ways to use Siri with the Calendar, Reminders, and Clock apps:

- You can change events with Siri, too. For example, if you have a meeting at 3 p.m., you can move it by saying something like "Move my 3 pm meeting to Friday at 6 pm."

- You can get information about your events with Siri by saying things such as "Show me today's appointments," "Do I have meetings on November 3?," "What are my appointments tomorrow?," and so on. Siri tells you how many events you have and shows you what they are on the screen. You can tap any event to view it in the Calendar app.

- You can speak to your iPhone to set alarms. Tell Siri what you want and when you want the alarm to be set. For example, you can say something like "New alarm *alarmname* 6 am tomorrow," where *alarmname* is the label of the alarm. Siri sets an alarm to go off at that time and gives it the label you speak. It displays the alarm on the screen along with a status button so you can turn it off if you change your mind. You don't have to label alarms, and you can just say something like "Set alarm 6 am tomorrow." However, a label can be useful to issue other commands. For example, you can turn off an alarm by saying "Turn off *alarmname*." Any alarms you create with Siri can be managed just like alarms you create directly in the Clock app.

- To set a countdown timer, tell Siri to "Set timer for x minutes," where x is a number of minutes (you can do the same to set a timer for seconds or hours, too). Siri starts a countdown for you and presents it on the screen. You can continue to use the iPhone however you want. When the timer ends, you see and hear an alert. You can also reset the time, pause it, and so on by speaking.

- You can get information about time by asking questions, such as "What time is it?," "What is the date?," and so on. You can add location information to the time information, too, as in "What time is it in London, England?"

- Tapping any confirmation Siri displays takes you back into the related app. For example, if you tap a clock that results from your asking what time it is, you can tap that clock to move into the Clock app. If you ask about your schedule today, you can tap any of the events Siri presents to move back into the Calendar app to work with them.

- When you use Siri to create events and reminders, they are created on your default calendar (events) or reminder list (reminders).

Using Siri to Get Information

There are lots of ways to use Siri to get information. There are lots of types information waiting for your command, such as topic information, places in your area, and so on. Just try speaking what you want to learn to best get the information you need. Here's an example looking for pizza places in my area:

1. Activate Siri by pressing and holding the Touch ID/Home button.

2. Say something like, "Show me pizza restaurants close to me." Siri presents a list of results that match your query. (You must have Location Services enabled for this to work. Refer to Chapter 4, "Configuring an iPhone to Suit Your Preferences," for information about configuring Location Services.)

You can also get information about topics. Siri responds by conducting a web search and showing you the result. For example, suppose you want to learn about William Wallace. Activate Siri and say, "Tell me about William Wallace." Siri responds with information about your topic. You can have Siri read the information by activating Siri and saying "Read." Siri reads the results (this doesn't always work; it works best when the results are presented via Wikipedia or something similar).

If you like pizza (or just about anything else), Siri can help you find it.

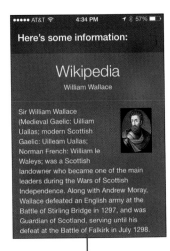

Want to learn about something? Just ask Siri.

Using Siri to Play Music

You can also play music by telling Siri which music you want to hear.

1. Activate Siri by pressing and holding the Touch ID/Home button.

2. Tell Siri the music you want to hear. There are a number of variations in what you can say. Examples include "Play album Time of My Life," "Play song Gone by Switchfoot," "Play playlist Jon McLaughlin," and so on. Siri provides a confirmation of what you asked and begins playing the music.

3. To move into the Music app to control the music with your fingers, tap Show Now Playing.

●●●●○ AT&T 🤖   4:39 PM   ⁕ 52% ▭⊃

Now playing album 'Time of My Life'...

Show Now Playing ────────────── ③

MORE SPOKEN COMMANDS FOR MUSIC

There are a number of commands you can speak to find, play, and control music (and other audio). "Play *artist*" plays music by the artist you speak. "Play *album*" plays the album you name. In both cases, if the name includes the word "the," you need to include "the" when you speak the command. "Shuffle" plays a random song. "Play more like this" uses the Genius to find songs similar to the one playing and plays them. "Previous track" or "next track" does exactly what they sound like they do. To hear the name of the artist for the song currently playing, say "Who sings this song?" You can shuffle music in an album or playlist by saying "Shuffle playlist *playlistname*." You can stop the music, pause it, or play it by speaking those commands.

>>>Go Further

Using Siri to Get Directions

With Siri, it's easy to get directions—you don't even have to stop at a gas station to ask.

1. Activate Siri by pressing and holding the Touch ID/Home button.

2. Speak something like "Show me directions from Indianapolis Motor Speedway to Lucas Oil Stadium." If you don't include the "from" part, Siri assumes you want directions from your current location (as in "Show me directions to Lucas Oil Stadium").

3. If Siri needs you to confirm one or more of the locations, tap the correct one. Siri uses the Maps app to generate directions.

4. To start turn-by-turn instructions, tap Start.

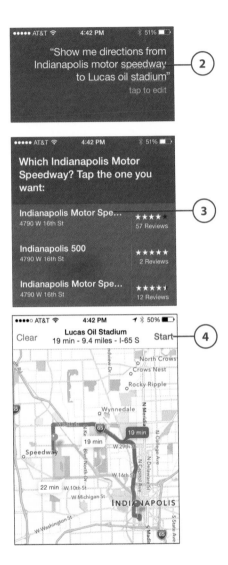

It's Not All Good

Voice commands work pretty well, but they aren't perfect. Make sure you confirm your commands by listening to the feedback Siri provides when it repeats them. Sometimes, a spoken command can have unexpected results, which can include making a phone call to someone in the Contacts app. If you don't catch such a mistake before the call is started, you might be surprised to hear someone answering your call instead of hearing music you intended to play. You can say "no" or "stop" to stop Siri should a verbal command go awry.

Using Dictation to Speak Text Instead of Typing

You can use the iPhone's dictation capability to speak text into any app, such as Mail, Messages, and so on. In fact, any time you see the Microphone button on the keyboard, dictation is available to you. Here's how this works:

1. In the app you are using, put the cursor where you want the text you will dictate to start. For example, if you are creating an email, tap in the body.

2. Tap the Microphone key.

3. Speak the text you want to add. For instance, when you create a new message, you can speak punctuation, but in this mode, you can create a new paragraph by saying "new paragraph." While you are speaking, you see the line that oscillates as you speak.

4. Tap Done when you finish your dictation. The text you spoke is processed and when that is complete, it is added to the message. From there, you can edit it just like messages you've only typed.

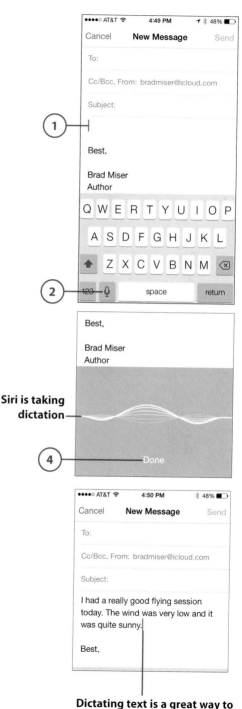

Siri is taking dictation

Dictating text is a great way to write without having to type

Tap to configure Safari

Tap to have the World Wide Web in the palm in your hand

In this chapter, you explore the amazing web browsing functionality your iPhone has to offer. Topics include the following:

→ Setting Safari preferences
→ Visiting websites
→ Viewing websites
→ Working with multiple websites at the same time
→ Searching the Web
→ Saving and organizing bookmarks
→ Sharing web pages
→ Completing forms on the Web
→ Signing into websites automatically
→ Using Safari's Reading List

Surfing the Web

The Web has become an integral part of most of our lives. It is often the first step to search for information, make plans (such as travel arrangements), conduct financial transactions, shop, and so much more. Fortunately, the Safari app puts the entire Web in the palm of your hand. Safari is a full-feature web browser; it doesn't need specially formatted, mobile websites to work (though it can certainly use those when available). Anything you can do on a website in a browser on a computer can be done with Safari on your iPhone.

Setting Safari Preferences

Like most apps, Safari offers settings you can use to adjust the way it works.

Configuring Safari's General Settings

Safari's General settings are as follows:

1. On the Home screen, tap Settings.

2. Swipe up on the screen until you see Safari.

3. Tap Safari.

4. To leave Google as the default search engine, skip to step 7. To change the default search engine, tap Search Engine.

5. Tap Yahoo! or Bing. The engine you selected is checked to show you that it is the search engine Safari will use by default.

6. Tap Safari.

7. Tap Passwords & AutoFill. These settings enable you to automatically log in to websites and to quickly complete forms on the Web by automatically filling in key information for you.

8. To use contact information stored on your iPhone to complete forms, set the Use Contact Info switch to on (green). If you don't want to allow this, leave it off and skip to step 11.

①

●●○○○ AT&T 🤖   4:44 PM   ❋ 98% ▰▰   ②

Settings

🧭   Compass   ⟩

🧭   Safari —————————————— ③

●●●●○ AT&T 🤖   4:44 PM   ❋ 98% ▰▰

⟨ Settings   **Safari**

GENERAL

Search Engine ————————— Google ⟩   ④

●●●●○ AT&T 🤖   4:44 PM   ❋ 98% ▰▰

⟨ Safari   **Search Engine**

⑥

Google   ✓

Yahoo! ⎤

         ⑤

Bing ⎦

Search Engine   Google ⟩

Passwords & AutoFill ——————— ⑦

●●●●○ AT&T 🤖   4:45 PM   ❋ 98% ▰▰

⟨ Safari **Passwords & AutoFill**

Automatically fill out web forms using your contact info, previous names and passwords, or credit card info.

Use Contact Info   ◯ ———— ⑧

9. Tap My Info.

10. Find and tap your contact
    information. This tells Safari
    which information to fill in for
    you on forms, such as your name,
    address, and so on. You move
    back to the AutoFill screen and
    see the contact you selected
    (presumably your name) in the
    My Info section.

Passcode

If you don't have a passcode active when
you perform step 11, you're prompted to
create one. You should not allow Names
and Passwords to be saved without a
passcode on your iPhone because that
means anyone who can get to your
phone can also get to your secured websites. (Refer to Chapter 4, "Configuring an
iPhone to Suit Your Preferences," for the
details of setting passcodes.)

11. To enable Safari to remember
    usernames and passwords for
    websites you log in to, set the
    Names and Passwords switch to
    on (green). If you don't want to
    allow this, skip to step 13.

12. Set the Always Allow switch
    to on (green) if you want your
    passwords to be saved on your
    phone, even for those websites
    that request that they not be
    saved. Some sites try to prohibit
    passwords from being saved
    for security reasons; this setting
    overrides that.

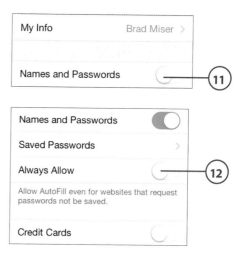

13. To allow credit card information to be saved on your iPhone, set the Credit Cards switch to on (green); if you don't want this information stored, skip to step 20.

14. Tap Saved Credit Cards.

15. Tap Add Credit Card.

16. Complete the required credit card information.

17. Tap Done.

18. Repeat steps 15–17 to add more credit cards.

19. When finished, tap AutoFill.

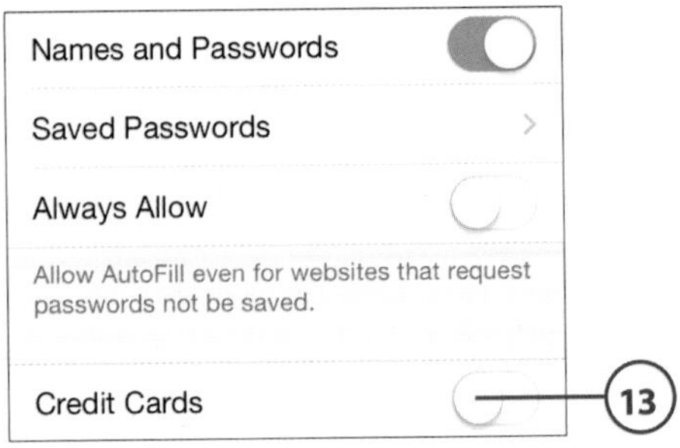

Names and Passwords	⬤
Saved Passwords	>
Always Allow	◯

Allow AutoFill even for websites that request passwords not be saved.

Credit Cards	◯ —⑬

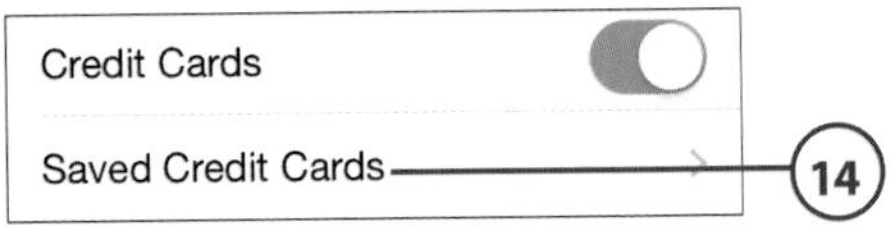

Credit Cards	⬤
Saved Credit Cards ———	> —⑭

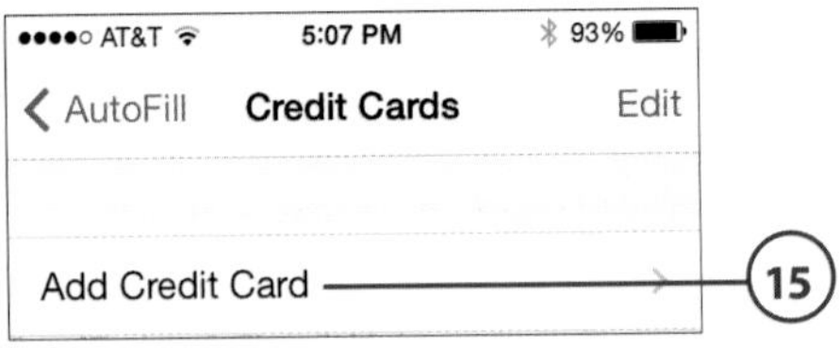

●●●●○ AT&T 🛜   5:07 PM   ≵ 93% 🔋

‹ AutoFill   **Credit Cards**   Edit

Add Credit Card ——— > —⑮

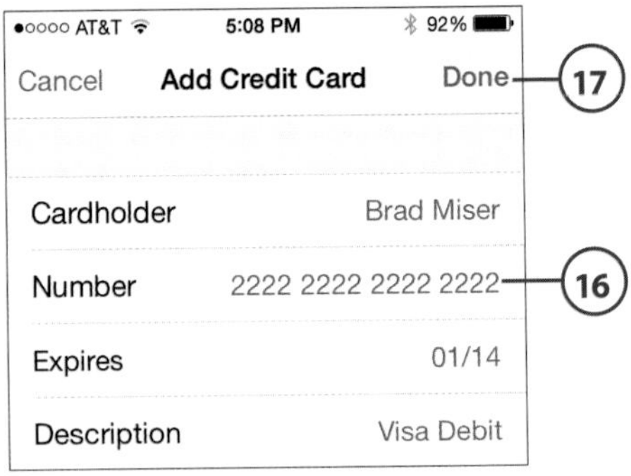

●○○○○ AT&T 🛜   5:08 PM   ≵ 92% 🔋

Cancel   **Add Credit Card**   Done—⑰

Cardholder	Brad Miser
Number	2222 2222 2222 2222—⑯
Expires	01/14
Description	Visa Debit

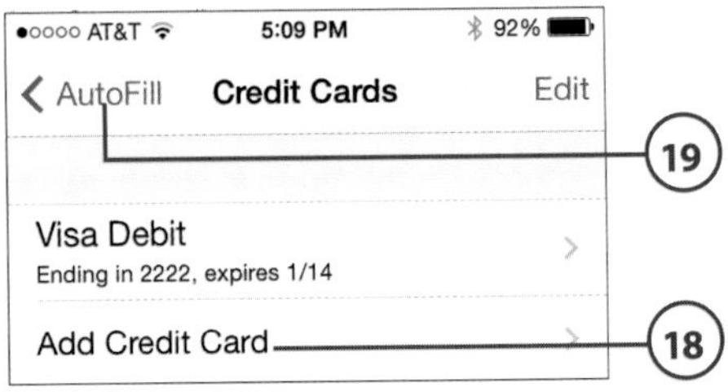

●○○○○ AT&T 🛜   5:09 PM   ≵ 92% 🔋

‹ AutoFill   **Credit Cards**   Edit —⑲

Visa Debit
Ending in 2222, expires 1/14   >

Add Credit Card ——— > —⑱

20. Tap Safari.

21. Tap Favorites.

22. Tap the folder of bookmarks that you want to be your Favorites. These are available when you enter a new URL, perform a search, or create new tabs so that you can get to them quickly and easily (you learn about creating and working with bookmarks later in this chapter).

23. Tap Safari.

24. Tap Open Links. This tells Safari how you want new pages to open when you tap and hold a link.

25. Tap In New Page to have Safari open and immediately take you to a new page. Tap In Background if you want Safari to open pages in the background so you can view them later.

26. Tap Safari.

27. To enable pop-up blocking, slide the Block Pop-ups switch to on (green). Pop-ups are now blocked. Some websites won't work properly with pop-ups blocked, so you can also use this setting to temporarily enable pop-ups by sliding the switch to off (white). Proceed to the next task to complete the rest of Safari's settings.

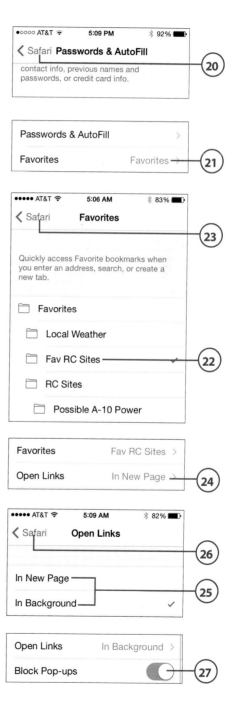

Revisiting Saved Passwords

If you enable usernames and passwords to be stored on your iPhone, you can get information about them by moving to the Passwords and AutoFill settings page and tapping Saved Passwords. On the Passwords screen, you see a list of websites for which information is stored on your iPhone. Tap a website and enter your passcode to view the details stored for it. To remove a saved password, tap Edit on the Passwords screen, tap the passwords you want to remove, and tap Delete. The next time you visit that website, you'll need to reenter your account sign-in information.

Configuring Safari's Privacy & Security Settings

Configure Safari's Privacy & Security settings by performing the following steps:

1. Swipe up the Safari Settings screen so you see the PRIVACY & SECURITY section.

2. To enable private browsing, which means Safari doesn't track and keep a list of the sites you visit, set the Do Not Track switch to on (green). If you have open web pages, you are prompted to close all tabs in Safari; tap Close All to close them or Keep All to leave them open. From this point on, Safari doesn't keep a list of web pages you visit.

3. Tap Block Cookies.

4. Tap the kind of cookies you want to block. The Always option blocks all cookies. The From third parties and advertisers visited blocks cookies from sites you didn't visit directly. This is the setting I recommend you choose because it enables websites you visit to store unnecessary information on your iPhone. The Never option accepts all cookies; I don't recommend this option because if you get directed to a site by another site that you didn't intend to visit, its cookies can be stored on your iPhone.

5. Tap Safari.

Making Cookies

Cookies are data that websites store on the device you use to browse them. Cookies can contain data about you, such as areas you last visited or things in which you are interested. Cookies are typically used to direct you back to these areas or point you to related areas. Most of the time, cookies are harmless and can even be helpful to you, at least from legitimate sites you intentionally visit.

6. Tap Smart Search Field.

7. To have Safari offer search suggestions, ensure that the Search Suggestions switch is on (green). These suggestions can make your searches more productive. If you don't want to use the suggestions, set this switch to off (white).

8. To have Safari preload the search results that are most popular based on what you search for, ensure that the Preload Top Hit switch is on (green). If you don't want these preloaded, set the switch to off (white).

9. Tap Safari.

10. If you don't want Safari to warn you when you visit websites that appear to be fraudulent, set the Fraudulent Website Warning switch to off (white). I recommend you leave this enabled.

11. To clear the history of websites you have visited, tap Clear History.

12. Tap Clear History again at the prompt. This removes the websites you have visited from your history list. The list starts over, so the next site you visit is added to your history list again— unless you have enabled private browsing, in which case the sites you visit are not tracked.

13. To remove all cookies and other web-related data from your iPhone, tap Clear Cookies and Data.

14. Tap Clear Cookies and Data again at the prompt. Any sites that require cookies or other data stored on your iPhone to function re-create the data they need the next time you visit them, assuming that you allow cookies to be stored on your phone.

15. Later, you'll learn about the Reading List that enables you to store web pages on your iPhone for offline reading; if you want to allow pages to be saved to your iPhone when you are using its cellular data connection, slide the Use Cellular Data switch to the on (green) position. Slide this switch to off (white) if you have a limited data plan and don't want to use it to store web pages (you can store them when you are using a Wi-Fi network). You're ready to browse the Web.

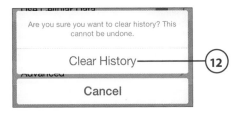

Advanced?

The Advanced option takes you to the Advanced screen. Here, you can tap Website Data to see the amount of data associated with websites you have visited; swipe up on the screen and tap Remove All Website Data to clear this data. You can disable JavaScript, which you aren't likely to want to do because many pages require this scripting language to work. You can also enable the Web Inspector. This enables website developers to check their websites on an iPhone for errors so that those sites can be updated to work properly. If you aren't a website developer, you probably won't need to use this tool. If you are a website developer, enable the tool when you evaluate your website using Safari on an iPhone.

Visiting Websites

If you've used a web browser on a computer before, using Safari on an iPhone is a familiar experience. If you've not used a web browser before, don't worry because using Safari on an iPhone is simple and intuitive.

Syncing Bookmarks

You can synchronize your Internet Explorer favorites or Safari bookmarks on a Windows PC—or Safari bookmarks on a Mac—to your iPhone so you have the same set of bookmarks available on your iPhone that you do on your computer and other devices, and vice versa. You can do this via the sync process or wirelessly using iCloud. Refer to Chapter 3, "Setting Up iCloud and Other Online Accounts," for information about using iCloud to sync bookmarks or Chapter 5, "Working with iTunes on Your Computer," for details of syncing your iPhone using iTunes. If you use Internet Explorer or Safari on a computer, you should synchronize before you start browsing on your iPhone so you avoid typing URLs or re-creating bookmarks. When you enable Safari syncing via iCloud, you can also view tabs open in Safari on other devices, such as a Mac or an iPad.

Using Bookmarks to Move to Websites

Using bookmarks you've synced via iCloud, or from a computer or other device, onto iPhone makes it easy to get to websites that are of interest to you. You can also create bookmarks on iPhone (you learn how later in this chapter) and use them just like bookmarks you've synced onto the iPhone.

1. On the iPhone Home screen, tap Safari.

2. Tap the Bookmarks button.

Back to the Bookmarks

The most recent Bookmarks screen is retained when you move away from Bookmarks and then come back. Each time you open your Bookmarks, you're at the same place you were when you left it.

3. Tap the Bookmarks tab if it isn't selected already. (If you don't see this tab, tap the back button in the upper-left corner of the screen until you do.)

4. Swipe up or down the list of bookmarks to browse the bookmarks and other folders of bookmarks available to you.

5. To move to a bookmark, skip to step 10; to open a folder of bookmarks, tap it.

Playing Favorites

You might see two Favorites folders on the Bookmarks screen. The one marked with a star is the folder you designated, using the Safari settings described previously in this chapter, as the place to store Favorites on your iPhone. If you use Safari on a computer, you can also configure bookmarks and folders of bookmarks on its Bookmarks bar. When these bookmarks are synced from your computer to the iPhone, they are stored in a folder of bookmarks also called Favorites and shown with the standard folder icon (see the figure marked with step 5). If you set this synced folder in your iPhone's Safari settings to also be its Favorites folder, you won't have to deal with this potentially confusing situation of multiple Favorites folders.

6. Swipe up or down the folder's screen to browse the folders and bookmarks it contains.

7. You can tap a folder to see the bookmarks it contains.

Change Your Mind?

If you decide not to visit a bookmark, tap Done. You return to the page you were previously viewing.

8. To return to a previous screen, tap the back button in the upper-left corner of the screen, which is labeled with the name of the folder you previously visited (the parent folder); this disappears when you are at the top-level Bookmarks screen

9. Repeat steps 5–8 until you see a bookmark you want to visit.

10. Tap the bookmark you want to visit. Safari moves to that website.

Browse in Private

If you tap the Private button at the bottom of the Bookmarks screen, Private Browsing is enabled, which means that Safari doesn't keep a list of the websites you visit. You're prompted to keep all the open pages open or to close them. After you make a choice, Safari stops tracking your web browsing.

11. Use the information in the section "Viewing Websites" later in this chapter to view the web page.

iPhone Web Pages

Some websites have been specially formatted for iPhones and other mobile devices. These typically have less complex information on each page, so they load faster. When you move to a site like this, you might be redirected to the mobile version automatically, or you might be prompted to choose which version of the site you want to visit. On the mobile version, there is typically a link that takes you to the "regular" version, too. (It's sometimes called the Desktop, Full, or Classic version.) Sometimes the version formatted for handheld devices offers less information or fewer tools than the regular version. Because Safari is a full-featured browser, you can use whichever version you prefer.

Using Your Favorites to Move to Websites

Using the Safari settings described earlier, you can designate a folder of bookmarks as your Favorites. You can get to the folders and bookmarks in your Favorites folder more quickly and easily than navigating to it as described in the previous section. (If you haven't set your Favorites yet, refer to the task "Configuring Safari's General Settings.") Here's how to use your Favorites:

1. On the Home screen, tap Safari. (If you are in Safari and have the Bookmarks screen open, tap Done to close it.)

2. Tap in the Address bar (if you don't see the Address bar, tap at the top of the screen to show it). Just below the Address bar are your Favorites (bookmarks and folders of bookmarks). The keyboard opens at the bottom of the screen.

3. Swipe up and down on your Favorites. The keyboard closes to give you more room to browse.

4. To move to a bookmark, tap it and skip to step 8.

5. To move into a folder, tap it.

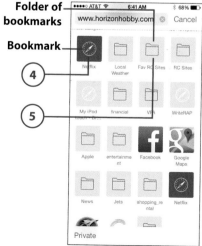

Folder of bookmarks

Bookmark

6. Continue browsing your Favorites until you find the bookmark you want to use. Like using the Bookmarks screen, you can tap a folder to move into it, tap a bookmark to move to its website, tap the Back button to move to the previous screen, and so on.

7. Tap the bookmark for the site you want to visit.

8. Use the information in the section "Viewing Websites" later in this chapter to view the web page.

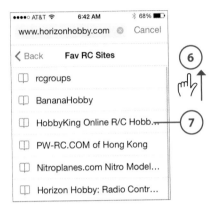

Typing URLs to Move to Websites

A Uniform Resource Locator (URL) is the Internet address of a web page. URLs can be relatively simple, such as www.apple.com, or they can be quite long and convoluted. The good news is that by using bookmarks, you can save a URL in Safari so you can get back to it using its bookmark (as you learned in the previous two tasks) and thus avoid typing URLs. Although it might not be fun to type URLs, sometimes that's the only way you have to get to a website.

1. On the Home screen, tap Safari. (If you are in Safari and have the Bookmarks screen open, tap Done to close it.)

2. Tap in the Address bar (if you don't see the Address bar, tap at the top of the screen). The URL of the current page becomes highlighted; if you haven't visited a page, the Address bar is empty. Just below the Address bar your Favorites are displayed. The keyboard appears at the bottom of the screen.

3. If an address appears in the Address bar, tap the clear button (x) to remove it.

4. Type the URL you want to visit. If it starts with www (which almost all URLs do), you don't have to type "www". As you type, Safari attempts to match what you are typing to a site you have visited previously and completes the URL for you if it can. Just below the Address bar, Safari presents a list of sites that might be what you are looking for, organized into top hits, suggested sites, or a web search.

Shortcut for Typing URLs

URLs include a top-level domain code that represents the type of site (theoretically anyway) that URL leads to. Common examples are .com (commercial sites), .edu (educational sites), and so on. To quickly enter a URL's code, tap and hold the period key to see a menu from which you can select other options, such as .net, .edu, and so on. Tap the code you want, and it is automatically entered in the Address bar.

5. If one of the sites shown is the one you want to visit, tap it. You move to that web page; skip to step 8.

6. If Safari doesn't find a match, continue typing until you enter the entire URL.

7. Tap Go. You move to the web page.

8. Use the information in the section "Viewing Websites" to view the web page.

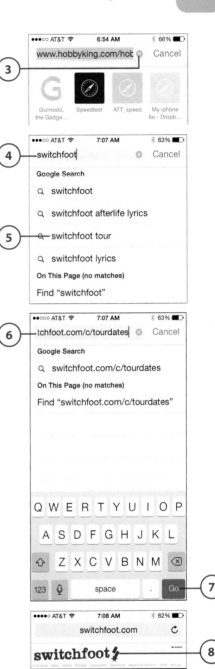

6. To close a tab, click its close button or swipe to the left on the tab you want to close. That page closes.

7. To open a new tab, tap the Add button and navigate to a page using the tools you've already learned in other tasks (bookmarks, typing a URL, and so on).

8. To close the tab view, tap Done. Tab view closes, and the page you were most recently viewing is shown.

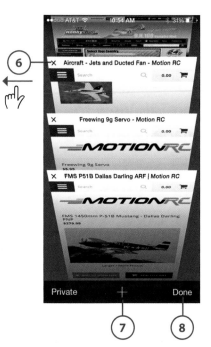

Tabs Are Independent

Each tab is independent. So, when you are working with a tab and use the back/forward buttons to move among its pages, you are just moving among the pages open under that tab. Pages open in other tabs are not affected.

Opening Web Pages That Are Open on Other Devices

When you enable iCloud Safari syncing, iCloud tracks the websites you have open on all the devices on which you have it enabled, including your iPhone, iPads, Macs, and so on. This is really handy when you have pages open on another device and want to view them on your iPhone. (Pages open on your iPhone are available on your other devices, too.) To view a page you have open on another device, do the following:

1. Open the tab view.

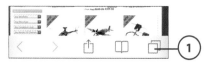

3. If an address appears in the Address bar, tap the clear button (x) to remove it.

4. Type the URL you want to visit. If it starts with www (which almost all URLs do), you don't have to type "www". As you type, Safari attempts to match what you are typing to a site you have visited previously and completes the URL for you if it can. Just below the Address bar, Safari presents a list of sites that might be what you are looking for, organized into top hits, suggested sites, or a web search.

Shortcut for Typing URLs

URLs include a top-level domain code that represents the type of site (theoretically anyway) that URL leads to. Common examples are .com (commercial sites), .edu (educational sites), and so on. To quickly enter a URL's code, tap and hold the period key to see a menu from which you can select other options, such as .net, .edu, and so on. Tap the code you want, and it is automatically entered in the Address bar.

5. If one of the sites shown is the one you want to visit, tap it. You move to that web page; skip to step 8.

6. If Safari doesn't find a match, continue typing until you enter the entire URL.

7. Tap Go. You move to the web page.

8. Use the information in the section "Viewing Websites" to view the web page.

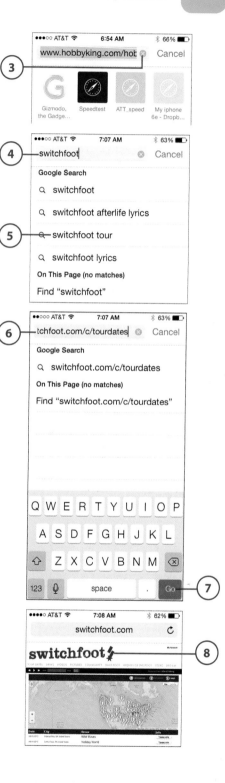

Using Your Browsing History to Move to Websites

As you move about the Web, Safari tracks the sites you visit and builds a history list (unless you enabled the Do Not Track option, in which case this doesn't happen and you can't use History to return to previous sites). You can use your browsing history list to return to sites you've visited.

1. Tap the Bookmarks button.

2. If you aren't on the Bookmarks screen, tap the back button (which is labeled with the previous screen you visited) until you move to it. (Safari remembers your last location, so if you were last on the Bookmarks screen, you don't need to tap any buttons to get back there.)

3. If necessary, swipe down the Bookmarks page until you see the History folder.

4. Tap History.

5. Swipe up and down the page to browse all the sites you've visited. The more recent sites appear at the top of the screen; the further you move down the screen, the further back in time you go. Earlier sites are collected in folders for various times, such as This Morning, Monday Afternoon, and so on.

6. Tap the site you want to visit. The site opens and you can use the information in the section "Viewing Websites" to view the web page.

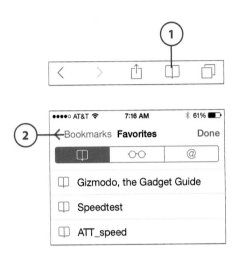

Erasing the Past

To clear your browsing history, tap the Clear button at the bottom of the History screen. Tap Clear History at the prompt, and it will be as if you've never been on the Web. (Don't you wish it was this easy in real life!)

Viewing Websites

Even though your iPhone is a small device, you'll be amazed at how well it displays web pages designed for larger screens.

1. Use Safari to move to a web page as described in the previous tasks.

Where Did the URL Go?

When you first move to a URL, you see that URL in the Address bar. After you work with a site, the URL is replaced with the high-level domain name for the site (such as sitename.com, sitename.edu, etc.). To see the full URL again, tap the Address bar.

2. To browse around a web page, swipe your finger right or left, or up or down.

3. To zoom in manually, unpinch your fingers.

4. To zoom in automatically, tap your finger on the screen twice.

5. To zoom out manually, pinch your fingers.

6. To zoom on a column or a figure, tap it twice.

7. To move to a link, tap it once. Links can come in many forms including text (most text that is a link is in color and underlined), graphics, and so on. The web page to which the link points opens and replaces the page currently being displayed.

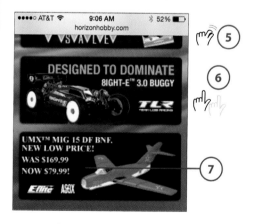

Do More with Links

To see options for a link, tap and hold your finger down for a second or so. When you lift your finger, a menu appears. Tap Open to open the page to replace the current page at which the link points (this is the same as tapping a link once). Tap Open in Background to open the page in a new Safari window that opens in the background, or tap Open in New Page to open the new page in the background. The command that appears depends on the Open Links Safari setting. Tap Add to Reading List to add the page to your Reading List (which is explained in the tasks in the section "Using Safari's Reading List" later in this chapter). Tap Copy to copy the link's URL so that you can paste it elsewhere, such as in an email message. Tap Cancel to return to the current page and take no action.

8. To view the web page in landscape orientation, rotate the iPhone so that it is horiztontal.

9. Scroll, zoom in, and zoom out on the page to read it, as described in steps 2–7.

10. To refresh a page, tap Refresh. (Note: while a page is loading, this is the "x" button; tap it to stop the rest of the page from loading.)

11. To move to a previous page you've visited, tap Back.

12. To move to a subsequent page, tap Forward.

13. As you move around, the Address bar at the top of the page and the toolbar at the bottom of the page are hidden automatically; to show them again, tap the top or bottom of the screen.

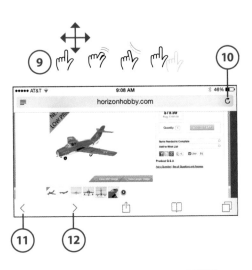

Working with Multiple Websites at the Same Time

When you move to a web page by using a bookmark, typing a URL, tapping a link on the current web page, and so on, the new web page replaces the current one. However, you can also open and work with multiple web pages at the same time so that a new web page doesn't replace the current one.

When you work with multiple web pages, each open page appears in its own tab. You can use the tab view to easily move to and manage your open web pages. You can also close open tabs, and you can even open web pages that are open on other devices on which your iCloud account has been configured and Safari syncing enabled.

There are two ways to open a new web page in a new tab. One is to tap and hold on a link on the current web page; you can use the resulting Open command to open the new page. There are two options for this approach. The one you use is determined by the Open Links preference set as described earlier in this chapter. The Open in Background option causes the new page to open and move to the background. This is most useful when you want to read the new page at a later time, such as when you are done with the current one. The In New Page option causes the new page to open and move to the front so you see it instantly.

The second way to open a new web page in a new tab is by using the Tab Manager.

All these options are described in the following tasks.

Opening New Pages in the Background

If you enabled the In Background option for the Open Links preference, you can open new web pages in new tabs by doing the following:

1. Tap and hold on the link you want to open in the background.

2. Tap Open in Background. The page to which the link points opens. The only result you see is the page "jumping" down to the Tab Manager button in the lower-right corner of the screen.

3. Continue opening pages in the background; see "Using Tab View to Manage Open Web Pages" to learn how to use the tab view to move to pages that are open in the background.

Opening New Pages in a New Page

If you enabled the In New Page option for the Open Links preference, you can open new pages by doing the following:

1. Tap and hold on the link you want to open in the background.

2. Tap Open in New Page. A new page opens and displays the page to which the link points.

3. Continue opening pages; see "Using Tab View to Manage Open Web Pages" to learn how to use the tab view to manage your open pages.

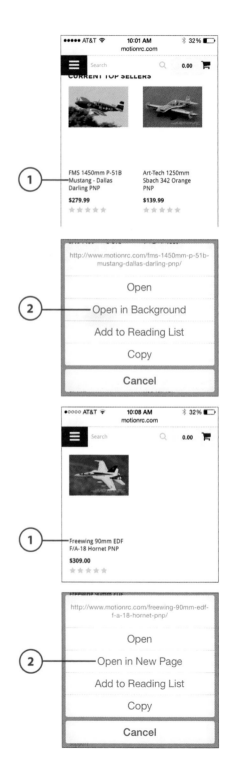

Just Open It

If you tap the Open command on the menu in step 2 of the previous tasks, the new web page replaces the one you were viewing on the current tab. This is the same as just tapping a link on the page.

Using Tab View to Manage Open Web Pages

As you open new pages, whether in the background or not, new tabs are opened. Safari's tab view enables you to view and work with your open pages/tabs. Here's how:

1. Tap the tab view button. Each open page appears on its own tab.

2. Swipe up or down on the open tabs to browse them.

3. Tap a tab/page to move into it. The page opens and fills the Safari window.

4. Work with the web page.

5. Tap the tab view button.

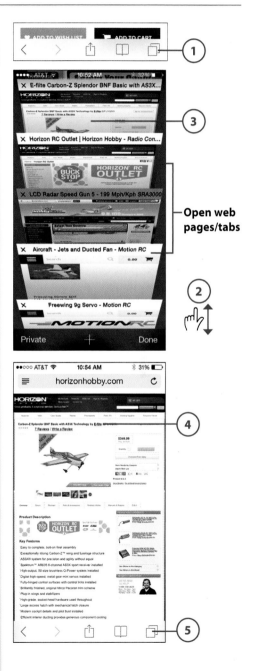

Open web pages/tabs

6. To close a tab, click its close button or swipe to the left on the tab you want to close. That page closes.

7. To open a new tab, tap the Add button and navigate to a page using the tools you've already learned in other tasks (bookmarks, typing a URL, and so on).

8. To close the tab view, tap Done. Tab view closes, and the page you were most recently viewing is shown.

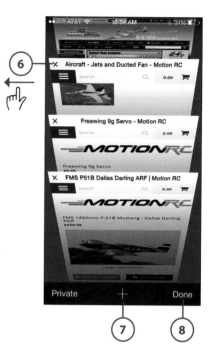

Tabs Are Independent

Each tab is independent. So, when you are working with a tab and use the back/forward buttons to move among its pages, you are just moving among the pages open under that tab. Pages open in other tabs are not affected.

Opening Web Pages That Are Open on Other Devices

When you enable iCloud Safari syncing, iCloud tracks the websites you have open on all the devices on which you have it enabled, including your iPhone, iPads, Macs, and so on. This is really handy when you have pages open on another device and want to view them on your iPhone. (Pages open on your iPhone are available on your other devices, too.) To view a page you have open on another device, do the following:

1. Open the tab view.

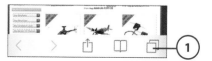

2. Swipe up the screen until you see the pages open on other devices. There is a section for each device; sections are labeled with the device's name. In each device's section, you see the pages open in Safari on those devices.

3. Tap the page you want to view. The page opens on the iPhone and becomes a new tab.

Searching the Web

In the first task of this chapter, you learned that you can set Safari to search the Web using Google, Yahoo!, or Bing. No matter which search engine you chose, you search the Web in the same way.

1. Tap in the Address bar. The keyboard appears along with your favorites.

2. If there is any text in the Address bar, tap the clear button.

3. Type your search word(s). As you type, Safari attempts to find a search that matches what you typed. The list of suggestions is organized in three sections. At the top of the list are potential website matches for your search. The center section, labeled with the search engine you are using (such as Google Search), contains the search results from that source. At the bottom of the list is the On This Page section, which shows the terms that match your search on the page you are browsing.

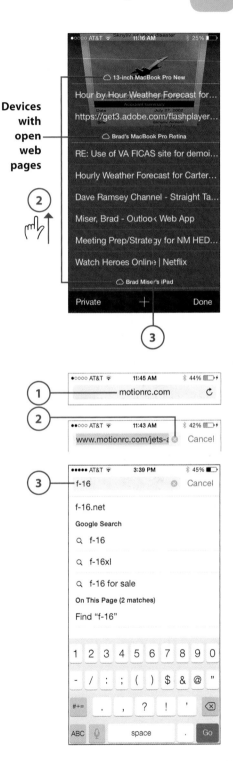

Devices with open web pages

4. To perform the search using one of the suggestions provided, tap the suggestion you want to use. The search is performed and you can skip to step 6.

5. If none of the suggestions are what you want, keep typing until you have entered the entire search term and tap Go. The search engine you use performs the search and displays the results on the search results page.

6. Use the search results page to view the results of your search. These pages work just like other web pages. You can zoom, scroll, and click links to explore results.

Searching on a Web Page

To search for words or phrases on a web page you are viewing, perform these steps, except in step 4, tap the word or phrase for which you want to search in the On This Page section. You return to the page you are browsing and each occurrence of your search term on the page is highlighted.

Saving and Organizing Bookmarks

In addition to moving bookmarks from a computer or iCloud onto your iPhone, you can save new bookmarks directly in your iPhone (where they can then move onto other synced devices, too). You can organize bookmarks on your iPhone to make them easier and faster to access.

Creating Bookmarks

When you want to make it easy to return to a website, create a bookmark. Do the following to create a new bookmark:

1. Move to a web page you want to save as a bookmark.

2. Tap the Action button.

3. Tap Bookmark. The Add Bookmark screen appears, showing the title of the web page you are viewing; its URL; and the Location field, which shows where the bookmark will be stored when you create it.

4. Edit the bookmark's name as needed, or to erase the current name, tap the Clear button (x). Type the new name of the bookmark. The titles of some web pages are quite long, so it's a good idea to shorten them so the bookmark's name is easier to find.

5. Tap Location. The Choose a Folder screen appears. The folder that is currently selected is marked with a check mark.

6. Swipe up and down the screen to find the folder in which you want to place the new bookmark. You can choose any folder on the screen; folders are indented when they are contained within other folders.

7. To choose a folder for the new bookmark, tap it. You return to the Add Bookmark screen, which shows the location you selected.

8. Tap Save. The bookmark is created and saved in the location you specified. You can use the bookmark to return to the website at any time.

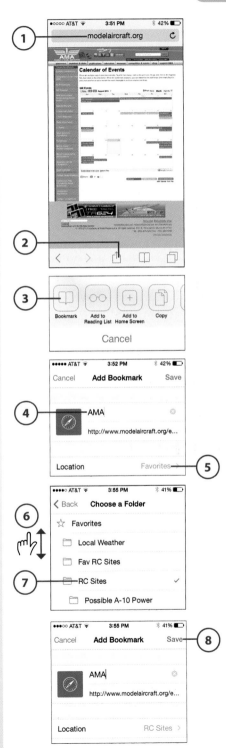

It's Not All Good

Unfortunately, bookmarks that you create on the iPhone are useful on the computer to which they are copied only if you use Internet Explorer or Safari (Windows PC) or Safari (Mac). If you use Firefox, Chrome, or another web browser, the bookmarks moved onto the computer from the iPhone are of little value to you because they appear in only one of the supported browsers (Internet Explorer or Safari). You can make them available in other browsers, but that requires going through extra gyrations, which can negate the value of syncing.

Organizing Bookmarks

You've seen how bookmarks can be contained in folders, which is a good thing because you're likely to have a lot of them. You can change the names and locations of your existing bookmarks and folders as follows:

1. Move to the Bookmarks screen showing the bookmarks and folders you want to change. (You can't move among the Bookmarks screens while you are in Edit mode so you need to start at the location where the items you want to change are located.)

2. Tap Edit. Unlock buttons appear next to the folders and bookmarks you can change; some folders, such as the History folder, can't be changed. The order icons also appear on the right side of the screen, again only for folders or bookmarks you can change.

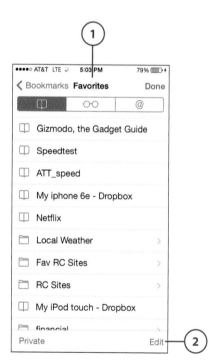

3. Tap the order icon next to the bookmark or folder you want to move and drag it up or down the screen to change the order in which they appear. When you drag a folder or bookmark between other items, they slide apart to make room for the folder or bookmark you are dragging. The order of the items in the list is the order in which they appear on the Bookmarks screen.

4. To change the name or location of a folder, tap it.

Can't Move?

If you have only one bookmark you've added, you can't move them around as described here because Safari won't let you "disturb" the default bookmarks and folders (such as Favorites and History). You can only delete default bookmarks.

5. Change the name in the name bar.

6. To change the location of the folder, tap the Location bar, which shows the folder's current location.

7. Swipe up and down the list of folders until you see the folder in which you want to place the folder you are working with.

8. Tap the folder into which you want to move the folder you are editing. You move back to the Edit Folder screen.

9. Tap Done. You move back to the Bookmarks screen, which reflects any changes you made.

10. Tap a bookmark you want to change.

Editing a Bookmark

If the bookmark you want to change isn't on the Bookmarks screen you are currently viewing, tap Done to exit Edit mode. Then open the folder containing the bookmark you want to change and tap Edit.

11. Change the bookmark's name in the name bar.

12. If you want to change a bookmark's URL, tap the URL bar and make changes to the current URL.

13. To change the location of the folder or bookmark, tap the Location bar and follow steps 7 and 8.

14. Tap Done. You move back to the previous screen, and any changes you made—such as changing the name or location of a bookmark—are reflected.

Can't Change?

You can't change default bookmarks, you can only delete them.

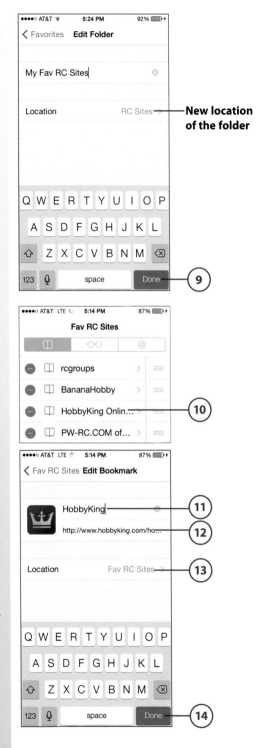

New location of the folder

15. To create a new folder, tap New Folder.

16. Enter the name of the folder.

17. Follow steps 6–8 to choose the location in which you want to save the new folder.

18. Tap Done. The new folder is created in the location you selected. You can place folders and bookmarks into it by using the Location bar to navigate to it.

19. Tap Done. Your changes are saved and you exit Edit mode.

Deleting Bookmarks or Folders of Bookmarks

You can get rid of bookmarks or folders of bookmarks you don't want any more by deleting them:

1. Move to the screen containing the folder or bookmark you want to delete.

2. Swipe to the left on the folder or bookmark you want to delete.

3. Tap Delete. The folder or bookmark is deleted. Note that when you delete a folder, all the bookmarks it contains are deleted, too.

Creating Bookmarks on the Home Screens

You can add a bookmark icon to a Home screen so that you can visit a web page from there; this handy trick saves you several navigation moves that would be required to move into Safari and type the URL or use a bookmark to get the page you want to see.

1. Use Safari to move to a web page to which you want to have easy access from the Home screen.

2. Tap the Action button.

3. Tap Add to Home Screen.

4. If needed, edit the name of the icon that will appear on the Home Screen. The default name is the name of the web page. It's best to edit it to a shorter name because it has a small amount of room on its icon on the Home Screen.

5. Tap Add. You move to the Home Screen and see the icon you added. You can return to the site at any time by tapping this button.

Website button on a Home screen

Location Is Everything

You can organize the buttons on the pages of the Home Screen so that you can place your web page buttons in convenient locations, and you can create folders on your Home screens to keep your web page icons neat and tidy there, too. Refer to Chapter 4 for details.

Sharing Web Pages

Safari makes it easy to share web pages that you think will be valuable to others. There are many ways to share, including AirDrop, Message, Mail, Twitter, and Facebook. A couple of examples of these will prepare you to use any of them.

Emailing a Link to a Web Page

You can quickly email links to web pages you visit.

1. Use Safari to navigate to a web page whose link you want to email to someone.

2. Tap the Action button.

3. Tap Mail. A new email message is created, and the link to the web page is inserted into the body. The subject of the message is the title of the web page.

4. Complete and send the email message. (Refer to Chapter 9, "Sending, Receiving, and Managing Email," for information about the Mail app.) When the recipient receives your message, he can visit the website by clicking the link included in the email message.

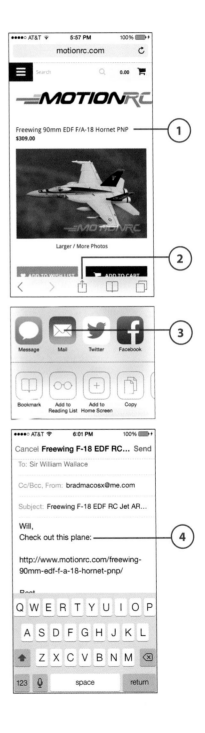

Tweeting a Web Page

If you come across a page that you want to share with someone via Twitter, Safari makes it easy.

1. Use Safari to navigate to a web page whose link you want to tweet to someone.

2. Tap the Action button.

3. Tap Twitter. A new tweet is created, and the link to the web page is inserted into the body.

Tweeting

To be able to tweet a page to someone, you need to configure your Twitter account on your iPhone. Refer to Chapter 3 for details.

4. Enter the message you want to tweet along with a link to the web page.

5. To add your current location, tap Location.

6. Tap Post. Your tweet is sent to everyone who is following you. They can visit the web page by clicking the link included in the tweet.

Reading Tweets

If you tap the Tweet tab (@) on the Bookmarks screen, you see tweets from people you are following. You can browse your tweets; read them; or tap them to move to where they link, such as a Facebook page. This tab appears only if you are currently signed into your Twitter account using the Twitter Settings screen.

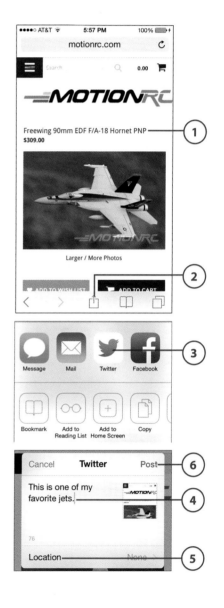

Completing Forms on the Web

Just like web browsers on a computer, you often have to complete forms on your iPhone, such as to log in to your account on a website or request information about something. You can manually enter information or use AutoFill to have Safari add the information for you. (AutoFill must be enabled using Safari settings, as explained at the beginning of this chapter.)

Manually Completing Forms

To manually fill in a form, do the following:

1. Open Safari and move to a website containing a form.

2. Zoom in on the fields you need to complete.

3. Tap in a field. If you tapped a text field, the keyboard appears.

4. Enter the information in the field. (If the site suggests information you want to enter, just tap it to enter it. You might have to tap Done to temporarily hide the keyboard to see all the suggestions. If a suggestion isn't the information you want to enter, just keep typing.)

5. Tap the Next button. If there isn't another field on the form, this button is disabled, so skip this step. If it is enabled, you move to the next field on the form.

Date Fields

When a form has a date field on it, tap in the field; a date selection tool appears. Navigate to and select the date you want to enter.

6. Repeat steps 4 and 5 to complete all the fields on the form.

7. Tap Done. If it's open, the keyboard closes and you move back to the web page.

8. Tap Continue, Submit, Go, Login, or whatever button is provided to send the form's information to the website.

Using AutoFill to Complete Forms

AutoFill makes completing forms faster and easier because Safari can enter information for you with the tap of a button.

1. Open Safari and move to a website containing a form. Zoom in on the fields you need to complete, and tap in a field. If you tapped a text field, the keyboard appears.

2. Tap AutoFill. Safari fills any fields it can, based on the information you designated when you configured AutoFill to use your contact information. Any fields that Safari tries to complete are highlighted in yellow.

3. Use the steps in the previous section to review all the fields and to type in what AutoFill wasn't able to complete or edit those that AutoFill completed but that need to be changed.

AutoFillin'

For AutoFill to work, it must be enabled in the Safari settings as described at the beginning of the chapter. If the data AutoFill enters is not correct, use the Safari settings to choose your correct contact info or, if the correct info is selected, update it in the Contacts app.

Signing In to Websites Automatically

If you enable Safari to remember usernames and passwords, it can enter this information for you automatically. When Safari encounters a site for which it recognizes and can save login information, you are prompted to allow Safari to save that information. This doesn't work with all sites; if you aren't prompted to allow Safari to save login information, you can't use this feature with that site. When saved, this information can be entered for you automatically.

1. Move to a web page that requires you to log in to an account.

2. Enter your account's username and password.

3. Tap the button to log in to your account, such as Continue, Sign In, Submit, Login, and such. You are prompted to save the login information.

4. To save the information, tap Save Password. The next time you move to the login page, your username and password are entered for you automatically. Tap Never for this Website if you don't want the information to be saved and you don't want to be prompted again. Tap Not Now if you don't want the information saved but do want to be prompted again later to save it.

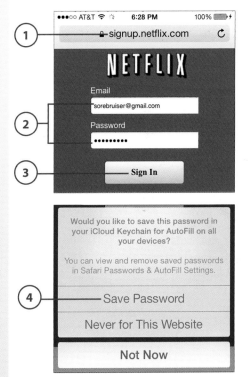

>>>Go Further

LETTING SAFARI CREATE PASSWORDS FOR YOU

If you have enabled the Names and Passwords setting, Safari can create passwords for you. Go to a website that requires you to create a password, such as when you register for a new account. When you tap in a field that Safari recognizes as requiring a password, tap Suggest Password. Safari presents a password for you; most of these will not be easy to remember, but that doesn't matter because it is saved for you automatically so you won't have to enter it manually. If you want to use the recommended password, tap Use Suggested Password; Safari enters the password in the password and verify password fields.

Using Safari's Reading List

The Reading List is a way to save pages you want to read at a later time. You can collect the pages you want to read on your Reading List as you browse. When you want to read the pages you have collected, open the Reading List and see the pages you have added there. The Reading List is useful to store pages that you do not necessarily want to bookmark because your use of them is temporary.

Adding Pages to Your Reading List

To add pages to your Reading List:

1. Using Safari, open a web page.

2. Tap the Action button.

3. Tap Add to Reading List.

4. Repeat steps 1–3 to add more pages to your Reading List.

Connection Not Always Required

To read the pages currently on the Reading List, your iPhone doesn't have to be connected to the Internet, which is what makes this feature particularly useful. However, to move to any links on a page on the Reading List, the iPhone does have to be connected to the Internet.

Using Your Reading List

To use your Reading List, do the following:

1. Open the Bookmarks page and tap the Reading List tab. You see the pages on your Reading List.

2. To see only pages you haven't read yet, tap Show Unread. The list is narrowed accordingly.

3. Swipe up or down to browse the pages you see.

4. Tap the page you want to view. It opens.

5. Read the page.

6. Tap the Bookmarks button to return to your Reading List.

Whittle Down the List

To remove a page from your Reading List, swipe to the left across the page you want to remove and tap the Delete button that appears.

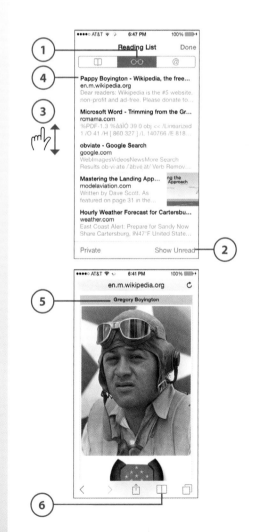

Tap here to
configure your
iPhone for music

Tap here to enjoy
musical bliss

In this chapter, you explore how you can use the Music app to enjoy all sorts of music. The topics include the following:

→ Stocking your iPhone with music
→ Configuring Music settings
→ Using the Cover Browser to find and listen to music
→ Finding music
→ Playing music
→ Creating and using Genius playlists
→ Using AirPlay to listen to your iPhone's music on other devices
→ Listening to music with iTunes Match
→ Listening to iTunes Radio

Finding and Listening to Music

The very first portable "i" device, the original iPod, did only one thing—though it did that one thing better than any other device ever—which was to enable people to take their music with them and enjoy it anywhere. While the iPhone has evolved way beyond anything the first iPod could do, one of the best reasons to have an iPhone is that they continue to be amazing devices for listening to all kinds of music and audiobooks. The Music app enables you to quickly move to and play any music in your personal music library. Using its iTunes Radio feature, you can also listen to music that is not in your library (kind of like listening to music on an old-fashioned radio only much better).

Stocking Your iPhone with Music

There are a number of ways to make music in your music library available in the Music app on your iPhone:

- Add music to your iTunes Library and then sync that music onto your iPhone (refer to Chapter 5, "Working with iTunes on Your Computer").

- Add music to your iTunes Library and then use iTunes Match to download and listen to that music on your iPhone (refer to Chapter 5 and the section "Listening to Music with iTunes Match" in this chapter).

- Download music directly from the iTunes Store onto your iPhone using the iTunes app (refer to Chapter 6, "Downloading Apps, Music, Movies, TV Shows, and More onto Your iPhone").

Yet Another Way to Listen

You can use iTunes Radio to listen to music that isn't stored on your iPhone. This is a great way to sample lots of music, some of which you might choose to add to your music collection. iTunes Radio is explained in the section "Listening to iTunes Radio," at the end of this chapter.

Configuring Music Settings

You can use an iPhone for music just fine without performing any of the steps in this section. However, because this book is named *My iPhone*, you should explore these options to make an iPhone your own for audio playback.

You can use the Music settings to configure various aspects of iPhone's music functionality.

1. Open the Settings app.

2. Swipe up the screen.

3. Tap Music.

4. If you don't want the Music app to shuffle to the next song when you shake the iPhone, slide the Shake to Shuffle switch to off (white). Slide the switch to on (green) to enable shuffling by shaking again.

5. Slide the Sound Check switch to on (green), if you want the Music app to attempt to even the volume of the music you play, so that all the songs play at about the same relative volume level.

6. To set an equalizer, tap the EQ bar.

7. Swipe up and down the screen to see all the equalizers available to you.

8. Tap the equalizer you want; the current equalizer is indicated by the check mark. To turn off the equalizer, tap Off at the top of the list.

9. Tap Music.

10. To set a limit to the volume level on your iPhone, tap Volume Limit.

11. Drag the volume slider to the point that you want the maximum volume level to be.

12. Tap Music.

13. To hide lyrics and podcast information on the Now Playing screen, slide the Lyrics & Podcast Info switch to off (white). When disabled, you always see only the album art for whatever is playing.

14. If you want music to always be grouped by the artist associated with its album, set Group By Album Artist to on (green). If you want music to be grouped by the artist performing it instead, set this to off.

15. Set the Show All Music switch to on (green) so that all the music you have purchased from the iTunes Store is shown—even if it is not currently stored on your iPhone. If this switch is off, only music currently stored on the iPhone appears in the Music app.

iTunes Match

The iTunes Match setting is covered later in this chapter, and iTunes Match is also discussed in Chapter 5.

16. Swipe up the screen.

17. To enable streaming content from iTunes libraries and other sources, tap Apple ID in the HOME SHARING section.

18. Enter the Apple ID and password associated with the music you want to share; in most cases, this should be your Apple ID.

19. Tap Done. You move back to the Music screen and your iPhone is able to stream music from shared sources.

20. Tap Settings. You're ready for some tunes.

HOME SHARING — 17

Apple ID bradmacosx@mac.com — 18

Password •••••••••••

An Apple ID is required to use Home Sharing.

Q W E R T Y U I O P

A S D F G H J K L

⇧ Z X C V B N M ⌫

123 🌐 space Done — 19

16

•••••○ AT&T 📶 10:00 AM 99% 🔋 — 20

‹ Settings **Music**

Using the Cover Browser to Find and Listen to Music

The Cover Browser shows you your music by its cover art; you can quickly peruse your entire music collection to get to and play the right music for your current mood.

To use the Cover Browser, perform these steps:

1. On the Home screen, tap Music.

2. If the Music app opens to any screen other than iTunes Radio, you can skip to step 3. If you see the iTunes Radio screen, tap one of the other buttons on the toolbar at the bottom of the screen. It doesn't matter which one. You learn what these buttons do and how to use iTunes Radio later in this chapter.

3. Rotate your iPhone so it is horizontal. The Cover Browser appears. Each cover represents an album from which you have at least one song stored on your iPhone.

4. To browse your music, swipe a finger to the right to move ahead in the albums or to the left to move back; the faster you swipe, the faster you scroll through the albums.

5. To see the songs on an album, tap its cover. The album "opens." On the left side of the screen are the album art and the playback controls. On the right side of the screen is a list of all the songs from that album that are available to you.

6. To browse the list of songs, swipe your finger up or down the screen.

7. To play a song, tap it. The song plays and is marked with a red "graphic equalizer" icon on the list of songs.

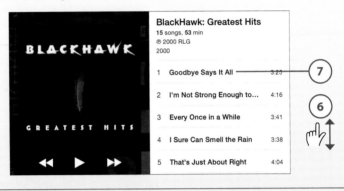

Turn It Up! (Or Down!)

No matter which technique you use to find and play music, you can control the volume using the Volume buttons on the left side of iPhone. Press the upper button to increase volume or the lower one to decrease it. While you are pressing a button, a volume indicator appears on the screen to show you the relative volume level as you press the keys. When you are on the Now Playing screen or viewing the Music control bar, you can use the Volume slider to set the sound level. And if you listen with the EarPods included with your iPhone, you can use the buttons on the right EarPod's wire to crank it up (or down).

8. To pause a song, tap the Pause button. The music pauses, and the Play button replaces the Pause button; tap Play to start the music again.

9. To jump to the previous song on the list, tap the Previous button.

10. To jump to the next song on the list, tap the Next button.

11. To play a different song on the list, tap it.

12. To return to the browser, tap the album cover. The music continues to play.

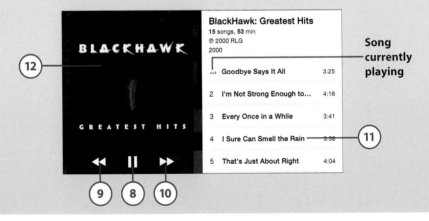

Shuffle Off (But Not to Buffalo)

If the Shuffle setting is active (you learn how to set this later), when you tap the Previous or Next button, the song that plays is random rather than being the previous or next one on the list. Unfortunately, there's no way to tell whether Shuffle is active from the Cover Browser. You have to move to the Now Playing screen for that.

13. While you're listening, you can continue browsing to find more music you want to listen to. When you select more music to play, it replaces the music currently playing.

14. Rotate the iPhone to be vertical to see the Now Playing screen.

15. Use the Now Playing screen to control the music (covered in detail in the "Playing Music on the Now Playing Screen" task later in this section).

Finding Music

Before you can listen to music, you need to find the music you want to listen to by using one of the many browsing and searching features the Music app offers. These include the Cover Browser you learned about in the previous section, working with playlists, browsing your music by artist, searching, and so on.

Finding Music by Playlist

Playlists are collections of music you create in iTunes on a computer or directly on the iPhone. A playlist can include music grouped for any reason, such as being from the same artist, your favorite songs, and so on. Finding and listening to music in your iTunes playlists that you have moved onto your iPhone is simple.

1. On the Home screen, tap Music.

2. Tap the Playlists button. The playlists on your iPhone appear. If you use folders to organize your playlists, you see those folders on the Playlists screen. For example, if you have a folder called "Best Rock" in iTunes, a playlist called "Best Rock" appears on the Playlists screen and contains all the playlists in the Best Rock folder. Playlists marked with the "nuclear" symbol were create by the iTunes Genius (you learn all about this feature later in this chapter).

3. Swipe your finger up and down the list to browse your playlists.

4. Tap a playlist or folder you'd like to explore. The list of songs in that playlist or the list of playlists within the folder appears with the title of the playlist or folder at the top of the screen.

Genius playlist

I See Music

If music is already playing when you open the Music app, you automatically move to the Now Playing screen. Tap the back button, which is located in the upper-left corner of the screen and you'll see the Playlists button at the bottom of the screen.

5. If you moved into a folder containing playlists, swipe up and down the screen to browse the playlists in that folder; if you moved into a playlist, skip to step 7.

6. Tap the playlist you want to see.

7. Swipe your finger up and down to browse the songs the playlist contains. (You can also search a playlist by swiping down from the top of the screen until you see the Search bar; learn how in the section "Finding Music by Searching" later in this chapter.)

8. When you find a song you want to listen to, tap it. The song begins to play, and the Now Playing screen appears.

9. Use the Now Playing screen to control the music (covered in detail in the "Playing Music on the Now Playing Screen" section later in this chapter).

10. Tap the back button to move back to the playlist's screen. (When you view a playlist's screen, the song currently playing is marked with the red graphic equalizer icon.)

>>>Go Further

ROLL YOUR OWN PLAYLISTS

You can manually create new playlists in the Music app. Tap New Playlist at the top of the Playlists screen. Name and save the playlist at the prompt. On the resulting screen, swipe up and down the list of songs to find a song you want to add to the playlist. Tap a song's Add button (+) to add it to the new playlist; the song's Add button is grayed out to show you it has been added. Add as many songs as you want in the same way. Tap Done. You move to the playlist's screen. Tap Edit. Change the order of songs in the playlist by dragging the Order button on the right edge of the screen up or down. Tap a song's Unlock button and then tap Delete to delete it from the playlist. Tap the Add button (+) in the upper-right corner of the screen to add more songs. When you're done changing the playlist, tap Done. You can listen to the new playlist just like any other playlist you have. The next time you sync your iPhone with iTunes, the new playlist is added to that iTunes so you can listen to it on the computer, too. (From there, you can sync it to other iOS devices, such as an iPad.)

Finding Music by Artist

You can find music by browsing artists whose music is stored on your iPhone. You can then see all the music by a specific artist and select the music you want to play.

1. On the Home screen, tap Music.

2. Tap Artists. (If you don't see the Artists button, tap the back button located in the upper-left corner of the screen until you do.) The list of all artists whose music or all authors whose audiobooks are available to the Music app appears. Artists are grouped by the first letter of their first name or by the first letter of the group's name (not counting *the* as the first word in a name).

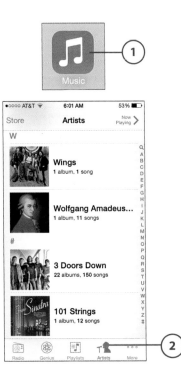

3. Swipe your finger up and down the list to browse all available artists.

4. To jump to a specific artist, tap the letter along the right side of the screen for the artist's or group's first name; to jump to an artist or a group whose name starts with a number, tap # at the bottom of the screen. For each artist, you see album art associated with the artist's music along with the number of albums and songs available to you.

Browse with Speed

If you swipe on top of the index, you can browse screens at a very fast speed. This is especially useful when you are browsing very long lists.

5. Tap an artist whose music you'd like to explore. A list of songs by that artist appears. If you have more than one album by that artist, the songs are organized by album.

6. Swipe your finger up and down the screen to browse the artist's albums. As you swipe up or down, you see the next album on the list. An album continues to appear on the screen as long as at least one of its songs remains on the screen, when you scroll past the last song on the album, the next album's art "bumps" the first album's art off the screen.

7. When you find the song you want to listen to, tap it. The song begins to play, and the Now Playing screen appears.

8. Use the Now Playing screen to control the music (covered in detail in the "Playing Music on the Now Playing Screen" task later in this section).

9. Tap the back button to move back to the artist's screen to find and play more music by the current artist.

To Now Playing and Back

Whenever music is playing or paused, the Now Playing screen is active even when it isn't visible. You can move to the Now Playing screen by tapping the Now Playing button located in the upper-right corner of the screen. You can return from the Now Playing screen back to where you were by tapping the back button, which is always located in the upper-left corner of the Now Playing screen.

10. Tap Artists to move back to the Artists screen to browse music by other artists.

Shuffling an Artist's Music

If you tap the Shuffle button next to any album on an artist's screen, music by that artist is randomly selected and begins to play. When the first song finishes, another is selected at random from that artist's music and it plays. This continues until you stop playing music or until all the artist's songs are played.

Finding Music in Other Ways

On the Music toolbar are five buttons. The first four are ways you can select music in which you are interested (you've already learned how to use two of these: Playlists and Artists). The More button takes you to the More screen that shows you all the content categories available in the Music app. (You see only categories that apply to you—for example, if you don't have any audiobooks in your collection, you won't see the Audiobooks category.) You can use this screen to access content when it can't be found by one of the category buttons on the toolbar at the bottom of the screen.

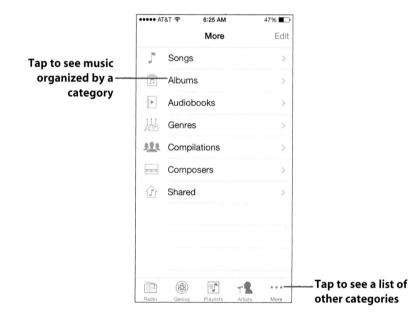

Tap to see music organized by a category

Tap to see a list of other categories

Open the Music app and tap More. The More screen appears. You see the categories that aren't currently on the toolbar (in a later note, you learn how to configure the toolbar's contents), including:

- **Songs**—This option shows you a list of all the songs available to you. The list is organized alphabetically; you can browse it or tap a letter on the index to jump to songs starting with that letter. Tap a song to play it.

- **Albums**—This view is similar to Songs and Artists except music is organized by album. You can browse albums. Tap an album whose music you want to listen to. You see a list of songs on that album and can tap a song to play it.

- **Audiobooks**—This takes you to a list of the audiobooks available to you. Browse the books and then tap a book you want to listen to. Listening to audiobooks is similar to listening to music.

- **Genres**—This list shows you music by the genre with which it is associated, such as Rock, Country, and so on.

- **Compilations**—This is similar to albums except a compilation can contain songs from multiple artists, such as greatest hits of the '70s, or a collection of songs grouped in other ways.

- **Composers**—Songs can have composers associated with them (composers are responsible for writing the music) while the artist is responsible for playing it. Sometimes these are the same people, but sometimes they aren't, especially for classical music. This shows you music organized by composer rather than artist.

- **Shared**—The Share source shows you music being shared via the Home Sharing feature. When you tap this, you see a list of all the iTunes Libraries being shared. Tap a library to see the music available to you. Browse, select, and play shared music as you do with music in your iPhone's music library. (If a shared library requires a password, you have to enter that to be able to access its music.)

>>>Go Further

CONFIGURING THE MUSIC TOOLBAR

As you have seen, the five buttons on the toolbar at the bottom of the Music app screen enable you to get to specific content quickly. You can choose four of the buttons that appear on the screen to make accessing content by the categories that are most useful to you even easier and faster. Tap More to move to the More screen. Tap Edit, and drag a button you want to add to the toolbar from the top part of the screen to the location of one of the buttons currently on the toolbar. Lift your finger when the button is in the location where you want to place it. The button you dragged replaces the button over which you placed it. The original button is moved onto the upper part of the screen and becomes available on the More screen. Drag the buttons on the toolbar to the left or right until they are in the order you want them to be. Tap Done. The Music toolbar contains the buttons you placed on it in the order you set for them along with the More button.

Finding Music by Searching

Browsing is a useful way to find music, but it can be faster to search for specific music in which you are interested. You can search most of the screens you browse. When a category, such as Songs, contains many items, searching can get you where you want to go more quickly than browsing. Here's how:

1. Move to a screen you can browse; this example uses the Songs screen, but you can search most screens similarly.

2. Swipe down to move to the top of the screen where you see the Search tool, or tap the magnifying glass icon at the top of the screen's index.

3. Tap in the Search tool.

4. Type the text or numbers for which you want to search. As you type, the items that meet your search criterion are shown; the more you type, the more specific your search becomes. Below the Search tool, the results are organized into categories, such as Albums and Songs.

5. When you think you've typed enough to find what you're looking for, tap Search. The keyboard disappears.

6. Browse the results.

7. Tap a song or album to get to the music you want to play.

Clearing a Search

You can clear a search by tapping the "x" that appears on the right end of the Search tool. Tapping Cancel does the same thing except it also closes the search screen.

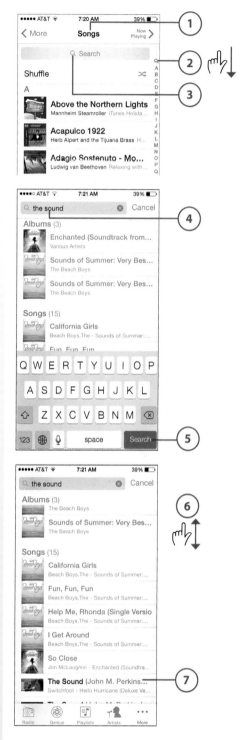

Playing Music

After you find and select what you want to hear, use the iPhone's music playback controls to listen to your heart's content. You can control music playback from a number of places.

Playing Music on the Now Playing Screen

As you have seen, the Now Playing screen appears when you play music and the iPhone is in vertical orientation (if it is horizontal orientation, you see the Cover Browser instead). In the upper part of the screen the cover art for the current song (for the album from which the song comes) is shown. In the lower part of the screen are controls for the music and information about it. The Now Playing screen has many features, including:

- **Timeline**—Just below the art, you see the timeline. The elapsed time is on the left side, and the remaining time is on the right. The red line is the Playhead that shows you where you are in the song. You can drag this to the left to move back in the song or to the right to move ahead.

- **Song information**—Below the Timeline is the song's name (in larger, bold font). Under that is the artist and album title. If any of this information is too large to fit on the screen, it scrolls across the screen to display it all.

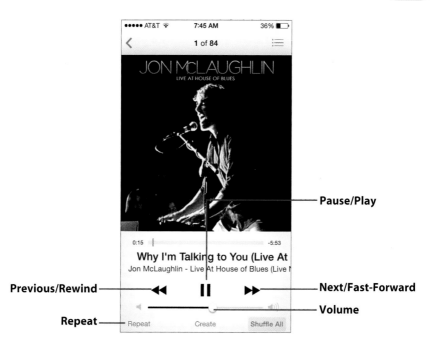

- **Previous/Rewind**—If the current song has been playing for more than a second or two, tap this button once to move to the beginning of the current song. If you are at the beginning of the current song, tap it to move to the previous song in the current source (album, artist, and so on). Tap and hold to rewind in the current song.

- **Pause/Play**—Tap Pause to pause the song. Tap Play to play it again.

- **Next/Fast-Forward**—Tap once to move to the next song on the list (or the next randomly selected song if you are shuffling). Tap and hold to fast-forward in the current song.

- **Volume**—Drag the slider to the left to lower the volume or to the right to increase it.

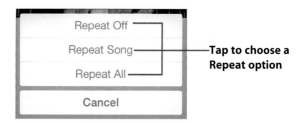

- **Repeat**—Tap Repeat to make the Repeat menu appear. Tap Repeat Song to repeat the current song. Tap Repeat All to repeat everything currently selected. For example, if you came to the Now Playing screen from the Artists screen, Repeat All causes all the artist's songs to be repeated. If you came from an album, all the songs on the album are repeated. Tap Repeat Off to stop repeating. The Repeat button changes to reflect the current state. For example, when Repeat All is selected, the button becomes Repeat All.

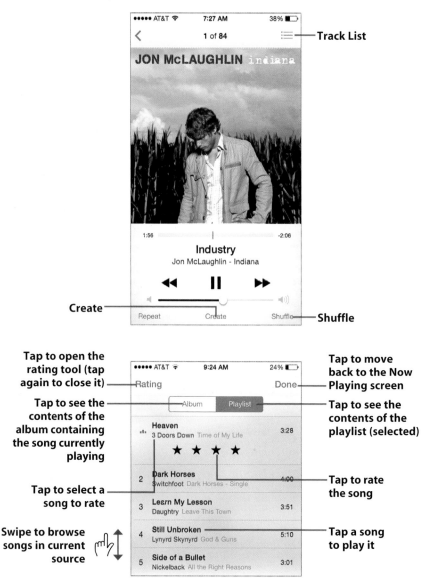

- **Create**—This creates a new genius playlist. The Genius is covered in detail later in this chapter.

- **Shuffle**—Tap Shuffle, which becomes Shuffle All, indicating that all the music in the current selection (artist, album, and so on) will be played randomly. When the current song finishes, another one from the group is selected randomly and played. Tap Shuffle All to turn off Shuffle so that songs play in the order in which they appear (top to bottom) on the screen from where you came to get to the Now Playing screen (such as an album's screen). (See the "Shuffling Music" section for more information).

- **Track List**—Tap the Track List button. The contents of the current source are shown. Depending on the source of music you are playing, you might see two tabs. For example, if you are playing a playlist, the Playlist tab shows the contents of the playlist while the Album tab shows the contents of the album that contains the song currently playing. Tap the tab for the contents you want to see. Swipe up or down the list to browse the songs. Tap a song to play it.

  To rate a song, tap Rating, tap the song you want to rate, and then tap the number of stars you want to give the song (between one and five). (Of course, the song plays when you tap it if it is not currently playing.) The ratings you apply to songs can be used to give you information about how much you like the song, and they can be used in smart playlists, such as to play songs in the Rock genre you have rated at four starts or higher.

  To return to the prior screen, tap Done. You see the album art and playback controls again.

Back to the Album

If you tap the Album tab and then tap a song on that album that isn't in the current playlist, you change the source of music from the playlist to the album. The Playlist tab closes and from that point on, you work with the album as the source.

Tap to move back to the source

Tap the album art to display lyrics (if there are any)

Swipe up or down to read the lyrics

Tap lyrics to hide them

- **Lyrics**—In iTunes, you can associate lyrics with songs. Assuming you haven't disabled the Lyrics & Podcast Info setting (see "Configuring Music Settings"), tap the art to display the song's lyrics. Swipe up and down on the lyrics to read them all. Tap the lyrics to hide them again.

  If a song doesn't have lyrics, when you tap it, the Rating tool replaces the song information (see the following note).

- **Back**—Tap the back button to move to the current source's (album's, playlist's, and so on) screen.

Another Way to Rate

If you tap the song information on the Now Playing screen, the information is replaced by the rating tool. Tap the number of stars with which you want to rate the song. Tap outside the rating tool to display the song information again.

>>>Go Further

COMPLETING ALBUMS

If you don't have all the songs on an album that is available in the iTunes Store, when you browse its contents, you see the Show Complete Album link. Tap this to see all the songs on the album. Tap a song's price button to buy and download it. Tap the Complete my album button, which shows the price to add all the songs on the album, to buy and download all the songs on the album that aren't currently in your library.

Playing Music from the Control Center

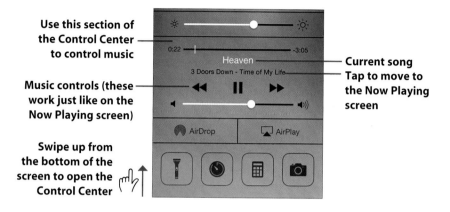

Use this section of the Control Center to control music — *(points to Music section)*

Current song
Tap to move to the Now Playing screen

Music controls (these work just like on the Now Playing screen)

Swipe up from the bottom of the screen to open the Control Center

As you've seen, the Now Playing screen provides lots of control for your music. However, it can take several taps to get back to that screen if you are using your iPhone for something else while you listen to music. To get to most of the music controls quickly, swipe up from the bottom of the screen to open the Control Center. Just above the AirDrop and AirPlay buttons is the Music section. Here you see some of the controls you can use for music playback; the controls here work the same as on the Now Playing screen.

Use the controls you see; then close the Control Center by swiping down from its top and continue what you were doing. Or, tap the artist—title information to jump to the Now Playing screen (the Control Center closes when you do this).

More than Just Music

What I've called the Music section of Control Center, I should have called the Audio Controls section because it changes based on the app you are using to play audio. For example, when you are using the Podcasts app to play a podcast, these tools control the podcast playback. Likewise, if you play audio with a different app, these controls work for that app. In other words, this section reflects the app currently playing audio.

Playing Music from the Lock Screen

When audio is playing and your iPhone is locked, it would be a hassle to move back to the Music app to control that audio; you'd have to tap the Touch ID/Home button or Sleep/Wake button to wake the iPhone up, unlock the phone, and then move to the Music app (which can require several steps depending on what you were last doing). Fortunately, you can control music playback right from the Lock screen.

Press the Sleep/Wake or Touch ID/Home button. Your iPhone wakes up and you see the Lock screen, which displays information about and controls for the music currently playing. Use the controls you see; these work like they do on the Now Playing screen (of course, there are more controls on that screen).

When you're done controlling the tunes, tap the Sleep/Wake button again if you want to prevent the controls from being on the screen (so that they don't accidentally get activated if you put your iPhone back in your pocket, for example).

Music controls (these work just like on the Now Playing screen)

Current song

Album art of current song

Shuffling Music

Shuffling music is a good way to keep your music fresh because you don't know which song will be played next. As you learned earlier, you can shuffle music from the Now Playing screen by tapping the Shuffle button. There are a couple of other ways to shuffle, too:

Tap to shuffle the playlist

Tap to shuffle music from the artist

- When you are browsing a source of music, such as a playlist, an artist, or an album, tap the Shuffle button. A song is randomly selected from the source and begins to play. You move to the Now Playing screen where you see the Shuffle All button is active. The first song plays; when it finishes, the next song is selected at random from the current source and plays.

- Start music playing and gently shake your iPhone in a back-and-forth motion. A song is selected at random and begins to play. You can shake your iPhone at any time to move to the next randomly selected song. (This requires the Shake to Shuffle setting to be enabled, as explained in "Configuring Music Settings.") (If you are carrying your iPhone around in a pocket or bag, it's a good idea to leave this setting disabled; otherwise, you might find your music shuffling in the middle of songs.)

Controlling Music from the EarPods

You have basic controls over music by using the switch on the EarPods that came with your iPhone. Press the upper part of the switch to increase volume or the lower part to decrease it. Press the center part to play or pause music.

Creating and Using Genius Playlists

The Genius feature finds music and builds playlists based on songs that "go with" a specific song. How the Genius selects songs that "sound good" with other songs is a bit of a secret, but it works amazingly well. You can have the Genius build a playlist for you in a couple of ways and then listen to or update it.

To create a Genius playlist based on the song currently playing, do the following:

1. Find and play a song using any of the techniques you learned earlier in this chapter; you see the Now Playing screen.

2. Tap Create.

3. Tap Genius Playlist. The Genius playlist is created, and you move to the Genius screen where you see the songs the Genius selected. The song that is currently playing is at the top of the list and is marked with the Genius and read graphic equalizer icons.

4. Swipe up and down the list to browse the songs the Genius included.

5. To save the playlist, tap Save. The name of the playlist changes from Genius Playlist to be the name of the song on which the playlist was based. The New button disappears, and the Delete button appears.

Song the genius playlist is based on

BECOMING A GENIUS WITH THE GENIUS

>>>Go Further

The Genius can be really useful. Check out these other genius tips:

- Here's another way to have the Genius create a playlist for you; with this method, you don't have to play the song you want to use first. Move to the Playlists screen. Swipe down the screen so you see the top of it. Tap Genius Playlist. You see the Songs screen on which all the songs available to you are displayed. Browse the list, use the index, or search to find the song on which you want the Genius to base the new playlist. Tap that song. The Genius creates the playlist, and you move back to the Playlists screen. Tap the new playlist, which is called Genius Playlist. You see the songs it contains. If you want to save the playlist, tap Save.

- Genius playlists appear on the Playlists screen like other playlists you have created, except they are marked with the Genius icon. You can play Genius playlists just like others on the Playlists screen.

- Genius playlists are also moved into your iTunes Library on your computer the next time you sync your iPhone.

- The Genius can change the songs in a Genius playlist for you so it becomes a new, fresh playlist. To do this, view the playlist and tap Refresh. The Genius selects a new set of songs based on the playlist's title song.

- To delete a genius playlist you have saved, open its screen and tap Delete. Tap Delete Playlist. The playlist is deleted. (If you have synced your iPhone since you saved the playlist, you won't see the Delete button because the playlist has been saved to your iTunes Library. To delete a playlist after you've synced your iPhone, delete it from your iTunes Library or remove it from the sync settings and then re-sync the iPhone.)

- You can also delete a Genius playlist by opening the Playlists screen and swiping to the left on the playlist you want to delete. Tap Delete. The playlist is deleted.

Siri and Music

You can use Siri to select, play, and control music, too. Refer to Chapter 12, "Working with Siri," for details.

Using AirPlay to Listen to Your iPhone's Music on Other Devices

With AirPlay, you can stream your music and other audio to other devices so you can hear it using a sound system instead of the iPhone's speakers or EarPods. For example, if you have an Apple TV connected to a home theater system, you can stream your audio to the Apple TV so it will play via the home theater's audio system. You can also stream to an AirPort Express base station to which you've connected speakers. Or, you can stream to AirPlay-compatible speakers that are designed to receive AirPlay signals directly. And for yet another option, you can stream music to Bluetooth speakers.

To use AirPlay, your iPhone needs to be on the same Wi-Fi network as the devices to which you are going to stream the music or your iPhone needs to be paired and connected to the Bluetooth speakers you are going to use (see Chapter 2, "Connecting Your iPhone to the Internet, Bluetooth Devices, and iPhones/iPods/iPads").

After you have set up the devices you are going to use, such as an AirPort Express base station and speakers, you can stream to them using the following steps:

1. Play the music or audio you want to stream.

2. Swipe up from the bottom of the screen to open the Control Center.

3. Tap AirPlay.

4. Tap the device to which you want to stream the music. It is marked with a check mark to show it is the active device.

5. Tap Done.

6. Use the playback controls you learned about earlier to control the music. If you are using an AppleTV, use the controls on the audio system to which it is connected to control the volume.

7. To return the sound to your iPhone, perform steps 2 and 3, tap iPhone, and then tap Done.

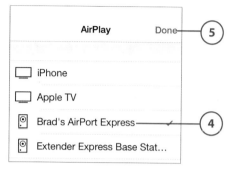

It's Not All Good

Unfortunately, you can only select and stream to one AirPlay device at a time.

Downloading Songs

If there are songs available but that aren't stored on your iPhone, you see the Download button, which is a cloud with a downward-pointing arrow. Tap this button to download the song to your iPhone. You also see the Download All command at the top of lists (such as the Artists screen) when there are multiple items that aren't downloaded. Tap Download All to download all the items on the list to your iPhone.

Listening to Music with iTunes Match

iTunes Match is useful because you don't have to worry about syncing the music in your iTunes Library to your iPhone; any music in your iTunes Library is available on your iPhone automatically. If the music you want to hear isn't already stored on the iPhone, when you select it, it gets downloaded and begins to play.

Listening to music with iTunes Match is similar to listening to music you've moved onto your iPhone by downloading or syncing it. The difference is that you might have to download the music to your iPhone before you can play it (it can download and play at the same time, which is called *streaming*). Music that needs to be downloaded to your iPhone is marked with the Download button; if you don't see this, the music has already been downloaded and you can listen to it immediately.

To start using iTunes Match, you need to add it to your iCloud account and configure iTunes on your computer and your iPhone to use it. These tasks are explained in "Working with iTunes Match" in Chapter 5.

After iTunes Match is set up, finding and playing music is just like when your music is stored on your iPhone. The following example uses the Albums option; working with other options is similar.

More than One Library?

If you have more than one iTunes Library, such as one on a work computer and one on a computer at home, you can configure each to use iTunes Match. The music from both libraries is available in the cloud and can be played on your iPhone.

To download and play an album with iTunes Match, do the following:

1. Open the Music app and tap the Albums button (if Albums is not on the toolbar, tap More and then tap Albums).

2. Use the techniques you learned in previous tasks to browse or search for the album you want to hear.

3. Tap the album. You see its information at the top of the screen and the list of songs it contains at the bottom.

4. To download the entire album, tap the Download button next to the album's information at the top of the screen; to download individual songs, tap their Download buttons. As each track is downloaded to your iPhone, you see each song's download status in the circle icon. When the song has been downloaded, the icon disappears. When all the songs have downloaded, the Download buttons next to the album and each song disappear.

Download album

Download song

5. Use the techniques you learned previously in this chapter to play and control the tunes.

Download and Listen with One Tap

You don't have to download music before you can listen to it. To download and play music from the cloud, simply tap the song you want to hear; it starts to download and you move to the Now Playing screen. As soon as enough has downloaded so that it will play with no pauses, it starts to play.

MORE ON ITUNES MATCH

Here are some more points to ponder when it comes to using iTunes Match:

- If you are going to be without an Internet connection for a while, make sure any music you want to listen to is downloaded on your iPhone so you can listen to it when you do not have an Internet connection.

- If you have a slow connection, it can take a moment for a song that is downloading to start playing after you tap it.

- If content is grayed out or has the cloud icon with a slash through it next to it, it is not available in the cloud so you can't download and play it. This is likely because it just hasn't been uploaded by iTunes Match yet. If you come back to the content at a later time, it will probably be available. Or, it might be content of a type that can't be uploaded to iTunes Match, such as a digital booklet that was included with an album.

>>>Go Further

- If you have enabled the setting to allow it (which is on the iTunes & App Store Settings screen), you can download content when you are connected to the cloud via a cellular network. However, music files are large and if your data plan has a limit, you might exceed that limit if you download a lot of music. If this is the case for you, it's better to download when you are connected to Wi-Fi because there is seldom a limit to the amount of data you can download over Wi-Fi.

- If you need to make room on your iPhone, you can delete songs by swiping to the left on the songs you want to delete and tapping Delete. The songs are removed from the iPhone but remain visible and are marked with the Download button so you can download them again later.

Listening to iTunes Radio

iTunes Radio streams music from the Internet onto your iPhone, much like listening to radio on a car or home stereo. However, with iTunes Radio you can create your own stations. The stations you create can be based on types of music you like or based on music that is similar to music you know you like. (If you've used Pandora, iHeart Radio, or similar services, you'll understand how to use iTunes Radio right away because it is similar to those services.)

Look Ma! No Ads!

If you use iTunes Match, you can listen to iTunes Radio free of advertising. If you don't use iTunes Match, you'll have to deal with a few ads here and there, but these are nowhere near as prevalent as on standard AM or FM radio stations.

In iTunes Radio, there are two basic types of stations. Featured Stations are those that are "default" and you can immediately listen to. My Stations are stations you create.

When you listen to iTunes Radio and discover music you'd like to have in your collection, it's simple to buy and download that music from the iTunes Store so you have it permanently.

You can also indicate music you like; over time, iTunes Radio tailors the music it selects and plays for you based on music you like (this is kind of like the Genius you learned about earlier).

Listening to a Featured Station

To listen to a featured station, do the following:

1. On the Home screen, tap Music.

2. Tap Radio.

The First Time

The first time you select Radio, you see the Welcome screen. Tap Start Listening to, well, start listening.

3. Swipe to the left and right on the Featured Stations to browse the stations available to you. (You might find the selection of music on the Featured Stations to be limited; most of the time, you'll probably listen to stations you create anyway.)

4. Tap the station you want to hear. The first song starts to play and you move to iTunes Radio's Now Playing screen, which is similar to the Now Playing screen you see when you are listening to your own music collection.

5. Use the controls you see to play the music; see "Playing iTunes Radio Music" for details.

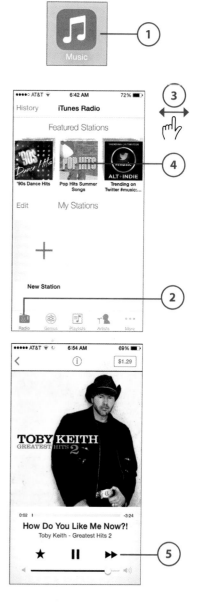

Creating an iTunes Radio Station Based on an Artist, a Genre, or a Song

To create your own stations, do the following:

1. On the Home screen, tap Music.

2. Tap Radio.

3. Tap New Station. (If you have created stations already, you might need to swipe up the screen because the New Station button appears at the end of the list of your stations.)

4. Enter an artist, a genre, or a song in the bar at the top of the screen. As you type, the app presents a list of possible matches.

5. If you want to use one of the matches, tap it. The station is created and it starts to play; skip to step 9.

6. Tap Search to see the full list of results.

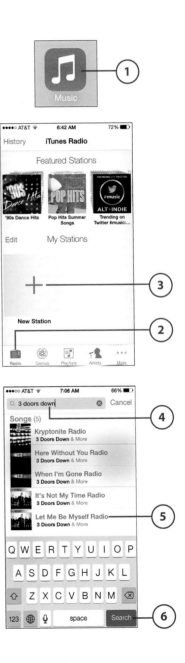

7. Swipe up and down the screen to browse the results. The results are grouped by type, such as Songs or Artists. The type you selected determines what the new station is based on. For example, if you tap an artist, the new station has music made by "similar" artists. If you tap a song, the new station Is based on similar songs.

8. Tap the song, artist, or other result on which you want your new station based. The new station is created and you move back to the iTunes Radio screen briefly where you see your new station. The station starts playing and you move to iTunes Radio's Now Playing screen.

9. Use the controls you see to play the music; see "Playing iTunes Radio Music" for details.

10. Tap the back button. You move to the iTunes Radio screen and see the stations you have created.

11. Swipe up the screen until you see the New Station tool.

12. Tap New Station and repeat steps 4–8 to create more stations.

Creating Stations from the Defaults

When you tap New Station, the Search bar that you use in step 4 appears at the top of the screen. Below that, you see a list of genres that you can use to create a station, too. Swipe up and down to browse the list. Tap a genre of interest. You see a list of stations that belong to that genre. Tap a station to sample the music it contains. Tap the Add button (+) to add the station to your stations.

Listening to Your Stations

To listen to one of your stations, do the following:

1. Tap Radio.

2. Swipe up and down to browse your stations. (The current station's name is in red.)

3. Tap the station to which you want to listen.

4. Use the controls you see to play the music; see "Playing iTunes Radio Music" for details.

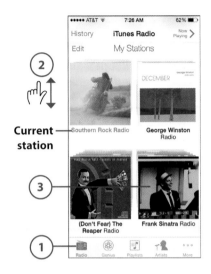

Current station

Playing iTunes Radio Music

Many of the controls you see on iTunes Radio's Now Playing screen are the same as on the Now Playing screen you learned about earlier. These include the back button, the Timeline (you can't drag the Playhead on this Timeline, however), Pause/Play, Next, and the Volume slider. Following are the controls unique to iTunes Radio you see and how you can use them:

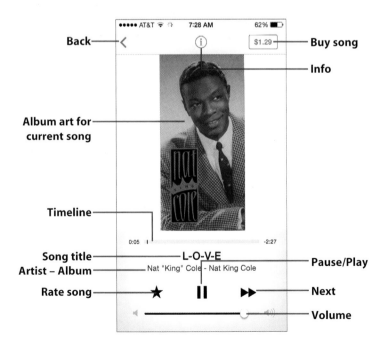

Tap to have iTunes Radio select more songs like this ——— Play More Like This ★

Tap to never hear ——— Never Play This Song ✕
this song again

Tap to add to ——— Add to iTunes Wish List ＋
your Wish List

- **Rate song**—Tap the star on the Now Playing screen. Tap Play More Like This to indicate you like the song so iTunes Radio should choose more songs like it; over time, the selection of songs you hear should get better as you "like" more songs. Tap Never Play This Song if you don't like the song and never want to hear it again. Tap Add to iTunes Wish List to add the song to your Wish List; you can go into the iTunes Store and buy the song from your Wish List at a later time.

  After you make a selection, the menu closes. If you tapped Play More Like This, the star becomes red to show you have "liked" the song. If you tapped Never Play This Song, the next song plays immediately. If you tapped Add to iTunes Wish List, the star is unchanged.

  If you tap the star again, you can undo your "like" (by tapping Play More Like This again) or remove the song from your Wish List. However, once you've "disliked" a song, it is gone forever (from your iTunes Radio playlist at any rate).

Info button ———  ——— Tap to buy the song

- **Buy song**—To buy and download a song, tap the button showing the song's price. Then tap BUY SONG. If you're prompted to sign into your Apple ID, touch the Touch ID/Home button if you are using an iPhone 5S or enter your Apple ID password and tap OK if you are using a different model. The song is added to your Music Library.

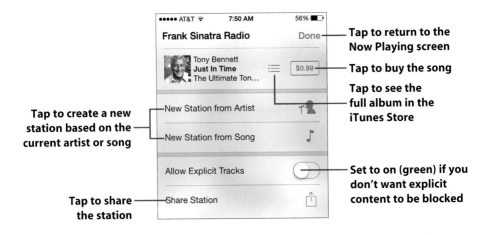

Tap to return to the Now Playing screen

Tap to buy the song

Tap to see the full album in the iTunes Store

Tap to create a new station based on the current artist or song

Set to on (green) if you don't want explicit content to be blocked

Tap to share the station

- **Info**—Tap the Info button to see a menu with a number of options. You can buy the song by tapping its price. You can see the full album containing the song in the iTunes Store. You create another station based on the artist or song, and you can even prevent or allow explicit content. You can also share the station with others. Tap Done to return to the Now Playing screen.

TURNING ITUNES RADIO UP

Here are a few more things you can do with iTunes Radio:

- To change one of your stations, tap Edit on the iTunes Radio screen (if you are on the Now Playing screen, tap the back button to move there). You see the My Station screen. Tap the station you want to edit. On the resulting screen, you can change the station's name and add more artists, songs, or genres that should be included in the station. You can also select songs, artists, or genres you don't want to play with the station.

- You can delete one of your stations by moving to the My Stations screen and swiping to the left on the station you want to delete. Tap Delete.

- At the top of the iTunes Radio screen, tap History. On the Played tab, you see a list of songs you have played, grouped by the station that played them. You can browse the list and tap a song to play it again. Tap the price button to buy a song, or tap Wish List to see songs on your iTunes Wish List. You can buy a song on the list by tapping its price button. To clear either list, tap the Clear button and then confirm that you want to clear it. Tap Done to close the History screen.

View, edit, and share photos, slideshows, and video

Take photos and video

Configure photo-related settings

In this chapter, you'll explore all the photo and video functionality that the iPhone has to offer. Topics include the following:

→ Setting your Photos & Camera preferences
→ Taking photos and video with your iPhone
→ Viewing, editing, and working with photos on your iPhone
→ Viewing, editing, and working with video on your iPhone
→ Using AirPlay to view photos and videos on a TV
→ Working with Photo Stream

Working with Photos and Video You Take with Your iPhone

The iPhone's Camera app takes very good quality photos and video. Because you'll likely have your iPhone with you at all times, it's handy to capture photos with it whenever and wherever you are. And, you can capture video just as easily.

Whether you've taken photos and video on your iPhone or added them from another source, the Photos app enables you to edit, view, organize, and share your photos. You'll likely find that taking and working with photos and videos are one of the most useful things your iPhone can do.

Setting Your Photos & Camera Preferences

There are a number of settings related to the Photos and Camera app that you can set with the following steps:

1. On the Home screen, tap Settings.

2. Swipe up until you see Photos & Camera.

3. Tap Photos & Camera.

4. To have your iPhone automatically download photos from and upload photos to your Photo Stream, set My Photo Stream to on (green); if you don't want photos to be downloaded or uploaded automatically, set it to off (white) instead. (Photo Stream is explained in more detail in the section "Working with Photo Stream" later in this chapter.)

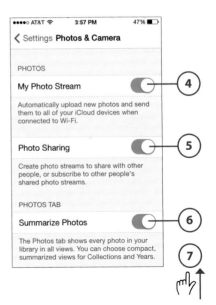

iCloud Required

To use Photo Stream, you must have iCloud configured and Photo Stream enabled on your iPhone (see Chapter 3, "Setting Up iCloud and Other Online Accounts" for details).

5. To share your Photo Streams with others and to subscribe to other people's Photo Streams, slide the Photo Sharing switch to on (green).

6. Set the Summarize Photos switch to on (green) to see a more compact view of your photo collections in the Photos app; you see thumbnails for only some of the photos in a collection and the timeframe of each group is larger. If you set this to off (white) instead, you see a thumbnail of every photo in your collections, which take up much more screen space and you have to scroll more to move among your collections. This setting impacts how you see your collections and years only.

7. Swipe up the screen.

8. Tap Play Each Slide For, which impacts slideshows you view on your iPhone.

9. Tap the amount of time you want each slide in a slideshow to appear on the screen.

10. Tap Back.

11. To make slideshows repeat until you manually stop them, set Repeat to on (green). When the status is off (white), slideshows play through once and then stop.

12. To view photos in a random order in a slideshow, set Shuffle to on (green). To have photos appear in the order they are in the selected source, set Shuffle to off (white).

13. To display a grid when you are taking photos, set the Grid switch to on (green). This can be helpful to keep your photos aligned vertically and horizontally. If you don't want to see this grid, set Grid to off (white).

14. If you want only the HDR version of photos (see the note in the following section for more on HDR) to be saved, set Keep Normal Photo to off (white). If you want both the HDR version and the normal version to be saved, set Keep Normal Photo to on (green); note that this creates two versions of every photo you take, which takes up more space on your phone.

15. Tap Settings.

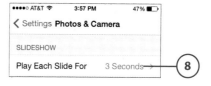

Taking Photos and Video with Your iPhone

Each generation of iPhone has had different photo and video capabilities and features. The current versions sport high-quality cameras, and in fact, there is a camera on each side of the iPhone. One takes photos of what you are looking at while one takes photos of what the screen is facing. Current generations also have a flash, the ability to zoom, and other features you'd expect from a digital camera.

An iPhone's photo and video capabilities and features are probably the largest area of difference between the models (except for the iPhone 5S's Touch ID feature, perhaps). Because of the fairly large variation in capabilities of the models that can run iOS 7, it's impossible to cover all the differences in this chapter; because the iPhone 5S is the most advanced model, it is the focus of this chapter. If you have a different model, some of the tasks described might not be applicable to your phone.

HDR

The High Dynamic Range (HDR) feature causes the iPhone to take three shots of each image with each shot having a different exposure level. It then combines the three images into one higher-quality image. You can choose to use HDR for specific photos when you take them. HDR works best for photos that don't have motion and where there is good lighting. (You can't use the iPhone's flash with HDR images.) Also, HDR photos take longer so you need to allow more time between photos when you use it. (This only matters if you are taking a series of images quickly.) When you use HDR for a photo and save the normal photo, too (step 14 in the previous task), you see two versions of each photo in the Photos app: One is the HDR version, and the other is the normal version. You might want to do this to see the difference between the two types. If you are happy with the HDR versions, set the Keep Normal Photo to off so that your photos don't use as much space on your iPhone and you don't have twice as many photos to deal with.

Taking Photos

You can use the Camera app to capture your photos, like so:

1. On the Home screen, tap Camera.

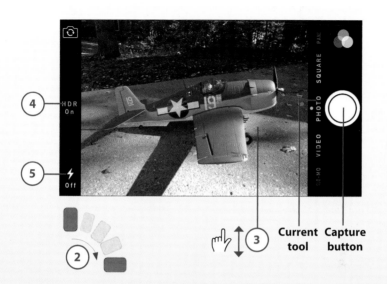

Current Capture
tool   button

2. To capture a horizontal photo , rotate your iPhone so that it's horizontal; of course, you can use either orientation to take photos just as you can with any other camera.

3. Swipe up or down (right or left if the phone is vertical) on the screen to choose the type of photo or video you want to take; as you swipe, the tool currently selected is shown in yellow just above the Capture button. Choose SLO-MO to take slow motion video (iPhone 5S), VIDEO to take standard speed video (more on video later), PHOTO to take a full-frame image, SQUARE to capture a square image, or PANO to take a panoramic image (steps to do this are in a later task). The PHOTO and SQUARE options work the same way, the only difference is the shape and proportion of the resulting photos.

4. To take an HDR image, tap HDR Off; it becomes HDR On in gold to show that you are taking HDR images. If you want to take only normal images, tap HDR On, which becomes HDR Off. This button indicates the current status of HDR, so you tap it to toggle this feature. (HDR is not always available, for example, when you turn the flash on.)

5. If you aren't using HDR, set the flash by tapping its current status. (When you enable HDR, flash is disabled automatically.) The flash menu appears.

6. Tap Auto to have the flash operate automatically, On to have it on for every photo, or Off to disable it. After you make a choice or after a few seconds of inactivity the Flash menu closes.

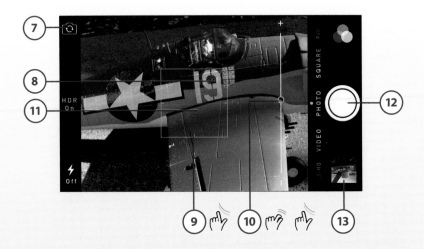

7. Tap the Lens Change button to switch the camera being used for the photo. When you change the lens, the image briefly freezes, and then the view changes to the other lens. The front lens (the one facing you when you look at the screen) has fewer features than the back lens. For example, you can't zoom when using the front lens nor does it use the flash. (The front lens is used most frequently for FaceTime and other video communication.) When you are using the front lens, some of the details in these steps won't apply, but the general process is the same.

8. Frame the image by moving and adjusting the iPhone's distance and angle to the image; if you have the Grid turned on, you can use its lines to help you frame the image way you want it.

9. To zoom in, unpinch on the image. The Zoom slider appears. (Reminder: You can't use zoom when taking photos with the frontside camera.)

10. Unpinch on the image or drag the slider toward the + to zoom in or pinch on the image or drag the slider toward the – to zoom out to change the level of zoom.

11. Tap the screen where you want the image to be focused. The yellow focus box appears where you tapped. This indicates where the focus and exposure are set.

12. Tap the Capture button on the screen, or either Volume button on the side of the iPhone. The iPhone captures the photo, and the shutter closes briefly while the photo is recorded. When the shutter opens again, you're ready to take the next photo. The process takes longer when HDR is on because the camera has to save three versions of the image and blend them together.

13. To see the photo you most recently captured, tap the Thumbnail button. The photo appears on the screen with iPhone's photo-viewing controls.

Lock It In

If you want to lock in the exposure and focus location, tap and hold your finger on the screen until the AE/AF Lock indicator appears on the screen. When you move the camera or the subject, the exposure and focus area remains locked in its position. Tap and hold on the screen until the indicator disappears to unlock it again.

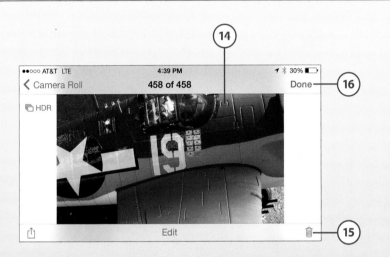

14. Use the photo-viewing tools to view the photo (see "Viewing, Editing, and Working with Photos on Your iPhone" later in this chapter for the details).

15. To delete a photo, tap the trash can, and then tap Delete Photo. The app deletes the photo, and you see the next photo in the Photo Roll album.

16. Tap Done. You move back into the Camera app, and you can take more photos.

Sensitive, Isn't It!

The iPhone's camera is sensitive to movement, so if your hand moves while you are taking a photo, it's likely to be blurry. Sometimes, part of the image will be in focus while part of it isn't, so be sure to check the view before you capture a photo. This is especially true when you zoom in. If you are getting blurry photos, the problem is probably your hand moving while you are taking them. Of course, since it's digital, you can take as many photos as you need to get it right; you'll want to delete the rejects (you learn how later) periodically, so you don't have to waste storage room or clutter up the Photos app with them.

Applying Filters to Your Photos

You can apply filters to photos as you take them as follows:

1. Use the skills you learned in the previous task to set up the photo you want to take.

2. Tap the Filters button. The Filters palette appears. You see a preview of the image as it would look with each filter applied to it.

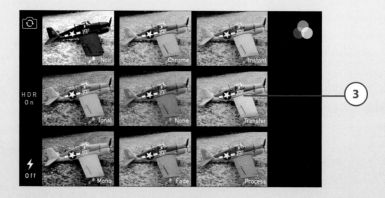

3. Tap the filter you want to apply. You return to the image you are capturing and see the filter applied to it. The Filters button is highlighted with color to show a filter is applied, in case you can't tell just by looking!

4. Tap the Capture button to take the photo with the filter applied.

5. To remove the current filter, tap the Filters button, and then tap None.

Location, Location!

If you allow the Camera app to use Location Services (you're prompted to allow this the first time you use the Camera app), the app uses the iPhone's GPS to tag the location where photos and video were captured. (Of course, you have to be in a location where the iPhone can receive the GPS signal.) Some apps can use this information, such as iPhoto, where you can use this data to locate your photos on maps, find photos by their locations, and so on.

Taking Panoramic Photos

The Camera app can take panoramic photos by capturing a series of images as you pan the camera across a screen, and then "stitching" those images together into one panoramic image. To take a panoramic photo, perform the following steps:

1. Open the Camera app.

2. Swipe on the toolbar or screen until PANO is selected. The app moves into Panorama mode. On the screen, you see a box representing the entire image and a smaller box representing the current photo.

3. Tap the Capture button. The app begins capturing images.

4. Slowly sweep the iPhone to the right while keeping the arrow centered on the line on the screen. This keeps the centerline consistent through all the images; the better you keep the arrow on the line, the better the photo will be.

5. When you've moved to the "end" of the image, tap the Stop button. You move back to the starting point and the panoramic photo is created.

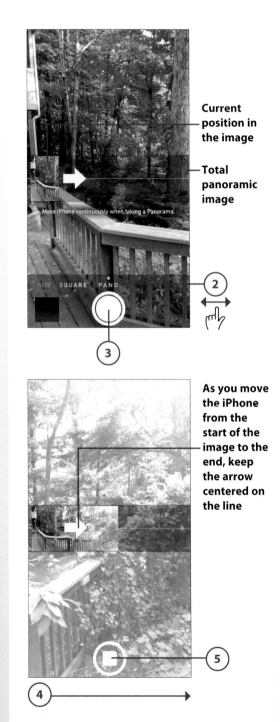

Current position in the image

Total panoramic image

As you move the iPhone from the start of the image to the end, keep the arrow centered on the line

6. Preview the image by tapping the preview icon. You see the image in the Photos app.

7. Use the photo-viewing tools to view the panoramic photo. (See "Viewing, Editing, and Working with Photos on Your iPhone" later in this chapter for the details.)

8. To delete a panoramic photo tap the trash can, and then tap Delete Photo. The app deletes the photo, and you see the next photo in the Photo Roll album.

9. Tap Done. You move back into the Camera app, and you can take more panoramic photos.

Panoramas Album

Panorama photos you take are automatically stored in the Panoramas album; you learn to work with albums later in this chapter.

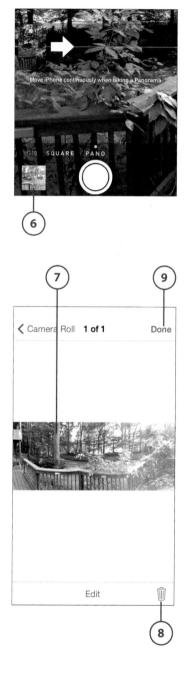

Taking Photos in Burst Mode (iPhone 5S)

With an iPhone 5S, you can rapidly take a series of photos, such as to capture action.

1. Open the Camera app and set the photo as you normally would.

2. When you are ready to start taking photos, tap and hold on the Capture button or either of the Volume buttons on the side of the phone. The Camera app rapidly takes a series of photos. As it captures images, you see the number of photos captured on the screen.

3. When you're done taking photos, lift your finger off the Capture button. (Later in this chapter, you learn how to work with Burst mode photos.)

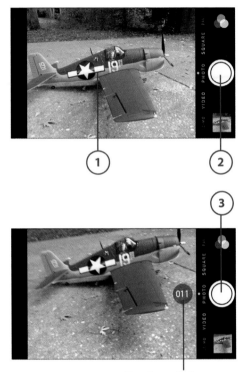

Number of photos you have taken in the burst

TAKING IPHONE SCREENSHOTS

>>>Go Further

There are times when it is useful to capture screen images of the iPhone's screen (such as when you are writing a book about your iPhone). The iPhone includes a screen capture utility you can use to take a picture of whatever is on iPhone's screen at any point in time. This is particularly helpful when you need to get help with a problem. Capture a screenshot showing the problem you are having and send it to whomever is trying to help you.

When the screen you want to capture appears, press the Home and Wake/Sleep buttons at the same time. The screen flashes white and the shutter sound plays to indicate the capture has been taken. The resulting image is stored in the Camera Roll album. You can view the screen captures you take, email them, move them onto a computer, or other tasks as you can with photos you take with the iPhone's camera.

Taking Video

You can capture video as easily as you can still images. Here's how.

1. On the Home screen, tap Camera.

2. To capture horizontal video, rotate the iPhone so that it's horizontal; of course, you can use either orientation to take video just as you can with any other video camera.

3. Swipe on the toolbar or screen until VIDEO is selected.

4. Choose the lens you want to use, configure the flash, or zoom in, just like setting up a still image. (The grid and HDR mode are not available when taking video.)

5. Tap on the screen where you want to focus. The yellow box indicates where you tapped.

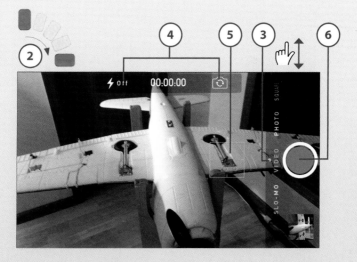

You Are Recording

When you tap the Record button, you hear the start/stop recording tone. When you stop recording, you hear the same tone. That's assuming you don't have the iPhone muted of course.

6. To start recording, tap the Record button. The Camera app starts capturing video; you see a counter on the screen showing how long you've been recording.

Length of video

7. To take still images while you take video, tap the Capture button.

8. To stop recording, tap Stop. Also, like still images, you can then tap the video's thumbnail to preview it. You can use the Photos app's video tools to view or edit the clip. (See "Viewing, Editing, and Working with Video on Your iPhone" later in this chapter for the details.)

Slow-Motion Video

If you have an iPhone 5S, you can also take slow-motion video. Choose SLO-MO on the toolbar; you see 120 FPS (Frames Per Second) on the screen indicating you are taking slow-motion video. Set up the shoot and take the video as you do with normal speed video. When you play it back, you can select the part you want to see in slow motion (see "Watching Slow-Motion Video (iPhone 5S)" later in this chapter).

Taking Photos and Video from the Lock Screen

Because it is likely to be with you constantly, your iPhone is a great camera of opportunity. You can use its Quick Access feature to quickly take photos when your iPhone is asleep/locked. Here's how:

1. Press the Touch ID/Home button. The Lock screen appears.

2. Swipe up on the camera icon. The Camera app opens. (If you don't swipe far enough up the screen, the Lock screen "drops" down again. Swipe almost all the way up the screen to open the Camera app.)

Bypass the Passcode

If you have a passcode set on your iPhone, you can use the Quick Access feature without tapping the Touch ID/Home button or entering your passcode. You can also view the photos you have taken since you started using Quick Access. To do anything else, you need to unlock your phone.

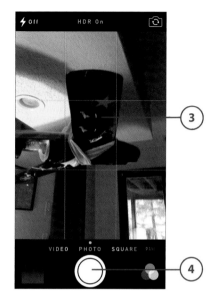

3. Use the iPhone's camera controls to frame and zoom the photo and set its options and filters as needed; these work just like when you start with the Camera app as described in the previous tasks.

4. Press either Volume button on the side of the iPhone, or tap the Capture button icon to take the photo. If you selected VIDEO, tap the Record button to start capturing video.

Taking Photos and Video from the Control Center

You can get to the camera quickly using the Control Center too.

1. Swipe up from the bottom of the screen to open the Control Center.

2. Tap the Camera button. The Camera app opens.

3. Use the Camera app to take photos or video as you've learned in the previous tasks. (In this figure, you see that the grid is turned on.)

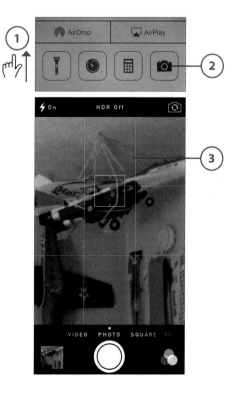

Viewing, Editing, and Working with Photos on Your iPhone

After you've loaded your iPhone with photos, you can use the Photos app to view them individually and as slideshows. You can also do some basic editing on your photos and use the photos on iPhone for a number of tasks, such as sharing your photos via AirDrop or email.

Finding Photos to Work With

The first step in viewing, editing, or doing other tasks with photos is finding the photos you want to work with. When you open the Photos app, you see three ways to access your photos: Photos, Shared, and Albums.

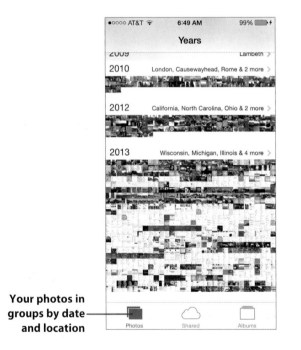

Your photos in groups by date and location

The Photos source organizes your photos with groupings of photos by date and location. (This is done automatically based on the data associated with your photos.) The top level is Years, which show your photos grouped by the year in which they were taken. You can then "drill down" into a year where you find collections, under which photos are organized by location and date ranges, which are determined according to the time, date, and location information on your photos. When you tap one of these collections, you drill down and see moments, which show you the detail of a collection. At the moment level, you see and can work with the individual photos in the collection.

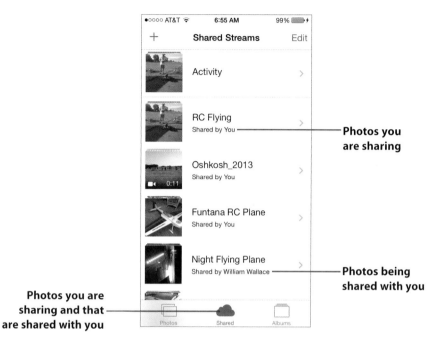

Photos you are
sharing and that
are shared with you

**Photos you
are sharing**

**Photos being
shared with you**

Shared shows photos you are sharing with other people and photos other people are sharing with you. For each group of photos being shared, you see the name of the group and who is sharing it (you, for photos you are sharing, or the name of the person sharing with you). When you tap a shared group, you see the photos it contains and can work with them. (Working with photo sharing is covered in detail in "Working with Photo Stream" later in this chapter.)

Albums allow you to organize your photos in a number of ways. Following are some of the albums or types of albums you see:

- **Camera Roll**. This album contains photos and videos you've taken with the iPhone's camera.

- **My Photo Stream**. This album contains photos you've taken with your iPhone or that have been uploaded from your other devices. (You'll learn about Photo Stream later in this chapter.)

- **Panoramas**. This album contains photos you've taken using the Camera app's Panorama tool.

- **Videos**. Videos you've taken with your iPhone are collected here.

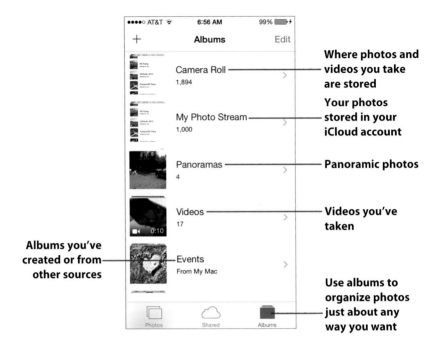

- **Albums synced from computers.** In Chapter 5, "Working with iTunes on Your Computer," you learned about syncing your iPhone with a computer. Photos can be included in the sync process, and you see any albums on a computer that you've included in the sync. These are identified by the source, such as "From My Mac," which indicates a folder synced from a Mac computer.

- **Albums you create.** Later in this chapter, you learn how to create albums for your photos. Albums that you've created on your iPhone are indicated by just having the name you give them (no "From" text).

Your Albums Might Vary
Some apps, such as Instagram, might add albums to those listed here.

While each of these sources looks a bit different, the steps to find the photos you want to work with are similar for all three sources; this example shows using the Photos source:

Collection Summary
Earlier, you learned about the Summarize Photos setting. This section assumes that setting is on. If not, your Collections screens may look a bit different.

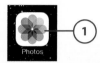

1. On the Home screen, tap Photos.

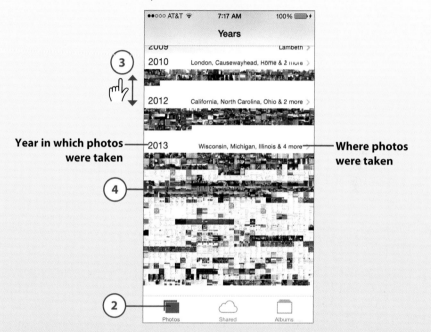

Year in which photos were taken

Where photos were taken

2. Tap Photos. On the Years screen, you see photos collected by the year in which they were taken. Next to the year, you see a summary of the various locations where the photos were taken.

Start at the Beginning

If the title at the top of the screen isn't "Years," tap the back button located in the upper-left corner of the screen until it is.

3. Swipe up and down the screen to browse all the years.

4. Tap the year that contains photos you want to work with. You move to the Collections screen that groups the selected year's photos based on locations and time periods.

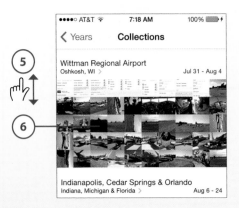

5. Swipe up and down the screen to browse all the collections in the year you selected.

6. Tap the collection that contains photos you want to see. Doing so opens the Moments screen, which breaks out the photos in the collection by location and date.

7. Swipe up and down the screen to browse all the moments in the collection you selected.

8. To see the photos in the moment based on their location, tap the moment's title. You see a map with photos collected at the various locations.

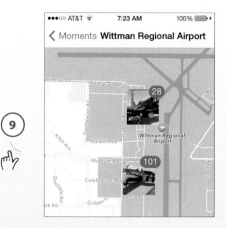

No Map Required

If you don't want to see photos in a moment shown on the map, just tap any photo in the moment to return to browsing that moment's photos as one group of photos.

9. Zoom in by unpinching your fingers on the map to get more detail. As you zoom, the locations of photos become more specific.

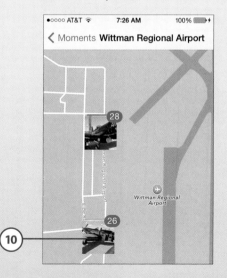

10. Tap the location that contains photos you want to see. You see a thumbnail of each photo at that location.

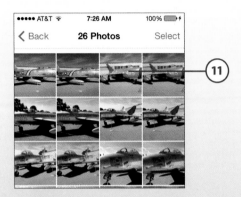

11. You're ready to view the photos in the group and can move to the next task.

Go Back

You can move back to the screens from where you came by tapping the back button, which is always located in the upper-left corner of the screen; this button is named with the screen it takes you back to. To choose a different source, you might have to tap the back button several times as the Photos, Shared, and Albums buttons at the bottom of the screen are only visible on the opening screen of the Photos app.

Viewing Photos Individually

The Photos app enables you to view your photos individually. Here's how:

1. Using the skills you learned in the previous task, open the group of photos that you want to view.

Orientation Doesn't Matter

Zooming, unzooming, and browsing photos works in the same way whether you hold your iPhone horizontally or vertically.

2. Swipe up and down to browse all the photos in the group.

3. Tap the photo you want to view. The photo display screen appears.

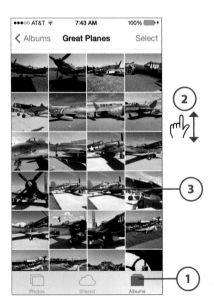

4. To see the photo without the app's toolbars, tap the screen. The toolbars are hidden.

5. Rotate the phone horizontally if you are viewing a horizontal photo.

6. Unpinch or double-tap on the photo to zoom in.

7. When you are zoomed in, drag on the photo to move it around.

8. Pinch or double-tap on the photo to zoom out.

9. Swipe to the left to view the next photo in the group.

10. Swipe to the right to view the previous photo in the group.

11. When you're done viewing photos in the group, tap the screen to show the toolbars again.

HDR Photos

When the app's toolbars are displayed, photos in the HDR format are marked with the HDR icon.

12. Tap the back button. You move back to the group's screen where you see the thumbnails of the photos it contains.

Viewing Photos in Slideshows

You can view photos in slideshows as the following steps demonstrate:

1. Using the skills you learned in the previous task, select and view the photo in a group of photos that you want to be the first one in the slideshow.

2. Tap the Action button.

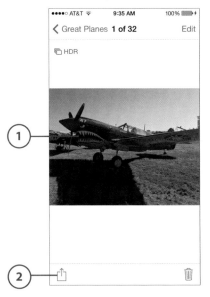

It's Not All Good

When you select a photo and tap the Action button, the app indicates that one photo is selected, which is true. However, when you play the slideshow, all the photos in the group are shown. The one you selected is just the first one displayed. This is a bit confusing, but as it appears to have no bearing on what plays in the slideshow, you can safely ignore the information about how many photos are selected. If you want to choose the photos that are shown, create an album containing only those photos and view that in a slideshow.

3. Tap Slideshow. You see the dialog you use to configure the slideshow.

4. If it isn't selected, tap iPhone to display the slideshow on your iPhone. (You learn how to use AirPlay to display photos from your iPhone onto other devices later in this chapter.)

5. Tap Transitions.

6. Tap the transition you want to be used between photos in the slideshow. That transition is selected and you move back to the previous screen.

7. If you want to hear music while the slideshow plays, set the Play Music switch to on (green); if you don't want to hear music, skip to step 11.

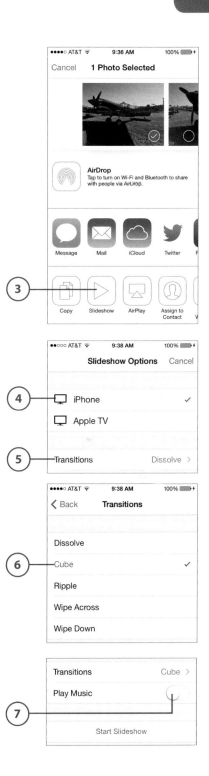

8. Tap Music.

9. Use the Music app to find the music you want to hear. (The Music app is explained in Chapter 14, "Finding and Listening to Music.")

10. Tap the song you want to hear play during the slideshow.

11. Tap Start Slideshow. The slideshow begins to play, and if you selected a song to play, it starts to play, too.

12. Rotate the iPhone if it includes horizontal photos. The slideshow plays, each slide appearing on the screen for the length of time you set. The transition you selected is used to move between photos. If you set slideshows to repeat, the slideshow plays until you stop it; if not, it stops after each photo has been shown once.

13. To stop the slideshow before it finishes, tap the screen. The slide-show stops and you see the Photo app's toolbars.

Working with Burst Mode Photos (iPhone 5S)

When you use the Burst mode to take photos, the Camera app rapidly takes a series of photos. (Typically, you use Burst mode to capture motion, where the action is happening too quickly to be able to frame and take individual photos.) You can review the photos taken in Burst mode and save any you want to keep as favorites; your favorites become separate photos just like those you take one at a time. Here's how:

1. View a Burst mode photo. Burst mode photos are indicated by the word Burst and the number of photos in the burst.

2. Tap Choose Favorites. The burst is expanded. At the bottom of the screen, you see thumbnails for the photos in the burst. At the top part of the screen, you see previews of the photos; the photo in the center of the previews is marked with a downward-facing arrow. Photos marked with a dot are "suggested photos," meaning the best ones in the series according to the Camera app.

3. Swipe all the way to the right to move to the first photo in the series; swiping on the thumbnails at the bottom makes them move faster.

4. Tap a photo that you want to save. It is marked with a check mark.

5. Swipe to the left to move through the series.

6. Tap each photo you want to save.

7. Continue reviewing and selecting photos until you've gone through the entire series.

8. Tap Done. Each photo you selected becomes a separate, individual photo; you can work with these just like photos you take individually.

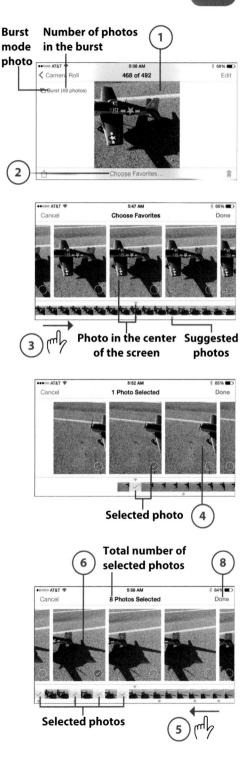

Burst mode photo — **Number of photos in the burst** ①

② — Choose Favorites...

③ Photo in the center of the screen — Suggested photos

Selected photo ④

⑥ Total number of selected photos ⑧

Selected photos ⑤

9. If you're done with the photos in the burst, tap the trash can.

10. Tap Delete *X* Photos, where *X* is the number of photos remaining in the burst.

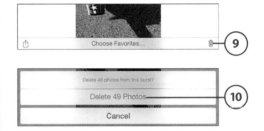

Burst Mode Photos and Photo Stream

Using Photo Stream, the photos you capture on your iPhone are automatically uploaded to your iCloud account from where they can be downloaded to other devices automatically. (You learn more about Photo Stream later in this chapter.) Only the first photo in a Burst mode series is uploaded to Photo Stream when you capture the burst. When you select your favorites, those photos are uploaded to your Photo Stream. The rest of the Burst photos are not uploaded to your Photo Stream.

Editing Photos

Even though the iPhone has great photo-taking capabilities, not all the photos you take are perfect from the start. Fortunately, you can use the Photos app to edit your photos. The following tools are available to you:

- **Rotate**. You can rotate your photos to change their orientation.

- **Enhance**. This tool attempts to adjust the colors and other properties of the photos to make them better.

- **Filters**. You can apply different filters to your photos for artistic or other purposes.

- **Remove red-eye**. This one helps you remove that certain demon-possessed look from the eyes of people in your photos.

- **Crop**. Use this one to crop out the parts of photos you don't want to keep.

Rotating Photos

To change the orientation of a photo,
use the Rotate tool.

1. View the image you want to rotate.

2. Tap Edit.

3. Tap the Rotate button until the
   image is oriented the way you
   want it to be. The image rotates 90
   degrees each time you tap it until
   it returns to its original position.

4. Tap Save when the photo has the
   orientation you want.

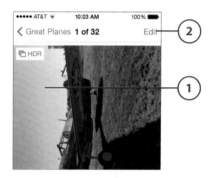

Enhancing Photos

To improve the quality of a photo, use the Enhance tool.

1. View the image you want to enhance.

2. Tap Edit.

3. Tap the Enhance button. The image is enhanced and you see the Auto-Enhance On message.

4. If you don't like the enhancements, tap the Enhance button again or tap Cancel.

5. To save the enhanced image, tap Save.

Editing Photos You Didn't Take on the iPhone

You can edit any photo stored on your iPhone, whether you used the iPhone's camera to take it or not. When you edit and save a photo that wasn't taken with your iPhone, such as one you imported from a computer, you are prompted to save the edited version in the Camera Roll album. If you save it, the edited photo is saved in your Camera Roll and from that point on, acts the same as photos you took with the iPhone. If you don't save it, the edits you made are not saved and the photo remains as it was.

Applying Filters to Photos

To apply filters to photos, do the following:

1. View the image to which you want to apply filters.

2. Tap Edit.

3. Tap the Filters button. The palette of filters appears.

4. Swipe to the left or right on the palette to browse all of the filters.

5. Tap the filter you want to apply. The filter is applied to the image and you see a preview of the image as it will be with the filter. Keeping trying filters until the image is what you want it to be.

6. Tap Apply.

7. Tap Save to save the photo with the filter applied to it.

Removing Red-Eye from Photos

To remove red-eye, perform the following steps:

1. View the image containing red-eye.

2. Tap Edit.

3. Zoom in on the eyes from which you want to remove red-eye.

4. Tap the Red-eye button.

5. Tap each eye containing red-eye. The red in the eyes you tap is removed.

6. When you've tapped all the eyes with red in them, tap Apply.

7. Tap Save.

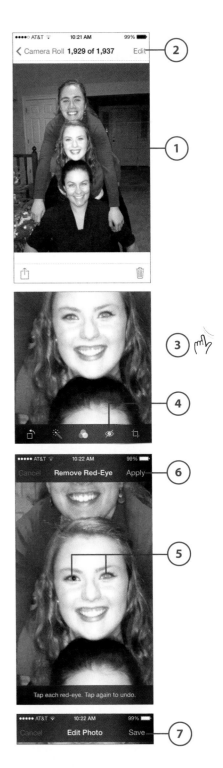

Cropping Photos

To crop an image, do the following:

1. View the image you want to crop.

2. Tap Edit.

3. Tap the Crop button.

Freeform Cropping

To crop the image to be any proportion you want, skip to step 6. Just drag the crop box's handles until the box contains the image as you want it cropped. Then tap Crop.

4. Tap Aspect.

5. Tap the aspect ratio to which you want to constrain the crop. The crop box is resized to be the proportion you selected.

6. Drag the crop box until the part of the image you want to keep is in the crop box. You can also drag on the photo inside the box to change the box's location on the photo. If you didn't select an aspect ratio, you can drag the corners of the crop box to change the shape and size of the crop box.

7. When the image you want is inside the crop box, tap Crop. The image is cropped to just that portion.

8. Tap Save. The cropped version of the photo is saved.

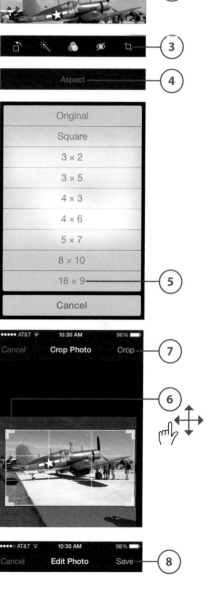

Working with Photos

Once you have photos on your iPhone, there are a lot of things you can do with them, including:

- Emailing one or more photos to one or more people (see the next task).
- Sending a photo via a text message (see Chapter 10, "Sending, Receiving, and Managing Texts and iMessages").
- Sharing photos via AirDrop.
- Sharing photos with others via Photo Stream (covered later in this chapter).
- Posting your photos on your Facebook wall or timeline.
- Assigning photos to contacts (see Chapter 7, "Managing Contacts").
- Using photos as wallpaper (see Chapter 4, "Configuring an iPhone to Suit Your Preferences").
- Sharing photos via tweets.
- Printing photos (see Chapter 1, "Getting Started with Your iPhone").
- Deleting photos (covered later).
- Organizing photos in albums (also covered later).

Copy 'Em

If you select one or more photos and tap the Copy button, the images you selected are copied to the iPhone's clipboard. You can then move into another application and paste them in.

You'll easily be able to accomplish any actions on your own that are not covered in detail here once you've performed a couple of those that are demonstrated in the following tasks.

Individual versus Groups

Some actions are only available when you are working with an individual photo. For example, you can send only a single photo via Twitter whereas you can email multiple photos at the same time. Any commands that aren't applicable to the photos that are selected won't appear on the screen.

Sharing Photos via Email

You can email photos via iPhone's Mail application starting from the Photos app.

1. View the source containing one or more images that you want to share.

2. Tap Select.

3. Select the photos you want to send by tapping them. When you tap a photo, it is grayed out and marked with a check mark to show you that it is selected.

4. Tap the Action button.

Too Many?

If the photos you have selected are too much for email, the Mail button won't appear. You need to select fewer photos to attach to the email message.

5. Tap Mail. A new email message is created, and the photos are added as attachments.

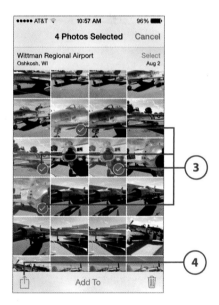

6. Use the email tools to address the email, add a subject, type the body, and send it. (See Chapter 9, "Sending, Receiving, and Managing Email," for detailed information about using your iPhone's email tools.)

7. Tap the size of the images you want to send. Choosing a smaller size makes the files smaller and reduces the quality of the photos. You should generally try to keep the size of emails to 5MB or less to ensure the message makes it to the recipient. (Some email servers block larger messages.) After you send the email, you move back to the photos you were browsing.

Images from Email

As you learned in Chapter 9, when you save images attached to email that you receive, they are stored in the Camera Roll photo album just like photos you take with your iPhone.

Organizing Photos in Albums

You can create photo albums and store photos in them to keep your photos organized.

To create a new album, perform these steps:

1. Move to the Albums screen by tapping Albums on the toolbar.

2. Tap the Add button.

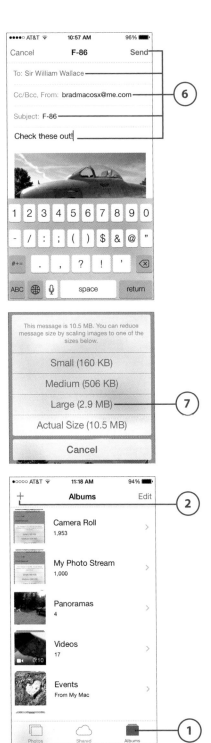

3. Type the name of the new album.

4. Tap Save. You're prompted to select photos to add to the new album.

5. Move to the source of the photos you want to add to the new album.

6. Tap the photos you want to add to the album. They are grayed out and marked with a check mark to show that they are selected.

7. Tap Done. The photos are added to the new album and you move back to the Albums screen. The new album is shown on the list, and you can work with it just like the other albums you see.

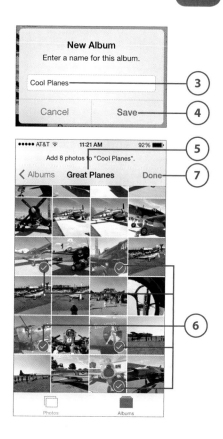

Adding Photos to an Album

To add photos to an existing album, do these steps:

1. Move to the source containing the photos you want to add to an album.

2. Tap Select.

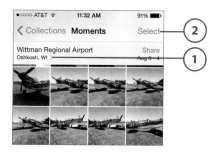

3. Tap the photos you want to add to the album.

4. Tap Add To. You move to the Albums screen.

5. Swipe up and down the list to find the album to which you want to add the photos.

6. Tap the album; if an album is grayed out and you can't tap it, that album was not created on the iPhone and so you can't change its contents. The photos are stored in the album.

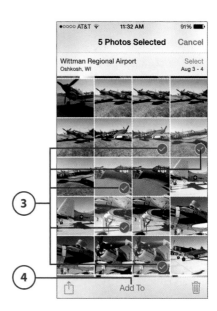

More Album Fun

You can change the order in which albums are listed by moving to the Albums screen, tapping Edit, and then dragging albums up or down by their List buttons. You can delete an album that you created in the Photos app by moving to the Albums screen, tapping Edit, tapping the Unlock button for the album you want to delete, tapping Delete, and tapping Delete Album. When you're done making changes to your Albums, tap Done. You can remove a photo from an album by viewing the photo, tapping the trash can button, and then tapping Remove from Album. Photos you remove from an album remain in the Camera Roll and Photo Stream; they are only deleted from the album.

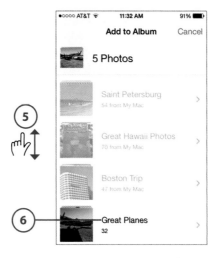

Deleting Photos

You can delete photos and videos that only you've taken with the iPhone's camera or have stored on it from another app on the phone. (To remove photos that are loaded onto iPhone via syncing with a computer, you must change the sync settings so those photos are excluded, and then resync. You can also delete photos from your Photo Stream as you learn later.) To delete photos or videos you've taken with iPhone's camera, captured as a screenshot, or downloaded from email, take the following steps.

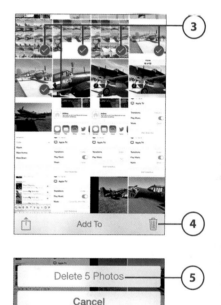

1. Open the source containing photos you want to delete.

2. Tap Select.

3. Tap the photos you want to delete. Each item you select is marked with a check mark and is grayed out to show you it is selected.

4. Tap the Trash Can button.

5. Tap Delete *X* Photos, where *X* is the number of photos you selected. The photos you selected are deleted.

Deleting Individual Photos

You can delete individual photos that you are viewing by tapping the Trash Can button and then tapping Delete Photo.

More Ways to Share

To share photos directly from a Moment, view the moment containing photos you want to share on the Moments screen. Tap Share. Tap Share this moment to share all of the photos in the moment or tap Share some photos to select the photos you want to share. Use the resulting Action menu to choose how you want to share the photos. The options you see depend upon the number of photos you are sharing.

Viewing, Editing, and Working with Video on Your iPhone

As shown previously in this chapter, you can capture video clips with your iPhone. Once captured, you can view clips on your iPhone, edit them, and share them.

Finding and Watching Videos

Watching videos you've captured with your iPhone is simple.

1. Move to the Albums screen.

2. Tap the Videos album. You see the videos you've taken on your iPhone. Video clips have a camera icon and running time at the bottom of their icons.

3. Swipe up and down the screen to browse your videos.

4. Tap the video you want to watch.

5. Rotate the phone to change its orientation if necessary.

6. Tap either Play button. The video plays. After a few moments, the toolbars disappears.

7. Tap the video. The toolbars reappear.

8. To pause the video, tap Pause.

9. To jump to a specific point in a video, drag the playhead to where you want to start playing it; if you hold your finger in one place for a few seconds, the thumbnails expand so your placement of the playhead can be more precise. When you lift your finger, the playhead remains at its current location; if the clip is playing, it resumes playing from that point.

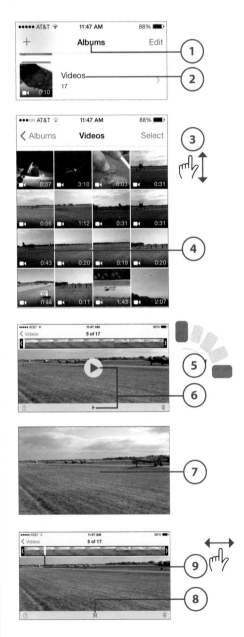

Deleting Video

To remove a video clip from your iPhone, view it, tap the Trash Can icon, and then tap Delete Video at the prompt.

Watching Slow-Motion Video (iPhone 5S)

Watching slow-motion video is slightly different than watching regular speed video. You have to set the part of the video that you want to play in slow motion, and then watch it to see the action slowed down.

1. Open a slow-motion video to view it.

2. Drag the left marker to where you want the slow motion to start; if you want the entire clip to play in slow motion, drag the marker all the way to the left.

3. Drag the right marker to where you want slow motion to end; if you want the entire clip to play in slow motion, drag the marker all the way to the right. When you play the video, the section between the markers plays in slow motion.

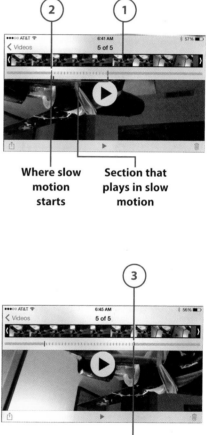

Where slow motion starts   **Section that plays in slow motion**

Where slow motion ends

Slow Motion and Only the Slow Motion

If you want the video to contain only the slow-motion section, trim it so the trim starts and ends where the slow motion does. (Trimming is described in the next task.)

Editing Video

You can trim a video clip to remove unwanted parts. Here's how you do it.

1. View the video you want to edit.

2. Drag the left trim marker to where you want the edited clip to start; the trim marker is the left-facing arrow at the left end of the timeline. If you hold your finger in one place for a few seconds, the thumbnails expand so your placement of the crop marker can be more precise. As soon as you move the trim marker, the part of the clip that is inside the selection is highlighted in the yellow box; the Trim button also appears.

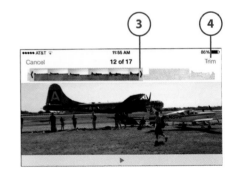

Trim from the Right

Some people I know find it easier to start trimming from the right side first as it makes it less likely you'll grab the play-head instead of the trim marker.

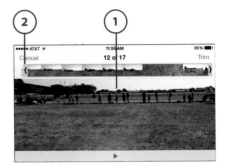

3. Drag the right trim marker to where you want the edited clip to end.

4. Tap Trim.

5. Tap Trim Original to edit the clip and replace the original version with the edited version or Save as New Clip to create a new clip containing only the frames between the crop markers. The frames outside the crop markers are removed from the clip. The clip is trimmed and replaces the original clip or a new clip is created depending on the option you selected.

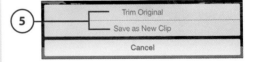

There's an App for That

For more powerful video editing on your iPhone, download the free iMovie app. This app provides a much more powerful video editor. You can use themes to design a video, add music, include titles and photos, and much more.

>>>Go Further

SHARING VIDEO

There are lots of ways to share your videos. View the video you want to share. Tap the Action button. Tap how you want to share the video. There are a number of options including Messages, Mail, iCloud, YouTube, Facebook, and Vimeo. Follow the onscreen prompts to complete the sharing process.

Using AirPlay to View Photos and Videos on a TV

Viewing photos and slideshows on the iPhone's screen is good, but seeing them on a big screen is even better. If you have an Apple TV connected to a home theater system, you can stream your photos and video so that you can see them on your TV and hear their soundtracks via the system's audio components.

After your Apple TV is configured, your iPhone needs to be on the same network as the Apple TV so the two devices can communicate.

To view photos on your TV, do the following:

1. View a photo in the source containing the photos you want to stream.

2. Tap the Action button.

3. Tap AirPlay.

4. Tap Apple TV. The photo is streamed to the TV and you return to the photo on the iPhone. You can swipe to the left or right to move to the previous or next photo and use the other viewing tools you learned about earlier. You see the same image on the iPhone and on the TV (at very different sizes of course!).

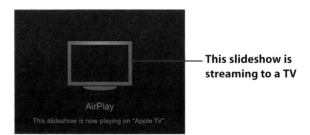

This slideshow is streaming to a TV

Previously in the chapter, you learned how to view photos in a slideshow. You can also stream a slideshow through an Apple TV by tapping Apple TV on the screen that appears after you tap Slideshow on the Action menu. When you start the slideshow, you see the images on the TV and hear its music on the audio device connected to the Apple TV. On the iPhone, you see the screen indicating the slideshow is being streamed. To stop the slideshow, tap the iPhone's screen.

This video is streaming to a TV

Similarly, you can stream videos to an Apple TV. View the video you want to stream. Tap the Action button and tap AirPlay. Tap Apple TV. The video plays on the device connected to the Apple TV. You can control the video using the controls on the iPhone's screen.

To turn streaming off, open the AirPlay menu and tap iPhone.

Working with Photo Stream

With iCloud's Photo Stream, devices can automatically upload photos to iCloud. Other devices can automatically download photos from iCloud, so you have your photos available on all your devices at the same time. Photo Stream has two sides: a sender and receiver. Your iPhone can be both. Photo applications, such as iPhoto and Aperture on a Mac, can also access your Photo Stream and download photos to your computer automatically. Windows PCs can also be configured to automatically download photos from your Photo Stream.

You can share your photo streams with others and view photos being shared with you. To get started with Photo Stream, you need to configure your iCloud account on your iPhone to use it; see Chapter 3 for the details to do that.

Viewing Photos in the Photo Stream Album

Accessing photos from the Photo Stream is much like accessing photos in albums:

1. Tap Albums to open the Albums screen.

2. Tap My Photo Stream. You see all the photos from your Photo Stream. You can work with them like any other photos on your iPhone.

Photos You've Taken with the iPhone

Of course, you don't need to access your Photo Stream for photos that you've taken with your iPhone since these are all stored in the Camera Roll album. You might want to access your Photo Stream to work with photos on other devices, such as those you've taken on an iPad.

3. Browse and work with your Photo Stream photos as you do with other sources. You can tap a photo to view it, play the photos in a slideshow, share photos, and so on. See previous tasks in this chapter for instructions.

Editing and Saving Photo Stream Photos

You can edit photos on your Photo Stream. When you save an edited photo, you are prompted to save it to your Camera Roll, which you must do if you want to save the edited version. You can't save edited photos directly to the Photo Stream.

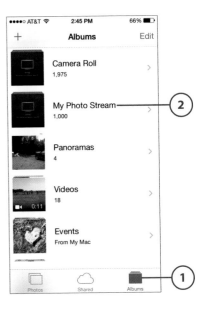

Adding Photo Stream Photos to Your iPhone

To save photos from your Photo Stream onto your iPhone, just move them into an album. That copies them from the Photo Stream and stores them on your phone.

AUTOMATIC DOWNLOADS FROM PHOTO STREAM TO A COMPUTER

>>>Go Further

One of the best things about Photo Stream is that photos you take on your iPhone are automatically uploaded to your iCloud account from where they are downloaded to a computer and permanently saved there. So, you don't need to worry about losing your photos, because they are saved on a computer automatically, giving you at least two copies of every photo you take.

On a Mac, the iPhoto and Aperture applications can automatically download your Photo Stream photos. To configure either of these applications, open the Preferences dialog and click the Photo Stream tab. Check the My Photo Stream, Automatic Import, Automatic Upload, and Shared Photo Streams check boxes. Photos you take on the iPhone are automatically added to your Photo Library. Any photos you add directly to the application are uploaded to your Photo Stream and available on your iPhone too.

On a Windows PC, open the iCloud control panel (you need to download and install the iCloud control panel first). Check the Photo Stream check box. Click Options. Use the upper Change button to choose the location in which you want your photos to be downloaded automatically. Check the My Photo Stream and Shared Photo Streams check boxes. Use the Change button to choose the location where you want Photo Steam photos to be stored. Click OK to close the choose folder dialog box, click OK to close the Photo Stream Options dialog box, and then click Close or Apply. You can move photos from the download folder into a photo application or work with them directly on the desktop. Any image files you place in the upload folder are added to your Photo Stream automatically.

Creating a Shared Photo Stream

You can share your Photo Stream with others. This is a great way to share photos, because others can subscribe to your shared photos streams to view and work with the photos you share. When you share photos, you can add them to a photo stream that's already being shared or create a new shared photo stream.

To create a new, empty, shared Photo Stream, do the following:

1. Open the Shared source. You see all the shared streams in which you are currently participating (as either the person sharing them or subscribed to them).

2. Tap New Shared Stream.

3. Type the title of the new stream.

4. Tap Next.

5. Enter or select the email address of the first person with whom you want to share the photos.

6. Add other recipients until you've added everyone you want to access the photos.

7. Tap Create. The shared stream is created and is ready for you to add photos. The recipients you included in the new stream receive notifications that invite them to join the stream.

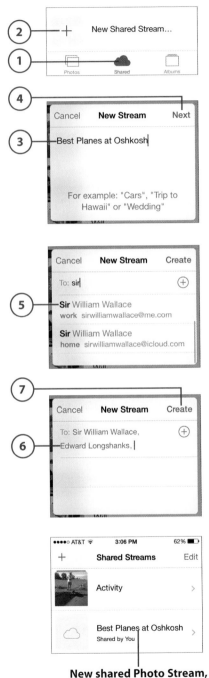

New shared Photo Stream, ready for your photos

Adding Photos to a Shared Photo Stream

To add photos to a Photo Stream you are sharing, perform the following steps:

1. Move to the source containing photos you want to add to a shared Photo Stream.

2. Tap Select.

3. Tap the photos you want to share.

4. Tap the Action button.

5. Tap iCloud.

6. Enter your commentary about the photos you are sharing. (Note, this commentary is associated only with the first photo.)

7. Tap Stream.

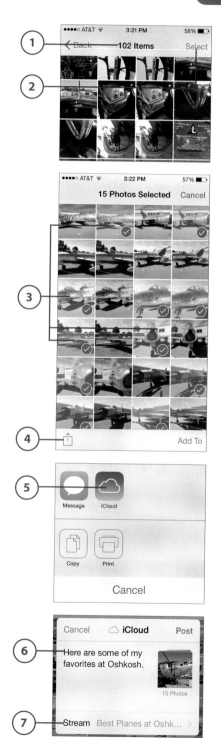

8. Swipe up and down to browse the list of shared streams available.

9. Tap the stream to which you want to add the photos.

New Shared Stream with Photos

You can create a new shared stream with the selected photos by tapping New Shared Stream.

10. Tap iCloud.

11. Tap Post. The photos you selected are added to the shared Photo Stream. People who are subscribed to the stream receive a notification that photos have been added and can view the new photos along with your commentary.

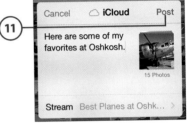

iCloud Account Required

The people with whom you share Photo Stream photos must have an iCloud account.

Adding Comments to Shared Photos

To add commentary to photos or to add more photos to a stream you are sharing, do the following:

1. Open the Shared source.

2. Tap the shared stream you want to work with. You see the photos it contains.

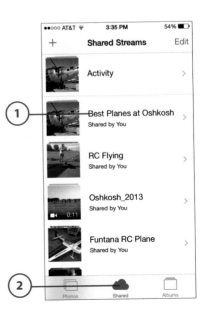

3. Tap the photo to which you want to add commentary.

4. Tap Add a comment.

5. Enter your comments.

6. Tap Send. People who are subscribed to the stream can read your comments.

7. To indicate you like a photo (though why you would share a photo you don't like I don't know!), tap the Like button.

8. Tap Back.

9. To add more photos, tap Add (+). You are prompted to select the photos you want to add. Use the app's tools to open the source containing the photos you want to add, select them, and tap Done.

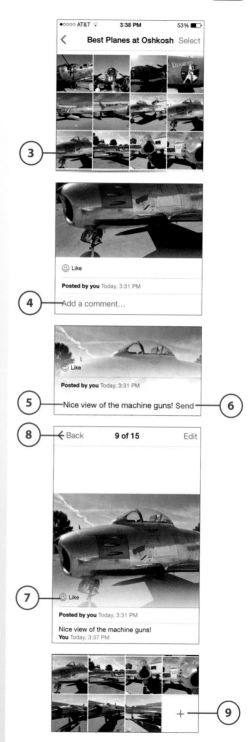

Inviting People to a Shared Photo Stream

To invite people to a stream you are sharing, perform the following tasks:

1. Open the shared stream.

2. Tap People. At the top of the resulting screen, you see the people you invited to share the stream. If they haven't accepted yet, you see Invited as their status.

3. To invite more people to share the stream, tap Invite People, and use the resulting Invite People screen to add people to the stream (type or select the person's email address and tap Add).

4. To allow others to add their photos and videos to the stream, set the Subscribers Can Post switch to on (green).

5. To enable anyone to see the stream by clicking a link you provide to them, set the Public Website switch to on (green).

6. If you enabled the Public Website setting, tap Share Link to share a link to the site.

7. To receive notifications when others post photos, add comments, or like the stream's photos, set the Notifications switch to on (Green).

8. To delete the stream, tap Delete Photo Stream and tap Delete at the prompt.

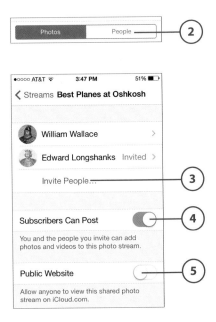

Working with Photo Stream Photos Shared with You

You can work with photo streams people share with you as follows:

1. Tap the notification you receive.

2. Tap Accept. The shared photo stream becomes available on your Shared tab.

3. Tap Streams.

4. Tap the new shared stream.

5. Tap a photo in the stream.

6. Tap Like to indicate you like the photo.

7. Tap Add a comment.

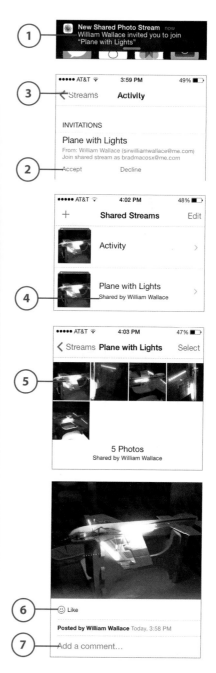

:omment.

к. View and work with
ɔhotos in the shared
n. As you add to the stream,
ications are sent back to the
ion who shared it with you.

on Shared Photos

n do most of the tasks with shared
ɔs that you can with your own, such
nailing them, using as wallpaper,
I so on.

ɔ unsubscribe from a photo stream,
move to its People screen and tap
Unsubscribe and confirm that is what
you want to do. The shared photo stream
is removed from your iPhone.

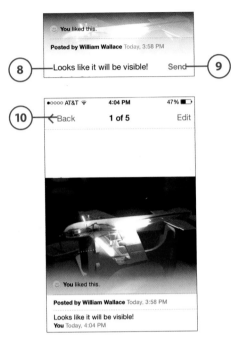

The Cloud Isn't Forever

You can store up to 1,000 photos on your Photo Stream. New photos are stored
on the cloud for only 30 days. Photos you've taken them with your iPhone or
other iOS device are stored in the Camera Roll album, and if you've configured a
computer to automatically download your photos, you have at least two copies
of all your photos. If you want to keep Photo Stream photos on your iPhone
that you didn't take with it, you need to move them to an album as described
earlier.

IMPORTING YOUR PHOTOS ONTO A COMPUTER

If you don't use Photo Stream to automatically save your photos on a computer, you can manually import them from the iPhone onto a computer. When you connect your iPhone to a computer, you are usually prompted to import the photos into a photo application. For example, on a Mac, you can import photos directly from the iPhone into iPhoto or Aperture. On a Windows PC, when you connect your iPhone to the computer, you should be prompted to choose how you want photos on your iPhone to be handled. From that point on, you should be prompted to import new photos from the iPhone to the computer each time you connect it to the computer.

>>Go Further

Watch movies
and TV shows

Listen to or
watch podcasts

Read ebooks
and PDFs

In this chapter, you learn about three really useful apps. Topics include the following:

→ Watching video with the Videos app
→ Listening to podcasts with the Podcasts app
→ Reading books with the iBooks app

Using Other Cool iPhone Apps

In previous chapters, you learned a lot about a number of useful apps, such as Mail, Messages, Safari, and so on. Your iPhone can run thousands of apps that can do just about anything you want to do. In this chapter, you learn about three apps that can bring a lot of enjoyment (and even some edification) to your iPhone: Videos, with which you can watch movies, TV shows, and video podcasts; Podcasts that you can use to subscribe and listen to or watch podcasts on your favorite topics; and iBooks that enables you to read books and PDF documents.

Watching Video with the Videos App

Your iPhone is a great way to enjoy different types of video, including movies, episodes of your favorite TV series, and video podcasts. Be prepared to be amazed; the high quality and portability are some compensation for the relatively small screen size. The Videos app enables you to watch lots of content right on your phone.

Getting Movies and TV Shows on Your iPhone

Of course, before you can watch video content, it needs to be stored on your iPhone. There are two primary ways to do this: using either the iTunes app on your iPhone or the iTunes app on a computer (of course, you can use both ways).

You can use the iTunes app to download movies and TV shows directly to your iPhone. They immediately become available in the Videos app. You can also rent movies. Refer to Chapter 6 , "Downloading Apps, Music, Movies, TV Shows, and More onto Your iPhone," to learn how to use the iTunes app on your iPhone.

You can download video content from the iTunes Store using the iTunes app on a computer; you can also add video content you've converted from DVD to your iTunes Library. To get video content from your iTunes Library onto your iPhone, sync the phone with iTunes. Refer to Chapter 5, "Working with iTunes on Your Computer," for information about working with iTunes on a computer.

After you've stocked your iPhone with content you want to enjoy, you're ready to watch it (after configuring a few, quick video settings).

Configuring Your iPhone's Video Settings

There are a few settings you use to configure various aspects of iPhone's video functionality. These steps show you how:

1. Open the Settings app and tap Videos.

2. Tap Start Playing.

3. Tap Where Left Off to have the Videos app start where you last were watching in a video when you play it again, or tap From Beginning to have your iPhone always start video playback from the beginning.

4. Tap Videos.

5. Ensure the Show All Videos switch is on (green) to show all your video content accessible by your phone; you can download video content not currently stored on your phone. If this switch is off (white), you can only see and access video content stored on your iPhone.

6. To access shared video through iTunes' Home Sharing feature, tap the Apple ID field.

7. Enter the Apple ID and password that are being used to share content through Home Sharing in iTunes.

8. Tap Done. Your Apple ID is shown in the HOME SHARING section. When you are on the same network over which iTunes is sharing content, you can access any shared movies, TV shows, and other video in the Videos app.

9. Tap Settings.

Home Sharing

To configure iTunes to share your library over your network, open its Preferences dialog, click the Sharing tab, check Share my library on my local network, and click OK.

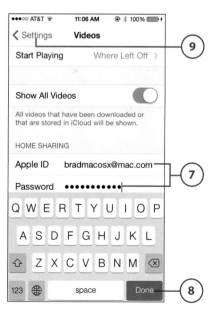

Finding Video

The first step in watching video is to find the movie, TV show, or other content you want to view. Here's how:

Videos

1. On the Home screen, tap Videos. The Videos screen appears, showing you the video content available to you.

2. Tap the tab at the bottom of the screen for the type of video you want to watch, such as Rented Movies, Movies, TV Shows, and Music Videos. You see tabs only when that type of content is stored on your phone; for example, if you currently don't have any rented movies, you won't see that tab. If you set the Show All Videos option, you see all the content of that type. You can access it regardless of whether it is stored on your phone.

   The tabs for each type of content look a bit different; the first figure shows Movies, while the second shows TV Shows. On the Movies tab, you see each movie available to you. On the TV Shows tab, you see content organized by series. Items marked with the cloud icon must be downloaded to watch them.

   The rest of these steps show selecting an episode of a TV series to watch; choosing other types of content is similar.

3. Tap the series you want to watch. At the top of the screen is the series' artwork. Just below that are tabs on which you can tap to get different kinds of information.

Download from the cloud

Number of episodes you haven't watched yet

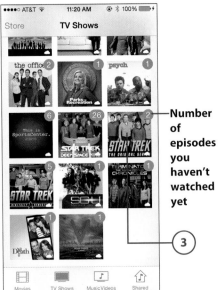

4. If it isn't selected already, tap Episodes.

5. Swipe up the screen to see the episodes currently available to watch. These are either episodes you've already moved onto your iPhone or those that you have purchased from the iTunes Store, even if they aren't currently stored on your iPhone.

Episodes you haven't watched yet are marked with a blue dot; as you watch videos, the blue dot empties to indicate how much of the video you have watched. If you've just started the video, the dot might still be full, but the more you watch, the more empty it becomes.

6. To get more information about an episode, tap Read More. A description appears.

7. Tap the episode you want to watch. If it is not stored on your phone, it starts downloading and begins to play when a sufficient amount is on your phone so that it can play without stopping. If the content is already on your iPhone, it starts playing immediately.

8. Control the video using the details provided in the next section.

8

FINDING VIDEO IN ALL THE RIGHT PLACES

The Videos app makes it pretty simple to find and start watching movies, TV shows, music videos, and so on. Here are a few more tidbits for you to find:

- If you tap the Store button, you move into the iTunes app, where you can download additional video (refer to Chapter 6 for details).

- The Details tab provides a detailed description of the video content you are browsing. When you tap this while browsing a movie, you see a description of the movie. When you are browsing a TV series, you see a description of the series (tap Read More to see a description of an episode).

- Movies have the Chapters tab. Tap this to see the movie's chapters. You can tap a chapter to start watching the movie at that point.

- The Related tab shows content related to the content you are browsing. You can tap the related content to explore and download it if it is something you are interested in watching.

- To return to a main tab (such as for Movies), tap the back button located in the upper-left corner of the window until you return to that tab.

- The Shared tab displays content being shared on your local network from iTunes (assuming you signed in to Home Sharing as described in the previous section).

- If you purchased only some episodes in a season of a TV series, tap Show Complete Season. All the episodes in that season are shown. Each one you haven't purchased has a price button; tap that to purchase and download the episode. You can also tap the Complete My Season price button to purchase all the episodes in that season that you don't have already.

Watching Video on Your iPhone

When you play video, it is always oriented horizontally so it can fill the screen as much as possible. The Videos app provides the following controls:

Tap to show the controls

- After the video plays for a few moments, the Videos toolbars disappear. Tap the screen to display them again.

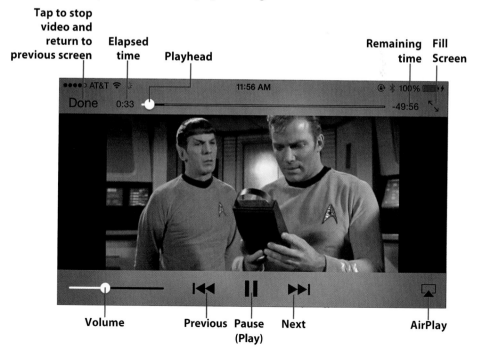

Tap to stop
video and
return to   Elapsed   Remaining   Fill
previous screen   time   Playhead   time   Screen

Volume   Previous Pause Next   AirPlay
                        (Play)

- Drag the Playhead to the right to move ahead in the content or to the left to move back in it.

- Tap the Fill Screen button to scale the content to fill as much of the screen as possible. Depending on the format of the content you are watching, some video might be cut off at the top or sides. Tap again to return to the previous scale; you may see black bars on the top/bottom or sides.

- Drag the Volume slider to the left to lower the volume or to the right to increase it.

- Tap Previous to move back to the start of the current content or to the previous chapter if you are watching a movie with chapters.

- Tap Pause to pause a movie; it becomes the Play button and you tap it to start it again.

- Tap Next to move to the next chapter if you are watching a movie with chapters or to exit the current content and return to the previous screen if you are watching something else.

- Use the AirPlay button to watch the content on a different device (see the next section).

- To stop the video before it finishes, tap Done. The video closes and you return to the previous screen.

- If you enabled the Where I Left Off setting, you can tap the video and it starts playing where you stopped it.

Audio Options

If a movie supports audio options, the Audio button (a quote bubble) appears on the bottom toolbar. Tap this to open the Audio & Subtitles screen. Here, you can choose a language for the audio and configure subtitles. Tap Done when you've made your selections.

Using AirPlay to Watch Your iPhone's Video on a Big Screen

You can use AirPlay and an Apple TV to display video that is stored on your iPhone on a TV (which likely has a much bigger screen than your iPhone!). As long as the iPhone and Apple TV are on the same network, you can use the AirPlay button to select the Apple TV as the output device.

To get started, play the video and tap the AirPlay button.

AirPlay

Tap the Apple TV connected to the TV on
which you want to watch the video

Tap the Apple TV to which you want to stream the video. The video begins
streaming to the Apple TV. You see the video on the screen and hear the
audio on whatever audio device the Apple TV is connected to.

Icons Matter

When a device is marked with the video screen icon on the AirPlay menu, you can
watch the video on the device. If it is marked with the speaker icon, only the audio
streams to the device.

Use the controls on the AirPlay screen to control how the video plays on the
AirPlay device. (You use the audio controls associated with the device to
which the Apple TV is connected to adjust the volume level.)

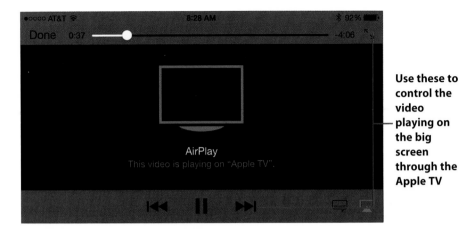

Use these to control the video playing on the big screen through the Apple TV

To display the video on the iPhone again, tap the AirPlay button and the tap iPhone or tap Done to stop video playback without switching back to the iPhone.

It's Not All Good

You can rent movies from the iTunes Store to watch on your iPhone or other devices. You need to be aware that rented movies have two time limitations. One is that you can keep rented movies on your iPhone for 30 calendar days, starting from the time you download the rented movies to your iPhone using the iTunes app or to your computer (not from the time when you sync the rented movies from your computer to your iPhone). The second limitation is that after you start playing rented movies, you have 24 hours (United States) or 48 hours (elsewhere) to finish watching it. (Though you can watch it as many times as you want within that 24- or 48-hour period.) When either of these time periods expires, the rented movie disappears from whatever device it is on.

You see warnings on your iPhone or other device where a rented movie is stored as the expiration time nears.

Another difference between rented movies and other kinds of content is that rented movies can exist on only one device. If you rent a movie on an iPhone, iPad, or Apple TV, you can watch it only on the device on which you rented it. When you move rented movies using iTunes on your computer to your iPhone, they disappear from the computer (unlike music or movies you own that remain in your iTunes Library where you can listen to or view that content). This also means that rented movies can be on only one iPhone, computer, iPhone, or iPad at the same time. However, you can move movies that you rented using iTunes on a computer back and forth among devices as much as you want. So you can start watching a movie on your iPhone and sync to move it back to your computer to finish watching it (within the 24- or 48-hour viewing period, of course).

Listening to Podcasts with the Podcasts App

Podcasts are episodic audio or video programs that are available on many, many topics. Using the Podcasts app, you can subscribe to and manage lots of podcasts so you always have something of interest available to you.

No Podcasts App?

If the Podcasts app isn't installed on your iPhone, you need to download and install it now. Use the App Store app to search for Podcasts, and then download and install Apple's Podcasts app. Refer to Chapter 6 for help downloading and installing apps.

Setting Your Podcast Preferences

Like most apps you've seen in this book, you can set some preferences for the Podcasts app, like so:

1. On the Settings screen, tap Podcasts.

2. To keep your podcasts in sync in the Podcasts app on iOS devices and iTunes on computers, set the Sync Subscriptions switch to on (green). This is nice because you can use different devices to listen to the same podcasts and you pick up on one device right where you left off on another.

3. Tap Auto-Downloads. Here, you configure the app to automatically download content for you (or not to do so).

●●●●● AT&T 📶 5:34 PM 🔋 ⚡ 90% 🔋	
Settings	
🅰 Podcasts ———————— ›	①

●●●●○ AT&T 📶 5:35 PM 🔋 ⚡ 90% 🔋	
‹ Settings **Podcasts**	
Sync Subscriptions ⬤	②
SUBSCRIPTION DEFAULTS	
Auto-Downloads ———— All ›	③

4. Tap the download option you want: Off, if you don't want content to be downloaded automatically; All, if you want all available content to be downloaded automatically; or Most Recent, if you want only recent content downloaded automatically.

5. Tap Podcasts.

6. Tap Episodes to Keep.

7. Tap the number and type of episodes you want the app to keep. For example, tap All Unplayed Episodes to keep any episodes you haven't listened to yet or tap Last 5 Episodes to keep only the five most recent episodes.

8. Tap Podcasts.

9. If you want the app to be able to download podcasts using your phone's cellular network, set the Use Cellular Data switch to on (green). Set this to off (white) if you have a limited data plan and want to download podcasts only when you are using a Wi-Fi network.

10. Tap Settings.

Using the Podcasts App to Subscribe to Podcasts

You can subscribe to podcasts you want to listen to so they are available in the Podcasts app. Here's how:

1. On the Home screen, tap Podcasts.

2. Tap My Podcasts. You see any podcasts to which you are subscribed in the center part of the screen. At the top, you see the Search bar and other tools.

3. Tap Store. You move into the iTunes Store, where you can use the buttons at the bottom of the screen to choose how you want to look for podcasts. The options are Featured, Audio, Video, Top Charts, and Search. The rest of these steps show using the Top Charts option; the other browse options are similar.

Searchin'

Searching can be the fastest way to get to a specific podcast. Tap the Search button, tap in the Search field, and type text or numbers associated with the podcast (such as its name, producer, topic, and so on). As you type, podcasts that potentially meet your search are listed. Tap a podcast to move to it.

4. Tap Top Charts.

5. Tap Categories.

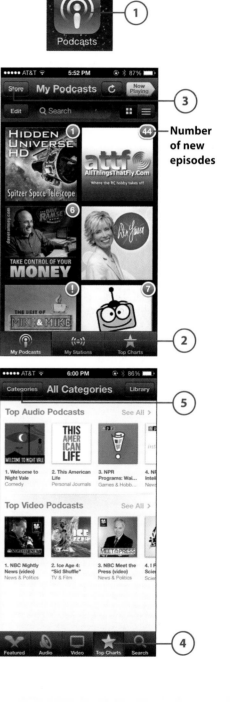

Number of new episodes

6. Swipe up and down to browse the available categories.

7. Tap the category you want to browse. You move to the screen showing podcasts in that category.

8. Swipe to the left or right on a group of podcasts to browse them, or tap See All to see all the podcasts in that category.

9. Tap a podcast of interest to you. You move to the podcast's Home page.

10. Tap the Details tab.

11. Read about the podcast and see a list of available episodes.

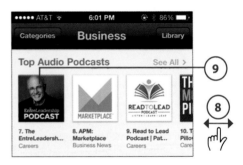

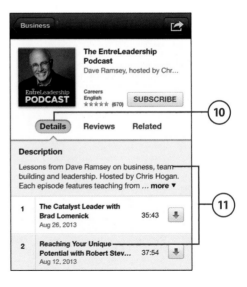

12. Tap the Reviews tab to see what other people think of the podcast.

13. Swipe up and down the screen to read all the reviews.

14. To subscribe to the podcast, tap SUBSCRIBE. You subscribe to the podcast and move back to the My Podcasts screen, where you see the podcast to which you subscribed. If you don't want to subscribe to the podcast, tap the back button located in the upper-left corner of the screen to continue looking for podcasts instead.

15. Tap the podcast to play it (details about finding and playing podcasts are in the following sections).

Going Back to Your Podcast Library Without Subscribing

When you subscribe to a podcast, you move back to the My Podcasts screen automatically. If you don't subscribe to a podcast, you can tap the Library button located in the upper-right corner of the screen. Sometimes, this button isn't displayed. If this happens, just tap one of the buttons at the bottom of the screen to make it appear again.

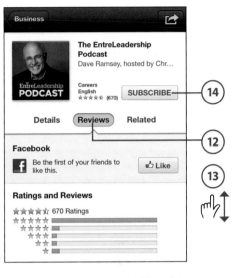

Choosing a Podcast to Listen To

When you're ready to listen, you can use the My Podcasts screen to quickly find the podcast you want to hear or see.

1. On the Home screen, tap Podcasts.

2. Tap My Podcasts to display the podcasts to which you are subscribed.

3. Swipe up and down the screen to browse all the podcasts to which you are subscribed.

4. Tap a podcast to view its episodes. You see the podcast's screen. At the top is the general information about the podcast. Below the description are the episodes available.

5. Swipe up and down the screen to find an episode in which you are interested.

6. Tap the episode to which you want to listen. If it is not currently downloaded, it starts to download and starts to play as soon as enough has been downloaded that it plays without stopping. If it is already stored on your phone, it starts playing immediately. You move to the Now Playing screen. See the next section for the details.

Episode that has been downloaded

Episode you haven't listened to

Tap to get more information about an episode

Download the episode

Not Downloaded?

If an episode hasn't been downloaded to your iPhone, the Download icon appears along the right side of the screen. You can tap the episode to download and play it while it downloads (streaming), or you can tap the download button to download it to your iPhone to play at a different time. (You might want to do this if you aren't going to be able to connect to the Internet later and want to be able to listen to the episode.)

Listening to Podcasts

The Podcasts app provides all the controls you need to listen to and watch podcasts. Here they are:

- Tap the Pause/Play button to pause a playing podcast or to play a paused one.

- Tap the Previous/Rewind button to move to the start of the current podcast. Tap and hold this button to rewind a podcast that is playing.

- Tap the Repeat last 15 seconds button to repeat the last 15 seconds. Tap the Move ahead 15 seconds to skip ahead by that amount.

- Tap the Next/Fast Forward button to move to the next episode in the podcast. Tap and hold this button to fast forward in a playing podcast.

- Drag the Volume slider to the left to decrease the volume or to the right to increase it.

- Tap the AirPlay button to stream the podcast to another device. On the resulting menu, tap the device to which you want to stream it.

- Drag the Playhead to the left to move back in the podcast or to the right to move ahead in it.

Playback speed — Sleep Timer — Action

- To change the speed at which the podcast plays, tap the 1x button; the podcast plays at 1.5 times normal speed. Tap again to play at twice the normal speed, tap again to play at one-half speed, and tap again to return to normal speed. The button reflects the current playback speed.

Tap to set the timer

Tap when you want playback to stop

- To set a Sleep Timer, tap the Sleep Timer button, tap when you want the playback to stop, and tap Done. When the timer expires, the podcast stops playing. When the sleep timer is on, the Sleep Timer button is highlighted in blue.

- Tap the Action button to share the episode via Mail, Messages, Twitter, Facebook, or AirDrop.

Managing Podcasts

Here are some pointers you can use to manage your podcasts:

Configure settings for a specific podcast

- To configure how a podcast is managed in the app, move to the episode list for the podcast and tap Settings. You see the Settings screen. These tools enhance or override the general podcast preferences you set earlier. Set Subscription to ON to subscribe to the podcast. Use Episodes to Keep to determine how episodes are retained; for example, tap Episodes to Keep, and then tap All Unplayed Episodes to have only episodes to which you haven't listened kept on your iPhone. On this screen, you can also change the podcast's Auto-Downloads setting and determine how episodes are sorted, played, and marked (played or unplayed). When you are done configuring the settings, tap Done.

- You can browse, select, and play other podcasts by tapping the Top Stations button on the app's Home screen and flipping through the various categories of podcasts available there. Tap a podcast you want to explore to see the list of episodes for that podcast. Tap an episode to listen to it. Tap SUBSCRIBE to subscribe to the podcast—at which point it appears on the My Podcasts tab just like other podcasts to which you've subscribed.

- To remove a podcast, tap Edit on the My Podcasts screen and tap Remove (x). You are no longer subscribed to the podcast. Tap Done when you are finished removing podcasts.

- To delete individual episodes of a podcast, swipe to the left on the episode you want to delete and tap Delete.

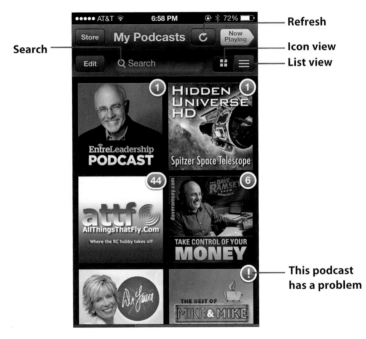

Refresh — Search — Icon view — List view — This podcast has a problem

- You can search podcasts by tapping in the Search field at the top of the My Podcasts screen, typing your search term, and tapping Search.

- You can change the view for the My Podcasts screen by tapping the List view button. You see your podcasts in a list. Tap a podcast to browse its episodes. Tap the Icon view to move back to the large icons.

- When a podcast is marked with an exclamation point badge, it has a problem. Tap the podcast to see an explanation of the problem at the top of the screen. Most commonly, it is that the app has stopped downloading the podcast because you haven't listened to any episodes in a while. Tap the message to refresh the podcast.

- Tap the Refresh button to cause the app to download any new episodes and to remove episodes according to your Episodes to Keep setting. (For example, if you keep only episodes that you haven't listened to, any that you have listened to are deleted.) You can also refresh podcasts by swiping down from the top of a podcast's episode list.

- To mark episodes as played, move to an episode list and tap Edit. Tap the episodes you want to mark as played, tap Mark, and tap Mark as Played. To delete episodes, tap Delete instead of Mark. Tap Done when you've finished marking episodes.

Reading Books with the iBooks App

The iBooks app enables you to download and read thousands of books on your iPhone. You can carry a library of books with you and enjoy the benefits of e-reading wherever you are. You can also download and read portions of books (samples) and then, if you decide that you want to read the rest of the story, you can easily upgrade to the full book. Once your digital shelves are stocked, you can use iBooks' handy tools to read books in a number of ways.

Where Is My iBooks?

If the iBooks app isn't installed on your iPhone, tap App Store, search for iBooks, and download and install the app. Refer to Chapter 6 for information on downloading and installing apps.

Using the iBooks App to Download Books

Similar to the Podcasts app, you can fill your iBooks' bookshelves with books by accessing the iTunes Store from directly within the app. When you move into the store by tapping the iBooks app and then tapping the Store button, you see tools you can use to browse or search for books in several ways:

Downloading Books from the iBooks Store

If you aren't sure you want to purchase a book, you can download a sample to read for free and then buy and download the entire book later when you are sure.

1. On the Home screen, tap iBooks.

2. Tap Store. There are a number of ways you can look for books in the Store; at the bottom of the screen, tap the option you want to use. The rest of these steps demonstrate browsing for a book by author and category; the other search and browsing tools work in a similar fashion.

3. Tap Top Authors.

4. Tap Categories.

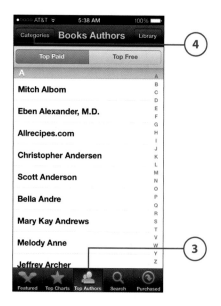

5. Swipe up and down the screen to browse the list of categories.

6. Tap a category you want to browse. A list showing authors with books in that category appears.

7. Tap Top Paid to browse books you have to pay for or Top Free to browse free books.

8. Swipe up and down the screen to browse the list of authors, or tap the index to jump to a specific section of the list.

9. Tap an author. What you see depends on the number of books the author has. For example, if you tap an author containing only one book in the category, you see a screen showing the book with a link to see other books by the same author. If you tap an author with multiple books in the category, you see a list of books by that author.

10. Swipe up and down the screen to browse the list of books by the author you selected in step 9.

11. Tap a book in which you are interested. The detail screen for that book appears. Here you see a description of the book, its user rating, and other information.

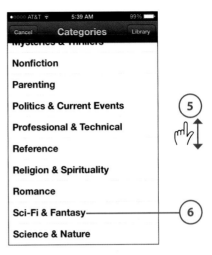

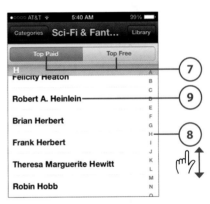

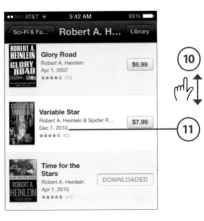

Are You Ready to Buy?

If you know you want to buy the book, you can just tap its buy button on the Books screen, which shows the price of the book or FREE if it is a free book. You then tap the button again to download it.

12. On the Details tab, browse the book's information, including its publication details, description, and so on; tap the More link to read all of the description.

13. Tap the Reviews tab and swipe up the screen to read reviews of the book.

14. Tap the Related tab to see related books.

15. To buy the book and download it, skip to step 16; to download a sample of a book to try for free, tap SAMPLE. You move back to your Library and see the cover of the book whose sample you downloaded. (Samples have the word "Sample" on their covers in a red banner.) You're ready to use iBooks to read the sample and can skip the following steps.

Happy with a Sample?

After you read a sample and decide you want the whole book, you can tap the BUY button that appears in iBooks when you are reading the sample. This takes you to a screen showing the price of the full book. Tap the Price button to start the purchase process.

16. To purchase and download a book, tap its Price button.

Buy a Free Book!

Quite a few free books are available; these are marked with the FREE button. When you tap this button, the process is the same as when you buy a book, meaning that you have to sign in to your iTunes account. Of course, it is different in that you aren't charged for the free book!

17. Tap BUY BOOK.

18. If the Sign In prompt appears and you're using an IPhone 5S, touch the Touch ID/Home button; if you're using a different model, type your Apple ID password and tap OK. The book is downloaded to your iPhone. New books are marked with the text New in a blue banner; samples are marked with a red banner. The book you just downloaded is ready for you to read.

Back to the Library

To move back to your Library without downloading a book, tap the Library button located in the upper-right corner of the screen.

New purchased book

New sample of a book

Finding Books to Read

When you launch iBooks, you see the Bookshelf where your books are stored. You can browse and search your bookshelf and, when you find a title of interest, you can take it off the digital shelf and start reading. You can browse books by their covers (steps 3 and 4) or use a configurable list (steps 5–7). You can also search for specific books (step 8). After you've found a book, reading it starts with a simple tap.

1. Move to the Home screen and tap iBooks.

2. Swipe down the screen to move the View buttons and search bar at the top of the screen into view.

3. Tap the by Cover button.

4. Swipe up or down the screen to browse your books by their covers. Skip to step 9 to start reading or continue with step 5 to view the books organized in lists.

5. Tap the List button to browse books by various categories.

6. Tap the category by which you want to see the books, such as Titles or Authors. The books are reorganized by the criterion you selected.

7. Swipe up or down the screen to browse your books. Skip to step 9 to read the book you've found via browsing, or continue with step 8 to search for a book.

8. To search for a book, type text in the Search tool; the text can be the book's title, author name, and so on. Books that meet your search criterion are shown on the shelf.

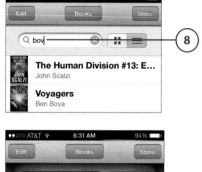

9. To read a book, tap its cover (whether you found it by browsing or searching). It opens and you see the most recent page you viewed, or the first page if you've never opened the book before. You also see the reading controls, which disappear after a few moments. To make them reappear, tap the screen.

Sync Up

When launching iBooks for the first time, you might be prompted to allow it to sync your iBooks content (books, notes, and so on) across multiple devices (such as an iPhone and iPad). If you tap Sync, the information is copied to your iCloud account. The next time you access iBooks with a different device that has the same account configured on it, your iBooks data is updated. This ensures you have the same data available in iBooks no matter which device you happen to be using.

Reading Books

iBooks offers many features that make reading digital books even better than reading the paper versions. The reading screen provides lots of information about and controls for your books.

Following are some of the great ways you can use iBooks to read:

- **Turn the page**—To move to the next page, tap on the right side of the screen or swipe your finger to the left to flip the page. To move to a previous page, tap on the left side of the screen or swipe your finger to the right.

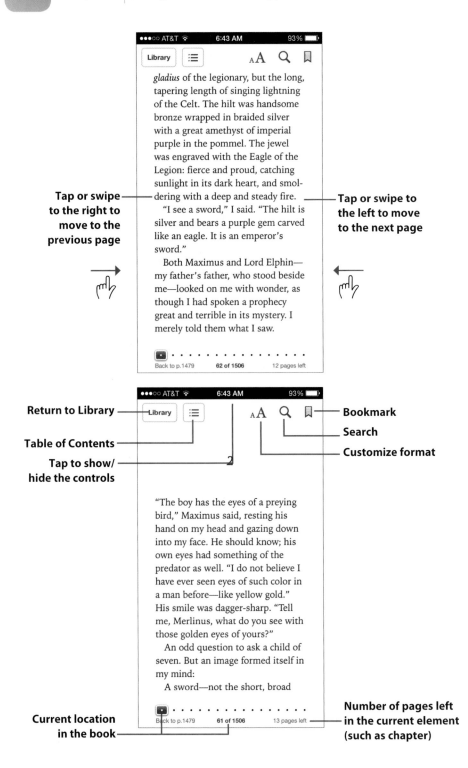

Tap or swipe to the right to move to the previous page

Tap or swipe to the left to move to the next page

Return to Library

Table of Contents

Tap to show/ hide the controls

Bookmark

Search

Customize format

Current location in the book

Number of pages left in the current element (such as chapter)

- **Hide/Show controls**—Tap the center of the screen to show or hide the controls; the book's title replaces the top buttons when the controls are hidden.

It's All Relative

The page numbers you see in iBooks are actually screen numbers. When you change the iPhone's orientation, font, or another factor that causes iBooks to change the layout of a book's screens, the page location and total page count also change to reflect the current number of screens in the book and element (such as chapter).

- **Rotate to read horizontally**—Rotate the iPhone to change the book's orientation. iBooks reformats and repaginates the book.

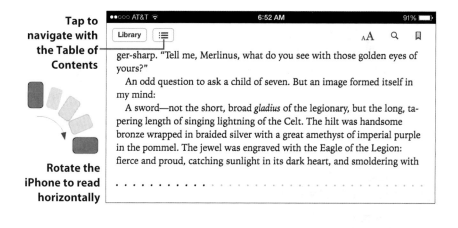

Tap to navigate with the Table of Contents

Rotate the iPhone to read horizontally

Tap to return to your current place in the book

Tap to view the Table of Contents

Swipe up or down to browse the Table of Contents

Tap to jump to an element

- **Navigate with the Table of Contents**—Tap the Table of Contents button; then tap the Contents tab. Browse the book's table of contents and tap the location to which you want to jump. To return to your previous location, tap Resume.

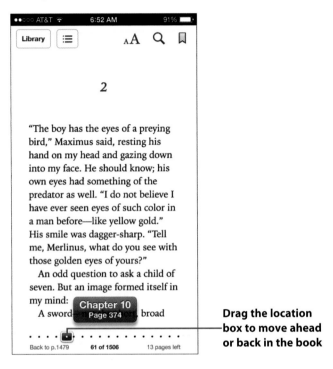

Drag the location box to move ahead or back in the book

- **Change pages quickly**—Drag the location box to quickly scroll ahead or back in the book. As you drag, the chapter and page number of the box's current location appear in a pop-up box. When you release the box, you jump to the new location.

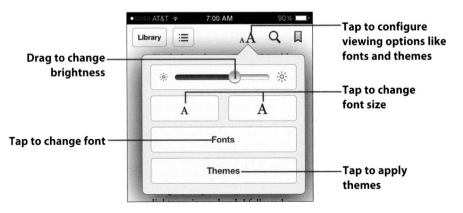

Drag to change brightness

Tap to change font

Tap to configure viewing options like fonts and themes

Tap to change font size

Tap to apply themes

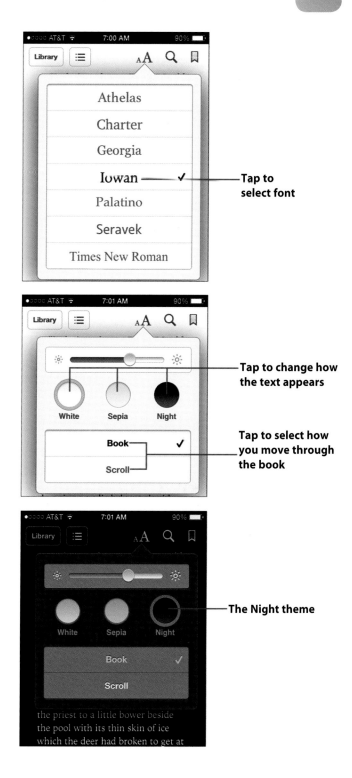

Tap to
select font

Tap to change how
the text appears

Tap to select how
you move through
the book

The Night theme

- **Change font and other layout options**—When you tap the Font button, the format palette appears. Drag the Brightness slider to the left or right to change the screen's brightness. Tap the larger font button to increase the size of the font; tap the smaller font button to decrease it. As you tap these buttons, iBooks reformats the book in the background. Tap the Fonts button, and a list of available fonts appears. Tap the font you want to use; again, iBooks reformats the book in the background so you can see the results. Tap the Themes button to see themes you can choose. Tap White to see standard black text on a white background, Sepia to see black text on a sepia background, or Night to see white text on a black background. Tap Book to see the standard book format, or tap Scroll to format the book on one screen that you swipe up or down on to read. When you're done making changes, tap outside the palette to close it.

It's Not All Good

When you tap the Fonts button, the list of font types replaces the other controls on the palette. Unfortunately, you can't return to the other controls without first closing the palette and reopening it. This is not a big deal, though, because it requires only a couple of quick taps. However, this makes adjusting both font type and size more difficult than it needs to be.

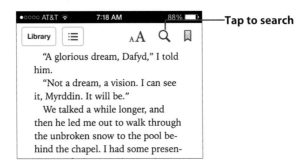

Tap to search

- **Search**—Tap the magnifying glass at the top of the screen to search for specific text in the book. Type the text for which you want to search. iBooks searches the book and presents matches to you; the more specific you make your search, the narrower the list of results are. When you finish entering your search text, tap Search to close the keyboard to see the full list of results. Tap a result to move to it in the book; the search term is highlighted on the page. To return to the search results page, tap the Search button again. When the keyboard is hidden, you can tap the Search Google button to perform a web search or the Search Wikipedia button to search the Wikipedia website.

Enter search text

Tap to move to the location of the found text

Tap to close keyboard to see all results

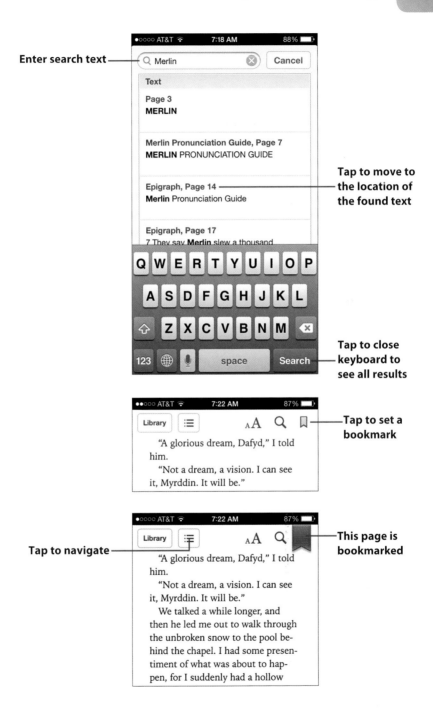

Tap to set a bookmark

Tap to navigate

This page is bookmarked

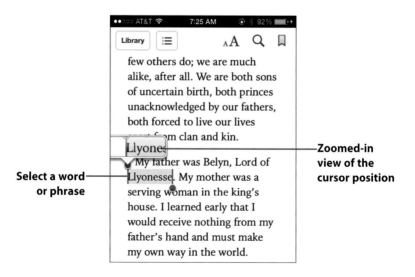

- **Navigate with bookmarks**—To be able to return to a specific location in the book, tap the Bookmark button. The page you are on is added to the Bookmarks tab and a red bookmark appears on it. To return to a bookmark, tap the Table of Contents button and then tap the Bookmarks tab. You see a list of all the bookmarks in the book; the chapter, page number, and the date and time when the bookmark was created are shown. Tap a bookmark to return to its location. To remove a bookmark, move to its location and tap the red bookmark icon; the bookmark is deleted.

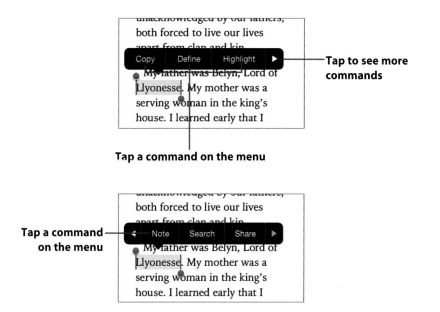

Tap to see more commands

Tap a command on the menu

Tap a command on the menu

- **Use other text features**—Select some text on a page; when you are done, a menu with the following commands appears:

  - Tap Copy (shown only for nonprotected works) to copy the selected text.

  - Tap Define to look up the selected text in a dictionary.

  - Tap Highlight to highlight the selection; when you select a highlighted term, a menu appears that enables you to change the highlight color, add a note, or remove the highlight.

  - Tap Note to create a note attached to the selected text. After you've created a note and tapped Done, the text is highlighted and you see the note icon on the right side of the screen. (Tap this icon to read or edit the note.) Tap text with a note associated with it to change the highlight color or remove the note. You can also navigate by note by moving to the Table of Contents screen and tapping the Notes tab.

  - Tap Search to perform a search for the selected text.

  - Tap Share to include the selected text as an excerpt via Mail, Messages, Twitter, or Facebook.

  - Tap the Collections button, which is labeled with the name of the collection currently being displayed, and then tap Purchased Books to access all the books you've purchased from the iBooks Store. Tap PDFs to see the PDFs in your library. You can create new collections by tapping New, typing the name of the collection, and tapping

Done. To put items in a collection, move to the Library screen, tap Edit, tap the books or PDFs you want to move, tap Move, and tap the collection into which you want to place the selected items.

Tap the Collections button to change the group of documents you are viewing

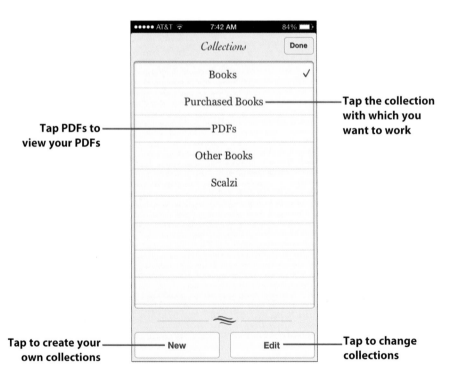

Tap the collection with which you want to work

Tap PDFs to view your PDFs

Tap to create your own collections

Tap to change collections

- **Reading PDFs**—iBooks is also a great PDF reader for your iOS device. To read a PDF, move to the Library and tap the Collections button. Tap PDFs, and when you return to the Library, you see the PDFs stored in your Library. Tap a PDF's cover to view it. It opens and you can use controls that are similar to those for reading books to view it. (If you open a PDF that is in black and white, the iBooks interface is in black and white, too.)

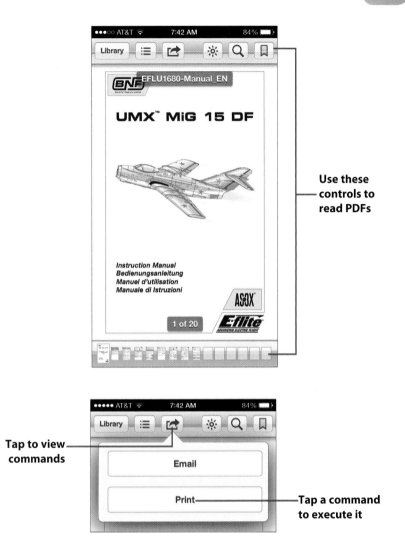

Use these controls to read PDFs

Tap to view commands

Tap a command to execute it

- **Take action**—If you tap the Action button, you are presented with commands available for the specific context in which you are working, such as Email or Print.

Loading Up on PDFs

When you tap a PDF document in another app, such as an attachment to an email message, you are presented with the option to open in iBooks. When you choose this option, the PDF is copied into your iBooks' Library and added to the PDF collection.

An iPhone is easy to maintain and isn't
likely to give you much trouble

In this chapter, you learn how to keep an iPhone in top shape and what to do should problems happen. Topics include the following:

→ Maintaining an iPhone's Software
→ Backing up your iPhone
→ Finding and securing your iPhone with Find My iPhone
→ Maintaining an iPhone's power
→ Solving iPhone problems
→ Getting help with iPhone problems

Maintaining and Protecting Your iPhone and Solving Problems

You probably noticed that this is a short chapter, and there is a good reason for that: An iPhone works very well, and you are unlikely to have problems with it, especially if you keep its software current. When problems do occur, you can usually solve them with a few simple steps. If that fails, there's lots of help available for you on the Internet.

Maintaining an iPhone's Software

Like software on computers, the software on your iPhone gets updated periodically to fix bugs, solve issues, and introduce new features. For best results, you should ensure the software you use is current to the latest releases.

There are two types of software you need to maintain: the iOS software that runs your iPhone and the apps you have installed on it. Fortunately, maintaining both types is simple.

Maintaining the iOS Software with the Settings App

You can check for updates to the iOS using the Settings app. If an update is found, you can download and install it directly on the iPhone. Here's how:

Update Notification

You might receive a notification when an update to iOS is available; you also see a badge on the Settings app's icon. You can tap in the notification to move to the Update screen (and so won't need to perform steps 1–3).

1. On the Home screen, tap Settings.

2. Tap General.

3. Tap Software Update. The app checks for an update. If one is available, you see information about it and should proceed to step 4. If you are using the current version, you see a message saying so and you can skip the rest of these steps.

4. Tap Download and Install. Depending on your iPhone's status, you might see different warnings, such as if you aren't connected to a power supply.

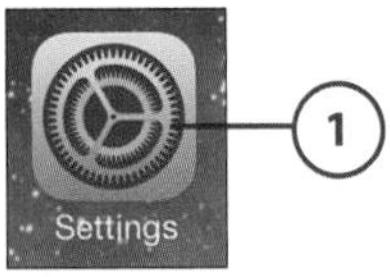

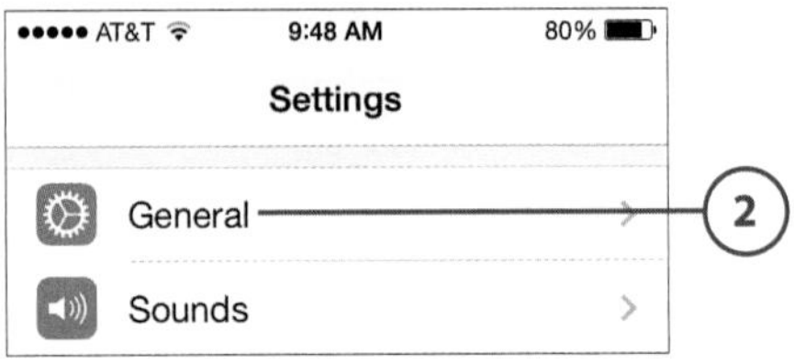

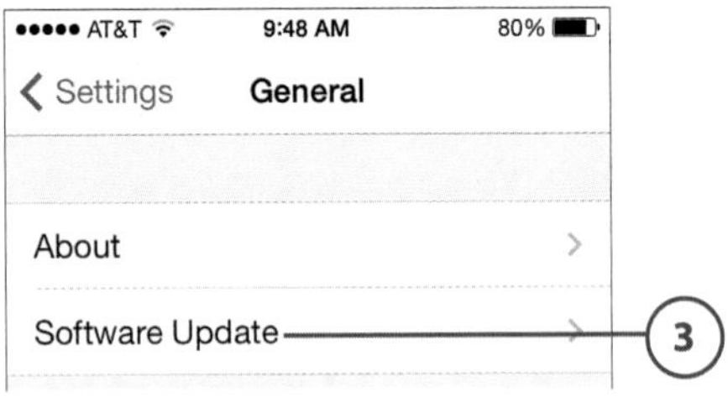

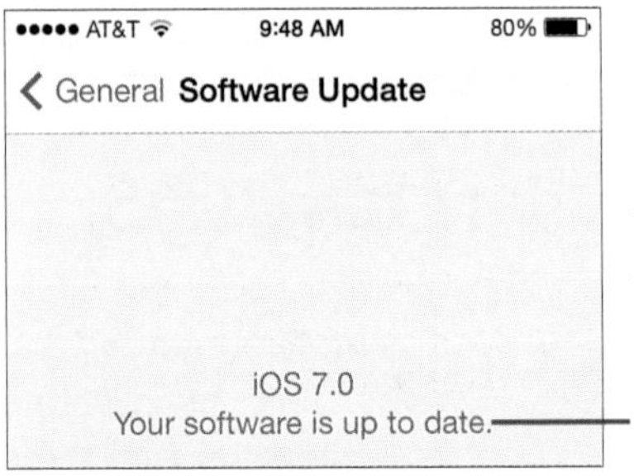

The iOS software is current; no update needed

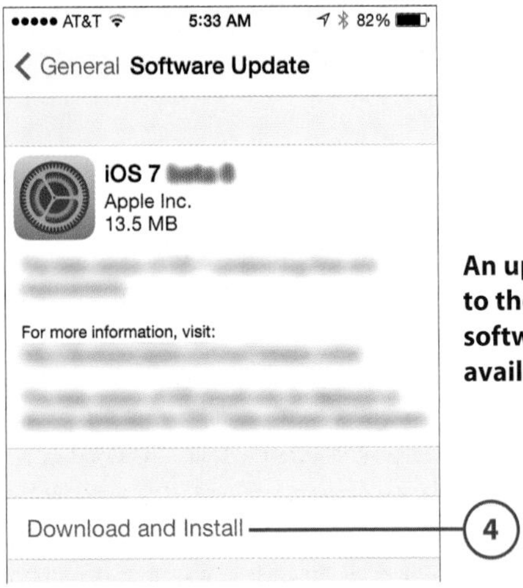

An update to the iOS software is available

5. If you see a prompt, tap OK; in some cases, the download starts immediately and you can skip this step. The software starts to download and you can see the progress of the download on the Software Update screen.

6. When the download is complete, tap Install or just let the iPhone sit because the software is installed automatically after the time indicated passes. After the install process is complete, your iPhone restarts with the updated software.

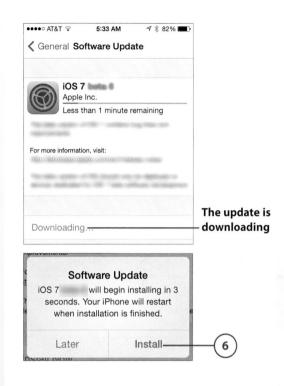

The update is downloading

Updating the iOS Software with iTunes on a Computer

You can also use iTunes on a computer to update your iPhone's iOS software. Connect the iPhone to your computer and move into the sync screen in iTunes. Click the Summary tab and then click Check for Update. iTunes checks for an update and prompts you to download and install it if one is available. If an update isn't available, you see a message saying so. If iTunes has downloaded an update previously, you see the Update button instead of Check for Update. Click Update, and iTunes installs the update on your iPhone.

Maintaining iPhone Apps

iPhone apps are regularly updated to fix bugs or add features and enhancements. If you enabled the Automatic Download setting for Apps in the App Store Settings (refer to Chapter 6, "Downloading Apps, Music, Movies, TV Shows, and More onto Your iPhone," for details), you don't need to worry about keeping your apps current because the iOS does that for you automatically whenever your iPhone is connected to a Wi-Fi network. If you enabled the App Store app to use cellular data (refer to Chapter 2, "Connecting Your iPhone to the Internet, Bluetooth Devices, and iPhones/iPods/iPads"), the updates occur at any time your iPhone is connected to the cellular network, too.

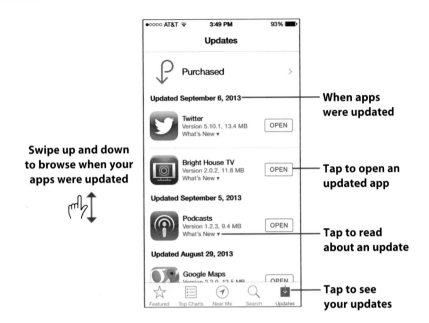

When apps were updated

Swipe up and down to browse when your apps were updated

Tap to open an updated app

Tap to read about an update

Tap to see your updates

To see how your apps have been updated, tap App Store on the Home screen. Tap Updates, and then swipe up and down to see the apps that have been updated. The updates are grouped by when the updates occurred. To see details about an update, tap its What's New link.

>>>Go Further

MANUALLY KEEPING APPS CURRENT

If you don't want your apps to be updated automatically, turn the Automatic Download setting for Apps in the App Store Settings (refer to Chapter 6 for details) to off (white). When updates are available, you see a badge on the App Store app icon showing how many updates are available. Tap App Store and then tap Updates. You see the available updates. Tap UPDATE for the updates you want to download and install, or tap UPDATE ALL to download and install all available updates.

Backing Up Your iPhone

Like all things data related, it's important to back up your iPhone's data. If you ever need to restore your iPhone to solve a problem or if you replace your phone with a new one, having a current backup can get you back to where you want to be as quickly and easily as possible.

There are two places where you can back up your iPhone. You can back up to your iCloud account or to your computer. In fact, you can back up to both places for maximum protection.

Ideally, you'll configure your iPhone to back up to iCloud so you can back up whenever your iPhone is connected to a Wi-Fi network that provides an Internet connection. Periodically, you can back up to your computer using the iTunes app.

To learn how to configure your iPhone to back up to your iCloud account, see "Configuring Your iCloud Account" in Chapter 3, "Setting Up iCloud and Other Online Accounts." With this enabled, your iPhone is backed up automatically. You can manually back up at any time as described in the following task.

Backing up to your computer is explained in the task "Manually Backing Up Your iPhone to Your Computer."

Manually Backing Up Your iPhone to iCloud

To manually back up your iPhone to your iCloud account, do the following:

1. Tap Settings.

2. Tap iCloud.

3. Swipe up the screen.

4. Tap Storage & Backup.

5. Tap Back Up Now, which is at the bottom of the Storage & Backup screen. Your iPhone's data is backed up to iCloud. You can see the progress on the screen; however, you can continue using your iPhone because the process works in the background. You just need to start it, and then do whatever you want while it completes.

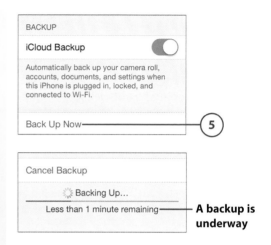

A backup is underway

Manually Backing Up Your iPhone to Your Computer

It's a good idea to back up your iPhone to your computer periodically.

1. Connect your iPhone to your computer and move to the Summary tab of the Sync screen (refer to Chapter 5, "Working with iTunes on Your Computer," for details).

2. Click Back Up Now. The backup process starts. You see information about the process at the top of the iTunes window.

This iPhone is being backed up to the computer

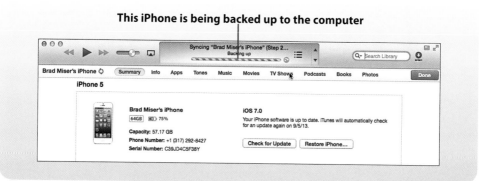

Finding and Securing Your iPhone with Find My iPhone

If you lose control of your iPhone, you can use iCloud's Find My iPhone feature to locate your iPhone and to secure it by locking it or, in the worst case, erasing its data. Hopefully, you'll never need to use this capability, but it's good to know how just in case.

Keep It Secure

For better security, you should configure a passcode, as described in Chapter 4, "Configuring an iPhone to Suit Your Preferences." When a passcode is required, it must be entered to unlock and use an iPhone. If you don't have a passcode, anyone who picks up your iPhone can use it. This section assumes you have a passcode set. If not, go back to Chapter 4 and set one before continuing—unless you've already lost control of your iPhone. If you don't have a passcode set, you're prompted to create one when you put it in Lost Mode.

After you configure Find My iPhone and use it to locate your iPhone, you can perform the following actions on it:

- **Play Sound**—This does just what it sounds like. A sound is played on the iPhone and an alert appears on its screen. This provides information to whomever has the device—such as if you've loaned the device to someone and want it back. The sound can help you locate the device if it is in the same general vicinity as you.

- **Lost Mode**—This locks the iPhone so it can't be used without entering the passcode. This can protect your iPhone without changing its data. You can also display contact information on the iPhone's screen to enable someone to get in touch with you.

- **Erase Your iPhone**—This erases the iPhone's memory as the "last chance" to protect your data. You should only do this in the worst-case scenario because when you erase the iPhone, you lose the ability to find it again using Find My iPhone.

Keeping You Informed

Whenever you use one of the Find My iPhone actions, such as playing a sound or using the Lost Mode, you receive emails to your iCloud email address showing the action taken along with the device, date, and time on which it was performed.

To use Find My iPhone, you must enable it on your iPhone. This is done using the iCloud Settings as explained in Chapter 3. When Find My iPhone is enabled, you can use it to locate or secure your iPhone.

Using Find My iPhone to Locate Your iPhone

To use Find My iPhone, perform the following task:

1. Use a web browser to move to and log in to your iCloud website located at icloud.com.

2. Click Find My iPhone.

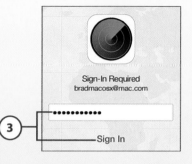

3. Enter your iCloud account password and click Sign In.

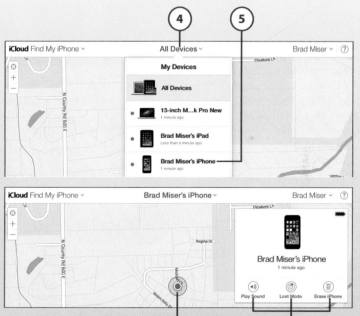

The iPhone's current location   Actions you can take

4. Click the All Devices menu. All your devices are shown on the My Devices list.

5. Click the device you want to locate. If the device can be located, you see it on a map. You can use the map's controls to zoom into the iPhone's location so you get the best idea of where it currently is. You also see a dialog box that enables you to perform the three actions described earlier. The details for each are provided in the following tasks.

Using Find My iPhone to Play a Sound on Your iPhone

Here's how to send a sound or message to an iOS device:

1. Locate your iPhone as described in the previous task.

2. Click Play Sound.

3. To stop the sound from playing on the iPhone, unlock it and tap OK on the message prompt. (If you don't require a passcode, anyone who has the phone can do this, which is another reason requiring a passcode is more secure.)

The Sound Remains the Same

When you send a sound to an iPhone, it plays even if the iPhone is muted.

The sound plays and the alert message appears on the iPhone

Using Find My iPhone to Put Your iPhone in Lost Mode

You can put your iPhone into Lost Mode by doing the following:

1. Locate the device using the steps in the previous task.

2. Click Lost Mode. (If you haven't entered a passcode, you're prompted to create one by entering and verifying it.)

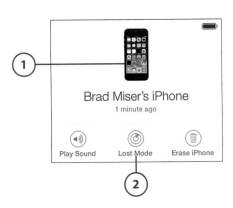

3. If you want to send a phone number to the device so that someone can call you about it, enter it at the prompt.

4. Click Next.

5. Enter the message you want to appear on the iPhone. This can be your request that whoever has the device call you, instructions for returning the device, and so on.

6. Tap Done. The iPhone is locked and the message you entered displays on the screen. While the iPhone is in Lost Mode, the Lost Mode icon on the Find My iPhone screen rotates and you see the Lost Mode indicator.

When the device enters Lost Mode, it is locked and protected with the existing passcode. The phone number and message you entered appear on the iPhone's screen. The person finding your phone can tap the Call button to call the number you entered.

The iPhone remains in Lost Mode until it is unlocked.

This iPhone is locked

The message and phone number you entered

The person who finds the phone can tap to call the number you entered

Using Find My iPhone to Erase Your iPhone

If you decide you've lost control of your device and want to protect the information it contains, take the following steps to erase it:

1. Locate the device using the steps in the task "Using Find My iPhone to Locate Your iPhone."

2. Click Erase iPhone.

Erase a Device

When you erase an iPhone, all its data is deleted and it is reset to factory conditions. This means you are no longer able to use Find My iPhone to locate it. Only do this when you're pretty sure the iPhone is out of your control or that you won't be getting it back any time soon.

3. Click Erase.

4. Enter your Apple ID password.

5. Click Next. All the data on your device is erased, and it is restored to factory settings.

6. If you want to send a phone number to the device so that someone can call you about it, enter it at the prompt.

7. Click Next.

8. Enter the message you want to appear on the iPhone. This can be your request that whoever has the device call you, instructions for returning the device, and so on.

9. Tap Done. The iPhone is erased and the message you entered displays on the screen. The person who finds it can tap Call to call the number you entered in step 6, hopefully to return your iPhone. If it does get returned, you have to restore the iPhone using a backup from iCloud or iTunes on your computer (the steps to do this are later in this chapter).

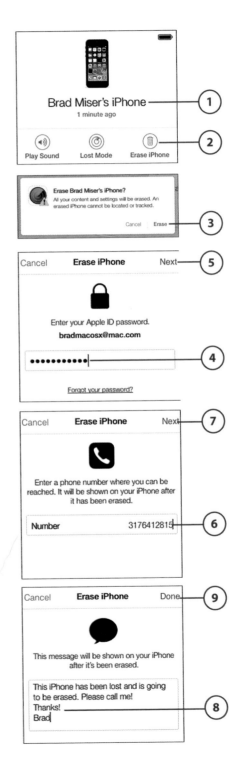

USING FIND MY IPHONE

>>>Go Further

Here are some more tips on using Find My iPhone:

- To update the locations of your devices, refresh the webpage and reopen the My Devices list.

- When you send a message to an iPhone that is in Lost Mode or when you erase it, you might want to include additional contact information in the message, such as your name and where you are currently located. You could also offer a reward for the return of the iPhone if you wanted to. Include enough information so that if someone wants to return the device to you, she has what she needs to be able to do so.

- If you lose control of your iPhone, use an escalation of steps to try to regain control. Look at the iPhone's location on the map. If the iPhone appears to be near your current location, play the sound because it might help you find it again. If the iPhone doesn't appear to be near your current location or it appears to be but you can't find it, put it in Lost Mode. This hopefully prevents someone else from using it while you locate it and allows someone who finds it to contact you. If you lose all hope of finding it again, you can erase the iPhone to delete the data it contains. When you do this, you lose the ability to track your iPhone and have to rely on someone finding it and contacting you. This is a severe action, so you don't want to do it prematurely.

- Erasing an iPhone is a bit of a double-edged sword. It protects your data by erasing your device, but it also means you can't use Find My iPhone to locate it anymore. You should use this only if you're pretty sure someone has your device because after you erase it, there's no way to track the iPhone's location. How fast you move to erase your iPhone also depends on whether you've required a passcode. If you do require a passcode, you know your device's data can't be accessed without that code, so it will take some time for a miscreant to crack it, and you might be slower on the erase trigger. If your iPhone doesn't have a passcode, you might want to pull the trigger sooner.

- As you use Find My iPhone, you receive email notifications about various events, such as when a device is locked, when a message you sent is displayed, and so on. These are a good way to know something about what is happening with your iPhone, even though you might not be able to see the iPhone for yourself.

- If Find My iPhone can't currently find your iPhone, you can still initiate the same actions as when the iPhone is found, although they won't actually happen until the iPhone becomes visible again. To be notified when this happens, check the Email me when this iPhone is found check box. When the iPhone becomes visible to Find My iPhone, you receive an email and then can take appropriate action to locate and secure it.

- There's an app for that. You can download and use the free Find My iPhone app on an iOS device to use this feature. For example, you can use this app on an iPad to locate an iPhone.

Maintaining an iPhone's Power

Obviously, an iPhone with a dead battery isn't good for much. As you use your iPhone, you should keep an eye on its battery status. As long as the battery icon is at least partially filled, you're okay. As the iPhone gets low on power, the battery status icon becomes almost empty. Two separate warnings alert you when the battery lowers to 20% and then again at 10%. If you keep going from there, the iPhone eventually runs out of power and shuts down. Of course, it gives you plenty of warning through onscreen messages before this happens.

Keep your eye on the battery icon so you don't run out of power

Getting Precise

To see the percentage of charge remaining along with the battery icon, move to the Settings app and tap General. Then tap Usage and slide the Battery Percentage switch to on (green). The percentage of charge remaining appears to the left of the battery status icon at the top of the screen.

This iPhone is being charged

Fortunately, it's easy to avoid running out of power by keeping your iPhone charged. The good news is that all you have to do is connect the iPhone to your computer, and its battery charges (you can sync your iPhone via iTunes at the same time). While this is occurring, you see the charging icon in the upper-right corner of the screen, and if you wake the iPhone, a large battery icon showing the relative state of the battery appears on its screen. When charging is complete, the battery status icon replaces the charging icon in the upper-right corner of the screen, the large battery icon disappears, and you see the iPhone's wallpaper if it's locked, or you see whatever screen you happen to be using if it isn't locked.

You can also connect an iPhone to an external charger if your computer isn't handy. This charges the battery but, of course, doesn't sync or back up your iPhone's contents via iTunes; if you sync and back up via the cloud-base services, such as iCloud and Exchange, you don't need to sync via iTunes anyway. And, using an external charger charges the iPhone's battery faster than connecting it to a computer does.

Topping Off

It's a good idea to keep your iPhone's battery topped off; this type of battery actually does better if you keep it charged rather than letting it run down all the way before recharging. Periodically, say every month or two, you might want to let your iPhone run completely out of power and the recharge it to maximize its life. The key point is, as Apple puts it, to "keep the electrons moving." So, don't let your iPhone sit with no activity for long periods of time.

Making the Battery Last Longer

If your iPhone's battery doesn't seem to last very long, the issue is likely that a service is very active and is requiring near-constant activity. Common causes of this problem are Push being turned on for an account that has a lot of activity, an application using GPS capabilities, and so on. Try these steps to find and stop the source of the power drain:

1. Open the Settings app, tap Mail, Contacts, Calendars, and then tap Fetch New Data.

●○○○○ AT&T 🔋 4:17 PM 100% ⬛▪

‹ Settings **Mail, Contacts, Calendars**

Fetch New Data   30 min ›

①

2. Slide the status switch for Push to off (white). This disables Push functionality. To update your information, set a Fetch schedule using the controls on the bottom of the Fetch New Data screen or just open an app, such as Mail.

3. Turn off any transmitting and receiving functions that you aren't using, such as Bluetooth. Using the Control Center is a handy way to do this quickly.

4. Press the Touch ID/Home button twice.

5. Swipe to the left or right on the apps to find any that might be using power without you realizing it.

6. If you find an app that might be draining your battery, swipe up on the app to shut it down.

7. Use your iPhone to see if the battery lasts longer. If it does, you know one of the changes you made was the reason; you can either leave the offending source of power drain shut down or just be aware when you are using it. If the battery still doesn't last very long, it may have a problem and you should contact Apple for assistance.

Solving iPhone Problems

Even a device as reliable as your iPhone can sometimes run into problems. Fortunately, the solutions to most problems you encounter are simple. If a simple solution doesn't work, a great deal of detailed help is available from Apple, and even more is available from the community of iPhone users.

The problems that you can address with the simple steps described in this section vary and range from such issues as the iPhone hanging (won't respond to commands) to not being visible in iTunes when connected to your computer (can't be synced). No matter which problem you experience, try the following steps to solve them.

Restarting Your iPhone

Whenever your iPhone starts acting oddly, restarting it should be the first thing you try. It's easy to do and cures an amazing number of problems. To restart your iPhone, do the following:

1. Press and hold the Sleep/Wake button until the red slider appears on the screen.

2. Drag the red slider to the right. The iPhone powers down.

3. Press and hold the Sleep/Wake button until you see the Apple logo on the screen. The iPhone restarts. When the Home screen appears, try using the iPhone again. If the problem is solved, you're done.

Can't Restart?
If your iPhone won't restart normally, press and hold the Sleep/Wake and Touch ID/Home buttons at the same time until the iPhone shuts off (about 10 seconds). Then, press the Sleep/Wake button to restart it.

Resetting Your iPhone

If restarting your iPhone doesn't help, try resetting your iPhone using the following escalation of steps.

All USB Ports Are Not Created Equal

If your computer can't see your iPhone when it's connected using its USB dock connector, try a different USB port. You should use a USB port on the computer itself rather than one on a keyboard or USB hub.

1. If an app freezes or starts acting oddly while you are using it, press the Touch ID/Home button twice. The Multitasking screen appears. Swipe to the left or right until you see the app that has frozen. Swipe up on the app to shut it down. Complete any tasks you have in other apps, and then proceed to the next step.

2. Restart the iPhone using the steps in the "Restarting Your iPhone" section. If the problem goes away, you're done. If not, continue to the next step.

3. If you can't restart the iPhone normally, press and hold down both the Touch ID/Home button and the Sleep/Wake buttons for at least 10 seconds. The iPhone should turn itself off and then restart; you can release the buttons when you see the Apple logo on the screen. If the problem goes away, you're done. If not, continue.

4. If you can use the iPhone's controls, proceed with the following steps. If you can't use any of its controls, you need to restore the iPhone, which is explained in the next section.

5. On the Home screen, tap Settings.

6. Tap General.

7. Swipe up the screen until you see the Reset command.

8. Tap Reset.

9. Tap the Reset command for the area in which you are having problems. For example, if you are having trouble with Wi-Fi or other networking areas, tap Reset Network Settings, or if you decide your Home screens are a mess and you want to go back to the default layout, tap Reset Home Screen Layout. If you are having lots of issues in multiple areas, tap Reset All Settings or Erase All Content and Settings (be careful because this erases everything on your iPhone).

10. Enter your passcode.

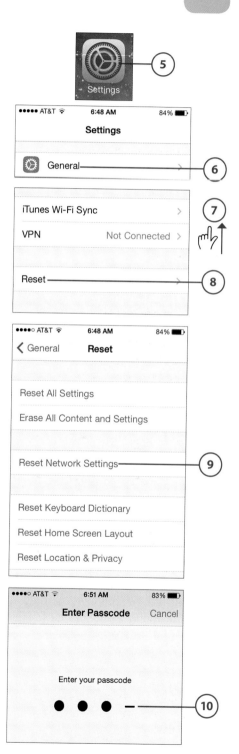

11. Tap the confirmation of the reset you are doing. The reset is complete and that area of the iPhone is reset to factory conditions.

12. Reconfigure the reset area. If you did a Reset All Settings or Erase All Content and Settings, you'll basically start from the beginning with your iPhone.

This will delete all media and data, and reset all settings.

Erase iPhone —————⑪

Cancel

Restoring Your iPhone

The most severe action you can take on your iPhone is to restore it. When this happens, the iPhone is erased, so you lose all its contents and its current iOS software is overwritten with the latest version. If you have added information to your iPhone since it was last backed up (when you last connected it to the computer or it backed up to your iCloud account), that information is lost when you restore your iPhone—so be careful before doing this. If none of the other tasks corrected the problem, restoring the iPhone should.

1. Turn off Find My iPhone (open the iCloud Settings screen, set the Find My iPhone switch to off (white), enter your Apple ID password, and tap Turn Off).

2. Connect the iPhone to your computer.

3. Click the iPhone button (if you have more than one iOS device connected, click the Devices button and then click the iPhone).

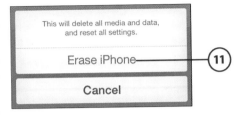

4. Click the Summary tab.

5. Click Restore iPhone. Remember that you lose everything on your iPhone when you restore it, so make sure that you have all its data stored elsewhere, such as backed up in your iTunes Library, before you do this.

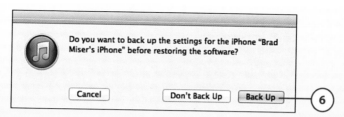

6. Click Back Up. This backs up your iPhone's contents.

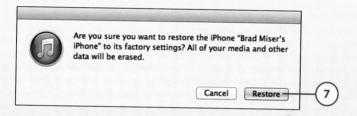

7. Click Restore in the dialog box. The Restore process begins and iTunes extracts the software and prepares to install it.

8. Read the information about the current version of the iPhone's software, and click Next.

9. Click Agree. The current version of the iPhone's software is downloaded to your computer, and iTunes reinstalls it on your iPhone. You see several progress indicators along the way, both on the computer screen and on your iPhone. Early in the process, the iPhone restarts and iTunes begins reinstalling its software. (If a firmware update is needed, iTunes handles that, too.) When the process is complete, you see a message explaining what has happened.

10. Click OK. The iPhone is restarted, and you see the Set Up Your iPhone screen.

11. Click the Restore from the backup of radio button.

12. On the pop-up menu, choose your iPhone's name and the most recent backup you see (which is the one that is not stamped with a date and time). If you want to go back to an earlier state, choose the time and date of the backup you want to use instead.

13. Click Continue. iTunes restores the iPhone from the backup.

14. Click OK in the completion dialog box. The iPhone is synced according to the settings stored in the backup. When the sync process is complete, the iPhone should be back in working condition with all your content restored to it. If you have a lot of content, this process can take a while because the sync is performed starting with the iPhone's memory being "empty."

Starting Over

If you want to start at the beginning, select the Set up as a new iPhone radio button in step 11 instead. Follow the onscreen prompts. When that process is complete, you're prompted to name and reconfigure the iPhone as you did when you first started using it.

How Does It Remember?

You might wonder how an iPhone can be restored. It's because iTunes backs up critical iPhone data and settings on your computer or on your iCloud account. Each time you sync, this information is backed up on the computer or to your iCloud account so that it is available again when it is needed, such as when you restore your iPhone. If you back up your iPhone to your computer, you should connect your iPhone to your computer or sync over Wi-Fi regularly even if the content you sync hasn't changed much. This ensures the iPhone's backup is current. iCloud backups happen automatically when your iPhone is connected to the Internet so you don't have to worry about backing it up manually.

Finding a Missing App

I've had more than a few emails from people on whose phones an app icon seems to have disappeared. In most cases, these were core iPhone apps that can't be removed from the iPhone, such as Settings or Photos. In almost all of these cases, the app's icon had inadvertently been moved into a folder and so was not visible in its expected location. If this happens to you, perform the following steps to restore the app to where it should be:

1. Move to the Home screen.

2. Swipe down from the center top area of the screen. The Spotlight Search tool opens.

3. Tap in the Search bar and enter the name of the app that is missing. As you search, Spotlight presents a list of items that match your search. If the app is found, you know it is still on the iPhone and it just has been accidentally misplaced; you can continue with these steps to find it. On the right side of the screen is the app's current location.

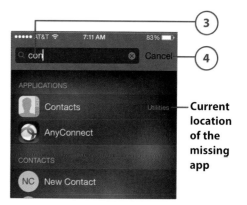

Current location of the missing app

If it isn't found, it has been removed from the iPhone and you need to reinstall it. Download and install it again using the App Store app. (Installing apps is covered in Chapter 6.)

4. Tap Cancel. You move back to the Home screen.

5. Open the folder where the app is currently located.

6. Tap and hold on the app icon until the icons start jiggling.

7. Drag the app's icon out of the folder.

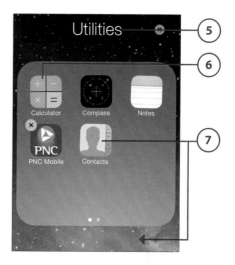

8. Place the icon where you want it to be (refer to Chapter 4 for details of moving apps on the Home screens).

9. Press the Touch ID/Home button to lock the icons in their current positions.

Making an iPhone's Screen Rotate Again

If your iPhone stops changing from horizontal to vertical orientation when you rotate the phone, you probably have inadvertently enabled the orientation lock. Unlock it again by doing the following:

1. Look at the top of the screen. If you see the Orientation Lock icon, the iPhone's orientation is locked.

2. Swipe up from the bottom of the Home screen to open the Control Center.

3. Tap the Orientation Lock button. When Orientation Lock is on, the button is white. When it is off, the button is black.

4. Confirm that the Orientation Lock icon has disappeared. The iPhone now changes orientation when you rotate it.

The orientation of this iPhone is locked

Blocking Unwanted Calls, Messages, or FaceTime Requests

If you want to block calls or texts from someone, do the following:

1. Create a contact for the phone number or email address used to send messages that you want to block. (Creating contacts is described in Chapter 7, "Managing Contacts.")

2. On the Home screen, tap Settings.

3. Tap Phone.

4. Tap Blocked.

5. Tap Add New.

6. Find and tap the contact you want to block. You return to the Blocked screen and see the person whose calls, messages, or FaceTime requests are blocked.

Unblock

To remove the block on a contact, move to the Blocked screen, tap Edit, tap the Unlock button for the contact you want to unblock, and tap Unblock.

Solving the Quiet iPhone Problem

If your iPhone stops ringing or making other sounds you believe it should, perform the following steps:

1. Make sure the iPhone isn't muted. The Mute switch on the left side of the iPhone should be in the position toward the front of the phone. If you see color in the switch, the phone is currently muted. Slide the switch toward the front of the iPhone to unmute it. You should hear sounds again.

2. With the iPhone unlocked, press the upper volume switch on the left side of the iPhone to make sure that the volume isn't set to the lowest level. As you press the button, a visual indicator of the current volume level appears on the screen. As long as you see a few "dots" on this, you should be able to hear sounds the iPhone makes.

3. Try a different app or task. If you aren't hearing sound from only one app and everything else sounds normal, you know there is a problem with that app. Try deleting and reinstalling it.

4. Move to the Sounds Settings screen.

5. Make sure the volume slider is set to at least the middle position.

6. Tap Ringtone.

7. Tap one of the default ringtones. You should hear it. If you do, you know the problem is solved. If not, continue.

8. If you aren't hearing sounds when the EarPods aren't plugged in, connect the EarPods and repeat the sound you should be hearing. If you hear the sound only when the EarPods are plugged in, your iPhone needs to be serviced by an Apple authorized repair center.

••••• AT&T 🔋	7:52 AM	🔋 75% 🔋
❮ Sounds	**Ringtone**	Store
train_ringtone		
Marimba (Default)		✓ —⑦
Alarm		

Getting Help with iPhone Problems

If none of the previous steps solve the problem, you can get help in a number of ways:

- **Apple's website**—Go to www.apple.com/support/. On this page, you can access all kinds of information about iPhones, iTunes, and other Apple products. You can browse for help, and you can search for answers to specific problems. Many of the resulting articles have detailed, step-by-step instructions to help you solve problems and link to more information.

- **Web searches**—One of the most useful ways to get help is to do a web search for the specific problem you're having. Just open your favorite search tool, such as Google, and search for the problem. You are likely to find many resources to help you, including websites, forums, and such. If you encounter a problem, it's likely someone else has, too, and has probably put the solution on the Web.

- **Me**—You're welcome to send an email to me for problems you're having with your iPhone. My address is bradmiser@icloud.com. I'll do my best to help you as quickly as I can.

Index

P

My iPhone
SEVENTH EDITION

COVERS iPhone 4/4S, 5, 5C, and 5S running iOS 7

que

Brad Miser

FREE Online Edition

Safari
Books Online

Your purchase of **My iPhone** includes access to a free online edition for 45 days through the **Safari Books Online** subscription service. Nearly every Que book is available online through **Safari Books Online**, along with thousands of books and videos from publishers such as Addison-Wesley Professional, Cisco Press, Exam Cram, IBM Press, O'Reilly Media, Prentice Hall, Sams, and VMware Press.

Safari Books Online is a digital library providing searchable, on-demand access to thousands of technology, digital media, and professional development books and videos from leading publishers. With one monthly or yearly subscription price, you get unlimited access to learning tools and information on topics including mobile app and software development, tips and tricks on using your favorite gadgets, networking, project management, graphic design, and much more.

Activate your FREE Online Edition at informit.com/safarifree

STEP 1: Enter the coupon code: GAYAOVH.

STEP 2: New Safari users, complete the brief registration form. Safari subscribers, just log in.

If you have difficulty registering on Safari or accessing the online edition, please e-mail customer-service@safaribooksonline.com